Fred Barton and
the Warlords' Horses
of China

ALSO BY LARRY WEIRATHER

The China Clipper, Pan American Airways and Popular Culture
(McFarland, 2007)

Fred Barton and the Warlords' Horses of China

How an American Cowboy Brought the Old West to the Far East

LARRY WEIRATHER

McFarland & Company, Inc., Publishers
Jefferson, North Carolina

LIBRARY OF CONGRESS CATALOGUING-IN-PUBLICATION DATA

Names: Weirather, Larry, 1944–
Title: Fred Barton and the warlords' horses of China : how an American cowboy brought the Old West to the Far East / Larry Weirather.
Description: Jefferson, North Carolina : McFarland & Company, Inc., Publishers, 2015. | Includes bibliographical references and index.
Identifiers: LCCN 2015040410 | ISBN 9780786499137 (softcover : alkaline paper)
Subjects: LCSH: Barton, Fred, 1889–1967. | Barton, Fred, 1889–1967—Travel—China. | Cowboys—Russia (Federation)—Siberia—Biography. | Horse breeders—Russia (Federation)—Siberia—Biography. | Americans—Russia (Federation)—Siberia—Biography. | Nicholas II, Emperor of Russia, 1868–1918—Friends and associates. | Warlordism—China—History—20th century. | Ranch life—Russia (Federation)—Siberia—History. | Intelligence officers—United States—Biography. | Cowboys—Montana—Miles City—Biography.
Classification: LCC DK766.W45 2015 | DDC 636.2/13092—dc23
LC record available at http://lccn.loc.gov/2015040410

BRITISH LIBRARY CATALOGUING DATA ARE AVAILABLE

© 2016 Larry Weirather. All rights reserved

No part of this book may be reproduced or transmitted in any form or by any means, electronic or mechanical, including photocopying or recording, or by any information storage and retrieval system, without permission in writing from the publisher.

On the cover: Fred Barton in Siberia, 1912. The horse may be a Russian half-and-half, but Barton brought his own saddle and tack (photo 940-763, Montana Historical Society Archives)

Printed in the United States of America

*McFarland & Company, Inc., Publishers
Box 611, Jefferson, North Carolina 28640
www.mcfarlandpub.com*

To Roy Knodel

Montanan with the 124th Cavalry Regiment,
Texas National Guard, the last cavalry unit to give up its horses.

His Mars Task Force in World War II
traded horses for mules and elephants and
fought behind enemy lines through the dark,
leech- and tiger-infested malarial jungles of Burma
into the freezing mountains of China, which is not to say,
despite loss of life and near universal loss of health,
they didn't take time out for a good rodeo.

Table of Contents

Acknowledgments — vii
Preface — 1
Introduction — 4

ONE • Fort Keogh Days, 1889–1905 — 11
TWO • A Young Bronc Peeler in Miles City, 1905–1911 — 23
THREE • Vladivostok and the World's Largest Horse Ranch, 1911–1912 — 36
FOUR • "Smoke 'Em If You've Got 'Em": The British-American Tobacco Co., 1912–1916 — 46
FIVE • Horses for the Warlords: The Longest Drive, 1917 — 60
SIX • 15th Infantry Cowboys and U.S. Intelligence, 1917 — 71
SEVEN • Khabarovsk, Siberia, to Hilar, Manchuria, 1917 — 87
EIGHT • Hilar, Manchuria, to Urga, Mongolia, 1917 — 94
NINE • Across the Gobi: Urga to Kalgan, 1917 — 103
TEN • Final Leg: Kalgan to Taiyuanfu, 1917 — 113
ELEVEN • Montana Cowboys in the Celestial Empire, 1918–1920 — 120
TWELVE • When to Hold 'Em, When to Fold 'Em, 1920–1937 — 134
THIRTEEN • Poor Little Rich Boy and Princess Xenia, 1920 — 144
FOURTEEN • The Many Wives of a Lifelong Bachelor, Here and Abroad — 148
FIFTEEN • Life Without Warlords: C.M. Russell and the Fred Barton Museum of the Old West, 1937–1967 — 164
SIXTEEN • Barton and the Hollywood Cowboys — 173
SEVENTEEN • Ruminating on Guys, Gussies and Morons at Trail's End — 190

Epilogue — 198
Chapter Notes — 207
Bibliography — 213
Index — 219

Acknowledgments

The acknowledgment pages of my earlier *Warlord Cowboys in China: The Fred Barton Story of the World's Greatest Horse Drive* (2009) said "the author would appreciate hearing from those who can provide additional clarity." At the time, much of the Barton story remained unknown or lacking context. Perhaps critical information would never come to light, lost forever. Since most of the paper trail had come to an end, I hoped my plea for additional information would reach hitherto unknown members of Barton's family or acquaintances who might have firsthand accounts. Response proved to be overwhelming and surprising.

All those earlier acknowledged share in this new attempt to come to grips with Barton's life. This project would not have been possible if not for the pioneering work done by Ralph Miracle, a story in his own right. Authors, historians, and others whose contributions, advice, or personal contact with Fred Barton proved immeasurably helpful include Craig G. Arnold of the Maritime Museum of San Diego; Bob Barthelmess, curator of the Range Riders Museum; Tom W. Clarke, Miles City historian; Edward M. Coffman, author of *The American 15th Infantry Regiment in China, 1912–1938*; Glen Dawson of Dawson's Books; Borein scholar and author Harold G. Davidson; Elizabeth A. Dear, curator of the C.M. Russell Museum; historian, author, and Russell scholar Brian W. Dippie; Scott Harrison of the U.S. Embassy, Beijing; C.A. "Andy" Hinton of the NAN Ranch; Dr. Frank Houle of the USDA Veterinary Services of APHIS; Dennis Noble, author of *Eagle and Dragon: The United States Military in China, 1901–1937;* Richard E. Oglesby of the Santa Barbara Corral of Westerners; Vivian Palladin, past editor of *Montana: The Magazine of Western History*; Michael Redmon of the Santa Barbara Historical Society; Koerner authority Fallis L. Oliver of Santa Barbara; Dick Raths, Montana veterinarian and chairman of the Cattle Health Brand Committee; C.M. Russell author and specialist Ginger K. Renner; Judith A. Sibley, assistant archivist at the United States Military Academy; John Taliaferro, author of *Charles M. Russell: The Life and Legend of America's Cowboy Artist*; and Richard Upton of Upton and Sons Publishers and Booksellers.

Special thanks go to families of the cowboys who went with Barton to China, particularly to Mr. and Mrs. Earl "Early" Camblin and family of Wright and Gillette, Wyoming. Also, thanks to the Perkins family of Miles City, and to Elaine Rhea for sharing family photographs.

The Montana Historical Society graciously opened all its files, including its Director's File and Magazine File, for this research. All the people there helped immensely, particularly Rebecca Kohl, photograph archivist. Other institutions who opened doors of knowledge included the National Archives, the U.S. Army Military History Institute at Carlisle Barracks, the Boise Public Library, the California Office of Vital Records and Statistics, the Portland State University Library, the Montana Stockgrowers Association, the Oberlin Shansi Memorial Association, the Clark College Library, and the Family History Center in Salt Lake City. Others who searched their holdings or allowed me to search for materials were various museums and art collections such as the Gene Autry Museum, the Cowboy Hall of Fame, the Buffalo Bill Historical Center, and the Richardson Collection. Great appreciation is also extended to personnel of Rocky Mountain College and Clark College who encouraged my time away from campus to pursue this path.

Among those who responded to the call to fill in the gaps and bring new context the author would particularly like to extend gratitude to Dr. Mary MacGregor-Villarreal, Jolaine Cowherd, Galia Ell, Robert Ell, and George Vitt. Their sharing led to an expansion and reevaluation of the Barton biography.

Also, special thanks go to all those folks who hosted the author's presentations about the cowboys in China at the Miles City Range Riders Museum, Bonita Miller in particular, and at the Pendleton Public Library for the 100th anniversary of the Pendleton Round-Up. Librarians and archivists at numerous institutions deserve much credit, particularly the Interlibrary Loan specialists who have been regularly kept busy over the years.

Friend of the literati and the wide, wide world of grammar, Doris Creelman deserves praise for her helpful suggestions.

The author's being married to his favorite librarian, Linda, the best supporter of this effort, did not hurt either. After Linda's father, to whom this book is dedicated, returned from the war in China, she sat with him through every B-Western motion picture that ran in Bozeman, Montana. Some of the on-screen cowboys were even real cowboys. Some appear in this book.

Thank you all for this group effort. The usual caveat applies. Any mistakes are mine, not yours. No man is an island, but the stacks of research files for the Barton story have created their own.

Preface

This book recounts the enigmatic life and times of Fred Barton, the Montana cowboy who went to China and raised horses for the warlords. Through print media, motion pictures, radio, television, and commercial artifacts, our popular culture has so seized on the iconic American cowboy of the Old West it may be hard at first to visualize a cowpuncher in a locale other than the plains of North America. Try Siberia and the Gobi Desert for starters. Barton rode through both on horseback.

Barton's stint as a bronc peeler occurred when cowboys faced dramatic changes. The first few decades of the twentieth century were a time of upheaval. Fences closed the open range, and long cattle drives ended. Range work was always seasonal, but staying employed in the saddle became even more difficult. The Old West era was gone, but not the cowboys.

To continue using their skills, many transitioned from the freedom of the open range to the more confining rodeo arena, Wild West show, vaudeville tent, and, most spectacular, Hollywood backlot. While Hollywood did provide jobs, motion pictures altered the cowboy image forever. As old-time cowboys said, celluloid cowboys in their fancy hats and blazing six-guns would have had a hard time being hired by any roundup boss. A few wranglers lit out for the country, or in Barton's case, out of the country. He hoped to find the Old West somewhere else. In his quest, he brought his version of Montana to China.

China underwent upheaval during the years Barton worked in the Far East (1911–1937). Caught between revolution, which overthrew hundreds of years of Manchu rule, and the China we know today, China's transitional decades became known as the chaotic warlord era. In this turbulence, Barton dared to create the biggest horse ranch in the world to supply the warlords with horses. He managed this ranch through the 1920s until the invading Japanese army commandeered it for their Shansi Province headquarters in 1937.

To stock his horse-breeding ranch, Barton embarked on the world's longest trail drive. For drovers, he was loaned the services of ex-cowboys serving with the U.S. 15th Infantry in Tientsin, China. This was no *Lonesome Dove*, for there were no cattle; only a massive herd of 3,500 big, hot-blooded Russian Orlov horses trailed through Siberia, Mongolia and Manchuria into China. There, they were bred with Mongol ponies and Morgans shipped in from the U.S and tended by Montana cowboys. And that was just part of Barton's adventures.

Barton followed his own long trail through the popular culture explosion of the first half of the twentieth century. He involved himself in the coffin business and cigarette advertising in China. Back in the States, he rubbed shoulders with the newly minted Hollywood set of artists and actors—Charles M. Russell, Edward Borein, Tom Mix, Will Rogers, William S. Hart, and Wallace Coburn. He spent much of his later years assembling his Museum of the Old West. He dedicated himself to preserving the memory of the open-range cowboys through his writings, his creation of the largest collection of Russell painting reproductions, and his continued interest in horse ranching.

The importance of this study resides in the timing of Barton's life (1889–1967). His timeline ranges from the Massacre at Wounded Knee to, on the day of his death, Mohammed Ali's indictment for refusing induction into the U.S. Army during the Vietnam War. Between those armed conflicts, much happened between the United States and China politically and culturally. The nineteenth and early twentieth century U.S. popular culture stereotype of the Chinese "Yellow Horde" had to change in the 1930s and 1940s to one of their being our democratic ally, more like us and less like the more "yellowed" Japanese enemy. Afterwards, the Chinese stereotype took on a different color, changing to "Red Horde." For the Chinese, American stereotypes passed through similar transformations, only Americans in China started out red, as "red-haired devils."

Fortunately for Barton, rural Chinese and Mongolians had never seen live ropers, riders, and shooters displaying their impressive skills as did cowboys at his ranch. Where movie theaters existed, and China did have them, city audiences admired cowboys by virtue of B-Westerns. As will be seen, the cultural clashes and exchanges between East and West inform Barton's biography. The opium and cigarette trade, Prohibition, dinosaur bone hunting craze, and the Roaring Twenties, jazz and prostitution scene all played roles.

When this project began nearly thirty years ago, other scholars and researchers warned the author not to get his hopes up. The warlord era in China was very difficult to research, particularly when it involved areas far from the big centers of population in Shanghai and Peking. How right they were.

Partly this was due to secrecy surrounding the "Great Game" being played by the major Western Powers, Russia and Japan in China. Prior to World War II, the U.S. government had little intelligence capability in the Far East. That meant that American commercial agents, travelers, and what little military the U.S. had in China became important sources of surreptitious information. Barton became part of that effort. As more records are found and declassified, the story of U.S. spy efforts in warlord China has only recently begun to be told. Barton's biography represents an attempt to do just that.

Chinese and Mongolian Place Names

Contemporary Names	*Current Names*
Amur River	Heilongjiang
Inner Mongolia	Nei Mongol Autonomous Region
Kalgan	Zhangjiakou
Mukden	Shenyang
Peking	Beijing

Contemporary Names	Current Names
Shansi	Shanxi
Sungari, Sunggari River	Songhuajiang
Tientsin	Tianjin
Urga	Ulan Bator

Pivotal Dates

1205–1279	Mongols invade China
1644–1912	Manchu rule of China
1894–1895	Sino-Japanese War
1900	Boxer Rebellion
1905	Russo-Japanese War over Korea and Manchuria
1911	Republican revolution, overthrow of Manchus
1917	Russian Revolution
1917–1927	Supreme warlord decade in China
1937–1945	Chinese war against Japanese invasion, World War II

Introduction

From Scythians to Roman chariots to Medieval mounted knights to Cossacks, warhorses played decisive roles in battle. The six-gun is said to have won the West, but not without the horse. Cowboys, Plains Indians, cavalry, all symbols of the Old West, owed their existence to the horse. And so did cowboy Fred Barton. As Old West icon, the horse was deeply rooted in the U.S. bedrock values of freedom, independence, the taming of nature, and the use of violence as justice. As will be seen, Fred Barton became the proverbial old warhorse in touting the virtues and preservation of the Old West. He grew up breaking Montana broncs and died with saddle and spurs in his Los Angeles apartment.

Even in modern times, military dependence on the horse was extreme. In World War I, Britain called up 165,000 mounts; Austria, 600,000; Germany, 715,000; and Russia, over one million.[1] In terms of sheer numbers, during World War I Russia ordered 3.3 million rifles, 4.5 million cartridges, 170,000 tons of barbed wire, and a staggering 20 million horseshoes from the U.S.[2] That was a lot of horse iron. The animals served as mounts for the cavalry and draft animals for artillery and transport wagons.

Consider World War II and what has been called the greatest tank battle ever fought, the Battle of Kursk. In this pivotal 1943 confrontation, Russian forces stopped and defeated the invading German army. Often overlooked is that the mechanized German blitzkrieg machine used more than a half-million horses, many more than vehicles. Horses could travel in mud. Tanks, mechanized artillery, and personnel carriers could not. Russia had a lot of mud.[3]

Perhaps no country realized the power of the warhorse more than China. Thirteenth-century mounted Mongol invasions changed China forever and proved the necessity of horses to Chinese rulers. Between the two world wars, China was caught in a transitional phase in trying to decide whether to modernize its armies in the Western style or not. After Western powers punished China for the Boxer Rebellion (1898–1900), many Chinese believed the country's military had to mechanize and organize on the Western pattern. Whereas some warlords saw cavalry as a powerful force, others saw armored trains, gunboats, airplanes, vehicles, and machine guns as the way to go. Generals like "Manchurian Tiger" Chang Tso-lin saw the merits of both ways. German military advisors were brought in. Officer candidates were sent off to modern Japanese military schools after the Japanese had defeated the Russians in the Russo-Japanese War of 1904–1905. Trained in Japan, these young Chinese officers came of age between the world

Warhorse Statue, Ming Tombs, Peking. Forced to import its horses through the centuries, China has revered the horse in art and on the calendar, as the Year of the Horse.

wars. For some, warlordism beckoned. Into this warlord free-for-all came Montana cowboy Fred Barton.

Barton joined other Western adventurers who became legends in China. The warlord period in China, which extended over most of the first half of the twentieth century, also became the golden age for soldiers of fortune in China. Anyone who went there during the warlord years was an adventurer, be they missionaries, merchants, mercenaries, military personnel, or explorers. Some Barton contemporaries became famous. Roy Chapman Andrews' expeditions into the Gobi Desert brought the "Indiana Jones" type Andrews world renown; one of Barton's North China/Mongolia acquaintances arranged vehicle and camel caravan transportation for the now-famous dinosaur bone hunter. Like Barton, Andrews became a civilian informant for U.S. intelligence in China, incorporating members of the U.S. and British armies into his museum expeditions; no wonder the Russians were accusing him of spying under the guise of science, even as their bevy of scientists were doing the same thing. Andrews thrilled the scientific community with his discovery of fossilized nests of dinosaur eggs. His velociraptor bones discovery would later be fleshed out, reanimated, and used to thrill *Jurassic Park* movie fans.

Although Andrews created his own colorful persona, it would be hard to beat that of "One-Arm" Sutton. Englishman Francis Arthur Sutton was injured in World War I at Gallipoli, where he came ashore carrying his golf clubs. As three soldiers sat on his chest, his right hand was amputated without the use of an anesthetic. This did not stop him from becoming a crack shot, bomb disposal expert, weapons inventor, news correspondent, island owner, champion golfer, Chinese Army general, and millionaire—just to mention a few of his accomplishments.

Sutton reached China on a path similar to Barton's, by first trying his luck in Russia. He sold boots in Russia, only to have the Cheka, or Soviet secret police, confiscate his consignment.[4] Similarly, Barton would have to change his plans due to the Russian Revolution. In 1919 Sutton tried his hand at gold mining in Siberia and ended up in Vladivostok, where Barton began his Siberian adventure as well. Sutton was known to walk around with a gold ingot, from which he would use his knife to peel off gold to pay bills and bribes. He ordered a huge gold dredge from the United States to be barged across the ocean, along with nails, women's shoes, and horseshoes for use in trade. Unfortunately for him, the war between the Russian Reds and Whites squelched this endeavor.

Sutton entered China, where he lost what money he had left on the Shanghai stock exchange, so he went to work as a munitions expert for various Chinese warlords, ending up with Chang Tso-lin in Mukden. "Manchurian Tiger" Chang was one of Fred Barton's warlord bosses. Sutton ran Chang's arsenal and trained his armies; Barton provided warhorses for Chang and associates. Chang so treasured Sutton that he gave One-Arm his own armored train and offered him as many fair Chinese maidens as needed. Before Chang was assassinated, he made Sutton a general in his army and a millionaire. Sutton fared better than Chang, surviving several assassination attempts and becoming a legend in China. Barton got the hell out.

One-Arm Sutton did not get out and was interned by the Japanese in Hong Kong with another equally colorful Old China Hand named "Two-Gun" Cohen. Obviously, when one self-promoting person named One-Arm has to share the stage with another self-promoting person named Two-Gun, one arm and two guns don't mix. The two couldn't stand each other's presence.

Unlike Sutton, Cohen and Fred Barton shared some of the same High Plains country, which extended from Barton's Montana into Cohen's Alberta and Saskatchewan. Whereas a Russian horse buyer coaxed Fred Barton from Montana to the Far East, Chinese railway workers and shopkeepers on the Canadian prairie would be Cohen's stimulant. Both men became High Plains drifters in North America and in the Far East.

Born of Jewish parents in Poland in 1897, Morris Abraham Cohen, and his family, escaped from the European pogroms and settled in London. Here, young Cohen became a pickpocket well-known to bobbies. To reform the young criminal, he was shipped off to a farm in Canada. As he came of age, he became a gambler, jailbird, lady's man, pimp, con artist, and real estate agent. Through his gambling, he became friends with Chinese who belonged to the Tongmengshui, an anti–Manchu-rule organization that supported Sun Yat-sen, revolution, and the formation of a republic in China. Cohen became a lifelong proponent of the Chinese cause—so much so that he was one of the few Westerners welcomed in China after the Communists seized control. Cohen trained Canadian Chinese in the military arts so that they could return to China to fight Manchu rule. After serving heroically with the Canadian Railway Troops in Europe in World War I, he went to China. He became "Father of the Country" Sun Yat-sen's personal bodyguard and lifetime devotee to Sun Yat-sen's wife, Soong Ching-ling, who would become the first woman president of the People's Republic of China (1968–1972). Her sister married Chiang Kai-shek, who ruled as president of the Republic of China on Taiwan.

Once, while saving Dr. Sun Yet-sen's life, Cohen was wounded in the left arm by a machine gun bullet. If it had been his right arm, he might not have been able to return fire. He decided then to carry two Smith and Wesson .45s, one on his hip and one in a shoulder holster. He also learned to shoot with either hand, hence, the name "Two-Gun."[5] Like many other soldiers of fortune in China, he advised and trained Chinese troops, to the point he was awarded the largely ceremonial rank of general.

Early in his China experience, Barton worked out of Shanghai, where resided a colorful yet unpleasant, rotund, bearded Buddhist abbot. Walking around in his Buddhist robe and sandals in the Bund gardens, the legendary Abbot Chao Kung bitterly heaped scorn on Europeans. He predicted he would someday walk on the ruins of London. Chao Kung was actually Trebitsch Lincoln, a Hungarian Jew and former Liberal member of Parliament from Darlington. *The Secret Lives of Trebitsch Lincoln* by Bernard Wasserstein explores what is known so far of triple-spy Trebitsch Lincoln's many identities. He had at various times been a curate in the Church of England, a Monte Carlo gambler, a failed businessman, a forger, an ex-convict, a postal censor, a would-be British spy, a confirmed German spy in the U.S., and an advisor to warlord Wu Pei-fu—all before entering a lamasery. He became a sworn enemy of Great Britain when his son was hanged for murder and he, racing back to Europe, was not permitted to land to see his son before the execution. Previously Lincoln's British citizenship had been revoked and he had been expelled.

Some colorful adventurers went to China in order to disappear if they were on the run. One, known simply as Kelley, was a seven-foot Texan who, like Barton, came of age as a cowboy. The redheaded Kelley wanted to see more of the world, so he became a Marine on an American man-of-war, going ashore in Mexico and other places around the world to quell disturbances. Assigned China gunboat duty up the Yangtze, he accumulated a fortune smuggling opium. Figuring he had enough money, he jumped ship and lived the wild life in the Shanghai clubs.

When things became too hot for Kelley there or he grew restless again, he spotted a blank space called Mongolia on maps of Asia. He filled his car with his remaining silver, kidnapped the prettiest "hostess" from the swanky Del Monte night club, and drove to Urga, Mongolia, without benefit of highways—a Hollywood movie in itself. Among his risky business adventures was his automobile touring company whose cars ran across the Gobi Desert from Urga to Kalgan. His Russian chauffeurs drove anyone anywhere on mysterious cruises, no questions asked. Such mysterious cruises included gunrunning. Due to his size, domineering nature, and the Colt he waved in the air, Kelley usually got his way. But the gunrunning was too much. He fled arrest, escaping back to China. Rumor had it that he had shot and killed his Shanghai flower, although she may have committed suicide. He had threatened to kick her out when he found her with one of his Russian chauffeurs.[6]

While Barton set up his horse ranch in China, Kelley was ducking the law and pursuing his wandering ways in the very places that Barton's friend Larson ran his businesses in Urga and Kalgan. It would be tempting to think that cowboy Kelley was an alias for cowboy Barton, but Barton was no seven-footer. There is the possibility that the two men met. If they did, Barton said nothing about it. They certainly traversed the same path across Mongolia and northern China.

This represents just a sampling of China legends. More will pop up as Fred Barton's story unfolds. Some people become legends; some do not. Why Barton's story heretofore has not stood with the others raises questions. As a top cowboy with proven credentials in line for legendary status, here is a man who

- was born at Fort Keogh on the frontier, the same year that Casey's Scouts of Cheyenne troops was formed at the fort, only to have Lt. Casey murdered at Pine Ridge the following year;
- canvassed the dangerous wilds of Siberia for the Russian czar to site the largest horse ranch in the world;
- trailed horses from Siberia, through Manchuria, and Mongolia into China—the world's longest horse drive—with the help of drovers from the U.S. 15th Infantry in China;
- assembled a group of Montana rodeo stars to create a quarter-million-acre horse ranch in Shansi, China;
- gathered intelligence for the U.S.;
- crossbred Russian, Mongolian, and Western horses to form a special breed for the Chinese warlords;
- became a tireless promoter of the Old West and artist C.M. Russell;
- owned the largest collection of Russell reproductions and created his own Museum of the Old West;
- married one of the richest widows in the Southwest and ran the famous NAN ranch; and
- hobnobbed with the Hollywood cowboy star crowd.

His horse drive alone would be worthy of a Hollywood film, yet Barton has remained in relative obscurity. Why?

Consider first what is necessary to create a legend or hero. In popular culture in the U.S., such a person needs to embody several characteristics. It helps if he is somewhat of a renegade to conform to our bedrock beliefs in individualism and freedom. The respected rogue succeeds by exhibiting special skills, pluck, and ingenuity to overcome overwhelming odds. Hence, such a person feeds into America's love of the underdog. Given American beliefs in democracy, the person must show commonality with everyone else. This includes not being elitist, overly intellectual, or perceived as being too far above everyone else. The person fights for and represents values we all share and is ready to sacrifice for those values. This is a far cry from the profusion of celebrities present today, whose popularity depends more on the creation of a persistent media image or persona rather than on personal, meaningful action. It's the difference between the 1920s' pre-eminent hero, Charles Lindbergh, and most everyone from the entertainment industry interviewed on television today. Lindbergh's historic 1927 solo flight across the Atlantic came just months after the death of Barton's hero, Charlie Russell.

Most of the people mentioned previously share some of these attributes, even those who are not American. As will be seen, Fred Barton embodies the attributes as well, but he still remains obscure. One reason might be that Barton was evasive, if not outright deceptive, about his past, so light could not be shone on it. Yet, others in China did the same. Often, such people as Two-Gun or One-Arm seemed to be such blowhards that, for biographers, truth was found in what these men refused to discuss rather than in what they enjoyed boasting about themselves. There is some of that in Barton's life.

Barton did not promote himself to the extent that Roy Chapman Andrews or Two-Gun did. Barton spent much of his life promoting the Old West and its values, particularly manifested in his promotion of cowboy artist C.M. Russell. Much of the time Barton promoted himself by indirect means. That is, he honored what for him what was the real American hero, the cowboy, which he considered himself to be. There would have been no Old West without the cowboy. Without the great cattle drives, the American West would have remained a trapped-out region where ragged miners moved from place to place across a landscape populated by dwindling numbers of Native Americans and buffalo. Without the cowboy, authors and motion picture makers would not have had the sheriffs, posses, gunslingers, railroads, rustlers, dance hall girls, gamblers, vigilantes, Matt Dillons, John Waynes, Ponderosas, Dodge Cities, Butches and Sundances, and Gary Coopers to quench audience thirsts. That iconic American six-gun and "six-gun" justice would not exist.

Independent and true to his beliefs, the cowboy was the true carrier of American values. Barton saw these qualities portrayed and exhibited by Russell and lived by old-school trail hands. Their actions and skills spoke more powerfully than their few words. To use a cliché, their word was their bond back when, for Barton, men were men. Barton most appreciated the comradeship formed by those who worked hard on the open range and the freedom the range offered. The cowboy represented most American bedrock values: Manifest Destiny, Western expansion, and the idea of the frontier coalesced around the cowboy. That the United States should be a beacon to the rest of the world, or the famous "City on the Hill" idea that this country should be a model for the rest of the world, clearly manifested itself in Barton's idealized cowboy. Barton measured all men and values against those of the cowboy. Triumphing over nature, another bedrock value, was how the cowboy made his living. A cowboy wasn't a cowboy without his horse. The tamed horse represented a triumph over nature in itself. If pushed, cowboys did not shy away from the slow-to-change bedrock belief in violence as justice either. This closely connected to another American value, that of technology as savior, which made Colt, Winchester, and other gun manufacturers famous. It also meant that Barton would not only want to ride a good horse, but also ride a good automobile when he no longer saddled up.

Barton might have become better known had he promoted himself directly. Instead, his writings do more implying than stating that he was part of this cowboy band of brothers. But he did not flinch in dropping the names of his cowboy heroes and friends that his listeners would be sure to recognize in order to create an association between him and them. He could bask in their glory, but this differs from the self-hype seen by many others of his time period. Of course, the others weren't cowboys. It was not in the cowboy code to extol oneself, and braggarts were distrusted.

After Barton engaged in occupations other than cowboying late in life, he came across to some as being an aging, windy blowhard. His story about China sounded unbelievable, so it was discounted, or at least treated with raised eyebrows. His stated friendship with famous people was questioned. Perhaps he rode on their coattails, inferior to their status, a wannabe. The jury remained out, sidetracking fame, waiting for his story to be confirmed.

Barton's identity problem also gets in the way. While his China contemporaries revealed fairly transparent lives, Barton's identity and past were hidden at various points. In part, this may have been the result of fearing for his life, protecting secrecy, and avoiding persecution, if not prosecution. Given his multiple identities or name changes, biographers are faced with difficult research problems in tracing the facts of his life. Likewise, divorces and litigations further complicated matters. A person who searches history for Fred Barton encounters many roadblocks. One who searches his other identities will be richly rewarded. Let us begin with his first identity.

• One •

Fort Keogh Days, 1889–1905

> *The Manchu Empire before 1898 had no Ministry of Foreign Affairs ... [so] contact had been dealt with by the Hall of Governance of Barbarians.*—Barbara Tuchman[1]

Fred Barton was not born Fred Barton. He was born Fred Kottmeier, Jr. So began his slippery history. From the get-go, his life embraced the Old West and rejected anything that wasn't the Old West.

Custer County, Montana Territory, did not record births in the 1800s, and Miles City newspapers reported few. Most went unnoticed. Death announcements overwhelmed those of births. The spring of Barton's birth, news accounts covered the great concern over the number of suicides in eastern Montana Territory—six within weeks. Why there were so many will be explained shortly, as those events helped shape Barton's life.

Lacking court records, Barton was able to change his birth date at different stages of his life. When he was eleven and sent to school in New Jersey, his birth was listed as April 1889, birthplace New York. As he grew into adulthood, he claimed he was born April 19, 1887, in Ekalaka, Montana. Later, the date became April 19, 1888, at nearby Fort Keogh just outside the town of Miles City. Finally, and throughout much of his adult life, he settled on April 19, 1889. In other words, he became younger as he aged. Wanting to appear older when younger and wanting to appear younger when older held certain advantages.

Barton and family members stated his father was a cavalry officer at Fort Keogh. Like Barton, Fort Keogh and Miles City were not born with those names. Both were the direct result of the 1876 Battle of the Little Big Horn and the defeat of the 7th Cavalry and death of General George Armstrong Custer. On the heels of the battle, Col. Nelson A. "Bear's Coat" Miles established the Tongue River Cantonment, also known as "the new fort on the Yellowstone." At the confluence of the Yellowstone and Tongue rivers, it could be resupplied by steamboats coming up the Missouri from St. Louis and down the Yellowstone. Infantry and cavalry patrols from this encampment served to block Cheyenne and Sioux from escaping to Canada. Miles was ordered out to campaign against various bands led by such chiefs as Sitting Bull, Gall, Crazy Horse, Lame Deer, and Chief Joseph, whose people were trying to make the arduous 1,200-mile flight to Canada to join Sitting Bull. The new fort was meant to force tribes to accept reservation life and to clear the way for the Northern Pacific Railroad.

Whiskey soon proved more of a problem than the tribes for Col. Miles. Mat Carrol, a nephew who traveled with the colonel, set up a whiskey tent for the soldiers eager for what Carrol's barrels contained. Other purveyors of the devil's tonsil varnish soon arrived. Miles ordered them off military ground. They moved two miles away, where they built shacks out of the cottonwood driftwood and deadfalls along the Yellowstone flats. This became Milestown. Drunken soldiers easily still made their way over the two miles, so Col. Miles moved the fort another few miles to the southwest, where it became Fort Keogh. In turn, Milestown with its saloons moved the extra distance towards the fort and became Miles City. As long as Col. Miles moved his fort along the river, Miles City probably would have dogged him everywhere, had it not been for the 1881 coming of the railroad, which fixed the town's location.

Less than a decade later, when Barton was born, memories of the Little Big Horn were still fresh. The fort was named for Capt. Myles Keogh of I Troop, 7th Cavalry, who died with Custer. Keogh's father had been a Royal Irish Lancer stationed at Garry Owen near Limerick, Ireland. "The Garry Owen" tune perhaps will be forever associated with Custer and the 7th Cavalry. Similarly, in the year after the battle, Big Horn County changed its name to Custer County in remembrance of the general.

Something is amiss with Barton's father's history as a Fort Keogh cavalry officer. None of the fort's monthly commissioned officer reports for the 1880s and 1890s list a Fred Kottmeier, Sr. He may have been a noncommissioned officer, but no service record for him has surfaced. However, not all military service records have survived. He may also have served under another name. As will be seen, the Kottmeier family did undergo name changes. Another possibility is that family members stretched the truth.

When Fred, Sr., died in New York in 1920, the commander of the Old Guard of the City of New York, a ceremonial guard consisting of veterans, requested that Old Guard comrades, members of the Veteran Battalion, and ex-members of the 22nd Regiment turn out for the funeral of Sgt. Kottmeier. This indicated Barton's father had served in some military capacity, somewhere, at sometime, even if only in the New York militia or National Guard.

While Fred Barton, Jr., was destined to go to China and travel the trails of Genghis Khan, his father worked for a Kahn in New York City for many years until his death. So valued and well thought of was he that the firm of Jacques Kahn, Inc., called a special meeting of its board of directors upon his death. The meeting had the sole purpose of passing resolutions to honor their friend and loyal employee of thirty-four years. The board took the extra step of publishing these resolutions in the *Sun and New York Herald* for all to see. Directors lauded Kottmeier's genial nature and sterling character, and pointed out that he had served with the original founder of the company, Jacques Kahn, recently deceased. Kottmeier worked as a salesman for Kahn, a prosperous Austrian Jew who became one of the largest manufacturers of plate glass and ornamental mirrors in the world. Much of that glass found its way into the still-existing fifty or more Art Deco skyscrapers and other buildings that his famous architect son, Ely Jacques Kahn, designed for New York City. Coining the term "New York Style" of architecture, Ely became known as "master of the 1920s loft building." Fred Kottmeier had become Kahn family.

The accolades present a dating problem. If Fred Barton's father worked continuously for Jacques Kahn, Inc., for thirty-four years, that meant he started with the firm around

One • *Fort Keogh Days, 1889–1905* 13

Left: Fred Barton's father (Frederick Kottmeier, later known as Fred Barton, Sr.). Photograph taken in 1888, a year before Fred Barton's birth. Fred Sr. died in 1920 (photograph 940-760, Montana Historical Society Archives). *Right:* Martha Barton, wife of Fred Barton, Sr. Photograph taken in 1888 just before her son Fred was born. Although her son was born a Kottmeier, the Kottmeiers adopted her family name of Barton. She outlived her husband by three decades, dying in 1950 (photograph 940-761, Montana Historical Society Archives).

1886. He didn't marry Martha Olive Barton in New York until June of 1888, around the time of Fred Barton's birth, give or take a year. Unless the elder Kottmeier was a Kahn merchant in Miles City or the company happened to be wrong about his length of service or his term of work was not continuous, it becomes problematic putting him at Fort Keogh in the cavalry when Barton said he himself was born.

The senior Barton may have worked for Fort Keogh's 8th Cavalry or 22nd Infantry in a civilian capacity, or both. At times the number of tradesmen at the fort outnumbered even the number of horses and mules. The month of his son's birth nearly 150 tradesmen worked at the fort. Another fifteen civilians worked for the Quartermaster Department, mostly as teamsters. Trade occupations included butcher, baker, barber, blacksmith, currier, cook, cabinetmaker, cooper, carpenter, engineer, fireman, molder, Moroccan leather finisher, machinist, miner, sawyer, tinsmith, painter, printer, tailor, wheelwright, telegraph operator, schoolteacher, locksmith, spinner, farmer, gardener, shoemaker, boilermaker, varnisher, brushmaker, coal miner, weaver, turnings finisher, brakeman, horseshoer, lathe worker, and stonemason. This does not include laundresses and side occupations. Fort Keogh was not a sleepy post.

Nor did the fort typify the frontier. Dispel any visions of Hollywood and television forts with their timbered stockades, main gates that swing open and shut just in time, and corner lookout towers or perches where soldiers hold off circling Indians mounted on ponies as arrows and bullets rattle the ramparts. Keogh looked more like a small town than a fort, hence the number of tradesmen. Rather than in a square or rectangle, its buildings were arranged around an open central diamond-shaped parade ground. Fourteen officers' quarter's buildings formed two sides of the diamond, with the commanding officer's quarters on the west point of the diamond. Officer accommodations were luxurious by frontier standards. Each wooden two-story duplex enjoyed a porch, dormer windows, and yard. Four sets of barracks for infantry and cavalry sat opposite. Other buildings included a granary, storehouse, bakery, various offices, guardhouse, photographer's studio, hospital, as well as others. "Suds Row" consisted of a series of one-story shacks. Here wives of the enlisted men did their family's laundry as well as that of the officers. These shacks for the enlisted men consisted of tarps, boards, logs, or a hodgepodge of materials available. Instead of a stockade, cords of firewood were stacked around the perimeter to serve as both partial fence and defensive perimeter. Very utilitarian.

Whatever Fred Kottmeier, Sr.'s position was in the 1890s, Fort Keogh offered much action for his growing child. Young Fred's preschool life at the fort would draw him back to Miles City for life. In summer, fort children could interact with Cheyenne boys and girls in the teepee encampments bordering Keogh. Families visited troops in the field. Sounds of shooting practice added to the excitement, as nearly every summer day soldiers competed to go up against teams from other forts. There were picnics, band performances, buggy rides, socials, parades, hunting and fishing family expeditions (even the schoolmarm and fort chaplain went hunting, in proper Victorian attire). In winter, the fort enjoyed its own skating rink. Children watched ice being sawn and harvested in huge blocks from the river. Pleasant smells from the bakery permeated all seasons.

Animals abounded. Kids grew up with them. Horses and mules ruled at Fort Keogh, but fort families also tended chickens, geese, and pigs for food. Pigs were fine until some people refused to keep them penned. Bullwhackers passed through with huge teams of oxen. Miles City stockyards filled with the restless din of cattle, horses, and sheep being sent to market. Sheepherders had first come to the Miles City area, followed by mostly English and Scottish interests in horses and then cattle.

Fortunately, photographers captured life at the fort and Miles City during Barton's early years. A succession of them documented Fort Keogh and Miles City, including John Fouch (1877–1879), Stanley J. Morrow (1878–1879), L.A. Huffman (1878–1891), and Christian Barthelmess (1888–1891). Barthelmess captured everyday life at the fort and in the field more than the others. As part of the military band, he was involved in most of the doings in and around the area, having set up his own studio at the fort. Much of what we know about Fort Keogh comes from the work done by Barthelmess. It was he who photographed the fifteen children old enough to attend the fort's school run by Laura G. Ritner at the time Barton was three years old. He avoided her teaching, being sent East instead upon reaching school age.

But it would be L.A. Huffman's photographs that Barton would collect throughout his life. For Barton, Huffman best captured the Old West, especially cowboy life on the frontier. What cowboy artist Charles M. Russell did in painting, Huffman did in photographs. Sometimes Russell used Huffman's photographs as the basis for a painting.

They captured the golden age of the open-range, long-drive cowboy just as the Old West was reaching its inflection point when Barton was born. For Fred, the Old West of the cowboy hit its heyday from 1875 to 1900. Although he would not become a cowboy until the early 1900s, he revered being trained by those old hands, who were captured in the art of Russell and Huffman rather than in the phony versions created by dime novels and, later, Hollywood.

They captured a period on the cusp of dramatic times that would change life at the fort, for Barton, and on the American frontier. Just prior to Barton's birth, Charlie Russell was himself trying his hand at cowboying. In the horrible winter of 1886–1887, he and the ranch foreman tended a herd up in the Judith Basin, far north of Miles City. The absent Helena, Montana, owner wrote to ask how his herd was fairing. The two men didn't have the heart to tell him that his investment was gone. Instead of writing a letter to describe the winter die-off, wrangler Russell sent a postcard-sized drawing he had done of a starving steer on its last legs being circled by wolves in the colorless snow void. He scrawled "Waiting for a Chinook" on the drawing, referring to a warming wind that might save the steers. Russell later painted a more detailed version of the drawing, entitling it *Last of the 5000*, which would become one of his more famous works. The disaster gave the young artist his start and forever embedded the iconic steer in American popular culture, a Western image perhaps rivaled only by sculptor James Earle Fraser's later sad *End of the Trail* portrayal of a slumped Native American on his horse.

That winter changed things forever. Severe drought had previously weakened the herds, steers growing thin as they overgrazed the little grass available, leaving little for winter forage. The howling Siberian Express whipped snow into drifts up to a hundred feet high. In places where wind stripped snow away, the blanket of white still remained deep enough to make it a struggle for animals to move or feed, or a solid crust of ice was exposed. The sharp crust further complicated survival, cutting the hair and hide off animals that tried to wade through the frozen landscape. Ice locked any exposed vegetation in its iron grip. In blinding, below-zero conditions, cowboys tried to keep herds moving to prevent stock from bunching up in coulees and dying. When drifting herds reached a fence or natural barrier, they refused to face into the wind, so they just stood there, starved, and froze. Cowboys literally froze to their saddles. Finally, they had to give up and let the wolves have their way. When Barton was a boy, the remains of the big herds were still being found in the coulees and hoodoos of the high plains. After spring thaws, some depressions turned white, not with snow, but with bones piled high.

At Fort Keogh the terrible winters and summers continued in the years before and after the Great Die-off. During the 1886–1887 winter, a Guinness World Record 15-inch diameter snowflake was recorded at the fort. Near record temperatures in the hundreds were recorded in successive summers, only to be followed by -65 F degrees in January of 1888. This record stood for forty years as the coldest temperature recorded in the U.S. Soldiers at the fort and the 900-plus Miles City townspeople also waited for a Chinook.

Because cattle paid the bills, the Great Die-off was generally regarded then and now as a cattle disaster. Horses, however, were not spared. Those horses unfortunate enough to be on the rolling prairies suffered the greatest death tolls. The snow became just too deep to paw through. Horses closer to the mountains could beat their way to steep, south slopes and dig down through thinner snowbanks to find some grass. Ranchers had no hay for horses. If they had some cattle feed, it meant days on snowshoes rather than horses just to reach livestock.

The disaster, which stretched across the West, convinced stockmen that the days of the open range and long cattle drives from Texas were over. Many cattle owners lost everything. For those who did continue the cattle business, one option lay in fencing cattle in, where they could be cared for and fed throughout the winter. Miles City sat at the heart of the reeling Montana cattle industry, so it was somewhat of a relief to find some respite from the troubles when the celebratory Stock Growers' Convention was held there in 1887, the year pastures began to be fenced in the area. It was also the year honoring one hundred years of U.S. presidents. Hundreds of cowboys "returning from the States" came to town "to see the elephant." They hoped for jobs and slept where they could, sometimes in the hills or under the cottonwoods. Theodore "Teddy" Roosevelt arrived on a train, but this would be his final year as a cattle rancher. (The winter of 1886–1887 cured him. Hundreds of his 5,000 head had perished on his two Dakota ranches.) Extra Pullman cars were brought in for housing to accommodate the numbers of people attending. Miles City teamed with excitement, temporarily masking the enormous changes.

To meet this changed world, stockmen dealt with immediate problems, such as the burgeoning wolf population that had feasted on the carcasses and weakened animals to the point the predators had become belligerent even towards humans. It was not just that wolves killed, it was the way they killed. A most revolting sight to a rancher was seeing a cow hamstrung by wolves. They would not kill the cow outright; rather, they would be eating on her, while she, still alive, would be trying to drag herself away on her front legs. The longer lasting solution to the disaster was in cooperation, pooling their efforts. Thus, the idea of the cattle pools was born.

This would be the world that cowboy Fred Barton would work in when he came of age.

Stockmen formed a roundup committee, which selected a captain of the roundup. This foreman oversaw roundups in designated regions where different ranches grazed their herds. The word of the foreman equaled or bettered that of God. In short, instead of each ranch's having its own roundup at different times and at different places with its own crew, branding and cutting out steers for market could be done all at once in specified areas at specified times with combined crews. Cooperation rather than competition was needed for the industry to make it.

Fred Barton was born during the 1889 Stock Growers' Convention held again in Miles City as this reorganization of the ranges was just taking hold. By 1890 the range had been divided into eleven districts. Newspapers announced the specific dates to ranchers when roundups would be held in their district—a far cry from the times when herds drifted everywhere and each rancher's cowboys kept to themselves. The Big Die-off had done its job. Bad winters persisted, but cattle industry survivors could go on.

Fences and hay pastures multiplied. As Montana cattle baron Granville-Stuart said of the disaster, "I wanted no more of it. I never wanted to own again an animal that I could not feed and shelter."[2] Like most disasters, the early signs were there and the causes many. The same pattern that led to the closing of the open range repeated itself preceding the "Dust Bowl" years of the Great Depression in the 1930s. Weather cycles suckered people. In the case of cattlemen, it wasn't "rain follows the plow" salesmanship, but rather "rain follows the cow." An 1875–1885 period of increased rain led stockmen to believe the prairie would support vast herds in perpetuity. Rich, abundant grass seemed the norm. The grass prairie existed throughout the West, making it easy to feed, water, and trail herds to Montana from Texas or Oregon to be fattened, placed in railroad cars, and shipped to the Midwest and East. Ominously, in the two years before the Great Die-off, a drought steadily crept northward from Texas. Temperatures fluctuated wildly, with hotter highs in summer and colder colds in winter. At times, it was hot when it shouldn't have been hot and cold when it shouldn't have been cold. More cattle died each winter.

Before the winter of 1886–1887, stockmen tolerated and expected a normal winter die-off of from 1 to 5 percent. Grazing cattle on the open range was cheaper than feeding cattle at that loss rate. During the good times, a cattleman could realize $40 in profit per head, over and above the paltry $1.50 it took to raise the animal and the shipping costs. If 1,000 steers were sent to market, the owner could realize a profit of a million dollars in today's money.

This led to inevitable overproduction, speculation, and greed. Instead of the overproduction of wheat just before the Dust Bowl years, the West experienced the overproduction of beef. Everyone who could afford to wanted to own a cattle herd. Butchers did so, former miners did so, retired army soldiers did so. It was another gold rush, only this one had horns. Tens of millions of dollars flowed into Montana from English investors. The demand for beef had been there, spurred by the earlier demand for tinned beef to feed Union forces during the Civil War. Now the railroads made it possible to ship beef east to meet increased U.S. urbanization. Processing plants sprang up along rail lines. Refrigerated railcars and ships made exporting beef to England and elsewhere a big business. As oversupply increased and prices began to spiral downwards, speculators still poured in. The frenzy is greatest when a bubble is about to burst.

Other forces also doomed this golden age of the West. Stricter cattle quarantine laws made it harder to move cattle from state to state or state to territory. The coming of the railroads also meant the coming of the farmer, meaning less contiguous grazing land for cattle. Although designed to capitalize on the cattle industry, the railroad curtailed long-drive cattle herds. Railroads began fencing their rights-of-way to prevent cattle from taking shelter in their road cuts. In effect, this amounted to a fence being placed across the waistline of the U.S.

Although the golden age of the long drives was over, the need for cowboys and horses was not. Young Barton would soon have his chance to realize the dream of so many youngsters of becoming a cowboy. The cattle industry changed, but Miles City remained a key shipping point for livestock. Cowboys would still be needed to break horses, brand cattle, and man the roundups. Their lives would be tough and challenging, a young man's game.

Another event shook Fort Keogh to its core the winter of 1890–1891, when Barton was going on two years of age. Just as changes occurred on the cattle range, relations with the tribes also changed. As more and more tribes had been forced to accept reservation life, the Indian Wars appeared over. Infantry and cavalry at Fort Keogh, the largest army fort in Montana, spent their time drilling and patrolling rather than campaigning. Earlier, at the time of Barton's birth in 1889, a unique change at the fort occurred when Lt. Edward "Ned" Wanton Casey asked the army for permission to form a new cavalry detachment consisting of 100 Cheyenne men. The army, such as Custer's Seventh Cavalry, had used riders from various tribes as scouts before, but never as an entire cavalry unit. Casey was a natural, creative leader as a West Point cadet. Even though he had attended the military academy with men such as 2nd Lieutenant John J. Crittenden III, who was killed and mutilated along with Custer on the Little Big Horn, he sympathized with the plight of the Native Americans, who called him Big Red Nose.

Despite doubters and protests, Casey believed the Cheyenne would make disciplined cavalry soldiers. Reservation life and attempts at farming had largely failed, so many Cheyenne were desperate. "Casey's Scouts" gave them a chance to feed their families. Casey's Scouts, L Troop, Eighth Cavalry, drew most of its men from the Northern Cheyenne in the Fort Keogh area and from Little Chief's band of Cheyenne, who had just returned in 1890 to the Tongue River from living with the Oglala Sioux at Pine Ridge. They earned forty cents a day more than a regular army private, and they needed to sign on only for six months. They furnished their own horses and tack, so they could ride on something they already knew.

Similar to another, later, West Point graduate, General George S. Patton of World War II fame, Casey wanted to distinguish the appearance of his unit. To promote unit pride and its uniqueness, Casey ordered special uniforms and insignia. Whereas Patton wanted his tank men to be adorned in gold helmets and bulky "Green Hornet" suits, which, of course, were rejected by the army, Casey still wanted his men to look like working cavalry, adapted slightly for the Native American. For instance, instead of the usual crossed-sabers insignia, Casey's Scouts wore crossed arrows. The Scouts' appearance most differed from that of regular cavalry in terms of winter dress. When artist Frederic Remington saw them in their bulky winter coats and towering hoods, he likened them to a cross between Russian Cossacks and Black Crooks.[3] Black Crooks referred to players and ballet dancers in a popular comic stage production of the time called *The Black Crook* (think men in tights). Casey's plan and training worked.

Casey's Scouts drew praise from everyone who saw them. Besides Remington, other notables such as naturalist and ethnologist George Bird Grinnell admired them. L Troop had nearly finished building its own cantonment for themselves and their families just upstream a mile and a half from the fort when they were ordered out to Pine Ridge in South Dakota. The trip ended in tragedy for just about everyone involved—in the events surrounding the massacre at Wounded Knee.

Another hard winter had already set in that December of 1890 when the column of Casey's Scouts moved out of Fort Keogh. They were riding into the teeth of a peculiar brand of millenarianism. The troop headed east to a natural fortress area known as the Stronghold to reconnoiter encampments involved in Ghost Dancing, which was causing panic among white settlers. Ghost Dancers followed the messages of Wovoka (Jack Wilson), a Paiute sheepherder that many Native Americans considered a messiah. So powerful was Wovoka's message that some of Casey's Scouts earlier had gone to hear him.

Within a year, the religion spread throughout Western tribes, particularly through its words of healing, clean living, and peaceful coexistence to create a better world. When Wovoka's message reached the Sioux, it was interpreted as a revelation to drive out the whites to herald in a new era. This generated great excitement, if not hysteria, among the Oglala Sioux on the Pine Ridge Reservation. The Ghost Dance was a variation of traditional circle dancing; only now warriors wore special Ghost Shirts with spiritual powers that made wearers immune to bullets.

Other military units had already arrived in the Pine Ridge area. Sitting Bull, his son, and eight others of his band were killed after Sitting Bull was arrested as an inciter. Six Indian policemen also died in the struggle. A band of Miniconjous left their reservation and headed to Pine Ridge. The Seventh Cavalry met them at the site of a tragic massacre, Wounded Knee, considered to be the last battle of the Indian Wars. Here, over 150 men, women, and children were slaughtered and buried in a mass grave, while 25 troopers died on the spot, many believed to have been killed by friendly fire.

Up to that point, Casey had kept his troops out of any of the preliminary confrontations, much to the disappointment of his troops. They hoped to heap revenge on recent enemies and to bring back horses as prizes. Casey forbade it. After the Wounded Knee massacre, he sought a peaceful solution. Leaving his troop behind so as not to create a misunderstanding and another slaughter, he decided to ride into a Sioux camp to risk a face-to-face talk with the chief. He was warned against doing this since the Sioux were in no mood to palaver, especially because of the horrific events of the previous day. Not far from the Sioux encampment, Casey was intercepted by messengers. One shot him in the back of the neck, killing him.

When Casey's Scouts returned to the fort with their leader's riderless horse, the cold January day became the saddest in the fort's history. The popular peacemaker was gone. The New Year seemed very bleak. Newborn Casey Barthelmess, son of the post's photographer, was promptly named after the popular lieutenant. Barthelmess saved the photo his father took of the sad homecoming of half-frozen Cheyenne cavalry. The photo has become one of the most published photos involving Fort Keogh. Barthelmess was born about the same time Fred Barton's brother, Lester, was born in 1890, both a year younger than Fred. Casey's path and Fred's would converge later on at Miles City as both became cowboys.

Also capturing events involving Fort Keogh and Wounded Knee in 1890 was Western artist Frederic Remington. When the visiting artist saw Casey's Scouts at the fort he said, "They fill the eye of a military man until nothing is lacking."[4] He rendered an image of one of Casey's Scouts at the fort. He also rode in a wagon along with Casey's Scouts at the time of Casey's death and captured events surrounding the tragedy in his art, recording in his book *Pony Tracks* how frustrating it was for Casey's Scouts to be shot at, and under orders not to shoot back.

Despite the thrilling adventures children had growing up at Fort Keogh, the history surrounding Barton's childhood was not the proverbial bed of roses. Not only was the cattle industry evolving through devastating events, but also the Indian Wars concluded. Consequently, life changed at the fort and Miles City as more settlers and speculators poured in. This created bubble resulted in the Panic of 1893. Railroads had overexpanded the same way the cattle industry had. New railroads and new trunk lines sprang up everywhere. Wall Street couldn't issue stock fast enough. People couldn't become rich overnight fast enough. The collapse of the beef industry only delayed by a few years that of the railroads.

Most railroads went bankrupt, including such stalwarts as the Northern Pacific, which ran through Miles City, the Union Pacific, and the Atchison Topeka & Santa Fe, the subject of popular songs. Some 600 banks failed, along with 15,000 businesses. Unemployment soared to nearly 20 percent. The same investors from abroad who had thrown money at the vast Western cattle herds and railroads now yanked their money out of the U.S. A run on gold began.

The new state of Montana was severely tested. The bottom had fallen out of grain and cattle prices. To make matters worse, the government repealed the Sherman Silver Act, which meant it had stopped buying silver. This forced Montana mines to close, mining being the second pillar of Montana's economy, behind agriculture. The boom-bust economic pattern of the U.S. stayed on course.

Dissatisfaction among the Montana unemployed directly affected Fort Keogh. A national worker's army, referred to as Coxey's Army, or more formally as the Army of the Commonwealth in Christ, planned to march on Washington, D.C. This constituted the nation's first planned protest march on the Capitol. Out-of-work miners and railroad workers in Butte, Montana, planned to join the 1894 march. When refused railroad transport to Washington, the men commandeered a Northern Pacific locomotive and some cars and set out anyway. Under their elected leader, William Hogan, these Hoganites, or Commonwealers, steamed across Montana, with the support of the populace in towns along the way. Right out of an early silent movie melodrama, close on their heels, steamed another train of federal marshals in hot pursuit, since the railroad was under court jurisdiction at the time. Some men died in a confrontation in Billings, Montana. Surviving federal agents were lucky to get away with their lives as residents of Billings besieged them in a railroad building while the Commonwealers got up steam and pulled out of town on another train.

By this time, soldiers at Fort Keogh were detailed to protect railroad property, particularly bridges, from being destroyed by the Hoganites. Five hundred soldiers from the fort met the 500 on the train at Forsyth, Montana, not far from Miles City. In the face of that organized firepower, Hogan and his men surrendered, averting a massive shootout. After that event, Fort Keogh settled back into a more normalized and peaceful routine.

For young Fred Barton and his brother, Lester, their militaristic, disciplined life was just about to begin and their free-ranging childhood end. Just after the Hoganite episode, five-year-old Fred was packed up and sent back East to begin school. This was not unusual for the time, as the West Coast did not have boarding schools and those in preparation for West Point needed to attend preparatory boarding schools and military academies for boys. Often unruly boys were also, in cowboy lingo, "eared" for the East to be straightened out, put on a career path, or both. Such was also the case of Charles M. Russell, Barton's cowboy-artist hero. Russell was sent back East from St. Louis to receive his schooling, to gain discipline, and to be dissuaded from wanting to go west. He chafed at the rules and made it to Montana and cowboy life as quickly as he could. A similar result occurred with Fred Barton, making it easy for the two men, though separated by an age difference, to feel a common bond. Both Charlie and Fred had been enrolled by their parents in New Jersey military academies.

Sending Fred and Lester to boarding school indicates their parents were somewhat well off. Tuition at the time was $400 a year, which would be approximately $11,000 in today's money. So to pay for both boys, Fred Kottmeier, Sr., and his wife, Martha, would pony up at least $22,000 a year in today's money for their sons' education at the Freehold Military School and the New Jersey Military Academy. The academy was arranged so that younger children "could benefit by the unquestioned advantages of military training and be free from the influence of boys of maturer years," according to school advertising. These younger boys had their own building and department at the Freehold Military School, billed as "a sub-preparatory school with a military system especially adapted to young boys." Older boys would graduate into the New Jersey Military Academy.

Fred hated it. The schools advertised themselves as institutions where boys prepared for business and college, but their strict military discipline was not for Fred, already inured to the freedom of the Big Sky. His first five years in Freehold, New Jersey, were spent under the direction of Major Charles M. Duncan, who had organized a unit to fight in the Spanish-American War. Upon entering the New Jersey Military Academy, Fred then encountered Colonel Charles J. Wright, principal and founder of the schools. Wright served in the Union army during the Civil War, having survived the New Orleans, Red River, and Port Hudson campaigns. During the Battle of the Wilderness, he commanded the 27th Infantry Regiment, United States Colored Troops. He was wounded at the assault on Petersburg and also at Fort Fisher. By the time Fred met him, Duncan had founded several other military academies, almost a cottage industry around the turn of the century. As if that weren't enough military for Fred, the army detailed officers to serve as teachers. While Colonel Wright made sure to tell parents that the school was certainly not a reform school, it was definitely designed to keep boys on the straight and narrow.

Barton spent six years at the New Jersey Military Academy at Freehold. Located near the site of the Battle of Monmouth, the academy was imbued with history. Folklore surrounding Molly Pitcher originated there. The Continental Army under George Washington confronted British troops at Freehold in June 1778. During that time, with the temperature over 100 degrees, it was imperative that women bring water to the soldiers and wounded, to the cannons to cool the barrels, and to the cannon swabs. These water bearers were nicknamed Molly Pitcher. Legend has it that one such woman manned a cannon after her husband went down. She so distinguished herself that General Washington made her an officer. After a British cannonball tore through the bottom of her skirt, she purportedly said, "It could have been worse."

As in any military academy, Fred had to dress in uniform, stand at attention, and perform military drills, all while attending to studies. No cavalry horses here. No Cheyenne scouts. No cowboys and herds. No smell of sage. Instead, the boys were called out to present colors and to march in services or special events in Freehold. That's about as good as it got, if you could call it good, although New York City and its enticements lay only forty-two miles away. Fred couldn't wait for his prison term to be over. While the New Jersey Military Academy offered excellent preparation for other officers' sons headed to West Point, Barton said he learned one great thing from his Eastern education: he never wanted anyone to give him orders again. Ironically, his future would have everything to do with the military.

Still, he must have made some friends during his years in Freehold. In the 1960s, before his death, Barton still paid for a gift subscription of *Montana: The Magazine of Western History* to be sent to his friend Joseph Treacy. The same age as Barton, Treacy and his wife were longtime residents of Freehold, the town that would rise to fame as the childhood home of musician Bruce "The Boss" Springsteen in another century.

• Two •

A Young Bronc Peeler in Miles City, 1905–1911

That s.o.b. had no head at all, just neck growed up and haired over.[1]—Fred Barton quotes an old cowman

It's okay to think you are a cowboy, unless, of course, you happen to run into someone who thinks he's an Indian.[2]—Richard S. "Kinky" Friedman, the "Good Ol' Texas Jewboy"

When Barton turned sixteen, he was gone.

Free at last, he made tracks back to Miles City and the life of a cowboy on the open range, which meant starting at the bottom. The bottom meant being a nighthawk, and this meant Fred started out exactly how Charlie Russell started, at the bottom. Russell stuck with it for eleven years. The job was dangerous during his tenure, since raiding parties killed several nighthawks in the Judith Basin where Russell worked. Nighttime was the magic time to steal horses. Fred would not face quite the same dangers, more removed from the Battle of Wounded Knee. Yet the nighthawk was still seen as being menial, expendable although important.

Barton's responsibilities included tending the remuda, the herd of saddle and work horses used by the cowboys to work the cattle. Ten head of horses usually were allotted to each cowboy, so it was typical for the nighthawk to be responsible for 150 horses in a remuda, including work horses and spares, although some remudas contained upwards of 250 head. The purpose of the remuda was to keep horses from straying at night so cowboys would not have to spend time each morning trying to round up mounts that had disappeared to hell and gone. The remuda and nighthawk also prevented rustlers and predators such as bears, wolves, and mountain lions from taking horses.

At its simplest, nighthawking meant keeping the horses calm and close during the night, and then finding some shade, unrolling the bedroll, and catching sleep during the day. Spring calving roundups and fall beef roundups were another story. The nighthawk's job never ended. Sleep had to be caught in snatches, for now the job entailed both day and night work. The trick at night was to give the horses enough space to graze so they would be good for the next day's work, but not so much that they couldn't be rounded up quickly. At its most complex, nighthawking meant quickly learning the names of all the horses and being able to recognize brands and ear cuts, even if they were old and haired over. It also meant keeping one's mouth shut after a night's work when ornery cowboys were awakened an hour or more before dawn and still had not had their second cup of coffee, whereafter they began to approximate something that might vaguely tolerate their own species.

Night posed its own problems. On inky nights when Barton rode blind, he could tell the disposition of the remuda only by the tinkling of the bell horses. The bell horses, or "bunch quitters," would try to sneak off with other followers, which is why they were belled. Clever horses learned to sneak into a ravine or coulee without making much sound. Barton had to outfox these horses and keep them close. Unforgiveable it would be for the raw nighthawk who fell asleep or let the herd drift in different directions. Gathering such a dispersed remuda in the morning took working cowboys off their job and could delay contracted cattle shipment at the railroad siding, costing the cattlemen thousands of dollars in railroad penalties if trains had to be delayed.

On nights shot through by lightning, cattle horns emitted eerie sparks of St. Elmo's Fire. Fireballs accumulated at the tips of horses' ears, setting the stage for a stampede. A cowboy dared not draw out any conductor of electricity such as a metal pistol or a rifle from its scabbard, although usually working cowboys did not carry rifles. Even holstered, a .45 charged and buzzing with electricity at a rider's side just added to the overall body tingling. Daytime was no peach either. When fattened beef were trailed a good hundred miles through the rough badlands to the railroad at Miles City, usually at least one river had to be crossed. During roundup, this was repeated several times, much to the delight of mosquitoes. Quicksand and treacherous currents stood in the way. Knowing how to swim helped, but sometimes the only way for a cowpuncher to get across and save his own skin was to hold on for dear life to his swimming horse's tail.

During busy times, roundup camps moved each day to cover a hundred-mile-square area at a crack. This might require five or six wagons and remudas, each with its own nighthawk. Upon arriving at a new campsite, the nighthawk was responsible for unloading the bed wagon and laying out a rope corral about 50-feet in diameter to contain the remuda. A front and back wheel of the bed wagon served as anchors for the rope corral. Forked sticks, ground pins, and guy ropes held the main rope a taut three feet off the ground. Setting up the rope corral, complete with rope gate, was an art the novice had to learn. Horses also had to learn. Part of breaking a horse was teaching it to stay within the rope corral. If one of the crowded horses grew frisky and jumped out, a shot-loaded whip or sometimes a couple of cowboys with ropes unceremoniously dragged him back in, teaching the horse it was much safer to stay inside with his comrades.

Once the night herd was corralled at daybreak and cowboys had selected their mounts for the morning's work and ridden out, the four-horse teams for the mess and bed wagons were harnessed. Fred could then let the remaining horses out to water, graze and trail to the noon camp. The same tedious procedure then occurred all over again, with the setting up of a new rope corral for the afternoon change of horses. The same thing happened at the night camp. While the cowboys slept, the nighthawk still worked watching the herd. As luck would have it, roundup always seemed to bring a miserable, slow, steady drizzle. You needed to be young, strong-willed, and independent or you wouldn't make it. Barton was all of those.

He was still in his teens when he began to realize his dream of riding the range.

He was not a teenager however, as the teenager concept had not yet been created. It was a question of whether a male was a boy or a man. Forget any transitional period. There was no between or "teen." He first hired on to work for pool outfits south of Miles City near Ekalaka, described in the June 16, 1911, issue of the *Miles City Independent* as "where the graveyard is closer to town then [*sic*] the new school house." His rebirth as a Westerner at Ekalaka may explain why Barton sometimes wrote down Ekalaka as his birthplace. After two years of wrangling horses, he became a full-fledged nighthawk for a year at $60 a month. After that, he hired on as a cowboy.

A cowboy took pride in doing everything from the back of a horse. In contrast, a nighthawk unloaded wagons, set up the remuda rope corral on the ground, and often had to help the wagon master with other chores. To a cowboy, that was no good. As the Western saying went, "If you want to fire a cowboy, just give him a shovel and tell him to dig a fence post hole. He'll break the shovel handle in two and quit on the spot." Even in Miles City, a cowboy would rather ride his horse across a street from one establishment to another before he would walk.

While achieving cowboy status was a step up, it actually meant a reduction in wages to $45 a month, plus board (beans, coffee, biscuits from the grub wagon), room (a bunkhouse or bedroll), and horses (from the remuda). Cowboys usually were hired in Miles City in April at the time of the Stock Growers' Convention and paid off in November after fall roundup. They didn't work year round, although some cowpunchers, such as Barton, could find winter work at ranches breaking horses for board and five dollars a head. Breaking horses could also mean breaking bones, so the job depended on how many horses needed breaking and how many cowboy bones were still intact.

Cowboys who did not find winter work on ranches either went back East to families or to warmer climes, or they took jobs in and around Miles City. Such work included tending bar, dealing faro in the many saloons or working in livery barns. Come spring, the newspaper mentioned who had returned to Miles City and at which boardinghouse they stayed. When cattle were shipped by train to market after roundup, some cowboys found a way back East by becoming true cowpunchers. That is, they rode with the cattle. At stops along the route, their job was to take a lantern and look into the cattle cars to see if any of the overcrowded steers had lain down. If so, they poked, or "punched," them with a long pole containing a spike on the end to get them back up. After a time, the term *cowpuncher* was applied to cowboys in general. Cowpunchers faced one problem: they could not work for railroad fare when returning in spring because steers had their tickets punched only one way, to the slaughterhouse. Cowboys arrived back in Miles City broke.

All was not work. Cowboys and townspeople alike looked forward to contests where cowboys competed against each other and the animals. Event organizers, often the cowboys themselves, became quite creative in thinking up ways they could test their skills and blow off steam after hard roundups. Ekalaka's 1910 fair featured an umbrella horse race. Riders tried to complete a circuit of the racetrack while gripping umbrellas used as giant wind-drags. Horses and umbrellas normally did not get along. Cowboys riding backwards on a variety of animals produced good laughs. Any nonstandard rodeo event was fair game. Competition at rodeos, roundups, and fairs did generally center on serious roping and riding, but some downright goofiness was expected. New inventions like the automobile and aeroplane became incorporated into various riding stunts. Some crazy events became standards, even main attractions, such as Miles City's wild horse race, which scattered cowboys "ass over tin cups" all over the track and infield. A cowboy who couldn't be smartly fearless while laughing at himself was not the kind of hand you wanted to trust with your life when the going got tough.

Being a cowboy was particularly special at the time Barton made his mark. The first decade of the new century saw the cowboy enshrined as the much-needed, new American hero. As John Taliaferro argued in his *Charles M. Russell: The Life and Legend of America's Cowboy Artist*, the Gay Nineties were a gloss covering the pessimism spawned by the panic of 1893, Coxey's March, and the bank and railroad failures. The trusts and titans of industry served as hollow models. America needed to pin its diminished pride and renewed hope on some icon.

During the nineties, when Barton was off at school, people desperate for jobs flocked to the cities and their skyscrapers, wondrous inventions, and supposed amenities. Many found a life of dirty, crowded tenements beset by crime. Neighbors differed from the country people they were used to. Immigration had shifted from their roots in northern and western Europe to southeastern Europe, a mass migration that many of the earlier settlers thought degraded and bastardized the race. America was being weakened, going downhill. Consequently, prejudice reared its ugly head. As Taliaferro pointed out, the "alien breeds" were blamed for what was going wrong, such as the Haymarket Riot (1886), Mafia riots (1891), Homestead Mine Strike (1892), Coeur d'Alene Strike (1892), and Pullman Strike (1894).[3]

What was needed was a good, strong, unblemished Anglo-Saxon hero harking back to bedrock values held dear. The cowboy fulfilled that role. Of course, those who spun the cowboy hero into popular culture had to largely ignore the number of African Americans, such as Bill Pickett, and many Mexican vaqueros who worked the range. They were okay to be seen in Wild West shows and at rodeo competitions, but not in the literature and motion pictures that were creating cowboy mythology. In speeches and in writing, Theodore Roosevelt proffered the white cowboy as American hero, along with his campaign for the strenuous outdoor life as a cure for personal and national ills. Owen Wister and his wildly successful bestseller, *The Virginian* (1902), the works of Frederic Remington, and the first Western movies in 1903 promptly backed up Roosevelt's campaign. Cowboys moved out of the pages of the post–Civil War dime novel melodramas into an iconic status that continues to this day.

Cowboys were to be emulated, representing a return to basic values. Rather than being weakened by the city, they were strong. They had been tested against nature and not found wanting. Though small in stature, they were perceived as being tough, loyal, and true to their word. They were courageous, as in Teddy Roosevelt's Rough Riders. In the face of a more mechanized, industrialized and politically obfuscating world, their uncomplicated "yup" and "nope" responses breathed fresh air, an air of certainty, in a world whose confidence seemed lost. The cowboy was cowboy. He could not be changed and was incorruptible in the face of social upheaval. On the flipside, enshrining the cowboy signaled collective nostalgia for a way of life whose golden age was over.

Nostalgia bred the rise of dude ranches, where sometimes Eastern women found husbands as they played at cowboy with real cowboys. Out-of-work or seasonal cowboys, former outlaws, and wannabes headed to the new film studios in Hollywood where Western films could be cranked out in a few days. Wild West shows proliferated. Popular culture went mad for the purified image of the cowpoke, or the Hollywood six-gun version that focused more on sheriffs, outlaws, and gunslingers than on the working cowboy, so much so the cowboy image was popularized in other countries, particularly Germany. Barton would put off his Hollywood years until later.

Fred Barton, still known as Fred Kottmeier, made the most of his seven seasons (1904–1911) as a Miles City area cowboy. Looking back on his early days on the range, the *Miles City Star* in 1920 waxed eloquent about him. After he had changed his name, the newspaper accorded him the title of "Mr." Barton, calling him "one of the best cowpunchers that ever forked a bronk [sic]." The newspaper could fork out a lot of what broncs leave behind. Fred must have been able to do so too. Somehow he convinced some of the best cowboys in Montana to pull up stakes and head with him to China. He would need the camaraderie formed on the range to realize his plans and what was about to be thrown in his lap.

To understand what befell Barton in 1911 is to understand the horse world as it existed then. Fort Keogh changed from being a fort to being an army remount station in 1900, when Barton was at the New Jersey Military Academy. The fort's focus became one of horses rather than infantry or cavalry. In 1907 the infantry was pulled out altogether, leaving Fort Keogh as the top supplier of horses to the military. Meanwhile, Miles City became the lively horse capital of the world. Horses were not only supplied to the U.S. Army by the Fort Keogh Remount Station, but also Miles City, as the largest primary horse market prior to World War I, shipped horses around the world.

Although mounted cavalry was no longer needed for the Indian Wars on the western plains, bigger wars required horses elsewhere. The Boer War in South Africa (1899–1902), particularly, made Miles City a source of superior stock. Boers could snipe at British infantry and then simply escape by mounting their horses and riding off. To counter this, the British needed mounted troops, meaning they needed horses fast and in numbers not available in Britain. The Boer War echoed the Plains Indian War. The Plains tribes mounted smaller, faster horses than did mounted cavalry, so warriors could attack and simply ride away. Smaller Boer horses provided the same edge over bigger English plodders. British buyers arrived in Miles City to buy what they could. What happened next tickled Fred Barton.

The vast Western ranges from the Dakotas to Utah were cleared of scrub stock. Miles City sellers then dumped them on the British government. As Barton put it, "Some of the damndest bucking horses and broncs in the world were sent there where they scattered British infantry all over the prairies of South Africa."[4] Cleaning out scrub horses left only the best, improving the herds on the northern plains for years to come.

In a historical twist, Englishmen sold scrub horses to other Englishmen. Most of the early horse ranches within a hundred-mile radius of Miles City were created by Englishmen or Scots. Some of the more famous names included Price of the Crown W, Archdale, and Major Dawson in the 1880s. These ranchers preceded even the big cattle outfits. They brought in fine Morgan stallions for the open range as soon as it was deemed relatively safe and the buffalo had been eliminated.

The market had an instant thirst for Montana and Wyoming horses sold out of

Miles City. Southern plantations, plus expanding Midwestern and New England farms, all needed horses. Buyers from Missouri bought Montana range mares, which they bred to produce the famous Missouri mules. The East Coast served as a tremendous market too. When war clouds loomed, horse ranchers saw the military as a main buyer. This was a time when U.S. Manifest Destiny turned its face to the Pacific and the Caribbean, as evidenced in the Spanish-American War and the Philippine-American War near the turn of the century. In addition to producing cowponies, or what are now known as quarterhorses, breeders favored Morgans because they were cold-blooded. Artillery and cavalry needed unexcitable horses. The Archdales produced a third type of horse, probably by breeding Percheron mares with thoroughbred studs. The military use of horses was building to a climax, which came for Barton in 1911. Revolution and what would be called the First World War was on the way.

Exporting horses to the rest of the world made Miles City sensitive to international events. In 1911 the *Miles City Independent* picked up on stories running in San Francisco newspapers relating to events in China. Something big was occurring in the "Celestial Empire." While early stories related how the Boy Emperor was being treated by an American physician for having eaten too many swallows' nests in the medieval conditions of the palace, a front-page story featured the secretary of the China Relief Commission at the Seattle Commercial Club pleading for westerners to fund aid to two million starving Chinese in the midst of a famine. Two dollars would save the life of a child. The dichotomy between Manchu power and the impoverished masses was boiling over. Revolution was coming. The old dynasty was collapsing. Heralding the change in the Far East, headlines turned political and martial. Strange names began to appear for Miles City readers: "Wu Ting Fang, Revolutionary, Captures Fort on Chunshan Hill"; "Manchus Hold Their Ground"; "Rebels Now in Control"; "Republic Is Likely for China"; "300 Men of 15th U.S. Infantry Arrived in Ching Wang Tau"; "Edict of Chinese, Abdication of the Throne Has Been Duly Signed."

Changes at Fort Keogh made Miles City sensitive to turmoil across the Pacific. By 1907, Keogh was in the process of being abandoned. Most troops shipped out for duty in the Philippines, leaving only a small caretaking contingent at the fort in 1908. The fort revived the next year as it became a remount depot to purchase and train most of the army's horses. By 1911 Fort Keogh Remount Depot had grown to nearly 800 horses. Most were singled out for cavalry, but a large number of more robust horses were slated for artillery use. A few were trained for riding and officers' horses.

Former troops at Fort Keogh began to write back to friends or family in Miles City from across the Pacific. For example, on May 17, 1911, the *Independent* published a letter from Capt. A.W.P. Anderson from Camp Bumpus in Leyte, Philippines. Some army retirees would return to Miles City after their tours. Later on, during and after World War I, the newspaper still ran letters or stories of Fort Keogh soldiers sent to the Far East. Some former Fort Keogh soldiers were actually out-of-work ranch hands or cowboys who entered the military for work.

Barton would not be the only cowpuncher to journey to China or the Far East. Sgt. Walter Mark, described as "a well known local horseman," in 1919 was first stationed at Corregidor but frequently visited Tientsin, China, accompanying the government money guards bringing pay to troops in China. The Tientsin, China, connection would become critical to Barton's future plans. In that same year, Marine A.E. Whilbricht returned from China, the Philippines, and Vladivostok,[5] where Barton would soon go. But these men went abroad because they were in military service. None went on his own. Barton did.

In that pivotal year of 1911, Miles City thronged with activity. The first big horse sale of the year was scheduled for March 1, but people placed much of their attention betting on when the ice breakup would occur on the Yellowstone. A fight between a badger and a bulldog cornered more wagering at the roller rink. Meanwhile, a hundred or so buyers descended upon the auction yards to buy some 4,000 horses over four days. Young scrub horses were brought all the way in from Yakima, Washington, to be sold. The June 16, 1911, *Miles City Independent* reported that by June the army alone had purchased 1,700 horses. The size of the Miles City horse market was staggering. Other sales that summer and fall usually ran between 2,000 and 4,000 horses sold over three- or four-day periods.

This kept the railroad quite busy. Northern Pacific agent E.B. McConnell said in the June 30 *Independent* that he had shipped out sixty-four cars of horses on his line alone to Alberta, Illinois, Wisconsin, Minnesota, Texas, Alabama, and California. Railway horse shipments created some unique job descriptions. The remount station employed "pusher boys," whose job it was to push horses out of railroad cars for unloading. By this time, Northern Pacific had been joined by the Milwaukee Railroad (Chicago, Milwaukee & Puget Sound Railroad). In May of 1911 in the *Independent*, Milwaukee representative Keeley spoke of a railroad innovation. The Milwaukee line would begin service with all-steel trains. He described the Olympian and Columbian cars in terms that would have made the *Titanic* blush. They were "immune from accident" and could "come through weeks of grind and grief with no more damage than losing a coat of paint." Barton would soon use the Milwaukee to ship his own horses and cowboys.

That spring the annual meeting of the Montana Stock Growers' Association rolled around. Charlie Russell was known to drop into Miles City for some of these conventions while Barton was there. Twenty-five cowboys rode into town firing their six-shooters to honor former President Teddy Roosevelt and his Rough Riders. Roosevelt was a charter member of the association. Not only had Montana cowboys gone to the Philippines and Far East, Western cowboys also invaded Cuba as Roosevelt's Rough Riders. Montana's volunteer unit did not quite make it all the way to Cuba, but a few cowboys did.

Symbolically, whether by luck or careful planning, the stockmen were greeted by a parade of traction engines. Talk about changing times. As the *Independent* began to fill up with ads for threshers and gas traction engines, the newspaper also announced efforts to hold on to the Old West. Groups such as the Master Horseshoer Protection Association were scheduled to meet. The day of the solitary range rider had morphed into the great age of joining. Fraternal groups abounded. Civic, recreational, and job-specific organizations proliferated. The prairie's lonesome dove was being overtaken by flocks of town pigeons.

Despite the celebrations in town, life on the range remained a tough proposition. Ekalaka country had not received any rain for a year. Ranchers sold off any horse that carried fat. Up north, W.R. Bass of Jordan shot himself when he lost half his band of 900 sheep. Scalps could still be taken, but not in the Old West way. Wolf trappers, known as wolvers, scalped ranchers' pocketbooks. Stockmen ended up wanting a bounty placed on the heads of unscrupulous wolfers rather than paying wolfers for ersatz wild wolf scalps. At first, wolf pup scalps received higher bounties than those of adult wolves. Trappers began to work the system, substituting coyote scalps for those of wolves. Bounties ranged from $3–10 per wolf scalp. When the higher bounty on wolf pups was removed to combat the chicanery, wolfers simply raised wolves rather than sheep or cattle, defeating the whole idea of ridding the range of predators. According to country clerk and recorder O.C. Haynes, from July 1910 to July 1911, bounties were paid on 3,805 coyotes, 211 wolves, and 374 wolf pups.[6]

Stock inspector Frank Biglin fought other ill-gotten gains by rounding up cattle rustlers. Meanwhile the state legislature wrestled with legislation having a modern ring to them: bills to keep the Yellowstone River free-flowing and bills to legalize slot machines. But what caught the eye of the *Independent* was the death of state Senator W.W. Beaseley of Livingston, who was well known in Miles City and at every other Montana horse track. Beaseley dropped dead of a heart attack playing the ponies at the Juarez, Mexico, racetrack. No one questioned whether his gains were ill-gotten or healthy.

Throughout the North American West, horse was king. Sometimes horses even made the newspaper obituary column, if facetiously. One lady's (old mare's) death read that she was "suspicioned to have come over on the ark." She had died "at her late home" on the ranch. Complications were said to be the cause. She had been a member of the "Calypso Church and Ricky Lodge." Fortunately, "she passed her last moments in peace, and was attended only by her relatives. The remains may be viewed by intimate friends all winter near the line fence." It was signed by R.E. Henderson, Undertaker.[7]

Names of cowboys who rode those horses, and would ride with Barton in China, began to appear in "Local Notes" in the newspapers, as did their family names. In May, just before the hiring seasons, C. ("Colie") Ward registered at the Milligan House, and after summer work he arrived late back in town a few days before Christmas. In August, Mrs. J.G. Perkins and family joined her husband in Miles City, having come in from Dickinson, North Dakota. Perkins had worked for the Dickinson Mercantile Company and had taken a new job with Larkin Brothers Furniture Company in Miles City. The Perkins name played a prominent role in Barton's later China adventure. News related to Barton's future Chinese cowboys was not always good. For example, P.A. ("Pinkie") Putnam was arraigned on a charge of grand larceny, with a bond set at the then princely sum of $750.

Barton's future China cowboys did shine at what would become the famous Miles City Round-Up, held in July, a tradition that continues to this day. In recent years the roundup has been known for attracting world-class rodeo contestants and world class salooning. In Barton's time in 1911, the roundup featured a variety of events. A series of entertainments began on the Fourth of July with the one-day-only Yankee Robinson three-ring circus combined with Texas Bill's Wild West and Congress of Rough Riders with, as advertised in the June 23 *Independent*, "seats for 10,000 people." Circuses were smart to team up with Wild West shows when touring the West. A circus by itself could

Opposite: **Yankee Robinson Circus and Texas Bill's Wild West advertisement (*Miles City Independent*, June 23, 1911).**

KIT CARSON'S
BUFFALO RANCH WILD WEST
AND
TRAINED WILD ANIMAL EXHIBITION.

TENTH TRANS-CONTINENTAL TOUR.

THE LARGEST WILD WEST SHOW ON EARTH

COMING DIRECT ON THEIR OWN SPECIAL TRAINS
OF DOUBLE LENGTH RAILROAD CARS FROM
THE BIGGEST RANCH IN THE WORLD.

Menagerie of Trained Wild Animals

From all parts of the Globe. Daring and death defying acts almost
beyond the realms of lucid imagination.

A COSMOPOLITAN COLLECTION OF COWBOYS AND GIRLS, VANQUEROS,
SEÑORITAS, GUARDIS RURALES, CHAMPIONS OF THE LARIAT,
ROUGH RIDERS, PONY EXPRESS VETERANS, DARING
ATHLETES, COMICAL CLOWNS, THRILLING
INDIAN FIGHTS AND WAR DANCES.

PRINCE BOTLOINE'S TROUPE OF RUSSIAN COSSACKS,

The most daring Horsemen in the World.

BANDS of SIOUX, CHEYENNE and COMANCHE INDIANS,

Fresh from the Camp-fire and Council, making their first acquaintance
with pale face civilization.

The Grand Ethnological Performance concludes with the Superb
Spectacular, Dramatic, Historical Fantasy,

be subject to hold-up by fun-loving cowboys—held up not for money but for an animal. One such incident occurred when a cowboy decided that he needed to have a Bengal tiger hide made into fancy chaps for special occasions.[8]

The circus featured what might be expected in all its glorified hyperbole—Tom Tom, the elephant "larger than Jumbo"; 300 circus artists; the roller skating bear; performing sea lions; the "finest horses on earth"; and trick riders, cowboys, and Indians. This presented an interesting situation: Cowboys and Indians performing before cowboys and Indians. In a weird juxtaposition, the show created an "Indian village" for spectators to enjoy, even though the Northern Cheyenne villages, the real things, stood close by.

Texas Bill could be excused for this, since his show was meant to play to Eastern audiences as well, but Westerners still got a kick out it. His show included Mexican bull fighting, fancy roping, and a race between an automobile and horse on a hippodrome track. Such sights were hard to resist, particularly with the "Marvel of the Century," the flying machine, or aeroplane, making its appearance. In Barton's generation, the West had moved from Indian War to flying machine. After flying at the Bozeman, Montana, Sweet Pea Festival that year, pilot R.C. "Lucky Bob" St. Henry (Lucky Lindy had not yet come along) liked Miles City so much that he decided to stay and raise alfalfa just across the Yellowstone opposite the city. More to the point, the show touted "7 Royal Tokio Japs," the Doos Imperial Russian Dancers, and the Esterz Troupe of Russian Cossacks. Barton did not realize he would soon be seeing Japanese, negotiating with Russian Czarist aristocrats, and riding with Cossacks in Siberia within the year.

However, a big difference existed between the Cossacks Barton rode with in Siberia and the so-called Wild West show Russian Cossacks of the Caucasus. The Wild West show Cossacks were not Cossacks at all. Rather, they were extraordinary Georgian riders who despised the czar's Cossack military detachments that butchered and suppressed Georgians. They hated being billed as Russians.[9] These performers rode atop strange pincushion-shaped saddles. The Georgian troupes entertained audiences with daring trick riding. They captured the audience's imagination with their colorful ethnic dances, songs, and clothes. The riders' derring-do inspired rodeos to adopt trick riding as regular features. Their showy outfits have influenced the wearing of fancy country-western clothing to the present day.[10]

After the Texas Bill extravaganza, the next week, on July 12, Kit Carson's Buffalo Ranch Wild West and Trained Wild Animal Exhibition rolled into town on its tenth transcontinental tour. It featured another group of "Russian" riders, Prince Botloine's Troupe of Russian Cossacks, "the most daring horsemen in the world." Though sounding like puffery to the cowpunchers, Barton would come to agree with this positive assessment of Cossack riding abilities. Among the acts and novelties, Carson offered airship flights; his own rough riders; bands of Sioux, Cheyenne, Comanche; and what was termed "The Battle of Wounded Knee," described interestingly as the culmination of a "Grand Ethnological Performance…. A Superb, Spectacular, Dramatic, Historical Fantasy." A fantasy it was. Miles Citians knew all about the real Wounded Knee, which was a lot less entertaining.

Opposite: **Kit Carson's Buffalo Ranch Wild West Show, with Prince Botloine's Troupe of Russian Cossacks (*Miles City Independent*, June 30, 1911).**

A 1909 Buffalo Bill Wild West French postcard photograph of a Georgian "Russian Cossack" trick rider. Note the elevated "pincushion" Georgian saddle.

Carson challenged locals to "bring in your bad horses and mules. Our cowboys will ride them free of charge. $25.00 will be paid to any person bringing a horse or mule they cannot ride." The outcome is lost in history, but the challenge was one worthy of horse country. Talented range cowboys were recruited as performers in the various Wild West shows, so that most likely many of the "outside" cowboys were not outside cowboys at all, but former locals or cowhands already known to the area. In fact, some cowboys later interested in accompanying Barton to China would miss their chance because of rodeo or other performing commitments. It was not uncommon for Montana cowboys to end up performing in Wild West shows before royalty in Europe. According to the *Independent*, these events marked the beginning of the annual Miles City Round-Up. It became a favorite stop for rodeo cowboys, as would the Pendleton Round-Up, Cheyenne Frontier Days, Calgary Stampede, and others.

It also marked the beginning of Fred Barton's new life abroad.

• Three •

Vladivostok and the World's Largest Horse Ranch, 1911–1912

It is an old saying that to scratch a Russian is to find a Tatar.[1]—Harry A. Franck, *Wandering in Northern China*

In the spring of 1911, prior to all the July celebrations, Barton was introduced to a Russian army officer. Russia was the biggest consumer of horses at the time. Like most European countries, Russia could see world troubles brewing and the need for a strong military but could not anticipate the horror that mechanized war would soon spawn. The Miles City market attracted the Russian because his country had no horse ranches of any kind. Instead, Russian horse procurers had to go from farm to farm, collecting a horse here and a horse there to supply its dragoons or artillery. In a quickly modernizing and arming world, this proved inefficient. Russia's other option, purchasing horses from potential European enemies, meant the supply line might be cut at any time. Contact with the British and Germans taught Russians how to raise horses, but Russia had no system for breeding horses in the vast numbers needed.

Barton and the officer engaged in long conversations about horses. Fred ended up escorting him to horse ranches to show how horse production was handled around Miles City. Whether the Russian bought horses that spring is not clear. What is clear is that the officer brought back something to Russia that was even more important: Barton and his knowledge. The Russians had big plans. Instead of buying horses and shipping them all the way across the Pacific Ocean, they would raise their own. The officer invited Barton to return with him to Vladivostok.

When Barton reached Vladivostok that spring of 1911, czarist bureaucracy went into overdrive. He was placed in the capable English-speaking hands of a government representative by the name of Lukmanov and then introduced to various officials of the Czar Nicholas II government, including the Viceroy of the Far East. Vladivostok, the Pacific gateway to Siberia, was also the gateway to Moscow, as it marked the end of the Trans-Siberian railroad linking Moscow to Vladivostok. Given its military and political importance, the city was filled with officialdom, both good and bad.

Ferdinand Ossendowski, a Polish geologist also sent to Vladivostok, described the world Barton entered in unflattering terms:

> [It was] composed of Russian officials who drank and made fortunes by extracting bribes or who found their way to prison; of drinking and card-playing officers; speculating

Three • Vladivostock and the World's Largest Horse Ranch, 1911–1912

merchants; small industrial operators using and abusing cheap labor unprotected by any laws; of banditti; of slave traders, counterfeiters, blackmailers, of being without any profession or with all sorts of profession from banditry to strangely regularized money making; of the scum of all countries and nations among whom one could find recruits for any adventure or expedition to look for gold on the shores of Okhotsk Sea, to go a-sealing to the Commander Islands, to barter with the natives of Kamchatka and Anadyr, where a glass of brandy and half pound of wet rifle powder were the price of sable or beaver skin.[2]

A place for an adventurer, indeed. Sitting on a deep bay called the Golden Horn, much of the city was modern, electrified, and built of brick. In the bay, the fortress on Russian Island watched over the city. Vladivostok was layered and climbed terraces up a mountain. The official buildings, port, railroad facilities, shops, banks, and barracks occupied the first European terrace above the bay. Not counting the military, over 53,000 Russians lived here. Above that layer sat the substantial Japanese quarter, with about 2,000 Japanese. The Japanese were keenly interested in iron reserves in the area. On top of the mountain, a meteorological station perched at the Eagle's Nest. Behind the mountain sprawled the Korean quarter of some 8,000 souls living in hovels where Ossendowski observed "people swarmed like rats."[3] Plagues began here so periodically the Russians disinfected the district by burning it down. Russians also were concerned about the nearly 30,000 Chinese living in the city, one of whom Barton would come to know very well. The Chinese would keep close tabs on Barton.

Barton was treated royally, enjoying the European district. The Russians intended to put Barton's knowledge to work right away. In just two weeks, a complete expedition had been planned and set out to survey locations where the biggest horse ranch in the world could be located. This was no crude expedition, for even the Viceroy of the Far East rode along to inspect his vast holdings. For a ruler, sometimes it was good to get out of Dodge.

Barton found himself riding with surveyors, government representatives, and, for protection, a contingent of Siberian Cossacks mounted on Mongol ponies. He came to respect the riding of the Cossacks on the small ponies. Their toughness in the face of the harsh Siberian climate showed. He filed this respect for the ruggedness of the ponies in the back of his mind. It would resurface and later be used when he went to China. Barton had his photograph taken with these Cossacks, not to be confused with the Cossacks from southern Russia who guarded the czar and rode much larger horses.

Peasants he saw along the way were also accomplished riders. Regular cavalry that rode English-style did not sit well with him. They posted, or raised themselves up and down on the saddle to match the trotting moving of their horses. Barton thought they looked like "monkeys on a postage stamp."[4] Since no one roped in Siberia or the Far East, Russian saddles had no horns. McClellan-type saddle and cruppers under the tail were used. Barton found the setup humorous at first and beneath the dignity of a cowboy, but then he saw their practicality, as saddle blankets notoriously slipped out from underneath McClellans used in the United States. Cruppers solved that problem.

The epic trip covered some 1,400 or 1,500 miles, much of it through Siberian wilderness. The scouting party sought an uninhabited open range with optimal grass, water, and climate for raising horses. Barton and the Russians planned to create a million-acre ranch that could support 100,000 mares, dwarfing any Miles City operation.[5] Barton would run the ranch using Miles City techniques.

Eventually the survey party came upon an area of southern Siberia that seemed perfect for the ranch. The vast mixed virgin grassland and pine hills lay on the southern exposure of mountains. Barton compared the climate to that of northern New Mexico, another area he would know much about later in life. Grass and water were plentiful. Furthermore, there were no people. The place was simply breathtakingly beautiful. In the 1930s, Will Rogers reacted similarly traveling by train just north of the proposed ranch area. Rogers, frustrated by riding the rails, wanted to get out and ride a horse. Upon seeing Siberia, he said, "It's exactly like the Indian Territory was when I grew up in it as a boy. And if you can find a finer one that that was before they plowed and ruined it, I don't know where.... Not a fence, all you would need would be one drift line between you and the Arctic Ocean."[6]

Having surveyed the area and confident of its suitability, the party returned to Vladivostok. For the next step, the Russians sent Barton to Moscow and St. Petersburg to meet with high officials. Although he did not have an audience with the czar, Barton was able to catch sight of him. It was nearly impossible for even provincial governors to see the czar. If they did, they would be lucky to have a five-minute audience. Russia lived under the severe peasant/master class system, but Barton found czarist officials particularly cordial to foreigners. It was a good time to visit Russia and be wined and dined, before it all came crashing down.

On the other hand, he saw the wretched plight of the peasants and commented on what he considered a misconception about Siberian exiles. Criminals were not sent to Siberia for the reasons the British transported wrongdoers such as thieves to Australia. Czarists permitted only the nobility and aristocracy to think. If a peasant began to think, to question why he was not educated or to question his status in life, he was condemned to Siberia. As Barton pointed out, many people stereotypically think of the Russian system as one of secret police sending people into exile. Under Stalin, this was true, but under the czar, such was not the case. As the Russians told Barton, no secret police force in the world can keep a country ignorant. Someone else might. Usually a peasant went to the only person he could trust with his concerns—a priest. As soon as the peasant showed an inquiring mind and asked why he and his descendants had to live like animals, the priest telephoned the secret police and the peasant was removed.[7] The same fate resulted under both Czarist and Stalinist regimes; the crimes and means simply differed.

After meeting with officials in European Russia, Barton returned to Vladivostok in the Far East, where he remained until 1912. He was told to return to the States and await being summoned to run the ranch. Meanwhile, the notoriously Byzantine Russian bureaucracy tried to move its slow wheels with wheels within wheels (think of Charles Dickens' Department of Circumlocution in *Little Dorrit*)—all slowed by paper and political maneuvering. The ranch could not be realized overnight.

His time in Siberia was not wasted. The Russians were not the only ones in Vladivostok. Future leaders of China resided there. Generals Chang Tso-lin and Chang Tsung-chang became very important to Fred Barton's future. They would want Barton to do for them what he planned to do for the Russians. These Chinese warlords took great interest in his plans.

The changing situation in China whetted their equine appetites. While Barton and

Three • Vladivostock and the World's Largest Horse Ranch, 1911–1912

Photograph taken in Siberia in 1912 of Fred Barton (on right) with his escort of Russian Cossacks on Mongolian ponies (photograph 940-762, Montana Historical Society Archives).

the Russians had been surveying and negotiating a horse ranch in Siberia, to the south—beyond Manchuria, Mongolia, the great Gobi Desert, and the Great Wall—China underwent revolution. The Manchu Dynasty had ruled China since 1644, but it was in trouble. Weakened by the failed Boxer Rebellion and its support of the opium economy, its grip on power was slipping. By the end of the reign of the empress dowager, the 1904 Japanese defeat of the Russians in Manchuria only fed the spirit of revolt. If "yellow-skinned" people could defeat the mighty Russians, they might also be able to defeat the Manchus, considered to be foreigners ruling China. Mongols also rebelled against the Chinese in Mongolia in 1911.

After ten armed revolts between 1906 and 1911, Dr. Sun Yat-sen proclaimed a short-lived republic. Even though Manchu rule was over, the republic fell apart nearly as soon as it was formed. A republic in name only, it could raise money only through customs taxes. Worse, Dr. Sun Yat-sen's government had to pay millions of dollars to provincial governors to fly the national flag. If China could not show the world it was a unified country, the Peking government could not obtain needed loans from international banks.

Each province acted independently with little or no respect for the central government (they even taxed the central government), and this led to the age of warlords. Over the next several decades, different generals partitioned off their own centers of power and vied to control Peking. This partitioning by military force depended on maintaining large, mobile armies. Though warlords favored using railroads as raceways for troops up and down the length of China, many areas lacked railroads—and railroads tended to switch gauges or track width from province to province. Generals needed horses for their own troops and mercenaries. Two such major players would be General Chang Tso-lin and his chief of staff, Chang Tsung-chang, whom Barton met in Vladivostok. They would also emerge as two of the most colorful Chinese characters in the early twentieth century.

Chang Tso-lin bought and fought his way from his meager beginnings as a common local petty bandit to being the major power in Manchuria and, at times, much of China. James Reid Marsh, who had been posted to Mukden for customs duty in 1917, observed that Chang was a superb horseman. On the celebration of the so-called birth of the republic, Chang rode through the streets on his cream-colored pony. He sat like a statue, letting the pony do all the prancing. A bomb suddenly exploded, but the assassination attempt failed. Chang deftly appeared out of the confusion of smoke, hurtling limbs, and burned clothing. He escaped to the Japanese consulate, since the Japanese were big funders for much of his adventuring. As Marsh stated, "Once more his dexterous horsemanship had saved him, and on the morrow the incident was forgotten."[8]

Called the "Manchurian Tiger" or "Mukden Tiger," Chang Tso-lin played both sides of the fence during the Russo-Japanese War. At one time he served as a lieutenant in the Japanese army to fight the Russians. After that war and a stint as a bandit, he received amnesty and was placed in command of a garrison outside Mukden, from which he quickly expanded his power. When traveler Harry Franck saw Chang, he noted that he kept the keys to prisoners' leg irons on his own person, that his American car was fitted with machine-gun emplacements, and that guards were strapped to the running boards so they couldn't bail out. Chang also routinely executed his own men for various offenses, usually involving money, so that many of his officers feared him.[9]

He was smart enough to surround himself with several Chinese graduates of West Point. Had Barton gone through with his schooling at West Point, he could have found another line of work in Manchuria. When Chang wasn't dressed as a general wearing a fur-fleeced hat against the cold, he wore a black satin skullcap and a famous pearl said to be the largest in the world. The halls of his provincial palace reflected his considerable wealth. Carved black teak, silk rugs, jade jars, scroll paintings, and porcelains filled his uncharacteristic French chateau.

He sustained his power longer than most Chinese generals by sharing his domain with the Japanese, by forming tentative pacts with other warlords, and by superior force and strategy. His power reached all the way to Peking, which he would finally take while his chief of staff, Chang Tsung-chang, took Shantung. In 1928 China would issue postage stamps commemorating the assumption of power of Marshal Chang Tso-lin and his president, Chiang Kai-shek, who would come to world prominence in World War II and, later, the Cold War. Indicative of disunity and warring in China, these stamps were available for postage only in the areas of Chang's control, the provinces of Chihli, Shantung, and offices in Manchuria.

The Japanese proved to be Chang Tso-lin's undoing. When he refused to follow Japanese advice, his personal train was bombed on June 4, 1928. He died a few days later after reaching his pinnacle of glory. The Japanese prepared to set up their puppet state of Manchucko in what was formerly Manchuria.

Three • *Vladivostock and the World's Largest Horse Ranch, 1911–1912* 41

Fred Barton with Russian horse in Siberia in 1912 (photograph 940-764, Montana Historical Society Archives).

Chang Tsung-chang, Barton's main Chinese contact in Vladivostok, was another rising star, described by U.S. general Stillwell as a man who was "dangerous even to look at."[10] Having been raised in Vladivostok and speaking fluent Russian, he made an imposing presence at a towering seven feet tall. Using his Russian language to advantage, he became known for the number of Russian mercenaries in his employ, as well as the brutality of his troops. Just as some U.S. army officers who served in China were accorded nicknames like "Vinegar Joe" (Stillwell), most Chinese generals or high-ranking officers had nicknames and loved to be connected to some legendary past or token of their personal charisma. Generals were referred to as the Dog-Eating General, Tiger, Big Tongue, Blue Sky, Dragon, the Long-Legged General, the Red-Bearded Bandit.[11] In a way, the descriptors paralleled the names of Casey's Scouts at Fort Keogh—Ridge Walker, Wolf Voice, Walks Fanning, His Bad Horse, Clubfoot, Man Bear, Shavehead, Turkey Legs. Chang Tsung-Chang was known as the "Dog Meat" general, but that had nothing to do with eating dog meat. Just as Chang Tso-lin was an inveterate poker player, Chang Tsung-Chang was hooked on *pai gow*, from which the card game of pai gow poker is derived. Manchurians referred to the game as "eating dog meat." Another Chang Tsung-chang nickname was "Three Things Not Known." His three mysteries consisted of people not knowing how much money, how many soldiers, and how many concubines he had.

In the field, Chang Tsung-chang lived in a luxurious yamen. Lavish meals were served on Belgian-cut dinner service with brandy and champagne. When he traveled the rails, he carried his own teakwood coffin on a flatbed car, sometimes sitting on it to smoke a cigar. He told his troops to bring him back in it if they were not victorious. Once he was not victorious, so he had his troops parade through town carrying his casket as he waved from it to the cheering crowd. Coffins were sometimes used to prime the troops for battle. As one observer mentioned when a Chinese army approached, "Oh-oh, they mean business. They brought their own coffins with them."

Chang Tsung-chang also hauled his concubines to the wars in two private railcars. At one point, the number of his concubines was known. Forty-two "ladies" occupied the cars. Twenty-one of them were White Russians, the rest were Chinese, Japanese, and one "bedraggled" American.[12] He numbered them so he did not have to remember names. He apparently lived up to his other nickname, "Old 86," so called because his penis was reportedly as long as a stack of eighty-six silver dollars. Considered by some to be the basest of all the warlords, he nevertheless seemed to be a momma's boy. Except for the days when he would be on the battlefield, he always brought his mother along in a well-appointed railway car.

The Russians kept a lively trade of whores going during this period. Most of the women supplied to bars and cribs around Peking and other major cities came from Odessa via Vladivostok. Every bar worth its salt, such as the Metropole in Peking, had its Olga. The Russians were not alone in supplying officials, generals, the international settlements, and the public with ladies of the evening. As described in *China Hand*, the most famous madam, Frankie, made a small fortune during the Sino-Russian War, throwing vodka and champagne parties for the Russian officers' staff in Siberia. After the war this American madam moved to Peking and bought three houses, which became "houses." One she owned; two she rented out. She became the wealthiest woman, and one of the wealthiest foreigners, in North China and was known to bankers and government officials alike. Frankie studiously avoided employing Russian women who had been poor slaves. She hired just about every other nationality to fill a niche.[13]

Barton must have either toured Mongolia during this time of waiting, passed through it on the Cossack expedition, or gathered information about it from contacts he had in the British-American Tobacco Company, because he knew the situation at Urga, the capital of Mongolia. He saw Urga across the Gobi Desert from China and south of the Siberian mountains of his projected horse ranch as another moneymaker. In 1912, as Barton recalled, he made a proposition to saddle maker Ed Bohlin in Miles City. Bohlin was single and working for the Coggshall Saddlery in Miles City. Barton offered to underwrite the expenses of establishing a saddle shop at the frontier town of Urga if Bohlin would move there.[14]

Urga was a city built by the Chinese so that they could trade with the Mongols. Given their nomadic life, the Mongols were not interested in living in cities or building them. Chinese merchants created huge compounds surrounded by ten-foot upright pine-log walls that could contain hundreds and sometimes thousands of head of stock. Annually Mongols journeyed to Urga to trade their Persian sheep wool brought in on camels. They would also bring horses and yaks to sell or trade. The Chinese offered them all manner of goods, particularly brick tea, to last the Mongols through the year, cloth, and saddles.

Barton wanted to move in on the saddle business and open his own compound in Urga to make saddles amidst the dusty Chinese compounds, the Mongolian religious

"The Manchurian Tiger" Chang Tso-lin (center) and his son, "Young Marshall" Chang Hsueh-liang (left), in charge of the warlord's personal bodyguard, meeting at Tientsin with Brig. Gen. Conner (right), commander of American Forces in China.

shrines, and the huge wolf-like dogs that waited outside the walls to eat the dead. Here, in Urga, where it was said that half the population were lamas in their saffron-yellow or brick-red gowns, thousands of them, even lamas rode ponies. Pedestrians had no right-of-way in Urga, just the riders in saddles did.

To Barton, it looked like a great deal that could make them both millionaires in time. Cheap saddletrees could be obtained from the Montana state penitentiary. For starters, Barton wanted Bohlin to order 1,000 small trees, 13–14 inches high, to be sent to Mongolia. There, he would employ Chinese agents and a staff of their excellent leatherworkers to build saddles for Mongol requirements. With all the stock found in Urga, cheap but quality leather was readily available. Bronze horns would be used that could be easily recovered. Bohlin would have nothing to lose.

Barton was disappointed when Bohlin turned him down to pursue his own course. Bohlin did not become a Chinese millionaire, but he did become a famous saddle maker. He moved to Los Angeles and set up shop at 5760 Sunset Boulevard, where he crafted saddles for the Hollywood crowd that Barton would also come to know. Today Bohlin saddles are exhibited as museum pieces or art objects. Bohlin became more interested in the challenge of individual design than in mass production. He would destroy whole pieces that were not unique and did not meet his idea of perfection. Barton had been talking to an artist.

Edward H. Bohlin (1895–1980) did not need to find the Old West in Mongolia, for he was about to create in California what would become most Americans'—and the world's—idea of the Old West. As a Swedish boy Bohlin dreamed of life in the Old West. Seeing Buffalo Bill Cody and his Wild West Show in Sweden fueled his desire to come to the States. At the age of 17 he worked his way across the Atlantic as a cabin boy on a freighter. He sought out Buffalo Bill, who gave him a job as a harness and tack repairer for his show. Bohlin then worked as a cowpuncher in Montana, which is when he and Barton ended up in Miles City at the same time. He opened his own saddle shop in Cody, Wyoming, in 1917. Shortly his life took a turn that made his decision not to go to Mongolia seem brilliant.

Cowboy motion picture star Tom Mix convinced Bohlin to move to Hollywood. At first Bohlin worked as a trick rider and roper in Western movies. After doing his homework and seeing that the Hollywood scene offered a big market for saddles and other gear, he opened his saddle shop where he could do his fancy leather carving and fine silver inlay.

"As they say," the rest is history. To use the title from James A. Nottage's book about him, Bohlin became "saddle maker to the stars." He outfitted Hopalong Cassidy and Topper, the Lone Ranger and Silver, Roy Rogers and Trigger, the Cisco Kid and Diablo, Lash Larue, Rex Allen, John Wayne, Gary Cooper, and as they say in Hollywood, "a cast of thousands, mostly horses." Today his saddles can best be seen in the Pasadena Tournament of Roses Parade, and classic Bohlin saddles can sell in the five-figure range.

The style of saddles, bridles, beltbuckles, holsters, spurs—just about everything seen in Hollywood Westerns—became icons either made by Bohlin or patterned after his designs and style. No brag, just fact, Pilgrim. People saw a Bohlinized West on the flickering screen, which, in turn, by capturing the imagination, became "The West." Bohlin sold everything from high quality silver-plated telephones to automobile hood ornaments featuring a saddle bronc rider atop a wild bronc. This was popular culture Sunset Boulevard style. More about Bohlin later. Barton would also reach Hollywood with some silver, but he would have to do it in his own way via Siberia and without Bohlin.

Ironically, horses doomed Barton's plans for the largest horse ranch in the world. Beginning in February of 1912, thousands of laborers working at the Lena goldfields on the Lena River in Siberia began a strike. The mines were owned by a consortium of British industrialist and czarist aristocracy. The mines cleared over 7,000,000 rubles in profit a year, making owners very, very rich. Workers, on the other hand, suffered in the harsh Siberian conditions, working 15–16-hour days. Nearly three-quarters of the thousands of workers at the mines suffered traumatic injuries. They were paid just enough to keep themselves and their families alive. The company took back in "fines" for doing poor work what little they were paid. Workers were paid largely in company scrip, redeemable only at the company store for food of poor quality, if it could be called food. Any worker wanting to eat had to give his money right back to the company.

It all came to a head when workers protested having to buy inedible meat comprising rancid horse penises. On April 17, czarist troops opened fire on strikers, killing hundreds and wounding hundreds more in what became known as the Lena Goldfields Massacre. In all, 10,000 people walked away from the mines, threatening Russia's move to the gold standard. Word of the slaughter spread across the country. What had been a failed revolution after Russia's humiliating defeat in the 1905 Russo-Japanese War found new wind. Strikes broke out across the land, sometimes up to 1,000 a month. These continued into World War I. This set in motion events leading to the 1917 Russian Revolution. Suddenly the Bolsheviks found a way to recover from their being recently arrested, exiled, or executed. As a young Stalin said, "The Lena shots broke the ice of silence, and the river of popular resentment is flowing again. The ice has broken. It has started."[15]

The Lena shot holes in Barton's Russian horse ranch. The public outcry over the massacre sent the bureaucracy in the Far East into a tizzy trying to keep order. At the same time in St. Petersburg, Russians worried over how much power the mystic Grigori Rasputin, sometimes referred to as the "mad monk," had over the Romanovs, particularly the czarina, who ran the country. The empire appeared weak and close to collapsing. The center could not hold. Preservation dictated that attention be diverted from Barton's horse ranch, but Stalin would be forever grateful for those horse penises.

Events coalesced to overtake Barton's long wait for the Siberian ranch to be approved. World War I loomed and then broke out. The Russian government turned its attention elsewhere. Just as revolution wracked China, Russia found itself in the throes of its own. Czar Nicholas and his family were killed along with countless representatives of the czar's government. Barton held out little hope that any of the people he had conferred with survived. He never heard from any of them again.[16] Fighting between Reds and Whites spread into Siberia and spilled into Mongolia. White Russian refugees tried to escape to the international settlements in China, often selling all they had—crystal, boots, jewelry, their own bodies—anything to survive.

Warlords like Chang Tsung-chang capitalized on the revolution to the north. Fleeing a country no longer theirs, White Russian cavalry enlisted in Chang's forces. They could scatter most military units and terrorize just about anyone by their distinctive appearance. They wore dark green, almost black uniforms with yellow leather boots that came up to their thighs. They carried pennant-tipped lances placed in their stirrup sockets, and each carried a dreaded da-bao, the Chinese executioner's sword, strapped over the shoulder in a canvas scabbard. Chang Tsung-chang also employed a Russian infantry brigade under General Netchaef of 3,000 men in four armored trains.[17]

Barton entered China during the golden age of warlordism.

• Four •

"Smoke 'Em If You've Got 'Em"
The British-American Tobacco Company, 1912–1916

> *We reached Tai-yuan-fu ... [and] thousands of posters and advertisements of the Anglo-American Tobacco Company, pasted up on walls, houses, gates, temples and every conceivable place, prove that the town has already attained a high degree of civilization. The posters of the Tobacco Company must surely mark the frontiers of civilization.[1]*
>
> —C.G. Mannerheim

Despite the collapse of the Russian horse ranch idea, Barton developed a taste for the Far East, its vast lands more like the Wild West, or at least what the Old West used to be. Thanks to an uncle who worked for the British-American Tobacco Company (BAT), by March 1912 Fred had signed on for a four-year hitch with the company. He was still known as Fred Kottmeier, Jr., when he set sail from BAT's New York offices for its main China offices in Shanghai. With his Montana roots, Barton differed from most company recruits. BAT usually drew its young men from Southern tobacco states, particularly North Carolina. Unlike other recruits, Barton packed his saddle.

Having already proven himself as being up for a big adventure in the Far East, Barton seemed a good choice to become a BAT agent. BAT hired only bachelors, who were not permitted to marry during their tenure. They could not be older than 25 for China duty. Barton met those restrictions. As one recruit later said, BAT needed adventurous young men "fools enough to risk what they proposed."[2] Barton was paid $1,500 per year plus living expenses. He could also earn a $500 bonus if he could learn enough colloquial Chinese to pass a BAT language examination offered every six months. To dissuade homesick young men from bolting right away, BAT made Barton and other recruits pay their own way to China. If they lasted a year, the company would then reimburse them. At the end of four years they could be granted a four-month leave of absence—if they lasted that long. Usually only two out of five recruits lasted out the first year. Culture shock, harsh conditions, and loneliness proved too much for many. To a nighthawk or cowboy, these posed not problems but familiar daily challenges, even seeming to be close friends.

Barton hired on just as BAT was making a big expansion and trying to monopolize the cigarette industry in China and much of the rest of the world. BAT dominated the commercial scene in China. Every Chinese city of any size had its BAT warehouse. Some of its facilities manufactured as many as ten million cigarettes a day. By 1916 the company would be selling a billion cigarettes—not per year, but per month. Even in congested Shanghai, the cigarette manufacturing plant consisted of 160 buildings on more than 32 acres of land.[3] Tens of thousands of Chinese were employed. Because of intensive advertising campaigns, giveaways, and various government edicts against smoking opium, the populace embraced cigarette smoking as a cheap replacement. Even better for Barton, the company was rapidly expanding into North China and Manchuria, areas under the control of people Barton had already met in Vladivostok.

Because Barton had already been in the Far East, he was not as much as a "griffin," or newcomer, as most new hires. Newcomers were surprised at their first head-office indoctrination into business life in Shanghai. First the "Old Man" in the head office would tell them about the opportunities that lay before them. Afterwards, they were lectured on not getting into trouble with women. As at the other big American establishment in Shanghai, Standard Oil, newcomers were given a pack of condoms and told that all Chinese prostitutes had syphilis or gonorrhea. Even Europeans, Americans, and White Russians were risky. Thus ended the lesson, and the job, if directions were not followed.

While Shanghai was commercially touted as the "Paris of the East" or the "Pearl of the Orient," it had not earned the nicknames of "Sin City," "City for Sale," "Babylon of the Far East," and "Whore of Asia" for nothing. International companies sent bachelors to Shanghai, swelling the ratio of men to women. These men had paychecks, time on their hands, and sex available everywhere. For the sexually deprived or world-class sexual deviant, Shanghai represented paradise. If you could dream it, Shanghai had it. As was said about the city, "If God created Shanghai, He owes an apology to Sodom and Gomorrah."

Along with destitute refugees, young Chinese women surged into this Jazz Age city fleeing traditional Chinese values, only to fall prey to prostitution. Gangs kidnapped girls or their families sold them into prostitution. By 1920, the Shanghai Municipal Council estimated 70,000 prostitutes worked the city; by 1930 there were around 100,000. Although Shanghai was the sixth most populated city in the world, it ranked first in number of prostitutes. Some International Settlements saw one out of every three women working the brothels, clubs, and streets, and that did not count the many underage girls.[4]

Griffins were also warned about how various triads, or gangs, ran the city, so it was important to know where to go, where not to go, and what legitimate and illegitimate services could be provided by the triads. For young men, life in Shanghai was either an untenable loneliness that sent them home or a thrilling adventure with touches of danger.

While recruits spent their days in city offices tending to paperwork, marketing campaigns, and the warehouses, Barton was one of those sent into the interior to "rough it" delivering and marketing BAT's many cigarette brands, such as Ruby Queen, Hataman, Pirate, Pin Head, Purple Mountain, New York, Vanity Fair, Belle of China, Legation, Victory, and Atlas. BAT was keen on expanding into North China, Manchuria and Mongolia to counter Russian cigarette influence there, and that is where Barton would go. BAT's Tientsin office on the coast was the main office for North China, with an adjunct office at Mukden (warlord Chang Tso-lin's headquarters) and another branch in Harbin. From Manchuria, BAT extended its business across the Gobi Desert to Urga, capital of Mongolia, by camel caravan. Barton would spend much of his time as an agent in Kalgan, the gateway to Mongolia and horse country.

Barton became a BAT agent just as the company was adjusting to momentous events in China. The 1911 revolution ended Manchu rule, and a brief republic was born. This required Barton and other field agents to change their advertising materials. BAT made sure that every conceivable space in every village was plastered with its advertising posters. During Manchu rule, BAT had exploited the Manchu's main power symbol, the dragon. Now, dragons had to be carefully avoided, but pretty Chinese young women were better eye candy than any dragon. The clothes that agents wore and the men illustrated in posters also had to be selective. For example, no one could be seen in a green hat, which symbolized a cuckold for the Chinese. Words had to be carefully selected as well due to cultural differences.

BAT was fortunate because the pronunciation of the word for bat in Chinese was auspicious, meaning prosperity, good fortune, and longevity. This meant that BAT could use bats as decorative elements on its posters along with pin-up lovelies or other Chinese scenes. In the United States or Great Britain, a poster featuring a young lady and bats might conjure scary vampiric voyeurism. Bram Stoker published *Dracula* in 1897, and by 1913 the silent film industry was already exploring the vampire myth, in which the lovely predatory woman was a "vamp." But the Chinese construed the juxtaposition as signaling the warmth of elite wealth and success. More feng shui than Fangs' way.

In 1974, during Ralph Miracle's research into Fred Barton's China exploits, Miracle wrote British-American Tobacco asking for any information it might have on Barton. Miracle had run into a brother of one of the cowboys who had gone to China with Barton. The Miles City man had a photo of the cowboys in China. Fascinated, Miracle wanted to know more about the story many people did not believe.

Miracle was no slouch when it came to horses and cowboy life. He was born of a pioneer Montana family. Though fifteen years younger than Barton, Miracle's life paralleled Barton's in many ways. Born in Helena, Montana, Miracle too was sent off to military school. At first, rather than heading east, he enrolled in Harvard Military Academy in Los Angeles. He then gravitated to the East and the New York City area. Returning to Montana, he managed the family ranch holdings and also the Westwood Ranch at Cascade, Montana, for Charles Bovey. He went on to become an executive officer of the Montana Livestock Commission, editor of the Montana Stockgrowers Association magazine, and author of many articles about the Old West.

As recorder of marks and brands, he enforced the registration of some 65,000 brands in Montana to help in identification, to curtail and prosecute rustlers, and to prevent brand duplication or confusion. The brands included Theodore Roosevelt's old Maltese Cross. As secretary of the Montana Stockgrowers Association, Miracle served with President Bob Barthelmess, whose father was Casey Barthelmess, named after the famous Fort Keogh lieutenant discussed earlier. Bob Barthelmess became director of the Range Riders Museum in Miles City. The museum was filled with cowboy memorabilia, including a photo of Barton. No wonder Miracle had interest in Barton. Late in life, Miracle retired to California, as did Barton.

Four • "Smoke 'Em If You've Got 'Em": 1912–1916

The British-American Tobacco Company informed Miracle that it could not give him any records of Barton's activities, but that everything he needed to know about Barton could be found in a book written by one of their lead advertising agents in China during Barton's tenure. This agent began his career nearly at the same time as did Barton. James Lafayette Hutchison published *China Hand* in 1936. The book covered his BAT China activities from 1911 to 1933. BAT said that Hutchison met an American cowboy who served as a BAT agent. Even though Barton went under a different name in Hutchison's book, BAT said that the cowboy was Barton.

Hutchison speaks of an American he met in Shansi province and Kalgan and kept running into during his years in China. This American, a company assistant at Kalgan on the main road into Mongolia, claimed to be an ex-cowboy and bronc buster from Arizona. He wore high-heeled cowboy boots for long trips just as Barton did. Hutchison called him "a wonder at breaking in and training Mongolian ponies."[5] He called himself Schneider, and said he had run away from his father at age sixteen, only to return at twenty-one to try to lick him. So far (1911 or 1912) he had failed to do so. He respected his father but needed to beat him before "he kicked off." He told Hutchison that he was going to go back home in about two years to try to knock him down again, since his dad was about sixty and not as spry as he used to be. With the exception of "Arizona," the dates and facts seem to fit Barton's life.

In 1916 Hutchison ran into "Schneider" again. This time it was in Tientsin, and Schneider seemed to be down on his luck, hitting the scotch. He said he had just received a letter that his dad had died and now he would never have the chance to defeat him. Rather than Arizona, now he claimed that his father had been an old rancher back home in New Mexico.[6] Barton stated that his father died in 1920, not too far removed from Hutchison's date of 1916. Barton would in later years ranch in New Mexico.

Hutchison mentions him again in his recollections of 1930. Now the cowboy is in his forties, Barton's age at the time. Hutchison says that tales of this cowboy drifted back to him over the years even when he was back at the company's main U.S. office in New York. To summarize, he claims that the ex-Arizona cowboy, while still working with the British-American Tobacco Company, managed to talk the local governor of Shansi province (the same governor Barton would work for) to permit him to gather a gang of riders and five hundred cattle and ship them to Shansi to set up a real Western open-range ranch on the plateau in back of the capital (which Barton would do to raise horses). But the upkeep was costly and the cows failed to reproduce on the strange grass. At the end of two years, the cowboy had to clear out in a hurry to avoid the fuming governor and the one hundred thousand dollar debt.[7] (Montana cowboys would have to clear out of Barton's Shansi horse ranch just a few years after its establishment when the winds of war blew against the local governor.)

When Hutchison met him in 1930 at the Astor House in Shanghai, the man who called himself Schneider said he was currently selling coffins to the Chinese under the name of the Artificial Flower Trading Company.[8] He said he had to use Chinese front men to run the business and stay in the background since the old governor general was still gunning for him. His coffins resembled fancy saddles all covered with silver and chrome (shades of the failed Bohlin saddle-making idea). He claimed to make a 1000 percent profit on each coffin, which meant in two years he could retire.

Coffins were ubiquitous in China. Even poor farmers kept them in their homes. Elderly family members chose their coffins and burial clothes in advance of their great event. These were kept stored in houses or dugouts. The soon-to-be-deceased also had a say about décor and ritual. For the sacrilegious, sometimes coffins served as temporary tables. Since Chinese had to be interred where they were born, railroads carried coffins on most runs. The deceased would be stored at a local temple until such time as the coffined corpse reached a state where it could be comfortably shipped. Then the coffin would be caulked until it was nearly airtight and loaded onto an open railcar; then a caged cock was put atop the coffin. The bird served as a receptacle for the spirit of the deceased on its journey home. It is not recorded what happens when two cock spirit-receptacles face off upon finding themselves side by side riding the rails.

Indeed, the Chinese funeral business provided a golden opportunity for accumulating wealth. The death of a rich person required an elaborate burial and ceremonial parade. In larger cities, several of these noisy, colorful parades marched down the streets each day. Professional mourners and funeral musicians, playing both Western and Eastern music, earned sixty cents a day; costumed street urchins earned twenty cents. Entourages pulled and carried elaborate floats and banners, as if it were eternal Chinese New Year or a version of Mardi Gras. Seeing these half-mile-long processions for the first time, Westerners thought the circus had come to town.

The dearly departed was housed under a colorful canopy in a fancy coffin, often lacquered or of expensive wood. Some coffins housed in their layered coverings looked the size of small temples or arks carried on bamboo poles by a 16-man hitch. Often processions carried

One of the ubiquitous posters BAT agents plastered across China. The Golf Cigarette poster blended East and West, and its film-star sex appeal lured men. Propitious symbols (flowers, crane, cat, mirror) appealed to liberated, modern Chinese women and those wanting to be.

effigies of deities or something identified with the person. These ranged from their birth animals, horses, ships, human figures, and sedan chairs, to tables loaded with money. In Tientsin, a rich man's Ford was duplicated in Chinese paper with bamboo and reed frames, right down to the last detail. Pedals were accurately placed. Interior upholstery was re-created in paper, and the effigy of the driver was a work of art. Much better than having the valet buried with the owner as in ancient times! The owner passed through the jade gates in style after the car was carried three miles through the city to the gravesite and then burned over the grave.[9] Nothing was spared. A fellow could become rich.

"Schneider" obviously had made his fortune, for he invited Hutchison to his apartment and drove him there in his Packard limousine (when Barton retired from China he favored large Cadillacs). There he introduced Hutchison to his Russian wife (Barton married a White Russian). He told Hutchison that she was dumb and couldn't understand English, but that she was sweet and would do anything he wanted, which was the kind of wife he wanted. "If she died tomorrow, I'd marry another Russian."[10] This attitude towards women and marriage showed up in a marriage tract that Barton would write later in life after the "sweetness and doing anything" wore off. Part of his attitude might have been Old China Hand masculine bluster, as his Russian wife occupied an important place in Barton's life long after their divorce.

Hutchison's account fascinated Miracle, who had borrowed *China Hand* from his friend Fallis L. Oliver of Santa Barbara, California. Oliver confirmed that Schneider and Barton were the same person. Fallis and Ruth Koerner Oliver, daughter of Western artist and illustrator W.H.D. Koerner, first met Barton, who was then retired, at the opening of the Cowboy Hall of Fame in Oklahoma City in 1965. Afterwards they visited Barton's apartment in Los Angeles. Oliver recalls reading about the cigarette and coffin business in Hutchison's book, but also believed Barton told him about the coffin business himself, saying that he had lined the coffins with cheap paper made to look like expensive fabric and had them shipped over from the U.S. As Oliver said, "If you find this book, and it (the information he recalled about the coffins) is not therein, you can surmise that Barton was the one. I would not have gotten the story from any other source. Maybe he did more than sell horses."[11] That information is not in the book.

Whether through memory lapse or trying to shield people, Hutchison also misnamed Barton's boss, BAT's no. 1 in Kalgan. Hutchison referred to him as a "lengthy, raw-boned Norwegian" named Ruckled who was away on a nine months' exploration trip, leaving Barton in charge.[12] The man's name was actually Alfred Rustad (a pronunciation close to "Ruck-led"), who was Norwegian as described. Since Fred Kottmeier, Jr., had not yet changed his very Germanic name to Fred Barton, that may help explain why Hutchison chose "Schneider," one of the more common Germanic names, for Fred.

And yet there seems to be more to it than that. Hutchison coyly dissembled or deliberately provided misdirection in what he knew about Barton. He passes off what he knows about "Schneider" as stories which came down to him over the years after he ran into Barton in a few chance meetings in Kalgan, Tientsin, and Shanghai. The truth of the matter is that he had to have known Barton well. For example, at the end of their four-year hitches working for BAT, both took their leaves back to the U.S. The two agents shipped out together on the SS *Siberia* (*Maru*) in June of 1915. With stops in Hong Kong, Yokohama, Kobe, and Honolulu before reaching San Francisco from Shanghai, the agents had plenty of opportunity to pass the time. Why Hutchison became elusive in properly identifying Barton may become clearer as later events unfold.

Hutchison did accurately name Larson, Barton's good friend in Kalgan. Hutchison's main base of operations was Peking, but on his visit to Kalgan, Barton took him to meet Frans August Larson (1870–1957). Few other foreigners lived in Kalgan, a fur, hide, camel, and horse trading center where Chinese and Mongols comingled. The climbing, torturous, switchbacking railroad that Hutchison rode up from Peking ended here, where everything including the people were brown and covered by dust, where long camel caravans plodded through the main street's foot-deep dust, and where Mongol ponies crowded the streets. Beyond Kalgan, only a rough camel trail followed an ancient tea and silk route to Mongolia. The trail's white streak, actually a streambed, climbed up the mountainous pass. Most times it was bouldered and dusty. Sometimes flashfloods roared down it, eradicating entire camel trains. Winter snow melt turned it into a muddy mess impossible to traverse. It was a rough trail and Kalgan was a rough place.

As BAT cigarette competitor Chien Chao-nan described it, the area was so primitive he was surprised BAT would even dare to do business there. The urbane Cantonese businessman saw no signs of civilization there. As Chien said, "No Western inns and even the Chinese inns are vile. Electric lights and jinrickshas have not been introduced. There is no way to get around except on horseback, in mule carts, and on foot. The wind fills the air with horse dung."[13] This meant that any foreigners wishing to travel to Kalgan or anyone entering Mongolia from China would stay with Barton and Rustad and eat at the BAT mess. This included Hutchison and all explorers and expeditions headed for Mongolia.

Just after Christmas, Barton, Larson, and Hutchison rode camels up through the northernmost arm of the Great Wall and the mountain pass above Kalgan. Breaking out of the pass, Hutchison was treated with a sweeping vista of the Gobi Desert plateau and the great Mongolian steppes that led to distant Urga, Mongolia. Urga lay some 1200 miles or four weeks by camel from Kalgan. Quite a contrast to Hutchison's relatively brief five-to-nine–hour train ride from Peking. As a griffin sent out to get to know the territory, Barton experienced just how far it was. He would need this knowledge for later endeavors.

Barton and Larson had unique connections to Urga, BAT's westernmost distribution center and capital of Mongolia. To resupply the warehouse there, Barton and Rustad dispatched two BAT camel caravans a month from Kalgan. Larson connected to Urga in a more intimate way. Because of those Urga connections, Larson became known famously throughout North China, Manchuria, and Mongolia as either "Larson of Mongolia" or "Larson, Duke of Mongolia." BAT's camels probably belonged to Larson since he was the biggest trader of Mongol ponies along with other stock in the Far East. He also traded in hides and furs. It was said that no Mongolian horse or pony entered China without passing through Larson's hands.

As a poorhouse resident in Sweden, Larson worked as a stable boy, acquiring his lifelong love of horses. That and his thirst for adventure brought him to Mongolia as a Swedish missionary. Traveling the land mostly on foot, he passed out Bibles carried by camel. Through his love of horses and wanting to learn the Mongol language, he was befriended by the Mongol prince of the Ordos, owner of vast herds of horses who set him up with a language tutor. For further language training, Larson went to Urga, where he studied the language for another year, being taken under the wing of the Bogdo Gegen, the Living Buddha of Urga. The Bogdo Gegen ranked third in Tibetan Buddhist hierarchy, and in 1911 he became emperor of Mongolia. Since Larson knew both Mongolian and Chinese, he was selected by the new Chinese president to negotiate peace with the Bogdo Gegen during Mongolia's 1911 war of independence from China. Later, leading up to World War II, Larson became a spy and advised Chinese Nationalist leader Chiang Kai-shek in his fight against both the Japanese and the Communists.

Larson became the go-to man for the Bogdo Gegen, supplying him with whatever he needed. Since the Living Buddha had a taste for things different and Western, Larson supplied him with everything from a Model T Ford to a ship. The ship presented a special case. It had to be transported piece by piece by camel across the desert and then reassembled at Urga. Larson dug wells to fill an artificial lake that would float the craft, only to find that the boat was too large. The Emperor didn't mind the boat's being converted into a teahouse. Ultimately, the leader proclaimed Larson a duke. With his title, close association with the various Mongol princes, and friendship with the Living Buddha, Larson had access to the best horses in Mongolia and land for breeding them. These Mongolian connections would aid Barton when he too became a horse rancher in China.

Larson also became the go-to guy for all the famous explorers heading into Mongolia and points west. He either supplied expedition parties with the needed camel trains, or, later, arranged for automobiles. He also could arrange for guides and at times served as guide himself. Along with Barton's boss, Alfred Rustad, Larson hosted and became lifelong friends with the famous explorers, soldiers of fortune, travel writers, reporters, and spies of the late nineteenth and early twentieth centuries, including Sven Hedin and paleontologist Roy Chapman Andrews. A young American engineer also came knocking as he staked out a railroad between Peking and the Mongolian border. Engineer Herbert Hoover would later become president of the United States.

Larson became indispensable for Russians, Chinese and Mongols by serving as an interpreter who spoke many languages. This did not come without a price. During the Boxer Rebellion of 1900, Boxers sought to slaughter any missionaries and their followers around Larson's missionary home in Kalgan. Larson, his wife, two daughters, and twenty other Swedish and American missionaries barely escaped. Larson had been pasturing some camels, horses, and oxen north of Kalgan on behalf of the British consul in Peking. C.W. Campbell wanted to embark on an expedition into Mongolia and had asked Larson to lead it. The Boxers ended that dream. The stock allowed the missionaries to escape, but they had to leave everything behind.

Ironically, Larson, who became the top horse trader and breeder of Mongol ponies, led the expedition riding not a horse but a bicycle. This at first caused some trouble. The caravan's horses bolted upon seeing the unfamiliar contraption. This unnerved the other missionaries he had put on the camels and horses. The bicycle created a sensation at Mongol camps as refugees crossed the desert. Larson would have been the first person to cross the Gobi and Mongolia on a bicycle if he hadn't tried to teach his wife to ride. Her skirt caught in the chain and sprocket, breaking the rear axel. The bike entered Urga on the back of a camel.

The Larson party's escape is an epic story in itself recounted in the plethora of books written about the Boxer Rebellion, including several books written immediately after their escape, including James Hudson Roberts' *A Flight for Life* (1903) and Mark Williams' *Across the Desert of Gobi: A Narrative of an Escape During the Boxer Uprising* (1901). Finding no safety from the Boxers in Mongolia, the small caravan was forced to continue on. They endured many hardships to reach Siberia, where Larson worked in gold mines to raise enough money for tickets on the Trans-Siberian railroad to Europe and boat tickets onward to his wife's home in Albany, New York. They later returned to Kalgan to start all over again. The Boxers had destroyed everything.

Barton and Larson shared a common bond, the love of horses. Thanks to his status, the Mongols allowed Larson to run his own horse ranch at *Tabo-Ol* (sometimes written as *Tab-Ol, Ta-Bol, Tabol*, and in some sources, even the more crazy *Taboo L*), about a five days' ride, or ninety miles, north of Kalgan. Tabo-Ol means "five mountains," but the mountains were actually hills on the undulating prairie. Thanks to the Living Buddha, Larson had been escorted to this region near the border with China, where he was given all the land he could see in every direction, plus all the land in every direction in an extra day's ride from that center.[14] He and his family sometimes stayed at the nearby lamasery in the hilly grasslands. At Tabo-Ol, Larson selectively bred and crossbred horses, bringing in some foreign horses as early as 1904. By his own estimation, he exported over 100,000 horses through Kalgan.[15]

This was the kind of scale and experimentation that Barton was looking for, and had almost pulled off in Siberia. Fred Barton, the most knowledgeable man in China about Western horses, was thrown together with Frans Larson, the most knowledgeable man about Far Eastern horse breeding. The conversations between the two must have been very stimulating. The result would become something electric.

When Larson wrote his own book about his Mongolian life, *Larson, Duke of Mongolia* (1930), he modestly revealed more about his love of the Mongolians and horses than his own exploits. The book devoted an entire chapter to "Horses." Larson went into depth describing why Mongol ponies were not afraid of people, why Mongols did not crossbreed, how Mongol pony qualities differed in each region of Mongolia, how ponies adapted to wolves, how foreign horses were introduced, how crossbreeding produced different kinds of horses, what some of the more famous racing horses and people were throughout Mongolia and China, and what happened to a Mongol horse when it was stabled and shod rather than allowed to roam. He knew his stuff, and the Internationals, Chinese, and Mongolians knew he knew it. All the famous winning race horses at the Chinese tracks and the polo ponies at the International polo fields were purchased from Larson. All horses purchased for the Chinese armies passed through Kalgan.

While no recordings exist of conversations between the two friends, both seem to have profited. Knowing Larson later opened channels for Barton to purchase ponies from Mongol princes for his own breeding experiments. On the other hand, Larson must have fallen under the Montana cowboy spell, because he took pleasure in riding on a Western cowboy saddle alongside Barton riding on his. This was country where most people had never before seen a Western saddle. As soon as people saw Larson's saddle, they asked for replicas. The saddle is lost, but likely stamped on it was "Miles City Saddlery, Makers of the original Coggshall Saddle."

Barton's Western influence must not have been lost on the Prince of the Ordos' people either. Beginning in 2011 and 2012, China news agencies touted the First and Second Ordos International Nadam fairs. These eight-day folk festivals in the Inner Mongolia Autonomous Region featured Mongolian music, horse racing, and traditional wrestling. Mongolians wore traditional, elaborate dress and headgear, but the preponderance of people wearing "ethnic clothing" were musicians, adults, and children wearing Western-style cowboy hats. It made no difference whether they rode in on their horses, motorbikes, or four-wheel drives. A century earlier, Barton's cowboy hat was the first they had seen. Now it is considered ethnic Mongolian. Some things last. Today, Western hats marketed to the Mongols is a Chinese industry.

Barton did not just tend business in Kalgan and Urga. Besides visiting headquarters in Shanghai, he worked Shansi province south of Kalgan, covered Manchuria, and returned to Vladivostok. Peking and Tientsin were just a train ride away, but he was on his own in rural areas. Like other agents, Barton had to adapt to whatever transport was available. That meant everything from water buffalo to mules to camels. Since saddling up steers for cowboy competitions in Miles City was a part of any good time at roundups, Barton did not hesitate to put his Western saddle on the broad back of a Manchurian water buffalo pulling a cart. It beat riding in crude carts with no shock-absorbing springs.

In 1915 Barton's four-year BAT contract ended when he sailed from Shanghai with Hutchison. Barton did not remain long in the States. Within months, he returned to China. He registered as an American citizen with U.S. consul-general Thomas Sammons in Shanghai. Sammons was sociable, likeable and in the good graces of Sun Yat-sen, the founder and first president of the Republic of China, but he was up to his eyeballs with problems in Shanghai due to World War I and the Chinese warlords. Shanghai was flooded with spies. The International Settlement and Shanghai Municipal Council depended on cooperation of the major powers represented in the treaty port. The major powers, however, not only warred with each other in Europe but also shunned talking to each other in China. This left the United States in a precarious position.

Sammons believed the best hope for China resided in a commercial rather than a military solution. Chinese needed experience in business management for the future. He saw what war and poverty did. This prompted him to organize a World War I Red Cross chapter and found a Rotary chapter to set up schools for immigrant Russian and physically handicapped children. Having already served as consul-general in Yokohama and the North China treaty port of Newchwang, he collected trade and other information from the major import/export players such as British-American Tobacco, Standard Oil, and Andersen, Meyer & Company. He became an expert on everything from opium to salt as China and the major powers struggled for control of Asia. Registered merchants like Barton certainly held his interest.

Barton no longer gave a BAT address, but instead that of the company his friend Larson worked for, Andersen, Meyer & Company. As will be seen, Andersen, Meyer, with offices in Shanghai, Kalgan, Harbin, Peking, Tientsin, and Vladivostok, proved a good source from which U.S. intelligence agents were recruited. The company worked hand in glove with BAT. Listed as "traveling tobacco salesmen" or "traveling merchants," these agents moved everywhere across China. When any salesman was asked who should be contacted in the event of his death or injury, he curiously named not a person, as was normal procedure, but the firm of George Borgfeldt & Company of New York City. The import/export firm became famous for its dolls and being the first company under contract to merchandise Disney characters such as Mickey and Minnie Mouse.

This time, Barton would not be a bachelor British-American Tobacco agent. He married Mabel Blanche Roberts (also known previously as Mrs. Mabel B. Newman or Mrs. M.H. Newman) in the city hall of Nagasaki, Japan, in September of 1916. They had met six months earlier and returned to Shanghai, where they lived at the Kalee Hotel. Later, they stayed at the posh Astor House Hotel. Three years older than Barton, Mabel had resided in Manila the previous year and was traveling the Far East.

One might think Shanghai a poor place for a new bride and housewife. First, the stench of the city assaulted the nose before travelers reached the city. Tidal flat muck, human excrement, rotting garbage, garlic, gas, industrial smoke, carcasses, sour sweat rags, all aromatically combined to waft on their own heavy current down Soochow Creek and the Whangpoo. Those who had lived in Shanghai for a long time often joked about the vileness when sailing back to their home countries. Once they reached open sea, they asked, "What is that horrible smell?" Came the reply, "Fresh air!" When Japanese propaganda extolled the "Greater East Asia Co-prosperity Sphere" and the "New Order in Asia," Shanghai radio called it the "New Odor in Asia." Almost anything could be gotten used to.

Shanghai's choked streets offered no place for a woman either. Teeming crowds jostled on the cramped sidewalks, a haven for pickpockets. Run by the criminal triads, the opium and heroin trade laid waste to lives by the thousands. Shrill, diseased, disfigured beggars grabbed at the shopper under a spider web of phone and electrical wires festooning the streets. The limbless rolled down sidewalks blocking already slow passage. Crossing or stepping into the street became perilous. The raucous stream of rickshaws, pedicabs, carts, streetcars, buses, lorries, and automobiles stopped for no one, even after a pedestrian was struck. Every available space was used for urination or defecation, so that summer flies swarmed the city. Given the poverty, disease, and crime, it is no surprise that each morning carts hauled away the dead bodies from the streets. In winter, corpses piled up to the tune of hundreds a day.

But that was Shanghai's outside world for the Bartons. The inside world was another story. Shanghai exhibited extreme disparity between rich and poor, the grandiose and absolute squalor. Just as non-Chinese men were not supposed to do any manual labor, housewives like Mabel did no cooking or housework. Anyone with even a modest paycheck could afford to pay two dollars a month for servants. Most BAT workers could afford full staffs of Chinese servants—a No. 1, a cook, a rickshaw boy, housecleaners, a washer, and so on. For those who lived in hotels, the settings were opulent, usually with large columned lobbies, billiard rooms, restaurants, and bars. With daily necessities taken care of, Shanghai's western employees and retirees could pursue leisure activities.

Shanghai offered much to Fred and Mabel. Stores exhibited products from around the world, from the best Paris had to offer to the illicit. Eating out at fashionable restaurants became ritual, as did exchanging social visits with friends and business acquaintances. Heavy British influence led to tiffins and teas. For night life, Shanghai transformed into a spectacular neon fairyland. The Russian influx put the city on the cultural map through ballet, orchestras, plays, and opera. Leading entertainers and touring groups such as the Bolshoi Ballet Company made Shanghai their stop. Art Deco movie houses showed the latest films for only seven cents in admission. Jazz played throughout the clubs and dance halls. Military detachments from the International Settlements paraded and hosted social balls.

Betting, races, sports and other events took place at the racetrack, which became more or less the social center or metroplex of Shanghai. Card and table gambling were enjoyed at popular grandiose casinos and dives. Shanghai was Las Vegas before Las Vegas had casinos. Casino limousines picked up "whales" at their residences and treated big betters to champagne and expensive foods. Many enjoyed riding, boating, golfing, strolling in Shanghai's parks, and renting summer cabins at a beach away from the city. For businessmen, joining social clubs was imperative. Much business was carried on within them and within business and fraternal organizations. These groups staged social affairs and receptions as well, keeping people busy. People needed to carry a wad of business cards to exchange at all times. With all the museums, sport clubs of every kind, and expositions, it was not a question of what to do but which to choose. One could live cheaply or richly. Either way, one could live well.

Mabel had plenty of time to arrange the social calendar. Fred had plenty of time too. Western business concerns in Shanghai generally kept a six-hour workday with a two-hour lunch. That gave workers plenty of time to engage in other activities in the morning, at lunch, and in the evening. It was a good life, even on a modest income.

The need for business cards led to a newspaper story about Fred. In December of 1915, prior to their marriage, Fred had gone to court in New York City to change his name from Fred Kottmeier, Jr., to Fred Barton. The story was picked up in Western newspapers. The *Laredo Times* enjoyed the true cowboy humor of the situation, reporting that Barton told the court that he was doing business in China and that the Chinese characters for his name were pronounced "Go-da-me," which served up too much profanity for him.[16] He did not find being called "God damn me" particularly appealing. His old bronc busting sidekicks must have gotten a charge out of that. As luck would have it, Barton's change-of-name notice sat right next to a photograph of the czar and czarina reviewing Cossacks. It was as if the newspaper intuited that Barton still had the Russian horse raising venture on his mind.

Barton's humorous court appearance made for good copy and may have contained some truth in it, but other family members also changed names from Kottmeier to Barton, including his mother and brother. Although his brother, Lester, obtained a passport to go to China with Barton in 1920, Fred's mother certainly was not going there. World War I provided the better reason for the name change. Anti-German sentiment gathered force in the United States from 1914 to 1918. It reached fever pitch on May 7, 1915, when a German U-boat sank RMS *Lusitania*, at one time the biggest ship in the world. Over one thousand passengers and crew perished, including 128 U.S. citizens.

Anti-German propaganda machines cranked up in the UK and the U.S. Some German-Americans were lynched, others were beaten, and windows of German-named stores were smashed. Particularly hard hit were German brewers, who produced most of the beer in the United States at the time. The association of Germany with beer hastened the process and made Prohibition possible. This was not the time to bear a Germanic name like Kottmeier. Even in China, German hatred spread. Because Fred Barton's mother's maiden name was Barton, reverting to that good English name proved easy and a safe thing to do. This was not an unusual practice. German family, street, and product names quickly underwent Anglicization during the war—something that drives genealogists to distraction today. Britain's royal family under King George V adopted "Windsor" to replace the "House of Saxe-Coburg-Gotha," and "Battenburg" became "Mountbatten." Furthermore, the Barton name was common in the U.S. and abroad—and who would impugn Clara Barton's legacy of the Red Cross during the meatgrinder of World War I?

A month after their wedding, Mabel accompanied Fred on a business trip to his old stomping grounds in Vladivostok. Over the next few years, they would bounce back and forth from their base in Shanghai to the U.S. and to Peking and Tientsin in North China as Barton put together his great plan for the biggest horse ranch in the world and the world's longest horse drive in modern times.

Two of Barton's aunts already lived in California, making Fred and Mabel's arrival and departure easier. Family members or friends could sign off on passport applications for Barton and his wife. His aunts were well known in California. Alice Kottmeier married musician Julius Stamm in 1893, the same year he, along with forty other musicians, founded the famous Los Angeles Philharmonic Orchestra and became its first conductor. He paid for many of the orchestra's instruments out of his own pocket. Music teacher Alice became much respected in music circles in her own right.

Alice's sister, soprano soloist Blanche Kottmeier, took lessons with Stamm. For several years she served as soloist church singer at the St. Vibiana Cathedral in Los Angeles, one of the few remaining buildings from early L.A. While Fred's music ability turned more to "cow"-traltos and "soap"-ranos than contraltos and sopranos, Aunt Blanche's opera and German Liederkranz music ability definitely ran in the family.

In 1901 Blanche married Dr. Ferdinand Butterfield, a capitalist from the eastern U.S. who became a mover and shaker in San Francisco, particularly in the wake of the near destruction of the city by the great San Francisco earthquake and fire of 1906. After the disaster, he represented various companies involved in trying to win franchises from the city supervisors to restore telephone, gas, electricity, water, and railroad services. His testimony led to graft and corruption charges against the supervisors in one of the great trials of the time. He served as president of some companies, and held controlling interest in the famous Best & Belcher Mine, part of the Comstock Lode in Virginia City, Nevada. Blanche and Ferdinand's daughter, Lillian Butterfield, tried her hand at Hollywood. She and Myrna Loy played "girls at Bacchanal" in *The Wanderer* (1925) starring Greta Nissen, Wallace Beery, and Tyrone Power Sr. The western branch of the Bartons was doing well.

Barton's temporary base in urban Shanghai might not have looked like horse country, but it provided plenty of equine interest. The city was dominated by the famous Bund with its skyscrapers of massive hotels worthy of Las Vegas such as Broadway Mansions, banks, customs house, and early Art Deco apartment buildings. Reminiscent of early immigrants sailing into New York harbor and seeing the city skyline for the first time, the scene amazed anyone entering the port. Behind the Bund lay another wonder, Shanghai's huge racetrack, a center of sport and social life for the city. The Race Club building towering over the track billed itself as the world's poshest race club. The racetrack also boasted the biggest grandstand in the world. It was said that the infield grass was as level as the surface of a billiard table. The expansive infield made it possible for team field sports to take place during the races.

Barton could watch Larson's horses race here. Despite there being no professional jockeys in China, horse racing was a mania for Shanghailanders. Nearly everyone who was someone raced horses at the track, played polo, or owned horses for recreational purposes. A horse named Bengal became Larson's most famous racer at the track. Bengal won more racers than any other in track history. The horse passed from "Duke of Mongolia" Larson to David Fraser, the Reuters correspondent in Peking. Fraser sold it to One-Arm Sutton, he who had lost part of an arm at Gallipoli and became advisor to northern China warlords. Finally Shanghai tycoon Sir Victor Sassoon purchased Bengal.[17] The names of horses Larson supplied to racetracks in Shanghai, Peking, and Tientsin were changed when the Japanese invaded. To erase vestiges of western influence, the Japanese rechristened horses with Japanese monikers.

Shanghai families from the International Settlement also liked to retreat to the countryside for rides on Larson's Mongol ponies. The British, who founded the Shanghai Race Track, heavily influenced these rustic recreational pursuits as well. The Paper Hunt provided a favorite equine recreational sport. Since Shanghai was not Great Britain with its foxes and fox hounds, a few riders rode out in front of the main hunting group. Instead of a leaving a trail of fox scent, they would drop scraps of white paper to be followed over ditches, hills, and dales. Wearing white pants and red jackets was of course de rigueur. Whoever figured out the trail, made the jumps across ditches, negotiated the mud, and reached the finish line first, won.[18]

Paper hunts mystified the Chinese. Jumping ditches and churning up dirt was not for them. The Chinese gentry shunned forms of physical exercise, looking upon riding as they did fishing. Fishing meant placidly sitting in one place, contemplating nature or composing poetry. Riding meant being rich enough to own a specially bred pacer giving the smoothest of rides, and never at a gallop or even a trot. The ride was to be as smooth as sitting in an armchair, a far cry from the devil-may-care riding of those "red-haired foreign devils."[19]

Such horses and pursuits served foreigners well. Barton had his eye on more military matters and a horse not yet seen in China, or anywhere, for that matter.

• Five •

Horses for the Warlords
The Longest Drive, 1917

> *The most interesting thing in the grave was a saddle upon which the man's head was resting.... The saddle was well preserved and when Nelson brought it to camp it proved to be a perfect McClellan type such as our army uses today ... quite unlike that used by Mongols or Chinese today or in the past. Nelson thought the grave must be at least a thousand years old and probably much more than that.... Thus far we have found no traces of horses in the very old formations.*[1]
> —Roy Chapman Andrews in Mongolia, 1922

In 1917 the dream of the great horse ranch came true. Warlords Chang Tso-lin and Chang Tsung-chang remembered the 1911 plans the Russians had for raising horses in Siberia. Now they wanted Barton to do the same for them. The trick was to find a location in China similar to that of southern Siberia with good water and grass. It needed to be close enough to rail lines for transporting stock to Peking yet far enough away from the capital and warring areas so that the ranch would remain safe in offering a consistent supply of horses. It needed to be close to Mongolia because all of China's horses came from there.

That China raised little or no stock, horses or otherwise, is surprising, considering that the Chinese back in the Jin Dynasty (AD 265–420) invented the harnessing system based on the breast strap, horse collar, and paired stirrups. The Chinese purchased most animals out of Mongolia. To understand why China was devoid of its own horses is to understand Chinese geography and history. No other animal was more important to the survival of China than the horse. Any study of Chinese art through the millennia reveals the horse as a favorite subject in statuary, scrolls, and paintings. The horse vies with, and even surpasses in some eras, the dragon as symbol and motif. The world was astounded in 1974 when the Terracotta Armies near Xian were discovered. Only partially excavated, the site has yielded thousands of life-size terracotta soldiers from around 210 BC. The site has become the premier tourist destination in China and has been dubbed "The Eighth Wonder of the World." As the soldiers were excavated from the earth, hundreds of chariot and cavalry horses also emerged to stand at their sides.

Ma Yuan (14 BC–AD 49), a famous Han general also known as General Fubo ("Queller of the Deep") said, "Horses are the foundation of military power, the great resources of the state but, should that falter, the state will fall." Throughout China's history, its chariot armies and cavalry units, along with the Great Wall, protected China from nomadic horsemen from the west and north. If the horse supply failed, China would fail, a lesson realized when Genghis Khan and Kublai Khan moved on the country. Like Russia, China depended on other areas for its horses, areas often inhabited by an enemy reluctant to give up its horses.

An ecological zone map of China reveals part of the country's problem. Southern and central China occupy a subtropical rain forest zone. Rice, the main crop, might feed a population of millions, but it is fairly useless as horse fodder. What little pasturage that could have been used had been converted to cultivated fields and paddies. Much of the area is also mountainous. Part of northern China lies in a deciduous forest zone, a thin strip of grassland, and high desert. Much of it, too, is mountainous. It lacks pastureland due to its highly cultivated terraces, fields, and loess hills built up from desert dust blowing in over the eons. The northern cold climate did not bode well for horses not acclimated to it. Looking north to Siberia for horses was stymied too. Raising horses in Siberian forests was difficult. With dense forests to the north, an ocean to the east, and rain forest to the south, China's only option for horses depended on nomads to the northwest across the Gobi whose herds could number in the millions. Their robust Mongol ponies were the exception in the harsh climate. Millennia of natural selection weeded out ponies unable to endure bitter winters, hot summers, sparse grass, lack of water, howling sandstorms, and suffocating dust storms. Wolves took care of the sick and weak.

For centuries, such a geography and climate frustrated invaders and Chinese alike. When imperial armies were sent out to meet invading nomads, put down rebellions, or forcibly obtain good horses from those reluctant to give them up, the mounted armies of the Chinese emperor needed a long supply chain to keep the horses fed. The transport and storage needed to feed a soldier was much less, at least ten times less, than the enormous amount of grain or hay needed to feed an army of horses. Defensive and offensive expeditions required enormous expenditures, taxing local supplies and risking the starvation of subjects for the sake of horses. Just as roundup cowboys in Montana required several mounts apiece, mounted armies needed the same. For example, a 50,000-man army required at least three horses per soldier. That meant 150,000 horses were needed right off the bat. For a four-year campaign, another 200,000 would be needed for replacements.[2] Complicating matters, the main grain-growing areas in the west of China were subject to drought, further diminishing supplies. The numbers are staggering for a country having to import horses.

Importing horses and setting up stud farms created another set of problems. The Chinese needed quality as well as quantity. Horse sellers outside of China liked to cheat Chinese civil officials by selling them their worst horses, figuring that officials would not know the difference. The quality of horses bred in China diminished in other ways too. Emperors and generals rode the best horses. Early in Chinese history, when an emperor, general, or nobleman died, his horse was killed and buried with him. He then rode his steed into the afterlife. Thus, the best horses were buried, not put out to stud. Corruption often ran rampant on stud farms without close military oversight. Unscrupulous horse masters wrecked good stallions by overbreeding and selling illegal colts bred to inferior mares on the side. Disease spread, weakening the herds.

Courtly tastes also interfered, particularly when emperors preferred white horses.

Chinese emperors in the seventeenth century demanded a Mongol tribute be paid to them of the "Nine Whites," comprising eight white horses and one white camel.[3] The animals were cherished much as Native Americans cherished rare white buffalo calves in the American West. Later emperors and warlords continued their predilection for white horses and white matching horses for their special military and ceremonial units. White works well for arctic hunting carnivores like the polar bear, snowy owl, and fox to blend in with the snow and ice, and it works well for hares, baby fur seals, and ptarmigan as camouflage to try to defeat those predators, but it does not work well for Mongolian ponies needing dark shaggy coats for warmth. The scarcity of white Mongol ponies meant that just about any white pony, no matter how inferior, ended up being sent to the Chinese, further diminishing the quality of Chinese herds.

While Barton was serving as a tobacco agent in China, explorer Robert Falcon Scott's ill-fated 1911–1912 expedition to the South Pole made the same mistake as the Chinese emperors. Instead of the "Nine Whites," Scott's ponies turned into the "Nineteen Dead Whites." Scott sent his agent to Vladivostok and to Chang Tso-lin's Harbin to purchase Mongolian ponies for the expedition. The agent knew more about selecting Siberian sled dogs for the expedition than he knew about horses. Scott had it in his head that white horses survived better on ice than darker ones. The inevitable result followed. Whites were few and far between. Savvy horse traders dumped the worst horseflesh in the Far East on the buyer. Some of the horses had long passed their prime, gone lame, and become broken-backed from carrying too much weight. On this lot, lives of the Scott party would depend.

Once a Mongol horse is taken out of its environment, it is headed for trouble. Winter's reduced sunlight in Mongolia triggers horses there to grow longer hair for warmth and protection from the wind. Summer sun causes them to shed and have shorter coats. Scott took horses from one hemisphere and one season to an opposite hemisphere and opposite season in the Antarctic, shipping them on a long journey through the hot tropics to boot. The suffering ponies' short hair did not equip them well for the Antarctic cold and howling white-outs. Some died before even reaching New Zealand, let alone Antarctica. Others weakened after they plunged through the ice and had to be saved from killer whales. New Zealanders who saw the ponies before they embarked on their final leg to the Antarctic knew they would never see these horses again. They would not see the people again either.

Scott encountered what Chinese expeditionary cavalry units did. If horses were used, most supply transport had to be dedicated to horse feed. The amount of feed for horses on Scott's ship dangerously decreased the space for food for the exploration party. This cost them. As horse owners at the Chinese racetracks learned, stabling Mongol ponies decreased their stamina, speed, and physical properties, such as that seen with hoof deterioration. They needed open spaces to run. Scott's ponies endured months of cramped, rocking quarters on ship, standing all the time while their health declined.

For the Chinese, just buying horses from the Mongols presented a hurdle. What would they accept in payment? Mongols cited prices for any goods or services in terms of how many horses it would cost. Horses served as currency, the only currency. Money was of little or no use to Mongolians. The Chinese certainly could not pay for horses with horses. The Chinese found tea to be the only thing they had that Mongols wanted, so they traded tea for horses, which meant inflating the price of tea as high as possible. Only so much tea can be traded. Demand for horses outpaced tea supply.

Finding enough horses was difficult, finding the right kind of horse even more so. The Chinese did experiment by bringing in some larger horses from central Asia and Europe. Big horses worked fine in the clearings of medieval Europe for knights jousting and engaging in sword play at close quarters, but they were not so fine on the expansive steppes of Mongolia where marauders armed with bows and arrows and riding fast, darting ponies could hit, run, and simply disappear by riding away. Even chariots were no match for that. Fred Barton would have to try his hand at developing the best warhorse for China.

World War I had concluded just as Barton planned to raise horses for the Chinese warlords. The world's first mechanized war created a slaughter carried out by armored tanks, machine guns, airplanes, and mobile gun platforms such as train flatcars. So why the interest in horses for modern warfare? Trench warfare's barbed wire and machine guns made cavalry charges suicidal if not impossible by the end of the war. Despite that, horses played a crucial role. Some felt a horse was worth more than a soldier. It was easier to replace a man than a horse. Horses could go where wheel and tracked vehicles could not. They did not require gasoline. They did not make the kind of noise vehicles made that would give away positions. To quote the old war saying, "Where there's war, there's mud. Where there's both, it's just plain hell." Horses could deliver messages, pull artillery, and carry supplies through mud and snow when nothing else could move. German defeat was preordained as soon as Germany became cut off from outside sources for horse replacements.

While the days of the cavalry were numbered, warhorse use was not. At the beginning of the war in 1914, while Barton worked in China for BAT, the Russians mustered over a million horses for battle, half or more of which were lost in the first three months of the war.[4] German and Austrian stud farms produced at capacity prior to the conflict, turning out hundreds of thousands of horses. Veterinary services during the war were as important as field hospitals were for wounded soldiers. British veterinarians estimated treating three-quarters of a million sick and wounded horses. The United States shipped nearly a million horses to France. Trying to prevent that, German agents in the U.S. tried to infect some horses with glanders disease and anthrax, as they had done on the Eastern Front to prevent the Russians from moving horse-drawn artillery.[5] Soldiers returning from the war had forever seared into their minds images of bloated horse corpses and the stench.

Horses were pivotal to World War II as well. Most images replayed today about this war show even greater technological advancements—aircraft carriers, battleships, fighters, bombers, panzer tanks, V-2 rockets, atomic bombs. For that greatest tank battle ever, the Battle of Kursk in 1943, horses outnumbered vehicles, proving to be a necessity as tanks and trucks bogged down in Russian mud. German technological advancement in the form of the vaunted Tiger tanks proved a liability in some ways. More than half the Tigers lost in Operation Barbarossa were not destroyed by the Russians but by their own crews when Tigers continuously broke down and could not be repaired. Their crews destroyed them to keep them from falling into Russian hands. Horses pulled most of the German artillery and shouldered most of the resupply burden. Winter forced the defeated army to eat its horses upon retreat, further causing artillery to be abandoned. Without horses, the German Army was lucky that anyone escaped.

In the Allies' China-India-Burma theater of operations, the Mars Task Force, composed largely of the last U.S. Army horse outfit, the 124th Cavalry, slogged its way behind Japanese lines through the jungles of Burma, along the Burma Road, and through the mountains of China depending on mules and even elephants. Off the Burma Road, tanks and trucks had no place to operate. They barely could negotiate the Burma road itself. In places it seemed to be a road in name only. Likewise, as the Japanese discovered upon invading China in World War II, China's size and rugged, roadless geography did not favor mechanized armies.

In the intervening period between the two world wars, "Tiger of the North" Chang Tso-lin needed horses, lots of horses, for his many brigades of cavalry, as did his eldest son and heir, "Young Marshal" Chang Hsueh-liang, and the Tiger's trusted "Dog-Meat General" Chang T'sung-chang. While machine guns and artillery pieces were always welcome, the Manchurian Tiger still needed the horse. He split the difference, organizing his army around the old (cavalry) and the new (mechanized). Some of his soldiers had been trained and equipped by the Japanese to fight in Europe in World War I. The war ended before most shipped out. To modernize, Chang Tso-lin was able to assimilate these troops and equipment into his own army.

Regardless of some defeats, Chang Tso-lin proved to be the most powerful Chinese warlord during the warlord period. He established his own arsenal to manufacture ammunition, rifles, mortars, and artillery pieces. He needed another factory to "manufacture" horses and not only Mongol ponies for his cavalry, but also more adaptable, bigger horses, strong enough to pull heavy artillery for modern war, yet fast enough for cavalry action and tough enough to survive the Manchurian winter. After the Russian Revolution of 1917, as thousands of White Russians fled from the Reds into Manchuria and China, the general also needed larger horses for the White Russian cavalry units who joined his army; but the defeat of czarist troops negated resupply of horses from Russia.

Barton laid out a plan to create such a horse factory for the general. Chang Tso-lin survived by being an opportunist who was not afraid to hire foreigners and rewarded them handsomely if they benefited him. For example, One-Arm Sutton, who ran Chang Tso-lin's arsenal and became his top military advisor, scored very well. The general gave him a beautiful home, rare gifts, and a pledge to scour Manchuria for the prettiest girls to service him. When events became too hot for Sutton in China and he left for safer Canada, he carried with him over a million pounds in profit, a staggering amount then, and even more staggering when converted to today's money.[6]

Working for a warlord was a dangerous game, so Barton had to be careful in negotiations. Warlords could be assassinated at any time, as well as those who worked for them. Sutton had many close calls. Chang Tso-lin was himself dangerous. Though seen by some as nothing more than an illiterate, diminutive, mahjong playing bandit, he knew how to survive and play the game. Like other warlords, he succeeded by forming allegiances, breaking them, and doing whatever it took to accumulate power. If crossed, he took action. If a newspaper editorialized against him, his soldiers would first harass newspaper offices. If that did not work, his soldiers liquidated the editor. Simple as that. Garroting was also in vogue.

Business meetings and banquets hosted by Chang could be pleasurable for people he liked or excruciatingly painful for those he disliked or wanted to test. He threw lavish banquets. Guests sat at prearranged places at tables draped with long tablecloths. Hidden under the tables, a prostitute was assigned to each guest with specific instructions. She went to work on her target, undoing his pants and either inflicting great pleasure or excruciating pain on his genitals. To avoid losing face, surprised guests had to grin and bear it. Evening soirees could either be too long or much too short.[7] Barton said nothing about the general's sense of humor.

Chang did have one weakness that any experienced cowboy from Miles City or any other Westerner could use to advantage to stay on his good side. Poker. Chang loved to play, and if you were the better player, it paid to let him win. Solomon Skidelsky, a leading businessman in Harbin, became the biggest winner by losing to Chang. The Skidelsky family was perhaps the leading Jewish-Russian family in the Far East, thanks to receiving a contract to build the final segment of the Trans-Siberian Railway running through northern Manchuria to Vladivostok. For that achievement, the Skidelskys became one of only ten Jewish families the Russians permitted to live in Vladivostok.

After the Russian Revolution, the Skidelskys fled Siberia for Harbin. They were part of a wave of Jewish-Russian families seeking shelter and a new start in Harbin. Many, like the Skidelsky family, claimed Odessa as their ancestral home.[8] Although Harbin was a Russian city in China, Chang Tso-lin was the regional warlord and governor.

Solomon Skidelsky, a millionaire from his substantial timber and mining interests in Siberia and Manchuria, won the local Mulin coal mine concession from Chang Tso-lin by letting him win for six months. The general felt so good about his incredible string of wins and poker talent that he willingly signed over the 30-year lease concession to Solomon. What money Solomon lost to Chang paled in comparison to profits from the lucrative coal mines. Skidelsky continued to supply coal to the railroad even after the Japanese occupied Manchuria.

Fred Barton's Harbin connections not only included poker-playing Chang, but also Barton's second wife and her stepsister, who were part of that Harbin community. Chang Tso-lin, however, was not the warlord Barton came to know best. Chang's territories offered no place for raising horses, but Shansi Province, home of Chang's ally warlord general and governor Yen Hsi-shan, did. Yen agreed to raise horses for the northern warlords and his own army. Having previously visited Shansi as part of his British-American Tobacco work, Barton found the perfect place for the horse ranch in Shansi just south of the Great Wall and near the border with Mongolia. Located about fifteen miles to the northwest of Taiyuanfu, the capital of Shansi, the ranch lay at the foot of the mountains and was watered by a stream.

Shansi Province proved an excellent choice. It represented the most politically stable province in China. Its governor, Yen Hsi-shan, was highly respected as a model reformer trying to improve the lot of his province rather than being one of the bandit barons seizing control in other provinces. The U.S. press called Yen Hsi-shan the "Model Governor" and the hope for China. *Time* magazine devoted the cover of one issue to his portrait. Other warlords trusted him because he had kept Shansi fairly neutral in the provincial and party wars.

Barton arrived at an optimal time for Yen. A graduate of Japan's Imperial Military Academy, Governor Yen believed that militarism and modernization represented the only hopes for unifying China. World War I changed part of that equation for him. As an admirer of the German war machine, to the point of bringing in German military advisors, Yen became somewhat disenchanted with militarism upon seeing the Germans defeated. He turned more to modernization instead.

Natural disaster also nudged him more towards modernization rather than isolation and militarism. Drought threatened a warlord's power by ruining his economy or tax base, starving his subjects and increasing the chance for invasion. As coal-rich as Shansi was, Yen's people preferred burning wood rather than coal. This denuded hillsides, silted rivers, and diminished irrigation. Shansi was particularly susceptible to the effects of drought-caused starvation because much of the agriculture had shifted from grain to opium poppies. Loan rates were too high to see farmers through drought years. They could never recover. As a last resort, farmers would have to eat their stock, so they had no field animals to till the soil. Starving inhabitants would also destroy their own homes in order to sell the wood or straw in the roofs. What dogs that hadn't been eaten turned into wolves desiring human flesh. The only hope then would be to migrate out of the province, which decimated the population and left a trail of human skeletons.

Beginning in 1919, severe drought struck the southern part of Yen's province and lasted for three years. Yen at least did have stored grain in the north. Though China would lose a half million people in this drought, Russia lost millions. As Donald Gillin pointed out in *Warlord Yen His-shan in Shansi Province, 1911–1949*, Yen faced having to find a way to transport grain from the north to people starving in the south. Without roads, even with 30,000 mules to transport the grain, relief would amount to a drop in the bucket. With the help of the American Red Cross and China International Famine Relief Commission, he put his army to work building roads.[9]

Since the Red Cross was an American operation that promised to build the roads and turn them immediately over to the Chinese, warlords trusted the Red Cross. Americans were held in higher esteem than colonialist British, Germans, French, and others who inhabited the international settlements imposed upon the Chinese. U.S. diplomats made it clear that the U.S. was not interested in making inroads into China. It only wanted free trade. In contrast, the Russians and Japanese had long vied with each other to make moves into China. Britain staunchly wanted to defend Hong Kong, its crown colony, as well as its naval port of Wei-Hai-Wei. Chinese resentment towards foreigners who claimed Chinese land and enforced their own laws kept bubbling up. The American approach paved the way for Barton to be accepted in important positions in the government of Shansi. It also helped that warlords generally were horsemen.

Further promoting modernization, Yen Hsi-shan experimented with crossbreeding livestock, so Barton's horse ranch well suited his plans. Yen also worked on crossing Mongolian and Merino sheep to come up with better textile wool. To do this, he enlisted the help of the other American in the area, Roger D. Arnold, who had become secretary of the Shansi International Relief Committee after taking a year of language class in Peking and receiving his first International YMCA posting to Taiyuanfu in the autumn of 1917.

While Barton created Yen's ranch, the friendly Arnold also made his way into the good graces of the warlord. He showed British World War I war movies to Yen, his wife, and his staff. These highlighted the work the Red Cross did in treating injured troops. So taken was Yen with the films he asked Arnold to show the movies for eleven consecutive nights to his troops, 800 at a time. He also requested that Arnold introduce his troops and students to Western sports to increase their physical education. Soon soldiers practiced track, basketball, tennis, and football while being encouraged to join the Anti-Narcotic League. This culminated in Arnold's creation of the first North China Amateur Track and Field Meet in Taiyuanfu. Even U.S. minister to China Paul Reinsch traveled from Peking to attend.[10]

Arnold provided great service to the United States. By the time the Japanese invaded China at the start of World War II, he had served longer than any American in Taiyuanfu, and later in Kunming, Yunnan, at the end of the Burma Road. He worked closely with Claire Chennault's Flying Tigers and the U.S. Army Air Force. He provided needed entertainment for the fliers and much-needed intelligence when it came to mapping the area. Highly thought of, he was listed as honorary pallbearer at a Flying Tiger funeral. In an area where few Americans resided, he and Barton knew a lot.

When it came to livestock, Governor Yen asked Arnold if he would arrange for the importation of 1,000 sheep from Australia. Arnold traveled to Tientsin on the coast and arranged for the shipment. Sheep were brought in the same way Barton brought in horses from the United States. The woolies were boated to the North China coast, then transshipped by rail through Tientsin to Shansi Province. Since Barton and Arnold became the warlord's livestock provisioners, they were well known to one another, particularly when Yen made Barton the director of his livestock programs. Both Arnold and Yen can be seen together in old photos as Barton's guests at the Shansi ranch.

Yen also crossbred pigs, and, of course, horses. Despite the well-meaning, sound ideas to improve Shansi livestock, as China Old Hand scholar Owen Lattimore pointed out, Yen's programs did not fare well. The culprit: corruption. Those in charge of stallions and rams simply wore them out by privately contracting their services.[11] To succeed, a ranch needed to be free of corrupt middlemen from the local bureaucracy. Putting a Montana cowboy in charge of breeding ingeniously sidestepped the usual rot at the core.

Aided by Shansi's geographical location, Yen was able to rule longer than any of the other warlords. He was the only provincial governor continuously to have been in office since the 1911 revolution. The rough, mountainous terrain that enclosed Shansi's high central plateau could be entered from only the north and east by narrow passes easily closed off and guarded. A few soldiers could bar many, and most trouble came from the north and east. Mongolia lay to the northwest, the Yellow River to the south and west with few crossings. Shansi was built like a fortress. Although railroads linked Taiyuanfu to Peking, Tientsin, and east coast ports, Yen Hsi-shan demanded that all foreign concession railroad companies build narrow gauge tracks. Because his tracks did not match those of the other railways in China, other warlords could not use their trains to attack his province. The changing track gauges slowed shipments because trains had to be loaded and unloaded at the border, but they improved safety from invasion.

Like Chang Tso-lin, Yen kept his independence by maintaining his own military arsenal and military academy in Taiyuanfu. At its height in the 1920s, the arsenal employed 8,000 workers. To modernize his army, Yen offered substantial rewards for any workers coming up with new weapons or improving old ones. And they did, developing a grenade launcher that could hurl grenades several hundred yards, an 88 millimeter howitzer, and more rapid firing weapons. Each day the plant churned out 4,500 grenades, 120,000 cartridges, and 3,200 mortar and artillery shells. This paralleled the 1,500 rifles, 500 pistols, 300 mortars, 30 machine guns, and an assortment of artillery pieces.[12] He went so far as to purchase two aircraft and to hire Japanese aviation instructors. Yen was still a warlord.

As an old fortress being modernized, Taiyuanfu's many walls had crumbled to the point that people could cross over them in places. Visitors still had to pass through arched gates to enter the city. When C.G. Mannerheim traveled to Taiyuanfu in 1908, he first reacted to the two slender towers of a Buddhist temple that stood above everything else. Streets were macadamized. Everywhere stood towers, pagodas, and old temples with glazed green and red roofs. Businesses were plentiful too, often with brightly colored, ornate storefronts. The town had the beginnings of a public park with a pond and many shade trees.[13] This was a far cry from the city's being the site of the worst slaughter of missionaries during the Boxer Rebellion less than ten years earlier. Missionaries, their children, and converts were publically beheaded before the then Western-hating Manchu governor. In 2000, they became part of the 120 Martyrs of China canonized by Pope John II.

Although a few missionaries had returned to Taiyuanfu and Shansi Province, those names still reverberated with massacre associations. Although half a world apart, the Boxers and the Ghost Dancers that affected Fort Keogh shared much in common. Drought precipitated both. Chinese blamed the terrible drought on foreigners and their foreign god. On the Great Plains, Native American reservations were reduced and divided into smaller parcels, which the Sioux were to farm. Drought eradicated the first season's crop. With the buffalo gone, this led to starvation. As in China, the white man had invaded native lands and brought disaster in the form of drought, disease, death, and cultural destruction.

In both instances, the Boxer and Ghost Dancer movements were part of a millenarianism that incorporated a return to the old ways and magic. The Boxers grew out of a religious sect, just as Wovoka had medicine-man training. With proper diet, prayer, martial arts training, and discipline, Boxers believed they could fly and become impervious to the weapons of the westerners. Wovoka was believed to be able to levitate, and followers of the Ghost Dance believed that through chanting, incantations, and dancing they became immune to the bullets of the white man.

The Boxer and Ghost Dancer beliefs in being impervious to white man's bullets were not isolated phenomena. At nearly the same time, Africa experienced Mumboism, another expression of millenarianism. Droughts and colonialism had driven African tribes to desperation. Rebels believed that spells could turn the bullets of the Belgians, British, French, Germans, and Portuguese to water. All these movements were curtailed with the same brutal results, a bloodbath and loss of more rights and land. Taiyuanfu was not so far from Miles City, after all.

The area Barton selected for the ranch resembled somewhat the Powder River area of eastern Montana—fairly barren grasslands interspersed with pine hills in a coal-rich region. Because Yen Hsi-shan maintained troops, a military school, and a munitions factory in Taiyuanfu, labor to build the ranch was readily available. Chinese army surveyors laid out the ranch to Barton's specifications. Soldiers cut cedars for fenceposts. Posts spaced every ten feet were run with six strands of smooth wire, also supplied by the military, so the horses would not be hurt by barbed wire. This major undertaking completely fenced off the ranch, which covered a quarter of a million acres[14]—not quite the size of the Russian ranch, but not bad.

Barton neither leased nor owned the land. He simply used it. His concern centered on two villages of about 250 families that occupied ground on the ranch. The villages appeared to be ancient, so he was troubled about disease. The governor relocated the villagers to other farmland and compensated those displaced. Once villagers had moved, troops burned the buildings and buried what was left. Barton did not want to take any risks. Under his direction, soldiers dug trenches and buried the remains twenty feet down, returning village soil to grassland.

Next came construction of a lavish eight-room headquarters house, followed by living quarters for the ranch hands a mile from the house. Barton required a big house for entertainment and business purposes. As governor, Yen Hsi-shan found little peace in the capital of Taiyuanfu, so at least once a month he retreated to Barton's house, where they parlayed and become close acquaintances. Photos from this time show Barton's personal interpreter, Li, at his side, not only at official functions but also in the corral to facilitate conversations with Yen and others. Barton did not have to pay any kickbacks to the governor and saw him as truthful in his dealings. Their relationship would last until 1937, when the Japanese overran the province. Barton's house literally became Yen's home away from home, his Camp David or country retreat. Barton also required space to entertain other dignitaries and Mongol princes from whom he bought ponies.

Thanks to his time with Larson and travel in Mongolia, Barton wanted to bargain directly with the Mongol princes at the ranch. If the princes felt they were dealing with Governor Yen, they may not have been willing to supply horses. They did not trust Yen, and for good reason. Yen encouraged his Chinese subjects to move into adjoining Mongol areas and cultivate the land. He needed more food production and needed to reduce unemployment to increase taxes, which supported his army and personal wealth. Taking away grassland from the princes reduced their power and gave them a distaste for Yen. In addition, Shansi merchants had long taken advantage of their western neighbors. Barton could sidestep those concerns.

With the problem of ranch location and construction resolved, Barton faced the next hurdle: acquiring enough breeding stock to supply military needs and his unique crossbreeding plan. He intended to incorporate three different breeds of horses to produce a horse of the right size, stamina, and demeanor. Breeding of these horses would be a bit complicated. Simply importing horses from the States or some other country would not work. The disastrous results of introducing a breed not suited to the climate had been demonstrated to the early cowpunchers in Montana. During the first years of the Texas cattle drives to the open range country around Miles City, many small Texas cow ponies, acclimated to warmer temperatures, died during hard winters, as did many cows. Many herds tried to shelter under the rimrocks along the Yellowstone River from Billings to Miles City, only to freeze or starve to death. Some froze standing up, creating bizarre statuary. Winter cut some herds by a third. Barton made sure that any imported horses from the U.S. would be acclimated and came from the Northern Plains or high desert areas.

Tough, winterized horses would form the core of the breeding program. Mongolian mares had to be bred to western light Morgan or thoroughbred stallions first. Though quite small, the Mongol mares made up for their lack of size in stockiness and strength. They could handle the severe cold and wind of Mongolia. They could also handle the typical Mongol rider, who averaged six-feet tall, and sometimes the additional weight of several members of his family. The idea was to cross Mongol ponies with Russian Orlovs, but the huge Orlovs represented a dramatic shift upwards in size, making breeding the two together impractical. It was like trying to breed a Pomeranian with a Great Dane. Morgans needed to be brought in first to produce a horse larger than the Mongol ponies that in turn could be bred to the Orlov strain. As Barton pointed out, the Orlov is a beautiful horse, but a bit flighty or warm-blooded.[15] The Morgan blood took the edge off the Orlovs to produce a more mild-mannered horse capable and big enough to be used with either cavalry or artillery. The Mongol blood made it tough and climate-ready.

• Six •

15th Infantry Cowboys and U.S. Intelligence, 1917

> *We're wild, we're wild. I'll say we're wild!*
> *We're the wildest bunch in town,*
> *From Wild Bill at the blinkin' Helm*
> *And the Top Kick straight down.*
> *We don't know the feel of a bit or curb,*
> *We're muddy and full of fleas,*
> *We don't give a damn for beast or man*
> *And we do as we damned well please!*
> —Anonymous 15th Infantry poem

Acquiring the horses, none of which were available in China, took some doing. Having been to Vladivostok and having toured southern Siberia, Barton knew where Orlovs could be gathered and purchased—in Khabarovsk, Siberia. Mongol ponies would of course come from nearby Mongolia, and the Morgans would have to be shipped across the Pacific from the States. None of this would be easy. Horses needed to be located, purchased, gathered, shipped, given veterinary examinations, and have their routes figured out with water and feed along the way. Given the international scope of gathering the horses, governments would have to be involved, railcars and ships reserved, and horse wranglers found to move the animals across land and sea. The problem was not just horsepower but also manpower.

Barton's connections with the U.S. military become very curious at this point. First, a ship, the U.S. Army transport *Dix* (formerly called the British steamship *Samoa*), was under orders to carry his Morgans from the States. Remember: Barton was civilian, not military. Second, soldiers from the U.S. Fifteenth Infantry in Tientsin were furloughed for at least four months to help him trail the Orlovs down from Siberia.[1] Let's consider the Tientsin furloughs first.

The Fifteenth Infantry was sent to China during Barton's first visit to the Far East in 1911 and 1912. With the fall of the Manchu Dynasty, the U.S. government worried about the safety of U.S. citizens living in China, particularly in Peking. Foreigners still felt uneasy about the massacres that had occurred during the Boxer Rebellion in 1900. Many a missionary had been killed. The Fifteenth Infantry was sent in to keep a communication and escape corridor open from Peking to the ports of Taku and the closest deeper-water port of Shanhaikuan, where the Great Wall meets the Yellow Sea in North China. After some moving around, headquarters was established at Tientsin between the coast and capital. Warlords knew that whoever controlled the railroad hub at Tientsin, with its access to arms shipments from the deep-water port, controlled all of North China.

Tientsin, or T'ien Ching, literally means an inland harbor. It is the port of Peking, though located forty miles inland on the banks of the Pei Ho. Tientsin surprised the soldiers. A fairly modern city on the main rail line of the Peking-Mukden Railway, Tientsin boasted multistoried buildings and one of the best bookstores in existence, where it was possible to find books censored elsewhere, such as the famed fourth printing of *Ulysses*.[2] What could not be bought in Tientsin could be purchased in Peking, just a train ride of about eighty miles.

The surrounding countryside left much to be desired. One soldier described it as looking much like dull parts of the Arizona desert. Actually, the area around the city was agricultural. That meant infantry needed to travel out of the area to conduct maneuvers, or it had to plan local outings between fall harvest and spring planting when fields were barren. Much of the time, soldiers just marched up and down the railroad right-of-way. Warlord armies did not concern themselves about incurring the wrath of farmers, but the Fifteenth had to be careful not to stir up anti-foreigner feelings.

Barton said he was friends with the colonel in charge of the Fifteenth Infantry in Tientsin.[3] Tientsin was home for BAT's operations in North China. Barton's former regional boss, William B. Christian, not only oversaw BAT operations in Peking and Tientsin but also transferred part of the company's buildings to the Fifteen Infantry for its headquarters. Christian started out as a typical BAT agent, hailing from a prominent Southern family from Richmond, Virginia. He also served as manager and vice president of the China-American Trading Company in Tientsin. Frans Larson, Barton's friend in Kalgan, used Christian to supply the Living Buddha in Urga with items he desired.

Larson ordered the Living Buddha's Model T through Christian's firm, which required an expedition in itself to make delivery. Christian ordered it disassembled and sent directly from Detroit. When it arrived by boat in Tientsin, it was reassembled, put on a railroad flatcar and transshipped to Kalgan. From there, its epic journey across the Gobi began. A team of bullocks had to pull the car up the steep pass leading into Mongolia. Early China photographer Ethan C. Le Munyon did the driving, taking photos as he went and delivering an English-speaking missionary woman to Larson's encampment at Tabo-Ol for a visit. Because of problems climbing steep terrain and perpetually becoming stuck in sand, Le Munyon knew the Ford needed extra gear ratios. This later resulted in improvements in the Moore Transmissions of Fords that Le Munyon patented. His documentation of the trip created a newspaper sensation and resulted in *National Geographic*'s extensive photo-essay of "The Lama's Motor Car: A Trip Across the Gobi Desert by Motor-Car" and *Motor Age*'s "Motorizing the Buddha of Urga."

Attracted by the need of motorized vehicles for expeditions bound for Mongolia, and also the commercial possibilities of creating an automobile service between Kalgan and Urga, Larson went into the automobile business. Staff in his company and Christian's maintained close ties and vouched for each other on legal documents. When automobiles were needed to dedicate the American Red Cross roads or for other grand events, a representative of the Fifteenth Infantry went along as well as diplomats to show the flag

Six • *15th Infantry Cowboys and U.S. Intelligence, 1917* 73

Fred Barton in 1918. By this time, Barton had traded Mongolian ponies for larger Russian and U.S. mounts, along with ditching his moustache (photograph 940-766, Montana Historical Society Archives).

and good will. The Tientsin/Peking/Kalgan American commercial community was a close one, which included officers of the Fifteenth Infantry.

Barton's request of the Fifteenth's colonel to use military men for a good part of the year for civilian purposes can sound a bit far-fetched. Historians who have studied the Fifteenth differ in their views of whether or not the colonel would furlough men for such a civilian endeavor. Dr. Edward M. Coffman, author of "The American 15th Infantry Regiment in China, 1912–1938: A Vignette in Social History," found it hard to believe that any regimental commander would have done such a thing, and suggested that maybe Barton latched onto some discharged veterans who stayed on in China.[4] Many did stay on because the rate of exchange was quite advantageous and booze was cheap during Prohibition, as were the women. Dr. Coffman did defer to Dr. Dennis L. Noble, whom Coffman favored as the authority on the Fifteenth. Noble, author of *Eagle and Dragon: The United States Military in China, 1901–1937,* said that normally he would agree with Coffman's position that no colonel would have done this, but not when it came to the Fifteenth.[5]

Etching depicting the Fen River, which watered Barton's China horse ranch, as it descends out of the rugged loess plateau into the central Shansi valley (from *The Earth and Its Inhabitants: Asiatic Russia*, 1884).

The differences in views of the Fifteenth might be explained by the rather schizophrenic nature of the unit. On the one hand, the Fifteenth was one of the best spit-and-polish units to be found anywhere. They had to be; they were constantly under the microscope in a foreign country where they had to compete against the other foreign units stationed on all sides of them—British, French, Italian, Japanese, Chinese. Against warlord armies, they were horribly outnumbered, so the Fifteenth maintained the peace through bluff and impressive displays of soldiering. Any sign of weakness signaled disaster. The Fifteenth most fiercely competed with the Legation Guards in Peking, the U.S. Marines. Fierce athletic contests on and off the field kept the soldiers sharp. The quality of the unit reflected itself in the names of its respected officers who became well-known leaders. This list includes such men as George C. Marshall, Philip L. Bolt, Joseph W. Stillwell, Earle G. Wheeler, and Mathew B. Ridgway.

Sometimes the Fifteenth carried its spit-and-polish too far for the locals, especially when on field maneuvers with the horses. Barbara Tuchman has described how, unlike the service in the U.S., this unit followed U.S. Army tradition to the letter. Campsites were completely policed. Not a piece of straw, horse dropping, or tin can would be left behind. Once, a delegation of elders from a local village pled their case. They needed what the Fifteenth was policing. The unit relented.[6]

On the other hand, the Fifteenth did not represent the typical military unit. As

Noble put it, in China, "they did just about what they wanted to do."⁷ If you knew where to look, the Fifteenth appeared as unorthodox as they come, perhaps even more than most Far East and western Pacific units who enjoyed unusual circumstances. Up to 80 percent of the unit could be "shacked up" at one time. Unlike at Fort Keogh, no officers' married housing existed, so houses had to be rented off base in one of the foreign concessions, usually the British or French since the United States owned no concession in Tientsin. At times the unit far exceeded any other army unit in incidences of venereal diseases and alcoholism. Some soldiers lived with their families; several married Chinese or other nationalities; and many hired Chinese servants cheaply who accompanied them even on field maneuvers. Photo scrapbooks kept by soldiers in the Fifteenth unabashedly show them being served beer in the field immediately after a ride, march, contest, or rifle practice. Training was hard, life was good, and the beer was safer than the water. The Fifteenth traveled with its own entourage.

Though not a cavalry unit, the Fifteenth employed horses. In fact, most military units, including the navy, used horses in China for both military and nonmilitary purposes. Thanks to Larson's supply of Mongol ponies, polo and horseracing were favorite pastimes. Many officers kept racehorses. Races were often the social and competitive events of the year. Much time was spent in betting and scouring the countryside for the best horses or figuring out how to bring in outside ringers. Shanghai featured some of the biggest races of all. Barton may have shared this interest in horseflesh with officers of the Fifteenth since he passed through Tientsin at least twice each year and could find good horses. Regular army officers at the time were also judged by how well they could ride; therefore, many officers took to their mounts as often as possible. For example, George C. Marshall rode all over the Chinese countryside. Some soldiers were even detailed as riders.

In addition, as Charles Finney points out in *The Old China Hands,* the Fifteenth enjoyed a mounted unit commanded at one time by "Wild Bill" Tuttle. The unit's one officer, twenty-seven enlisted men, and fifty-two Mongol ponies were tasked with being ready to ride hard and fast outside the city to warn foreigners of imminent attacks and to evacuate them. This required the officer to know Mandarin to deal with situations in the countryside.

Thanks to Larson, Tuttle rode Gobi Sun, a buckskin Manchurian pony said to be the best polo pony in all China. Tuttle's unit consisted of ex-cavalry, and they were superb horsemen.⁸ Captain Tuttle exemplified the close connection between the tobacco agents, horsemen, and the military in North China, for he was the very first "Marlboro Man." A full-page advertisement by the Tobacco Products Corporation (China) for Marlboro cigarettes appeared in the *Sentinel,* the publication of the Fifteenth Infantry in Tientsin. A caricature of Tuttle stated, "Wild Bill says: I'm from Texas. Give me a Horse and a Marlboro Cigarette and Watch My Speed."⁹ Although the Tobacco Products Corporation competed with British-American Tobacco in China and Manchuria, the same people who ran BAT financed the company. This manly Marlboro Man advertising campaign represented a radical departure for Marlboro, named after Great Marlborough Street in London where the cigarette was first produced. The brand was first marketed to women as being "Mild as May."

El Paso's Wild Bill was not mild as May. When Feng Yu-Hsiang, called the "Christian

MONGOL PONY
Tough, strong, winterized

2,000

MORGAN
Fairly even tempered, mid-sized

650

ORLOV
Big, serves many military roles, spirited

3,500

Chart showing the number and type of horses Barton interbred to perfect a warhorse for the Chinese warlords. Tall Russian Orlovs were first bred to medium-size Morgans to produce a smaller horse that was then bred to the smaller Mongol ponies.

Warlord," attacked Tientsin with his army, Tuttle took nine men and met them on the outskirts of the city. As Feng's massive army advanced with fixed bayonets, Tuttle advanced towards them alone, demanding that they detour around the city. The heroic bluff worked. Tuttle was indeed the rugged Marlboro Man. To cap off his cowboy image, "the Pride of Eagle Pass" organized a regimental horse show in which he exhibited Texas "Wild West" riding. Always the cowboy.

The cavalry connection to Barton and his father's past at Ft. Keogh can be seen. Barton could certainly speak the language. Before being transferred to Tientsin, some of the soldiers of the Fifteenth served in the Philippines, where Fort Keogh soldiers had been sent. Furthermore, within that U.S. Army contingent in the Philippines, the army established an advanced intelligence unit for the Far East called the Military Information Division of Army Headquarters.

At the time, the U.S. had little intelligence capability in China, that is until Ralph Henry Van Demon, "the Father of American Military Intelligence," created the Manila

MID. After the Boxer Rebellion, he had slipped incognito into China in 1906 to reconnoiter and map lines of communication around Peking. Sometimes on bicycles, he and Capt. Alexander Coxe traveled, took notes on distances, and drew maps from Shanghai to Peking. Even before the Fifteenth Infantry arrived in China from the Philippines, in 1910 Van Deman returned secretly to Tientsin to complete the project, only this time mapping railways, roads, and rivers. The Japanese had their eyes on expanding their Asian empire, and their protests led to Van Deman's expulsion. His Manila division dispatched about a dozen officers to China and Formosa to prepare maps and collect intelligence from 1906 to 1911.[10] This spy-vs.-spy in Asia became part of what the British called the Great Game, or what the Russians called the Tournament of Shadows.

Besides showing the flag before other countries wanting to slice up China, the U.S. State Department focused on a more worrisome and immediate problem, which was, oddly, why the State Department rather than the War Department controlled the Fifteenth.[11] When China underwent its revolution in 1911, the United States feared another bloodbath against foreigners. Evacuating U.S. citizens from all over North China could have turned into a fiasco without the U.S. military and State Department having knowledge of roads, railroads, and rivers. Without maps, any relief force traveled blindly. Isolationist America did not want to commit troops to China to protect U.S. interests, but it would tolerate a few Marines and army personnel there to protect the legation and evacuate citizens by rail to coastal ships if the situation blew up. By the time the army could issue evacuation orders from Washington or the Philippines, it would be too late. The U.S. minister to China, however, was right there and could communicate immediate orders.

The Fifteenth was a conduit to North China. The "Can Do" Fifteenth, with its Chinese dragon symbol, possessed capable riders, some of whom like Tuttle were Westerners in the Old West sense of the word. These were just the kind of men Barton needed to trail horses. No time to train greenhorns. Barton specifically asked that the men furloughed to him come from Texas, Wyoming, Montana, and other western states.

They certainly sought adventure. Men of the Fifteenth asked for duty in China, and, once there, most preferred not to leave. The unit spirit they described resembled in words that of the American Volunteer Group or Flying Tigers of World War II fame. Before they joined, these men were already accomplished soldiers who sought to test themselves to find out how good they really were. Like the Tigers, they sought challenging new adventure not found elsewhere. To even be admitted into the Fifteenth, a soldier had to have at least six years' service, be an expert rifleman, and excel in at least two sports. He had to hold his liquor (recruits were tested on this on their first train ride in from the coast to Tientsin), and he had to act as a good ambassador to the Chinese (which meant he could not get into trouble during his two-week layover in the Philippines en route to China). Many never made it to China. He who passed the tests was "a 14 karat soldier from his bald spot to his heels."[12] As will be seen, this penchant for adventurous yet older, more experienced men matched Barton's taste. He would seek the same type of individuals for his Montana cowboys on the Shansi ranch.

Barton could secure army cowboys because it was in the War Department's and State Department's interest. A story that still needs to be told about the Fifteenth and U.S. military in China concerns information gathering. The U.S. government needed intelligence about what was going on in China and nearby countries at the time. Anyone travelling into the interior could be an intelligence source. Roy Chapman Andrews, adventurer and paleontologist for the American Museum of Natural History's expeditions into Mongolia, served this function. As he said in *Heart of Asia*, "During World War I, I was doing an intelligence job in China that often took me across the Gobi Desert to Urga, in the north. I needed a headquarters at Kalgan, the entrance to the Mongolian plateau. Les Whitman, a trader (at Kalgan) who dealt mostly in ponies, had to go to America on business...."[13] Not only did Andrews serve an intelligence function, but also he had contact with the horse industry in the same area through which Barton would acquire his Mongolian ponies each year, making friends with Whitman and Frans Larson.

Andrews (Office of Naval Intelligence agent #241) also recounted a nearly fatal 1926 intelligence mission. He and a group of scientists set out from Peking for the Gobi at the time of warlord battles between Chang Tso-lin and "Christian" General Feng. Though flying the Stars and Stripes, their car was machine-gunned and stopped. They were lined up to be executed, only to be saved by a Chinese officer who understood Andrews' Mandarin. Andrews explained to the officer: "We were American Intelligence officers, from the Military Attaché's office, on reconnaissance. He nodded. 'Yes, I know your colonel, but I'm a staff officer. I can't control these men. Get off the road ... quickly.'"[14]

The clearest indication of civilians used as agents appeared in public papers of Paul S. Reinsch, U.S. minister to China, during the years Barton first went to Vladivostok and first created the Shansi ranch. Reinsch was not unknown to Montanans. His book *Civil Government with Montana Supplement* became the standard text for civics classes across the state, as well as being used for naturalization classes in the mining town of Butte. As Noel H. Pugach pointed out in *Paul S. Reinsch: Open Door Diplomat in Action*, Reinsch formed "an unofficial group of advisers, informants, and agents" who "had access to Reinsch twenty-four hours a day, by means of correspondence, chits, the telephone, and under cover of night, the backdoor of the chancery."[15]

Reinsch depended on adventurers, such people as Roy S. Anderson. Anderson, son of an American missionary in China, worked variously as a journalist under the name of "Bruce Baxter," as an adviser to both military and civilian leaders in the Chinese government, and as an agent for Standard Oil, the American International Corporation, and other companies. Like Barton, he lived as an adventurer with an eye to commercial success. Likewise, agent William H. Donald, an Australian newspaperman, wrote for the *China Mail*, the *Far Eastern Review*, and the *New York Herald* and was "not above dabbling in intrigue and even a little blackmail." He first attached himself to Sun Yat-sen and later to Chiang Kai-shek as a faithful adviser.

A third known informant, James A. Thomas, served for many years as manager of the powerful British-American Tobacco Company.[16] This was the "Old Man" Barton met in BAT's Shanghai office. Reinsch sent his agents into the provinces to do the work of the U.S. government, including negotiating with provincial warlords or governors. Barton traveled the length and width of China, and he certainly enjoyed an inside track with warlord governors. These agents could in turn recruit their own agents out of their own companies or acquaintances. The BAT certainly maintained the greatest number of employees or biggest information loop of any U.S. company in China.

When Reinsch and Barton were both getting their feet wet in Asia, China and the

U.S. were negotiating the designation of the British-American Tobacco Company as the selling agent for a Chinese government tobacco monopoly. The Chinese government desperately needed money, so it was interested in offering commercial concessions worth millions.[17] At the same time, the Japanese were trying to keep the government weak by not allowing Chinese naval or port expansion while strengthening their own military and commercial presence. The BAT plan countered the Japanese by putting U.S. firms into China while supporting a central Chinese government.

Concurrently, the Chinese negotiated with the U.S. to have Standard Oil explore oil potential in Shensi Province (right next to Shansi) and also in Chihli. If that worked out, the next province drilled would be Shansi, home of Barton's ranch. The dream was to make Shansi the new Texas, or what the Bakken oil fields of Montana and North Dakota look like today. Reinsch hoped this oil development could be used to make the U.S. the predominant player in China's natural resources. Shansi also sat on the richest coal deposits in China, but they had seen little development. Superstitions still abounded about evil spirits in the earth that sought revenge on anyone digging. Dragons were known to spit fire (methane explosions) on those who dug for coal in shafts. Meanwhile the Japanese tried to create new superstitions, forging documents to discredit and scare Chinese away from U.S. companies. After much political intrigue and protests by British, Dutch, and particularly Japanese companies, the oil deal fell through the year Barton started the ranch, in 1917.[18]

Warlords also wanted to sour the deal. The Peking government had to nationalize the oil reserves to benefit financially. Provincial warlords wanted individually to own their mineral and oil reserves, and Yen Hsi-shan, Barton's governor, was rumored to be richest of all the warlords. When the Japanese invaded Shansi in the 1930s, Yen moved the bulk of his wealth to nearby Shensi Province. Eighty carts filled with 520 tons of opium and silver made the move. The Japanese found another CH$300,000 of silver buried on the grounds of his palatial estate. This occurred after he had given CH$870,000 to his defenders to help stave off the invaders, and he had used his own fortune to stop a run on the Provincial Bank of Shansi by loading up three truckloads of silver and delivering it to the bank. This fortune did not even reflect his other holdings or sources of wealth. Money flowed into his coffers from whatever central Chinese government had seized power momentarily. The Peking government was forced to pay him for his allegiance, however transitory it might become.[19]

U.S. State Department staff found themselves caught in a welter of commercial wars, warlord wars, and an embryonic stage of a world war. Thus, they were tied down in Peking and major ports such as Shanghai and watched by the Japanese and other foreign powers. The military had limited intelligence capability as well. U.S. military presence was quite small, a few marines relegated mostly to consulate guard duty, a few sailors at major ports or on a few river gunboats (made famous in the movie *The Sand Pebbles*). The Fifteenth, the largest land group, was actually quite small, rarely numbering over a thousand men and usually lucky to make 800 with no more than forty officers. Moreover, once World War I began and European countries pulled troops from the Chinese treaty ports to fight on the European front, the Fifteenth had to absorb the patrol duties of the other troops. Unlike some other countries, the U.S. had no centralized intelligence agency of any kind.

The U.S. used a piecemeal variety of informal methods and covert spying to gather information. For example, a catcher was planted as a spy on a U.S. baseball team touring the Orient.[20] Shipmates in the U.S. Asiatic Fleet were supplied with horses and cameras by their superiors and told to just have fun riding in opposite directions along the Great Wall snapping pictures of "things of interest." Each sailor was assigned a different section of the Great Wall to photograph, with trips lasting up to three weeks. They were not to take photographs of any Japanese soldiers who might try to confiscate cameras. If they did, the photographs would seem to be innocent scenic travel shots. Sometimes Asiatic Fleet sailors found ancient weaponry on the Great Wall, including 30-foot repelling pikes and shields nearly as big as a man was tall. Chinese secretly aided these spy trips by supplying feeding stations for both men and animals along the way.[21]

Another tantalizing story is that of famous Taos painter Leon Shulman Gaspard (1882–1964), a self-professed World War I aviator and international spy. Much like the story Hutchison told of "Schneider" (Barton), unraveling Gaspard's story is fraught with fabrications and false leads. Most of what is known about his adventures stems from stories Gaspard told Southwest writer Frank Waters just prior to the painter's death. Waters constructed Gaspard's 1965 biography out of these stories recounted around the kitchen table. How much Gaspard exaggerated, deceived, or fell prey to faulty memory is open to question. He certainly loved to tell stories, punctuated by Russian folk songs from his youth in Vitebsk, Belarussia, and on the Siberian steppes as he traveled with his fur-and-rug trading father.

He traveled and sketched in China during the critical years Barton established the Shansi ranch. Gaspard's story intertwined with that of Paul Reinsch's successor. As minister to China, Reinsch was followed by Charles R. Crane, philanthropist and president of the famous Chicago plumbing fixtures company. Crane products grace bathrooms yet today and made most outhouses irrelevant. Crane was primarily responsible for Reinsch's position as U.S. minister to China (1913–1919). He had successfully lobbied the administration to pick Reinsch for the job. Reinsch may have accepted the nomination after his friend Crane said he would purchase Reinsch's art collection if he would take the posting.

The two both believed in progressive causes and enjoyed close Chicago and University of Wisconsin family connections. When it came to China, both fought to keep China independent and free from Japanese dominance. Crane, a Russophile who founded Russian studies in America, had traveled extensively in Russia and needed to keep in touch with what was happening in Japan, China, and Russia in the throes of revolution. Crane inherited Reinsch's information network when he took over duties in Peking, 20 March 1920 to July 2, 1921.

Gaspard's tale of his time in China sounds fishy. At the end of March 1921, he and his wife sailed for Japan and Shanghai from the U.S.[22] They then traveled north to Peking and stayed with the Cranes. This part of Gaspard's story makes sense. Being on the governing board of the Chicago Art Institute, Crane knew the Gaspards from at least the time the institute hosted Gaspard's exhibition of New Mexican scenes and portraits in 1920. Taos art was all the rage in the Windy City. Some of the earliest Taos artists were Chicago transplants. Because Gaspard and his U.S.-born ballerina wife, Evelyn Adell, were Russian citizens (they took their two-year honeymoon on horseback through Siberia in 1909), the Cranes and Gaspards shared immediate links.

Gaspard said that after spending a month in Shanghai, they met the Cranes in Peking. Evelyn stayed with the Cranes while he embarked on a nearly two-and-half-year horseback tour of Mongolia, Siberia, Turkestan, and Tibet, riding back to China and thence by rail to Peking. Five months of painting followed in Peking before he returned to Taos. Sources differ about his trip. Some say Crane accompanied Gaspard on his trip.[23] Crane may have accompanied him on the train to Kalgan, where Barton's friend Frans Larson may have supplied Gaspard with a pony for his trip to Urga and points west. Gaspard related that he purchased his pony and traveling supplies in Kalgan.[24] However, it would have been impossible for Crane to travel any farther than Kalgan with Gaspard. Crane departed China in 1921, just months after the Gaspards arrived. A change in administration in Washington cost Crane his ministerial job.

Other sources claimed that instead of being accompanied by Crane, Gaspard was given a military escort from Kalgan to retrace in reverse the trail Barton had taken from Urga to Kalgan with the Orlov horses. This might have been true, if "military escort" meant one man. In interviews with Waters, Gaspard said he traveled alone northwest out of Kalgan heading for Urga until he met Stzanim Nagumba at Koko-nor at the edge of the Gobi Desert. The man was clearly dressed as a Chinese army general. Nagumba served as his protector against bandits the rest of the trip. Nagumba had served as a general under Barton's warlord boss, "Manchurian Tiger" Chang, or Chang Tso-lin. Nagumba told Gaspard that Chang's forces had been defeated and disbanded in a battle with the Japanese, so he was broke and jobless.[25]

This scenario also lacked credibility. Koko-nor lay in a different direction than the track to Urga, and was far from Kalgan. Just happening to run into a lone Chinese general at the edge of the Gobi in itself stretched credulity. Chang Tso-lin did suffer a defeat, but not in 1921. Later in 1922 he struggled with other Chinese warlords over control of Peking. He certainly had not suffered defeat at the hands of the Japanese (yet), as they supported him. Even more telling, ship manifests show the Gaspards returning to the United States on September 11, 1921. They had been in China less than six months, not three years as claimed. Their short stay paralleled Crane's short tenure.

Confusing matters more, Gaspard spent the next several years in Taos painting from the sketches he made on his trip and backdating them. As an example, *Manchurian Forest*, painted in Taos (c. 1924), was backdated to 1921. *American Art News* in December of 1922 announced that Gaspard, now in Taos, planned a big exhibit based on his trip to China, Mongolia, the Siberian border, and mostly Peking for the following March. He would have returned from China earlier but because of fighting, some of his paintings disappeared in transit between Peking and Mukden. The April 1926 issue of *El Palacio* reported that Gaspard had returned to Taos in 1921 or 1922, and that the paintings had been lost due to the Russian Revolution and World War I. But now, after four or five years, the paintings of Mongolian subjects had arrived in New York after traveling halfway around the world. Gasp! Had they?

Gaspard dropped names of important people he met when circling Central Asia. On his way to Urga, he met Roy Chapman Andrews' expedition. Chapman was embarking on a bone hunting expedition into Mongolia in 1922, but Gaspard appeared to have already shipped out. Likewise, Gaspard said he arrived in Urga, where Polish adventurer and writer Ossendowski introduced him to "Mad Baron" von Ungern-Sternberg. Ungern-

Sternberg controlled Urga at the time and was arranging for the Urga's Living Buddha to become emperor of Mongolia. The Ossendowski/ Sternberg dates nearly match those of Gaspard's.

Gaspard's claiming he met Swedish explorer Sven Hedin in Tibet seemed completely off base. Gaspard said he was on his way back to China from the Tibetan border when he met Hedin on horseback disguised as a Tibetan. Hedin, however, had wanted to organize an expedition to Tibet in 1923, but hostilities in southwest China and Tibet between Tibetans and Chinese Muslims forced him to cancel. Instead, he rode from Peking to Urga and into Siberia with "Duke of Mongolia" Frans Larson in Larson's Dodge, and then by rail on the Trans-Siberian Railway to Moscow. It was highly unlikely that Larson's Dodge suddenly, Pegasus-like, converted itself into a horse and flew across two deserts to materialize half a continent from where it actually was just to support Gaspard's story.

Despite all of Gaspard's apparent dissembling, he did spend time in Central Asia and enjoyed the patronage of powerful people such as Crane and Crane's friends the Rosenwalds of Chicago. Julius Rosenwald, president of Sears, Roebuck & Company, supported Jewish causes and supported Jewish migrant artists, of which Gaspard was one. Gaspard and Marc Chagall came from the same Russian town and purportedly were fellow art students. The Rosenwalds and others were concerned about pogroms in Russia and the plight of Jews who fled to Asia.

Crane, on the other hand, due to family connections, was most eager for information about the plight of the Czechoslovakian Legion stranded in Siberia after the war. The legion of mostly Czech and some Slovak volunteers wanted independence from the Austro-Hungarian Empire. To achieve this, they fought on the Eastern Front with Russian troops. However, when the Bolsheviks gained control of most of Russia, the legion, which had supported the White Russian cause, found itself trapped. The Bolsheviks had no interest in fighting on the Eastern Front. That was the Czar's war, and the Czar was dead. An evacuation plan was negotiated to transit the more than 60,000 Czechs and Slovaks by Trans-Siberian Railway to Vladivostok. Ships would take them back to Europe to rejoin the fight on the Western Front. Instead, the evacuation bogged down as World War I ended. Strung out across the rail line in Siberia, the legion fought the Reds to survive in very uncertain circumstances. This forced Japanese, U.S., British, French, Italian, and French Colonial troops to intervene in a very messy international situation. Everyone needed information, and not just of the military type. Humanitarian and commercial information gathering rose in importance.

Another of Gaspard's powerful patrons was George D. Pratt. Gaspard made a start in the art world when Pratt, a director of Standard Oil, offered him help. Standard Oil had vested interest in, or near monopoly of, the kerosene business in China. As a trustee of the American Museum of Natural History, Pratt also approved the museum's funding of Chapman's Mongolian expeditions. A big-game hunter and traveler, Pratt traveled to the Orient and donated to various institutions mounted trophy heads and souvenirs of his trips. He had some idea of the situation in China.

Even Gaspard's paintings leave unanswered questions. Many do reflect places he said he visited. Some also depict some pretty big places he failed to mention to Waters. Several of his more important paintings capture Manchurian, Siberian or Russian scenes dated around 1921. More questions are raised about where he really was, for how long, and for what purposes. In the spy-vs.-spy world of intrigue that was China, a gregarious, multilingual traveling painter offered something quite apart from sailors with cameras, hunters, baseball catchers, cigarette sellers, mapmaking bone hunters, and even a Montana cowboy with his soldier drovers.

One of the duties of U.S. military officers in China was to gather information. To aid this and to aid communications with the Chinese, officers of the Fifteenth took five hours of language training each week, which gave them a certain advantage over other foreign military units in Tientsin. Since members of the Fifteenth fancied themselves as adventurers, and leaves or travel passes were generally granted, they traveled all over North China, sometimes with camera in hand. Marines and infantry loved hunting and collecting trophy heads.

These favorite pastimes offered exciting travel and served as cover for information gathering. Soldiers could jump a train from Tientsin or Peking to the interior mountainous regions. Within days they could be on leave shooting elk, bear, tiger, pheasants, rams, wild pigs. Although Christian missionaries in China are generally stereotyped as peace-loving stewards of God rather than gun-toting hunters, the Belgian Scheut missionaries, like "Duke of Mongolia" Frans Larson, were exceptions. After the Boxer Rebellion, they did not mind arming themselves, some with Winchesters.[26] Above all, they loved to hunt and offer hospitality and local knowledge of game in Inner Mongolia to visiting hunters. The Missions of de Scheut went so far as to publish their own hunting picture postcards. As long as the fathers did not offend Buddhist sensibilities by blasting vultures that cleaned up human corpses, the black robes' hunting practices were accepted. Nearby in northern Shansi Province, one hunting cabin was jokingly referred to as "the American Legation."[27] If soldiers could be sent into the Chinese hinterland, what could be better than sending a group of "cowboys" into Siberia, Manchuria, Mongolia, and a fairly remote part of China?

The United States was playing catch-up in gathering intelligence about China and Mongolia. For much of the nineteenth century and early twentieth century, Victorian England and czarist Russia played the Great Game to determine which empire would control central Asia. The English sent agents into the central Asia interior from India, the economic jewel they were trying to protect. Russia sent information-gatherers in from the north through Mongolia in the form of scientific expeditions—geologists, botanists, cartographers. Agents and expeditions on both sides sometimes did not return. The two empires pitted themselves against each other under the guise of merchants or scientific expeditions long before U.S. adventurers like dinosaur-hunter and spy Roy Chapman Andrews or horse raiser Barton.

Missionaries offered another possible source of U.S. information-gathering. At the time Barton was establishing the Shansi ranch, American missionaries in China totaled about 5,000 if missionary wives were also counted.[28] Missionaries faced a peculiar information problem. Their stay in China depended on fund-raising back home. There were never enough donations to meet physical needs in China, let alone spiritual needs. Hence, despite harsh conditions, messages and images from the missionaries needed to be positive so that church members back home did not become discouraged and cease giving. Postcards sent by missionaries back to the U.S. pictured "good works" or "good sights"—

usually views of missionary schools, hospitals, chapels, pagodas or other buildings representing Chinese institutions not threatening to Christianity or Chinese leaders believed to be Christian[29]—not photos of beheadings, poverty, troops, floods, summary justice, and disease like those experienced by U.S. troops stationed in China.

With the rise of Chinese nationalism, churches increasingly worried about negative publicity that could undermine missions in China. For example, Frank Gamewell played his own Great Game. The Methodist Board's Associate Secretary for the Far East in the 1920s began censoring or editing letters sent by missionaries in China. Even President Bowen of Nanking University had his mail held up because of his outspokenness.[30] Missionaries simply did not enjoy the freedom to provide accurate accounts that could aid intelligence gathering.

Barton certainly fit into the Reinsch era, explaining the availability of army transport ships for his horses, his draft deferral, his secretiveness, and his friendship with the colonel of the Fifteenth. Barton had an enviable pipeline into the highest ranks of the Chinese army, was on good terms with a provincial governor, knew conditions in revolutionary Russia/Siberia, and had contacts in Mongolia and Manchuria. Nearly everyone Barton knew in China served in intelligence in one way or another. BAT agents collected intelligence, commercial travelers spied, journalists spied, ex-missionary Frans Larson spied. Given the paucity of Americans in North China, it would be hard to find any who were not collecting information for naval intelligence, the War Department, or Reinsch.

That Barton's name was put before the highest circles in Washington survives in a tantalizing paper trail. Part of the mystery surrounding how an army transport could be used for civilian purposes is explained by State Department and War Department letters. In 1920 the charge d'affaires of the Chinese Legation in Washington, D.C., requested Secretary of State Bainbridge Colby to aid in the shipment of horses Barton was collecting throughout the West. The State Department had to forward the request to the War Department since a military ship was involved. The State Department's Alvey A. Adee wrote a letter to secretary of war Newton D. Baker, dated May 3, 1920:

> I have the honor to enclose herewith a copy of a note from the Chinese d'Affaires ad interim at Washington stating that the Governor of the Province of Shansi,
>
> China, having in view the development of the natural resources of the Province, is desirous of obtaining horses for the Livestock Bureau which he has recently established. This Department has been informed by Mr. Fred Barton, Manager of the Live Stock Bureau, who is now in the United States for the purpose of purchasing about two hundred and fifty horses for the Bureau, that they are to be used solely for breeding purposes.
>
> In view of the statement made by the Chinese Charge d'Affaires that it has been found that there are no ships on the Pacific equipped to carry live stock except the United States Transport DIX, I have the honor to inquire whether the War Department finds it practical to allot space on that transport for the shipping of the horses to China, the expense of which, the Charge d'Affaires states, will be borne by the Chinese Government.

Secretary of War Baker signed off on the request on May 7, 1920. His letter was then passed on to the Chinese through the State Department.

The letter indicates that Barton had already made contact with Reinsch's superiors in the State Department and that the diplomatic niceties had already been worked out. For example, the letter spells out that the horses were to be used for breeding purposes only. Why? What other purposes were there? War materiel, for one. Saying that the horses would be used only for breeding is like some counties saying they need nuclear breeder reactors just to light their homes. But it was important that the United States remain neutral and not be perceived by the Japanese and other powers as intervening militarily. The same went for the other warlords in China. If it were known that Yen Hsi-shan and Barton were raising military horses for Chang Tso-lin to be used against the other warlords—and using a U.S. military ship to aid in the process—trouble could only follow. Barton and the Chinese knew enough to go to the State Department first rather than the War Department.

Representing the State Department, Reinsch not only handled the bureaucratic paperwork with the Chinese, but he also coordinated with the military in China under State Department, rather than War Department, control—an unusual situation to say the least. Reinsch handled all the paperwork for clearing the clandestine and not-so-clandestine Andrews' expeditions through China and into the Gobi. The usual movie and magazine image of the Andrews' expeditions to find bones and record wildlife has been one of a group of scientists all working on behalf of a museum. However, each expedition had among its staff a U.S. military representative, sometimes a surgeon, sometimes a mapmaker, sometimes a photographer.

The timing of the letter is curious, suggesting a "done deal." In two weeks or less after the Chinese received approval notification, Barton and his Montana cowboys were already hopping the rails to Reno to pick up the horses collected there from around the West and move them on to the West Coast to load the USAT *Dix*. Obviously Barton did not scour the many states of the West for the small Morgan stallions he desired and

Inner Mongolia postcard photograph of an unidentified American hunter with Belgian missionary R.P. De Wilde and trophy argali sheep, the world's largest mountain sheep. U.S. intelligence was gathered during such trips.

arrange for pasturage, corrals, and transportation while recruiting all his hands in just a few weeks. Much had been done beforehand. The timing of the War Department's having the *Dix* almost immediately available, in the right place at the right time, with that much hold space seems very fortuitous.

The War Department and the Fifteenth Infantry had to keep their eyes on one of its Chinese nemeses, Chang Tso-lin, whose troops at times threatened Tientsin and the corridor to Peking. Because Chang Tso-lin, through his chief of staff, brought Barton to China in the first place, Barton was a good person for the Fifteenth to know. After all, he alone would supply Chang with horses. Barton could move freely without drawing attention. If he were not recruited outright as a spy, it is hard to believe he would not at least have been told to keep his ears and eyes open. Likewise, the furloughed soldiers seemed to have kept their mission under wraps. In a unit of great storytellers, so far no written or oral history of their "cowboy" trip has surfaced as told by the riders themselves.

Since Barton did not name the colonel who furloughed men to tend to the Orlovs, duty rosters might shed some light. In 1914 the colonel for the Fifteenth was J.C.F. Tillson. The next extant roster in 1928 shows Col. I. Newell in command. Lt. Colonel Albert Brevard Sloan served as interim commander in 1921. But in 1917 the Fifteenth was still just moving into new quarters, and everything was still in flux. Over time, Barton probably knew these men. Col. William M. Morrow departed in the summer of 1921, so he could very well have been in command when Barton borrowed his riders. A rigid control officer, Morrow was considered a martinet by his men, who would have been glad to grab a four-month furlough. Whichever officer was in command, Barton asked if he had any men from Western states with cowboying experience and got them. In spring, eight ex-cowboys from Texas, Nevada, Utah, and Wyoming were furloughed to go with Barton.[31] They wanted adventure. They got it—the world's longest horse drive, or, more precisely, they "trailed" the horses the longest distance.

• Seven •

Khabarovsk, Siberia, to Hilar, Manchuria, 1917

I had no place to hide from thunder, so,
I am not afraid of it anymore.
—Genghis Khan

Much of the route crossed vast stretches in Mongolia where local knowledge of water sources was a must. Therefore, Mongol guides joined Barton and his furloughed cowboys. Mongol guides could navigate when both land and sky were featureless. Like camels, they seemed able to find the trail by smell when no one could see from the dust storms. They could placate evil spirits at the *obos*, religious rocks and shrines, by tearing shreds from their clothing or hair from their horses to hang from the obo. They could scout ahead to route the herd around areas where prints of unshod horses signaled dangerous marauders. They could see camel caravans on the horizon and know instantly if they were Chinese or Mongol. They could collect the dried dung that was the only source of fuel for fires.

Barton planned a route that would avoid all towns to deflect interference of any kind and the possibility of disease. Not only would the circuitous route be long because of geography, it would also be a big drive. In Khabarovsk, 3,500 Orlov mares had been assembled and awaited them. The herd began to move in spring of 1917. If Barton had waited a few months more, the venture would likely have failed. Because of the timing, the U.S. was keen on finding out what was occurring in Siberia, Manchuria, and Mongolia.

Russia fell into turmoil. The Russian Revolution in February 1917 had deposed the czar and installed the provisional government. Barton's horse drive was sandwiched in those few months between that event and the Russian 1917 October Revolution that brought the Bolsheviks to power and set off civil war between the Reds and the Whites across the land. The next year the area around Kharbarovsk and along the Trans-Siberian Railway and its spurs became the scene of untold atrocities committed by Reds, Whites, Japanese, bandits and others.

The American Expeditionary Force Siberia (AEF) would find itself caught in the middle. It was tasked with securing the railroad lines. The AEF prevented tons of war supplies that had piled up at the ports from falling into Japanese hands. The U.S. earlier sent these shipments to its World War I ally Russia, but they had been abandoned during the Russian Revolution. Doing anything in Siberia at this uncertain time proved risky business. Fortunately for Barton, the Bolsheviks' drive to control all of Russia took time to work its way to the Far East, but when the Reds did reach it, bloody consequences ensued, particularly for Mongolia and Manchuria. Anarchy unleashed horror. In the great famine that followed, Mother Russia ate most of her horses. The Orlovs were lucky. For this horse drive, cowboy-soldiers served better than plain cowboys.

Much is still not known about the coordination that went into trailing the herd through so many provinces and countries. Chang Tso-Lin and his right-hand man, Chang T'sung-chang, certainly helped smooth the way through Manchuria and probably Siberia. Born in Vladivostok, Chang T'sung-chang spent much of his time there and spoke Russian fluently. Barton, accompanied by his wife, Mabel, in the fall of 1916, took a business trip to Vladivostok, where most likely he met with Chang.

Just months later the Orlovs were on the move, complete with Mongol guides as well as the soldiers. Just as Frans Larson had arranged Mongol guides for scientific and mapping expeditions in Mongolia, he probably devoted the best guides to Barton. Finding enough water for a herd of that magnitude was critical, particularly if the trip was to be kept as secret as possible and the herd was to be moved off the beaten paths. It's one thing to cross the Gobi with a caravan of a hundred camels that can go long stretches without drinking. It's quite another to water more than three thousand horses out of wells that are no more than small holes in the ground. Crossing that much of Mongolia with that many animals also may have required the blessings of local Mongol princes and the Living Buddha, which could have been arranged through Larson.

Never had there been a drive of this magnitude, not even in the U.S. West. When Texas cattlemen first trailed herds the long distance from Texas to Montana, horses were brought along to supply their cowboys, usually at the rate of a dozen or so horses per drover. As a consequence, the smaller horse herds hardly compared to the size of cattle herds. No real thought was given to breeding horses at the end of the line; they were just there to use to move cattle herds north, and then they were cut loose at the end of the line.

The drive took four months to reach the ranch. The herd passed through the range of the Siberian tiger into desert strewn with camel bones. It first moved from Khabarovsk through the rugged terrain of southern Siberia via Hilar (also spelled Hailar, Chailar and Khaylar). While the Chinese Eastern Railway and the Trans-Siberian Railway and its spurs connected Kharbarovsk, Vladivostok, Harbin and Hilar, using railroads in time of war was out. Russians needed the railroad system through Siberia and Manchuria to ship war supplies to the fierce World War I battles raging on the Eastern Front. Meanwhile, Germans planned to sabotage rail lines near Hilar by blowing a tunnel. Major von Pappenheim, German military attaché to China, along with nine Germans, three Chinese, twenty camels, five horses, and two dogs, departed from Peking as if on a hunting trip. Disguising themselves as Russian soldiers, they tried to win Mongols over to their side. The Mongols instead robbed them and denounced Pappenheim, curtailing the saboteurs.[1]

How Barton was able to purchase that many Orlovs when Russians suffered so many horse casualties at the European front bespoke of good contacts and serious warlord money. Barton described the Orlov drive as having four segments. The first proceeded from Kharbarovsk to Hilar. The second skirted the northern edges of the Gobi Desert and the mountains of Siberia to Urga. The true crossing of the desert occurred on the leg from Urga to Kalgan. The homeward-bound last leg plunged south from Kalgan to Taiyuanfu. Because of the vast distances traversed from east to west and north to south, each leg differed from every other in terms of its character and challenges. Regardless of the segment, to protect this valuable investment, Barton kept the herd away from towns and established paths as much as possible. Despite this furtive routing, it is still easy to map much of the drive. Water and geography dictated it.

To ensure adequate grazing, water, and weather, the trip from Khabarovsk meant leaving in the spring. If the herd left too early, rivers and water holes could still be frozen in March in this area to the south of the Siberian permafrost zone. Departing too close to ice-out risked losing horses to flood. Waiting too long meant facing the unbearable mosquitoes plaguing the river and marshlands southwest of Khabarovsk. Moving horses across the Amur from Khabarovsk was made easier by the timely construction of the first permanent bridge across the river in 1916, the year prior to the horse drive. Before the Trans-Siberian Railway bridge, crossings had to be made by ferry boat in summer, or by laying down tracks on thick river ice in winter.

Three possible routes existed from Khabarovsk to Hilar. Two involved traveling even more northward, following the Amur River valley for some 800 miles in order to cross mountain defiles to reach the grasslands of Manchuria. Such an option would have required slogging hundreds of miles through thick taiga forest along the Amur. In the American West, even moving small herds of cattle, horses or sheep through small sections of thick forest from winter to summer ranges results in royal pain. The Amur was no way to go.

Instead, most Russians took another path when entering Manchuria from Khabarovsk. The Sunggari River (or Songhua), a tributary of the Amur, flowed into the Amur near Khabarovsk. It was this river that allowed the Russians to enter Manchuria and found such cities as Harbin. The Sunggari flowed through flat plains and skirted some of the worst impediments on this segment, the Lesser Khingan Mountains. Often snow-capped, the Khingan range drove north-south spines through Manchuria. Following the river across the Great Manchurian Plains not only solved water problems, but also prevented getting lost and slowed by heavy timber. It also meant there was space enough to bypass population centers like Harbin. The trade-off was contending with marshland and crossing many tributaries coming out of the mountains along the way. Once the Sunggari rounded the nose of the Lesser Khingans, the herd could follow the oxbows and meanderings of its tributary, the Nen (Nonni) River northwest to Quiqihar and Tsi-Tsi-har.

But first the herd must negotiate passing around the metropolis of Harbin, "the Paris of the East," also called the "city of music." Harbin was an anomaly. Dropped down into North China, this Russian creation of 70,000 souls resembled no frontier town. As Julie M. Fenster pointed out in *Race of the Century*, "In the American west, the charm of frontier towns was that they were in a rush to prosper, but often didn't appear prosperous. Russia, on the contrary, wanted Harbin to look like a great city before it was one."[2] This was no Miles City, Montana, although it too was a young railroad and river town, with a riverfront of crowded steamboats rivaling those in Mark Twain's days.

Russian and Japanese department stores competed in this garden city. Wide boulevards, manicured lawns, statuary, baroque and art nouveau edifices, cupolaed and spired mansions, and cobblestone streets graced central Harbin. But for a few rickshaws in the streets, it was hard to comprehend that this was China. Although neapolitan, the city sat amidst the frontier. Its cuisine reflected this dichotomy. Jamie Bisher in *White Terror: Cossack Warlords of the Trans-Siberian* described French haute-cuisine existing side by side with servings of bear paws, deer nostrils, and Siberian tiger testicles.[3] Not exactly Montana prairie oysters, but close.

A growing Jewish presence spurred Harbin's expansion. The Russian government encouraged Jews to colonize Harbin. According to David Wolff in *To the Harbin Station: The Liberal Alternative in Russian Manchuria, 1890–1914*, Russia wanted to develop the area with merchants and people the government thought were strong enough to stick it out—Georgians, Latvians, Ukrainians, Poles, and Jews. Previous Russian expansionism depended on sending in the Cossacks and military rather than commercial interests.

In the decade before Barton arrived on the trail, Russia seriously discussed the Jewish territorial, or homeland, issue. Other than Palestine or Zion, other lands discussed for a Jewish homeland included Uganda, Morocco, and Canada. Harbin was chosen as a great Russian experiment, a place where Jews could live, work, and practice their religion free of ramped-up Russian pogroms. This served partially to solve the Jewish "problem" in Russia. Encouraging Jewish settlement also countered the even more pressing problem of Chinese colonizers, seen as the "Yellow Peril" in their own country. The flood of Japanese colonizers into Manchuria and a similar threat by Japanese business concerns were further eroding Russian influence in the Far East after Russia's humiliating defeat in the 1904–1905 war with Japan.[4] Russia, China, and Japan would continue to struggle for control of Manchuria through much of the twentieth century.

Though Harbin was Russian in character and overseen by officers of the Russian-controlled Chinese Eastern Railway, Barton's client, General Chang Tso-lin, controlled Manchuria. As Chang played all the sides of the fence in order to consolidate his power and build his army, all parties interested in Manchuria sought to either help or placate him. Given his sponsor and previous Russian connections, Barton probably faced no problems in traveling around Harbin.

The irony was that Chang began his career as a *hunghutze*, a bandit or highwayman, from the Kirin Mountains separating Manchuria from Korea and the Russian Far East. Many hunghutze hung around the approaches to Harbin waiting to divest travelers of their valuables. Since Chang had once been their leader, Barton made it through. The Chinese did not have to send a messenger to keep the bandits at bay. They simply rounded up as many as they could and cut off their heads. Anyone like Barton, who rode into Harbin from the countryside to present papers, saw heads on poles lining the roads into town—a stark contrast to the cultured city of churches, synagogue, ballet, opera, and posh dressers at the sulky-track races. Message received.

Thirteen-year-old Yafracina Ashia Paschenko was living in Harbin at the time Barton passed by. She and her stepsister Elizabeth, who was about the same age, were born in Harbin. Jews transplanted to Harbin were considered stateless. Thus, when needing to record her nationality to obtain travel visas or fill out ship manifests, Ashia would sometimes leave blank the space that asked about her nationality, but she would indicate

Seven • Khabarovsk, Siberia, to Hilar, Manchuria, 1917

Covering a good portion of Asia, as the arrows show, this is the approximate route of Barton's 3500 Orlov horses accompanied by Mongolian guides and herded by Barton and eight cowboys furloughed from the U.S. 15th Infantry.

she was Russian when asked about her race or people. Elizabeth would generally say she was of Russian nationality but Hebrew when asked about race or people. They were part of the great experiment. Little did Barton know that Ashia would later become his wife and they would remain friends for life.

In his cowboy hat, Barton would have cut quite a figure in Harbin. Cowboys were well known in the Far East as movie stars, and Harbin loved its cinemas. The Hotel Oriant, the Grand Hotel, across from the railway station, and the famous Jewish-owned Hotel Moderne on Harbin's main street contained cinemas that also hosted theatrical performances, ballets, and concerts. The showpiece Hotel Moderne, a touch of Paris with its restaurant, bar, billiard room, barber shop, and cinema, had only recently opened.[5] Watching silent Westerns starring early cowboy stars like Tom Mix differed in Harbin from the U.S. cinematic experience. Piano players in movie houses stateside made Western shorts and multi-reelers more suspenseful, but the Hotel Moderne featured an entire philharmonic orchestra accompanying the films. Theatergoers could have seen the real thing if they had ventured outside the city to see Barton's cowboys.

Early Hollywood began receiving fan mail from Harbin for such stars as Monte Blue. Born Gerard Montgomery Bluefeather, Monte was of mixed blood, including French and Cherokee or Osage. Had he not been in Hollywood working for D.W. Griffith, he could easily have been a good choice for Barton's trail drive or Shansi ranch. Nearly the same age as Barton, Blue had worked as a cowpuncher, ranch hand, circus rider, and Hollywood stuntman (as in the 1915 *The Birth of a Nation*) before becoming a B-Western star and more. It would not be long before Barton had his own Hollywood connections.

Much of the land that opened up after one passed Harbin was flat and had some grass, but it was hard like desert pan, which made for easy going. Although the Greater Khingan Mountains still blocked the way to Hilar, located below their western slopes, an old post road crawled through a pass over the mountains; also, the Chinese Eastern Railway had punched its way through timber and mountain meadows in the same area. If all else failed in conquering the mountains, railroads offered the solution as a way through, as long as tracks were cleared before a train chugged up or down the pass. Participants in the Peking to Paris race of 1907 and the subsequent New York to Paris Auto Race of 1908 had to resort to using the tracks to reach Mongolia.

Passing through deciduous and pine woods could not be avoided in crossing the Khingans. At night the herd became vulnerable to stampede and predation by Barton's old Montana nemeses, the wolf and bear. In Montana, bears sat atop the food chain, but in the Khingans they did not. Twiggy tree nests that bears slept in for safety and the scarcity of timberwolves signaled the presence of Siberian tigers. An occasional tiger would drift out on the steppes, but the woods harbored the worst danger. Mountain lions caused some problems in Montana. They averaged a bit over 100 pounds in weight, but that barely measured up against the tigers. This top predator could weigh a formidable quarter of a ton or more and could take down anything on two or four legs. The royal Bengal tiger of southern Asia was said to be the real man killer, whereas the Siberian, or Amur, tiger has had a reputation of rarely taking a human. However, Chinese Eastern Railway construction was stopped at times because of severe tiger predation on Chinese workers. This wasn't Montana. A cowpoke could lose his scalp here and have it eaten along with everything else. There were better ways to keep saddle leather supple than having a tiger chewing on it.

Fortunately, no horses were lost on this longest drive. Once the herd was safely through the Khingan Range, Barton dropped down into grasslands and headed for Hilar near the Mongolian border. Hilar was also the major railroad stop before the Chinese Eastern made its way north to Chita, Siberia, and eventual connection with the Trans-Siberian Railway connecting the Russian Far East and the Pacific to Moscow. More Mongolian yurts began to appear as the country transitioned from forest to treeless expanses, and from China and Russia to Mongolia.

As Barton described it, he kept the herd away from centers of population. Hilar was one such place. His horse-raising friend Larson had helped C.W. Campbell, British consul in China, mount an expedition from Kalgan to Hilar in 1902, which Campbell described in *Travels in Mongolia, 1902*. They planned to stop in Hilar, but upon seeing the hordes of Mongols streaming westward fleeing the city and other area villages, they bypassed it to avoid the cholera outbreak. Such outbreaks bedeviled many towns and outposts sooner or later. Barton wanted to take no chances with the diseases, particularly considering Hilar's past.

A reasonable question to ask is why Barton did not retrace the route Larson had taken in 1902 from Hilar southward to Kalgan. Why did he take the herd west to Urga in the middle of Mongolia and then have to travel all the way back east through the Gobi Desert? Why not just drive southward and avoid the Gobi altogether? That cutoff would result in saving hundreds of miles. A trade route did exist between Kalgan and Hilar. The southern route involved traversing the flanks of the Khingans. The mountains spawned many streams on their east side but few of any permanence on the drier west side where sand hills appeared. Barton needed permanent sources of water. The one river that could be depended on was the Kerulen that ran west to east across eastern Mongolia. It popped out of the Kentai Mountains not too far from Urga, providing a narrow band of vegetation on the northern fringes of the Gobi. The Kerulen enabled Genghis Khan in the thirteenth century to move out of Mongolia to conquer Manchuria and ultimately create the vast Mongol Empire.

• Eight •

Hilar, Manchuria, to Urga, Mongolia, 1917

Chinese Emperors avoided open war with the Living Buddha, because it might arouse protests of the Chinese Buddhists. At one time they sent to the Bogdo Khan a skillful doctor-poisoner.... Very soon the Chinese died from some unknown cause.[1]
—Ferdinand Ossendowski

Barton's herd shadowed the old caravan route that followed the Kerulen upstream. Barton intersected the river at Kulun Nor (Kulun Lake) where the Kerulen flowed into this giant freshwater lake on lush grasslands to the west of Hilar. The lake stretched over sixteen miles across, farther than the eye could see, preparing the herders for the Big Sky that was to come. The Kerulen's irregular meadows varied from nearly nothing at all to swaths more than four miles wide separated by brown marsh. The river flowed through arid steppes of low alkaline hills with sandstone and other rock outcroppings, somewhat like eastern Montana. Except for some dwarf willows along the river, no trees covered any slopes. After several days of traveling, the herd maneuvered around some sandstone hills which confined and speeded up the river's current at Mergen Ul. Whipped by strong winds, clouds of red dust made the closeness of the Gobi known.

Continents stretched before them. To the north, just out of sight, ran the endless Siberian taiga stopped only by polar ice; ahead and around them lay the vastness of the largest temperate grasslands in the world. The scientist who came up with the term temperate ought to have been shot. The high Eastern Steppe of Mongolia was a colder, shadeless Serengeti. It bordered on Martian sands and pebbles, a half-million square miles of Gobi desert. If not for the curvature of the earth and a few mountains, the men could have seen Europe, and nary a fence. They traveled days without seeing anything human. This was true, staggering freedom. Grass rippled like the waves of antelope or gazelles.

Barton pushed on to the principal trading post on the Kerulen, Sam Beise Urgo. Caravan routes from Urga, Hilar, and the Siberian and Chinese frontiers passed through this outpost with its two large monasteries. Silks, cattle, ponies, hides, and wool were traded here. Even with the blessing of the Living Buddha in Urga, Barton needed to stop to pay his respects to the local ruler out of necessity and courtesy. He could keep the herd off the well-traveled routes as much as possible, but hiding a dust cloud of 3500 large horses on a plain was impossible. Passing caravans exchanged information, creating a "desert telegraph" across Mongolia.

At least Barton did not have to worry overly much about rustlers on his way to Urga. In Mongolia, stealing a horse meant death. Besides that, there was no need to steal. Horses could be easily borrowed and returned. Being without a horse in the Gobi and the open steppes was a death warrant in itself. Thus, the open horse ranges of the nomadic Mongols owed their very existence to the prohibition against horse stealing. Cattle rustling was a different matter, a source of clever notoriety rather than one's demise.

Regardless of the diminished threat of rustlers, Barton's riders kept close herd on the Orlovs trailing through unfamiliar country. Like Montana, the steppes contained half-breeds and others who did not subscribe to the Mongol code. As to the code of the West, had there been rustlers and they had been caught no tree limbs existed over which to stretch a rope.

Paying respects to the local prince or chieftain of a Mongol banner, a political division in Mongolia, was generally straightforward and ceremonial. Like all yurts, or ghers, that of the ruler and dispenser of justice faced south, so a rider needed to approach the yurt from the south to show peaceful intent. Weapons would be left outside above the door flap. The ruler sat inside facing the southern doorway, which was draped with prayer ribbons. Felt mats covered the floor. Guests were invited to sit on woolen rugs on the appropriate side of the tent, which wasn't much bigger than the normal Mongolian family yurt. Snuff or tobacco would be exchanged as a sign of greeting and friendship. This would be followed by the ritualistic asking about the weather, the animals, family health, and how the trip was going—in short, not much different from Iowa farmers' beginning discussions at a local coffee shop, only here mare's milk and cheese were served.

As many as ten other officials, messengers, and scribes sat to the other side of the prince. A copper prayer wheel that he could spin rested at his side. In the center of the tent, a brazier threw off heat and light from burning argol or dry camel dung. At home with people, swallows darted in and out of the entrance to their nest on a board hung inside near the opening. They kept the flies in check. After the scribes examined Barton's papers, he was off. As with most abodes, the blue prayer cloths strained in the wind outside the entrance. Their prayers flew continuously on the winds to build up merit for its owner. They kept the lies in check.

While drinking kumiss with local officials went smoothly, care had to be taken to avoid merchants along the way, or at least to avoid drinking with them. On the northern route around the Gobi, these scattered buyers and sellers had a penchant for offering guests tarantula wine. This wine differed from the tarantula wine that now is served in Cambodia to give tourists the feeling of going "local" and doing something daring. In Southeast Asia the wine usually consists of spiders fermented or pickled in rice wine. In Barton's time, spiders were maddened with hot iron rods to up their poison level. After they had been soaked in alcohol, they were reduced in boiling water with a secret recipe of berries and herbs. A few drops of that brew added to a drink and the imbiber experienced faintness, loss of speech, movement, and memory. The guest was then robbed and dumped far out in the desert. He had no recollection of what had happened. With his watchful armed men, Barton could avoid that.

Cowboys knew about tarantula alcohol. They had a long tradition of passing the story of the U.S. equivalent, Judge Roy Bean's version of the drink, from one campfire to the next. The Texas justice of the peace, self-styled as "The Law West of the Pecos," listened to a stranger who showed up in his saloon. Not knowing who the scoundrel judge was, the man belittled the strength of Bean's drinks and began shooting up the place. As the legend went, Bean walked outside, turned over some rocks, and whacked a poisonous tarantula and a couple of vinegarroons (scorpions) residing underneath. He returned, floated the creatures in a glass of pure alcohol, and forced the stranger to drink it all down. So much for the gunslinger.

But having a drink out here by the Gobi was much different than leaning over the mahogany in Miles City. Montana hooch caused "a man to see northern lights at noon time, rainbows at night, and a total eclipse of the sun anytime."[2] It could make a jackrabbit spit in the eye of a rattlesnake. Kerulen River hooch made a man see nothing, but he prayed for total eclipse as he stood naked in the desert expanse. He could not even spit in a jackrabbit's eye, as he had no spit.

A few days later, after paying respects to the local prince, the herd passed the ruins of Para-hota, or Tiger Town, now nothing more than some ditches, large rubble and earthen grass-covered mounds where buildings had stood, heaps of stones, and a few ruined brick pyramids about thirty feet high. So much for the fourteenth century. No tigers here, and no town, just several hundred miles of toiling ahead to reach Urga.

The monotony of the track to Urga was interrupted by more interval stops to parlay with chieftains. Some held forth in yurts, others in wooden or brick structures not far from Buddhist monasteries with Tibetan features. Sometimes hills intervened. Mostly the drive moved through a featureless vastness. About two hundred miles out from the Tiger City ruins and after the Kerulen had drifted more to the southwest, the river took an abrupt turn and headed northward—the final leg to Urga.

It is not known how Barton planned to feed his crew along the drive. Had this been Montana, a chuckwagon would have accompanied the men on such a long journey. Something was needed, as they traversed long stretches with no towns and no habitations or possibility of resupply. Earlier expeditions and some caravans used camel carts as chuckwagon substitutes. Some employed Chinese carts pulled by bullocks. Whatever Barton used, he probably had to employ more than just his furloughed soldiers and Mongol guides to tend the food wagon in whatever form. Hunting antelope, waterbirds, and other wildlife could certainly supplement their grubstake, but they would need to supply at various points along the way. Barton had in mind Hilar, Urga, and Kalgan, but the drive also depended upon haggling along the way for sheep to eat, which others traveling across Mongolia also did.

As the drove of horses moved the final hundred miles northwest to Urga, the land began to change. The waters of the Kerulen flowed colder, clearer, faster—clearly a mountain river. Grass grew thicker, more hills appeared to break up the plains, mountains rimmed the north with the first visible trees since crossing the Kinghans weeks ago. Marmots and prairie dogs riddled the landscape with their rockpile diggings. This was no time for a horse to break a leg or throw a rider by stepping into a hole, but certainly it could be the place to do it. Horse and sheep herds appeared with more regularity.

Urga lay on the other side of a divide separating the Kerulen from the Tola, or Tuul, River, which flowed through the sacred city. For hundreds of miles, the Kerulen had served as the herd's lifeline. Now it had to be left behind. The herd pushed up the green hills, some of the hills with pine groves on their tops. When the other side of the divide was reached, there it was—Urga, seat of the Living Buddha, the only city in Mongolia, which made it completely out of place in a land of nomads.

Barton and his party could see it from fifteen miles out. There was cause for celebration. Urga marked the halfway point in their journey. They had made it that far without losing any stock. The Orlovs had already been on the trail longer than the first Texas herds trailed to Montana. Those herds had traveled nearly 1500 miles to reach Miles City; the Orlovs, though just halfway, had covered hundreds of miles more than that.

Urga sat in a bowl rimmed by mountains and directly at the base or in the shadow of Bogdo-ol, "God's Mountain." Heavily forested and standing thousands of feet above Urga, this was not only a sacred mountain but also the Living Buddha's game preserve patrolled by a few thousand lamas. The *hutukhtu*, or Living Buddha's main palace, sat right at the mountain's base. Its shining gilded cupolas could not be missed. His other three palaces (alternately green, red, and blue) and temples were scattered across the city, although it would be hard to call Urga a city. It was more like three separate cities (Chinese, Russian, Lamaist Buddhist) strung out along the river and separated by pastureland. Clearly it was a sacred pilgrimage city, the seat of Mongolian Buddhist power. This trading and caravan hub linked Mongolia with Russia to the north, China to the east, Tibet to the south, and distant middle Asian lands to the west.

The cultural collision made a train wreck of the architecture. This was no Harbin, or Paris of the East. Instead it looked mostly as if Tibet had somehow collided with the American frontier. Much of Urga was stockaded, similar to early forts in the American West. It was as if every stockade the West had ever known had been reborn and transported here. Given the close proximity of the mountains, logs and poles were easily obtained. Since the Mongols lived as nomadic herders, they did not build. Instead, their yurts were scattered throughout the city and around its perimeter, except for the sacred mountain.

Barton left the herd in the lush pastureland away from the city, but his ride into town was not without interest. Whereas the Chinese and Russians respected the dead and buried them, Mongolians showed no such respect. Once a person died, the corpse was considered vile, corrupted, and a dwelling place of evil spirits. The body was loaded into a cart and driven towards the hills. At some point the rocky, bumpy ground would shake the body out of the back of the cart. When the driver returned to Urga, he would not even know where the body was shaken out, for he did not look back. Some bodies were dumped into the river, others hung on trees.

Huge Mongolian dogs resembling black Tibetan mastiffs made fast work of the corpses. If they didn't, wolves would. Each Mongolian family kept one such dog and left it out each night to forage. The downside: corpse eaters had no fear of living humans either. Barton made sure he stayed on his horse when approaching any habitation. He would be ripped apart on foot. Shoppers in the city needed to carry a stick with a sharp nail at its end in daytime. Thus, the way into Urga was covered with human bones from corpses that ended up in the stomachs of dogs. In daytime, ravens, or "Mongolian coffins" as the Chinese called them, worked over whatever tidbits were left.[3]

The stark black birds and white skulls could not prepare Barton for what followed.

Not only was he met with colorful prayer ribbons and elaborately painted prayer wheels, but also the people themselves wore kaleidoscopic color. Urga was a living hat museum, with everything from what looked like wizard hats to helmets sprouting peacock plumes. Thousands of lamas garbed in crimson and flaming yellow paraded the streets and streamed among the blue-clad Chinese and embroidered Russians. Mongol horsemen wore plum-colored robes cinched at the waist with a colorful sash. Most wore hats that rode like saucers on their heads. The saucer appeared to be of black felt while a yellow or red pointed cone rose above it.

Most striking, married Mongolian women wore elaborate headdresses. Their long dark hair had been plaited and flattened over a huge wooden framework, resembling the downward curving horns of a mountain sheep ram. These women were not rams, but butting heads with all that metal, glass, and wood was not a good idea. An ornate saucer-shaped cap stood atop each woman's head and framework. It was ornamented with jewels or bits of glass. Jewelry hung from her ears, and her ornate robe reflected geometric puzzles. Both Mongol men and women wore huge leather boots, whose toes pointed up, making riding easy, walking nearly impossible. In winter, they stuffed the oversized boots with wool for warmth. In summer the tops of the boots served as storage for personal objects in lieu of pockets.

Barton entered the town to pay his respects to Larson's old friend, the Living Buddha, to resupply, and to pass muster with the other officials. He first passed through the Chinese quarter upon entering Urga from the east. The Chinese constructed their own temples and compounds behind the stockades. Next came the Russian quarter with its rows of typically ornate Russian-style cottages, white Orthodox church with its Byzantine gilded domes, and ugly red brick consulate building on a knoll. In back of the consulate, an eroded ravine held the bleached skulls and other bones of the many beggars who died in the frigid night winds that swept the market square of its refuse, dust, and them. The bodies of beggars too infirm to beg were collected each morning and dumped here after other beggars had scrounged their rags. This ravine bore a terrible ornamentation. It had the look of what was left by a bad Montana winter after cattle stacked up in a coulee.

Completing a nearly two-mile ride along the Russian houses, Barton reached the main square, where all the architecture collided in a pastiche of palisaded compounds, tents, Chinese shops, ornate houses, and yurts. At the eastern end of the main street, alive with colorful horsemen, stood the customs house and the ministry of foreign affairs. The customs office was surrounded by an enormous compound filled with camel caravans. In order for one to clear customs, business had to be conducted not in the wooden customs building but rather in the yurt at its side. Mongols didn't cotton to buildings. Because the wooden building was empty—just for show—metal filing cabinets and a telephone box arranged on the yurt's felt walls looked out of place to a Westerner.

Barton had little to worry about in passing through customs. One of Frans Larson's Mongol friends, Soliin Danzan, served as the customs agent for the Ministry of Finance, a ministry Danzan would soon run. Most of Urga's ministers were Larson friends. Danzan purportedly started his career as a horse thief. He must have been a good rustler during times of upheaval, as he had obviously ducked the death penalty. He later became a Mongolian revolutionary leader and war minister.[4] He traveled to Moscow to meet Lenin in 1921 but became a capitalist as the Mongolian agent for a British-American automobile company and Larson business associate.

While Barton was conducting business in Urga, it was good he could leave the Orlovs on pastures outside of town. The horses needed to rest and regain weight for the strenuous ordeal of crossing the Gobi. The herd was lucky not to be around the customs agent. Danzan owned the first motorcycle in Mongolia. He rattled and banged down the streets of Urga on his 1912/1913 Harley Davidson X8E, sending terrified camels and ponies running in all directions. Unlike the Living Buddha, who just parked his automobile, Danzan relished riding his miniature iron horse.

Not far from the customs house, Urga's horrible prison stood behind its palisades. This was another reason why there was no horse stealing in Mongolia, or more accurately, that there was little horse stealing. Apparently a lama had once stolen a horse. Mongol riders went after him. Although he was a lama, he was not heard from again. Frontier justice. Another time, two Russians stole and ended up in this prison. In its dungeons, prisoners were locked into four-by-two-and-a half-foot boxes. Each box contained a small slit where the jailer could slip food scraps into the prisoner, whenever the jailer felt like it. The torture seemed worse than medieval. Unable to move in the restrictive boxes, prisoners' limbs shriveled up and became useless, even if they were later released from life sentences. Boxes were not cleaned. Those incarcerated survived as long as possible in their own filth and in temperatures often well below zero. Women were not excluded.

The city's tent market and animal market contained everything a caravan or sojourner might need. Just beyond the market stood various blacksmith and leather shops. Pots and pans, custom bridles and other tack could be made within the hour—at very stout prices. Chinese merchants dominated the market and knew how to fleece customers. Only horses were cheap, the currency of the Mongolians. Buyers and sellers also haggled over sheep and camels. Herders from across Mongolia's treeless expanses came here, on the edge of the forests, to select their long birch "roping poles," which stood in bundles like cane-pole fishing rods in the marketplace.

Riding uphill through the lama city brought Barton to the Living Buddha's main palace at the base of the mountain. He passed through lines of whitewashed stupas, sitting like monstrous fat chess pieces waiting for black's next move. The air hummed with the tenseness of a chess match held in suspension. Time was running out for black's move, but black would move within the year. The pieces foreshadowed a ruthless Chinese chess player who would threaten to wipe the board clean, only to be checkmated by an even blacker Russian master.

Instead of an unpeeled log palisade, the palace grounds were surrounded by eight-foot tall white posts trimmed in red. The palace was also white, with gilded cupolas above the Tibetan-style roofs curled upwards at their ends like nodding lily blooms. Its side pavilions were roofed a rich blue-green. An elaborately painted, tiered gateway led to the complex. The palace dominated the landscape. It wasn't Lhasa, but it certainly proclaimed the Mongolian version of it.

Getting in posed a problem. Pilgrim multitudes circled the complex in sort of a Buddhist version of the circling the Kaabah at Mecca. They formed a living prayer wheel. A phalanx of red and yellow lamas led up to the main entrance. After long journeys, many pilgrims knelt and beat their heads upon the ground. Others piled up outside the fence of the red building that was the Living Buddha's private residence near the palace. A red rope was thrown over the fence from the building. Pilgrims approached the end of the rope on their knees, touching it as it jerked, believing the Living Buddha held onto the other end and was their telegraph to Heaven. Sometimes an electrified line was thrown over the fence just for kicks.

Inside, incongruous objects filled rooms and hallways. The palace seemed a museum celebrating the Victorian machine age. Rather than being lighted with argol fires, candles or kerosene lamps, the palace was electrified. Gramophones stood side by side with typewriters, microscopes, bicycles, automobiles, surgical instruments, pianos, clocks, and sewing machines, none of which were used. Whatever novelty the Living Buddha fancied, it was ordered and shipped. Likewise, whatever animals he desired for his zoo behind the palace were procured. Some of the animals, such as monkeys, snakes, and parrots, lived in the palace. Quite Victorian.

Treasures brought by pilgrims filled other rooms. Statues of the Buddha in every size and out of every precious material imaginable filled one room. Others contained tortoise-shell boxes, rubies, diamonds, chunks of jade, rare furs, jewel-encrusted elephant tusks, carved walrus tusks from the Bering Sea, perfumes, and other riches. Library rooms were stacked with books and manuscripts that lamas worked on transcribing.

The vast throne room was bathed in semidarkness. Before the throne, Mongol nobles sat at a low table, as did scribes. On the dais, the Living Buddha sat on a red throne framed in gold and cushioned in yellow. He was surrounded on either side with yellow screens framed in heavily ornamented black Chinese wood. Rather matching the screens, the aging man wore a Mongolian coat of yellow with black binding. Although his eyes were wide open, he was blind.

Some said alcohol had blinded him. Others said his bisexual escapades linked to venereal disease had done the deed. Usually such incapacitated Living Buddhas were secretly poisoned and removed. His veneration continued by virtue of his followers building a huge shrine on the west side of Lama City, in which resided one of the largest golden statues of the Buddha. Apparently this had propitiated the gods. He was revered because he was the Living Buddha. He was liked because he was generous, charitable, and helped anyone who came to him with problems. His charity extended to all living things, as evidenced by the animals living on the sacred mountain behind the palace. After three centuries of animals being protected and coddled there, the elephant, cheetahs and other exotics had lost any fear of man. The stewardship applied even to Urga's corpse-eaters. It was best to be out of Lama City by four in the afternoon. At that time lamas in a feeding cart passed through the streets. They ladled out kitchen scraps from a barrel to the mob of ravenous canine carnivores. They knew what the cart was. Best also to be in the cart, not near it.

Barton had but a window of a few months to move the Orlovs out of Siberia before political conditions and fighting would make the trip impossible, although he could not know that. Now that the herd had made it as far as Urga, again his timing or luck could not have been better. Mongolia enjoyed some measure of independence at the time, but all that was about to change. Urga was about to become the scene of told and untold horrors, years of it. With Russia tied up in World War I and its own revolution, China sensed weakness, as did the Japanese. General Hsu Shu-tseng, "Little Hsu," was ready to invade, encouraged by the Japanese. The Japanese hoped he would drive a Manchurian wedge between Russia and China that they could exploit in their plans to rule Manchuria and the trade routes to Russia. Hsu did not mind the encouragement, because in true warlord style he simply hoped to expand his territory and grab more loot. By 1919 even the Living Buddha would be under house arrest.

That year, Hsu sent thousands of his troops into Kalgan and across the Gobi to Urga under the guise of protecting the city from bandits about to attack. He, of course, was the bandit. He gave the ruling Mongolian council and the Living Buddha forty-eight hours to renounce Mongolian autonomy and be subject to China, meaning to Little Hsu. Through bribes, intimidation, and physical force, this was accomplished. All Russian businesses were confiscated, and the terror began. The prison overflowed. Beheadings and shootings were the norm. Hsu ruled with an iron fist.

Nothing compared to what happened shortly when Hsu's troops at Urga were themselves destroyed by one of history's zaniest figures, the Mad Baron, also called the Bloody White Baron, also called sadistic and demented. As James Palmer has pointed out in *The Bloody White Baron: The Extraordinary Story of the Russian Nobleman Who Became the Last Khan of Mongolia*, Baron Roman Nikolai Maximilian von Ungern-Sternberg was a born horse soldier.[5] Chang Tso-lin would later even consider Ungern as possible head of his cavalry divisions. Ungern commanded the White Russian Asiatic Cavalry Division, nicknamed the Savage Division. This independent Cossack unit contained Buryats, Bashkirs, Mongolian freedom fighters, Chinese, Manchus, Japanese, and Polish exiles among others. Virulently anti–Bolshevik and pro-monarchy, Ungern fought to restore the monarchy in Russia and Mongolia. After an initial defeat, Ungern took Urga and rescued the *Bogda gegen*, or Living Buddha. His thousand men routed 7,000 entrenched Chinese soldiers by virtue of the baron's superior tactics, intelligence, and psy-ops that played on the fears and superstitions of the encircled soldiers.

Having taken Urga in 1921, the Living Buddha bestowed Ungern with the honorific title of khan. Some Mongols saw him as Genghis Khan reincarnated, a white war god on a white horse forecast in some prophecies. He was sent to restore the Mongol Empire. The anti–Semitic Ungern first purged the city of all Jews. One of horse-raiser Frans Larson's business associates had married a Russian Jewish woman, and he had to quickly get her out of Urga before Ungern's henchmen could kill her.

After dispensing with the Jews, Ungern set his sights on anyone who had any connection, real or imagined, with the Reds or Chinese. All travelers were suspect and subject to torture or death. Where Ungern went, death followed. Before "freeing" Urga, he had been headquartered on the Chinese Eastern Railroad, where he received "death trains" stuffed with Bolshevik prisoners to be tortured and executed. He had them hanged, sometimes eighty at a time, and left in trees to rot. Soon the stench in the countryside around his headquarters outdid anything in *Apocalypse Now*.

Baron Ungern did believe in the end of the world, or apocalypse, and believed it was near. His sadism in part copied the Buddhist carved visions of hell depicted in local temples.[6] Unfortunate sinners were shown dying from exposure on ice, burning alive, and being ripped apart by wild beasts. Ungern brought these scenes to life, and more, even in disciplining his own men. Drunken men were stripped and made to stand out on the river ice all night, having to fend off wolves with their bare hands—a clever way of combining two visions of the Buddhist hell: exposure on ice and rending by beasts. The baron was known to have kept wolves in his attic for special occasions, and he drove through town using wolves in place of sled dogs. It was a good thing that Ungern's political views precluded the alcoholic Living Buddha from this vision of hell.

Others prisoners were burned, flayed, shot, put to the sword, quartered, beheaded. Instead of administering a hundred lashes as punishment, Ungern ordered a hundred lashes to every body part until flesh separated from bone. He was said to feed the bones of the dead to his horses. The baron gave vent to his sadism and mystical nationalism, foreshadowing the coming Nazi terror; but just as for General Hsu, power and loot also stood at the heart of his endeavors. The baron was savvy enough to arrange his political marriage to a Manchurian princess related to the governor of Kalgan, which helped the baron control the entire trade route from Kalgan to Urga and beyond. Had Barton tarried another year or two to make his horse drive, he would have blundered into the horror. Fortunately for him, now was the time to put hoof to ground and cross the Gobi.

While Barton and his cowboys did not have to sing to keep a herd of cattle calm, they did have all those horses, and they did share the customary cowboy campfire singing and storytelling, sometimes with a military twist. Some of the standard tales would have made the baron proud—tales of sewing shut the eyelids of recalcitrant steers that kept bolting from roundup herds for the hinterland, and tales of cowboy King Fisher, who raided Mexico for horses and cattle and returned with sixteen human ears strung on his bridle reins. The Old West was still close, very close.

• **Nine** •

Across the Gobi
Urga to Kalgan, 1917

This desert is reported to be so long that it would take a year to go from end to end; and at the narrowest point it takes a month to cross it. It consists entirely of mountains and sands and valleys. There is nothing at all to eat.[1]
—Marco Polo, *The Travels*

Gone were the days of easy water and fodder along the Kerulen. Survival on the route from Urga to Kalgan depended on knowing the location of desert wells built long ago to service caravans. Missing one of these small holes dug into the expansive Gobi assured the same fate as that of castaways missing an island and their only chance for survival in the vast Pacific. The word *Gobi* translates as "big, dry, waterless place." Although the Gobi does contains some ponds, the water is usually brackish, undrinkable; and although the water table is fairly close to the surface, death would come before a person could dig a hole deep enough to reach it.

Many misconceptions exist about crossing the Gobi. The trade route to and from Urga existed for centuries. Thousands of caravans had crossed it carrying silks, tea, and furs, so it was easy in Barton's time to see the well-marked road on maps as a comforting, nearly straight, distinct line. Near its ends, particularly near Kalgan, it was a definite trail, so well worn by carts and hooves that it carved itself into the loess in some places to a depth of several feet or yards. A city slicker sitting backwards on a blind horse could not get lost. But that was not the Gobi, not what lay between the ends.

Each caravan found its own way across the route, meaning that hundreds, if not thousands, of paths crisscrossed, wandered, came together, and parted across the desert in confusing patterns. Bleached bones and camel dung led everywhere. No central route existed except on maps. Many confused travelers found themselves not even on the main route. They mistakenly followed a cutoff route that led to an isolated monastery or a shortcut to the Kerulen to the north or to points south. Such wrong turns cost days and lives.

Many photographs, such as those taken on the Roy Chapman Andrews expeditions, popularized the Gobi in classic images of caravans trekking along the spines of massive sand dunes as camels cast long shadows in the relentless sun. While this image can be found in some parts of the Gobi, most of this desert does not contain sand dunes. Much of the Gobi is flat, not duned, consisting of a hardpan floor, often covered with pebbles, gravel, and thin, sparse grass. Sometimes a shield of barren rock serves as the floor for this northernmost desert. Such a combination of harsh surfaces quickly wears on the hooves of camels, cattle, and horses.

The image of caravans pictured in daylight is not necessarily correct either. Though depicted and defined as desert animals, camels do not fare well in the intense heat of midday. Caravans generally moved at night, with bells on the stock. This held true for Mongol camel caravans and Chinese bullock cart trains. Animals grazed and watered in late afternoon and early morning. Sleep occurred during the day. Many caravans chose to cross the desert in winter rather than summer to avoid the deadly heat. A good former nighthawk like Barton knew all about working at night and sleeping during the heat of the day.

"Just follow the telegraph poles from Urga to Kalgan, and you'll not become lost." That saying was another misconception. Mirroring the trade route, the telegraph line could help. It could also provide false security. Given the complete lack of wood in the Gobi, the desperate and the unscrupulous found that telegraph poles teasingly provided great sources of firewood, building materials, and repair wood for broken wheels, axles, and carts. Wire wasn't a bad find either. Sometimes the line was sabotaged as an act of rebellion or war. Telegraphs poles began disappearing shortly after the line was established. This went on until the Living Buddha ordered the beheading of anyone putting ax to pole. As if missing poles were not enough of a problem, the telegraph line had been surveyed in as straight a line as possible. That meant instead of going around hills, mountains, dunes, and rock outcrops, it went over them. It was impossible for caravans or a herd of horses to maintain a course on the line. Desert mirages also made poles appear where they were not and made them appear at times as something other than telegraph poles, sometimes something to be avoided rather than followed.

Several days out of Urga, the forests and mountains had been left behind. The herd was still passing through hilly grasslands sprinkled with yurts and a few monasteries. Marmot burrows and prairie dog holes again pitted the ground. Changes in the Gobi's surface color warned of danger, as the prairie dogs brought up fresh dirt. The tunneled areas were not so easy to spot where the desert prairie had been scorched a uniform color by caravans letting their campfires burn after departure. Despite the danger, the rat-like animals were entertaining. When the dogs became separated from their burrows by the herd, they feigned death and simply toppled over. Marmots chirped and went subterranean.

The vast colonies of prairie dogs had to be avoided to prevent injury to horses and riders. A hoof suddenly plunging into a underground rodent gallery as the roof collapsed could send a rider flying or bring a horse down. When Barton and his Cossack escort had surveyed Siberia six years earlier looking for a site for the proposed Russian horse ranch, marmots caused many people to topple as if they were no more than prairie dogs.

When they were prime, marmot hides provided a major source of trade for Urga. Hide caravans headed east to Kalgan, where millions of hides continued on by train or caravan to Peking and Tientsin for export. Many of them went to the United States. The turn-of-the-century fashion craze for fur continued well into the twentieth century. Furs were prerequisites for the Hollywood and East Coast socialite scenes. Little did starlets, gun molls, the old rich, and the nouveau riche know that dyed marmot hides could be marketed as expensive mink or sable. So great was the demand for marmot that thousands of hunters traveled up the Amur River from Khabarovsk or took the railroad out of Manchuria to cash in. The seasonal influx of these hordes forced people to stay in cramped, squalid housing, ripe for disease. Marmots carried the deadly plague bacillus *Yersinia pestis*. As William C. Summers chronicled in *The Great Manchurian Plague of 1910–1911*, the plague quickly spread by boat and railroad, with 50,000 people dying in Manchuria within a few months.[2] Barton avoided the plague then, and did so again now as part of his plan to stay away from the main track, people, and their animals as much as possible.

Numerous large horse herds grazed this region and had to be navigated. Staying away from caravans, except at wells, and herders' flocks was relatively easy, but other animals roamed the steppes besides camels, cattle, horses, and sheep. As the landscape leveled more into prairie and softer rolling hills, some hills were not hills at all but were alive, and they were no optical illusion. Thousands of antelope or gazelles presented a solid yellow mass on a hill, making it seem as if the hill moved, until it was realized the entire hill was covered with animals. Montana had its antelope, but nothing like this, reminiscent of how buffalo herds had covered the prairies before becoming only memory and earning a pittance for destitute bone hunters.

Clouds cast their own moving shadow herds across the prairie. As the grass thinned, the ground provided color. Every color of the rainbow covered whole stretches of the trail with pebbles of chalcedony or agate. The ornate carpet broke up the otherwise monotonous dry grass and dust. After several days of moving between wells, all eyes were guided by a dark bulwark on the horizon. From a distance the mountain looked sheer; some called it the Gibraltar of the desert. As the herd drew closer to it, the mountain became a huge jumble of massive rocks. The mountain, Tuerin, served as an important marker on the caravan route. First, its well was spaced thirty miles from the last well. Second, somewhere in the rock jumble stood a telegraph station offering contact with the outside world. Third, and perhaps most noteworthy, Tuerin marked the true start of the Gobi.

That the desert was about to get serious was driven home to the riders upon passing the final huge *obi*, or prayer pile, marking the entrance to the desert. Each traveler knew to place another stone on the pile to ensure good luck in making the crossing. Obis were common across Mongolia, and the men had seen plenty of them. This one was different. Not only had it grown to enormous proportions and was covered with blue prayer strips streaming in the wind, but also it had a peculiar central pole. Its top was spiked with a bleached animal skull, a warning to all who were about to do what they were going to do. The white death mask clearly stated it was not too late to turn back. Everyone threw a rock on the pile, whether they were believers or not.

As the Mongol guides led the herd to the well in what seemed like a rocky, waterless wasteland in which nothing could survive, there in a basin between the rocks sat an astounding vision, an entire town, a Buddhist lamasery. No vestige of green could be seen anywhere, yet four golden-domed temples rose out of the desert. Their roof corners curved upward. Some of the temples used the big boulders as walls. Hundreds of tiny white houses of lime and wood lined the broad streets. Tall stockpiles of camel dung marked the town's entrance. How this fairy-tale place survived was anyone's guess.

Nearly hidden in another basin stood the lonely hut that housed the telegraph station. Progress across the Gobi could be measured by these evenly spaced stations. Three of them were scattered between Urga and Kalgan. This was the first. Progress also could be gauged in the desert void by counting telegraph poles, although in the shimmering heat a pole could easily be mistaken for a person or horse. Twenty-four poles equaled a mile. Counting at least gave the mind something to do in the daily grind. Only 14,400 poles to go.... This worked only when poles were close enough to be seen and not obscured by blowing dust.

Few travelers, if any, sent messages from these stations, but telegraph operators necessarily staffed these most desolate stations on earth. The operators struggled to preserve their sanity. Because there wasn't enough "juice" in the line to carry messages across the desert or continent, relay stations were needed to pass on messages. One saying held that the only thing alive in the Gobi was the telegraph line—when it was working.

Barton and company knew exactly where and when they entered the Gobi proper. It sat in the basin of an extinct sea. The men could feel it. The horses dropped twenty or thirty yards down the layered rim of the ancient beach onto the flat, barren plain of nothingness before them. No more sound of larks singing. No more big herds of antelope. No more ravens and golden eagles perched atop telegraph poles. All that remained were slowly moving dust devils, the cold of night, the heat of day, the plodding of many thousands of hooves, the occasional yip or whistle of a drover, the bones scattered across the desert floor like dots and dashes—the desert's Morse code of death.

Like ships at sea, caravans passed the herd after dark going in the opposite direction across the dunes and flats. Usually the wind died down, so that the sound of tinkling bells worn by the trains of oxen and camels carried for miles. Small flashes of light sparked on the horizon as camel drivers used their strikers to light their pipes. Desert travelers customarily traveled in two shifts to avoid the heat: predawn to midmorning, late afternoon to late night. This way, animals had time to eat, drink, and rest, as did the men. Depending on the distance between wells, sometimes it was necessary to travel all night or to go without water for a day. The oxen from the huge oxen cart trains ate most of the grass available around the wells, if there was any, so Barton's guide had to search farther from the wells to rest the horses.

Since antelope could not drink from the wells, whose water lay underground, they migrated each morning to their own hidden sources of water in the desert. This caused the "moving mountains" of their herds to swell before they dispersed for the rest of the day. Mongol guides knew some of these hidden water sources, which meant a quicker drink for the horses since water would not have to be drawn from a well. On the other hand, because the antelope were so fleet, they could cover more ground in a day to reach a water source than could a caravan or horse herd. Sometimes an antelope's water source was too rank for a horse.

Days out of Tuerin the men and horses came to a well. The land was absolutely flat, the horizon boundless. All caravans had to stop in this stony, deserted zone, but they could not stay. There was nothing for a camel, ox, or horse to eat to stay alive. Getting an early start from the well was imperative. Ahead lay some thinly grassed prairie alternating with sand blows and gravel patches.

After a long haul, Barton found a pond in the least expected place. It was muddy, but water was water. Horses had no trouble with it. This desert anomaly teemed with water birds. Ducks swam while cranes and ploverlike birds probed its receding edges. The sparsely grassed area around the pond harbored desert larks and partridge. Again the desert filled with sound, and again the desert took on added features. Thicker grass grew up little valleys on the swells of low, small hills.

After a few days of this terrain, the worst seemed over, but then the desert changed again. The herd left the grass prairie and entered what seemed an endless series of valleys channeled between reddish sand hills punctuated by a few stony passes. The number of plants seen in one dried-up channel could be counted on one hand; otherwise the place lay barren.

All of this country was dangerous. The danger of not having water was a constant, but the reverse was true as well. The Gobi could behave like Texas or New Mexico, where freak rainfall, even a hundred miles away, could result in an unexpected flash flood when there was not a cloud in the sky. This happened to caravans and explorers alike. Some lived to tell about it. A huge dust cloud would appear on the horizon signaling the mass movement of gazelles, a big caravan, an army, or an oncoming windstorm. Suddenly the wave of liquefied desert rolled through, carrying all before it—rocks, sand, plants, camels, people, yurts. Nothing could withstand the battering ram of a mud flow speeding across the desert like a lahar racing down a volcano. Whole caravans and communities had perished in the debris flows. It was not good to dwell on this aspect while riding through the channeled landscape, to ask where the plants that could be counted on one hand had washed in from or what fertilized them.

Ude, or Udde, "The Gate" marked another of those places on maps that was not a town at all but was actually a desolation rather than a destination. It did contain a log buttressed well and a nearby telegraph station nestled in the boulders at the base of a layered mountain called Ertni Obo, or Treasure Mountain. It was more or less a big mound of rocks, hardly a treasure. The corrugated tin shack held on against the desert as the second telegraph station on the Urga-Kalgan route. How the telegraph operator did not bake his brains out in that oven was hard to comprehend. A mud hut would have given more insulation. Barton could take some comfort in the fact that Ude represented the halfway point between Urga and Kalgan. That put the herd about 400 miles out of Kalgan. A couple of forlorn-looking trees that barely qualified as vegetation clung to existence here, the first to be seen since departing from the Urga area.

Beyond Ude, patches of rock interrupted the ground. Like low reefs, they sat on the sea of the plains. Although the miles were barren of pasture, wells contained cold, clear water. This was not the case at the Iren Dabasu, also known as Erhlien, the next telegraph station. Iren Dabusu sat in a basin near a marshy lake. Its water was fetid, yellow, salty, and undrinkable, but it was loved by water birds of all types. Two yellow mud huts and a telegraph station sat at some distance from the stinky mess. A more desolate place could not be imagined. Salt had risen to the surface of the encrusted ground, blinding white under the sun. Small drifts of sand on the lee side of a few struggling thorny shrubs provided the only visual relief.

While a few blades of grass held promise that the herd had passed the zone of absolute aridity, the Gobi punished them with the most intense heat and illusions yet before they could exit the basin. It was easy to see why *Gobi* also meant "cavity." The basin was indeed a cavity, strewn with the rib cage cavities of dead camels on the hard sand. Strips of desiccated hide still held some of the bleached cages together as they teetered on collapse and the wind played atonal music through them.

Just as heat mirages created falsehoods on the horizon, another illusion rolled across the ground, which came alive with rugs of what looked like giant woolly worms. Caravan camels shed their winter coats in great clumps that tumbled across the plains like Montana tumbleweed. With no fences to stop them, legions of hair balls continued mile after mile, combining in ever larger bundles. The moving ground unnerved men and spooked horses, particularly if the woolly masses suddenly swirled upward. Beatrix Bulstrode, in her *A Tour of Mongolia* (1920), described encountering this same phenomenon. The boluses picked up dry grass as they rolled and zipped by her at tremendous velocity.[3] It was as if the desert spirits that made strange, unaccountable sounds at night had hacked up hair balls and sent them like flying badlands banshees to scour the desert floor.

At last the herd climbed the steep, southern, giant bathtub rim of the Gobi. Desolation gave way to clouds of antelope herds floating across meadows and quartering ahead of the horses. Twenty miles out from the last telegraph station, a miniature Lhasa hove into view. The white temple trimmed in red provided a splash of desert color, as did the monks in their red and gold robes. A quick stop at their well, and then it was on to Pan-kiang.

Weeks earlier, ominous teeth in the skull perched atop an obi had marked entry into the Gobi. At the other end of the desert another set marked departure from it. The telegraph station at Pan-kiang consisted of three low huts forming three sides of a square. They were surrounded by a mud wall with an entrance facing south. Like white teeth, a gruesome line of telegraph insulators lined the top of the entranceway. The ceramic bicuspids could have been the teeth of the wind, which never seemed to stop sandblasting, choking, and swallowing everything. Sand piled up against the north side of the station and threatened to bury the whole thing. The station was lighted by large grilles covered with paper in the Chinese manner. At least the attraction of the well afforded the Chinese telegraph operator with some human contact besides what came over the wire and out of an opium pipe.

Barton's group had traveled 170 miles from Ude to Pan-kiang. They could feel good about conquering the heart of the Gobi, but the toothy insulators still warned that perhaps the most dangerous part of the journey confronted them on their way into Kalgan. And it would not be a problem with the desert, although the desert had not given up yet. The Great Wall above Kalgan remained a long way off. Curiously for the men, the herd now moved across what appeared to be the badly crumbled remains of another great wall. What was it doing out here? Whoever dreamed of a great wall out in the desert?

The herd traveled for ten miles at a time over pebbly or bedrock country resembling Western sagebrush country. Then the men and horses were met with intervening rises of barren earth and reddish undulations, only to drop back down into another ten miles of marbled flatness. For variety, nature threw in some sandy sterile areas, rocky passes, and thin prairies. No herds or yurts out here. The antelope had again disappeared. After this much time on the trail, the Orlovs had become conditioned. Still, the herd needed to reach good grass to regain weight. Water can keep a horse going for some time, but sooner or later it has to eat. Orlovs are not wild mustangs.

One area was greener than its surroundings, but the guides made the herd circumvent the grass. The detour seemed counterintuitive. The Mongols explained that the grass grew thicker here because of a famous battle where many soldiers had perished. Blood made the grass grow greener. The site was lonelier than the Little Big Horn, just sitting out in the flats in the middle of nowhere. If the story were true, hundreds must have been killed. The Mongols believed the place was cursed, and that was enough.

In the final week of the push to Kalgan, the horses enjoyed grazing on thicker grass on the plains and hills. This was horse country, the great Mongolian prairie, evidenced by the growing number of yurts and herders dotting the far landscape. Antelope intermingled with Mongol herds. Wolves could be heard at night, but they were not much threat to Barton's big Orlov horses. Wolves went after colts or sheep but were kept in check by the Mongol herdsmen, who rode the wolves down, caught them in the loop of their long roping poles, bound their jaws, and then skinned them alive, except for the head, before releasing them. It was not enough to kill a wolf, they wanted it to suffer. Any Buddhist respect for other living things vanished when it came to wolves.

Mongolia almost took the same path as Montana Territory did in regard to wolves. Montana wolfers liked to use strychnine to poison them. Russians tried to convince Mongolians to do the same. Mongolians quickly found that setting out poisoned carcasses for wolves ended up poisoning their own guard dogs left out at night to forage. Besides, baiting with strychnine was not something a Mongol could do from a horse. If something could not be done from a horse, it probably was not worth doing.

Wolves might not take on an Orlov mare or stallion, but they would take on a human. They attacked Russians and Chinese, but left Mongolians alone. When facing an attack by a wolf, Russians and Chinese usually impulsively ran, whereas Mongols attacked. A human's impulse to run triggered the wolf's instinct to chase prey. It was an open question about what wolves thought of Americans, so it paid to have a saddle rifle at hand.

As was the case back in Urga, a far greater threat came from a herdsman's massive dog that could outmuscle any wolf. These black beasts wanted more than a chunk of any human. In approaching any yurt, Barton's Mongol guides hollered, "Nuhuio!" (Mongolian for dog). The call brought out the dogs, and also their owners, who were then under obligation to control them. This part of Mongol etiquette avoided any sneak attack. Chains heavy enough to contain bears restrained the beasts. These were not Miles City cattle dogs or sheepherder sheps. These dogs were no bluff; they meant intentionally to do bodily harm.

The herd passed near Frans Larson's horse operation at Ta-Bol and its nearby lamasery. Ta-Bol, meaning five mountains, showed some slight elevations, but overall the country was grassy prairie. Barton and his guides had to keep the telegraph poles on their right, or else it was easy to become confused and head up the wrong trail. Trails split off in different directions to both north and south. Curiously, the Mongol ponies in this area looked smaller than those seen back in Urga and along the Kerulen. Since this area of Outer Mongolia sat closest to China, Chinese warlords had purchased the bigger horses from this area for years, leaving behind the smaller ones. The Orlovs resembled sleek giants from another planet compared to these stubby ponies.

Now came the most dangerous part of the journey, the final seventy miles or so into

Kalgan. Mongolia was losing its grip on the land, and China was rapidly pushing onto the prairie from the east. Here the prairies ended and cultivated land began. Each year Chinese farmers plowed more horse prairie under, creating more dust. Unpaid soldiers and other brigands had been drawn to this area in gangs, finding travelers and farmers easy prey. There was plenty of plunder to be had from the camel caravans and Chinese ox carts. Caravans were concentrated here into a single track, as opposed to the myriad of desert wanderings. Bandits could pick their targets of opportunity. In lieu of caravans, they could always pillage, rape, and kill in local farm huts and villages.

The new generation of bandits, half-Mongol and half-Chinese, proved most dangerous. As the Chinese moved in on the Mongol pasturelands, they enticed or tricked Mongol herders into debt, debt they could never pay. Ultimately herders lost their herds and their rights to their land and would even end up having to sell their wives to the Chinese merchants. Since Mongol women could stand the severe climate and endure hard labor better than Chinese women, the Chinese male immigrants were glad to have them. As Danish explorer Henning Haslund pointed out, the despised mixed breeds, or offspring, of these forced marriages inherited what some considered the worst traits of both peoples. They were clever, they could ride, they could fight, and they were merciless. Women were not excluded, for they too could lead bandit bands. Their beauty worked to great advantage in lulling unsuspecting travelers into a false sense of security.[4]

The area seemed drawn right out of the pages of some Wild West dime novel, and one needed to be armed and to travel in force. Vigilance replaced the monotony of the desert. Anyone seen on a rise scouting the herd needed to be investigated to make sure other riders were not lurking behind that hill. Like the wolves, usually these ne'er-do-wells who lived off the land shrank at the sight of any force that could stand up to them. Barton had come too far to lose men or the herd now. Like a force of nature, his herd made an imposing impression in itself, and its escort of American soldiers, armed with sidearms and rifles, intimidated bandits carrying mostly rusty, outdated weaponry at best.

Barton's saddle rifle echoed his own life in many ways. Winchester lever action rifles were synonymous with the Old West. Magazine and dime novel writers and illustrators would not have been caught dead portraying cowboys pulling a bolt-action rifle from the scabbard to fend off Indians, grizzlies, banditos, mountain lions, and perverted wolverines with blood in their eyes. Westerners needed a rifle that slid easily from a scabbard, not something that had a bolt that could snag. As a cowboy rifle, the Winchester handled much differently than the bolt-action standard Springfield army rifles that the 15th Infantry soldiers were used to.

Just as the Far East contacts first had intended Barton to create a ranch for the Russian czar, Barton's Winchester Model 1895 was meant to go to Russia too. It was manufactured for the czar's army from 1915 to 1917 for World War I before the Russian Revolution. The U.S. Army also ordered the military 30–40 Krag cartridge version (Barton's version) of the Model 1895 for the Spanish-American and Philippine-American wars in which some Fort Keogh soldiers participated. The same held true for their participation with Theodore Roosevelt's Rough Riders in Cuba. Roosevelt personally purchased twins of Barton's rifle to equip Rough Rider officers. Some Winchesters also found their way into the hands of Pancho Villa's army and also became the favorite of

Pinkerton agents, the Texas Rangers and the Arizona Rangers. Ever the hunter, as he had been in Montana and Dakota, Roosevelt's later Winchester Model 1895 became the famous "Teddy's African gun," or, as he called it, his "medicine gun." The rifle had bloodlines. Now the herd passed through along with the Winchester.

Hara-Ossu with its temple and a few houses appeared near a river. For people traveling to Urga, this was the last Chinese inn they would see on this side of the Gobi. Not too far away stood a Swedish mission, another sign of civilization. Beyond that, some more small Chinese villages, usually only a few huts or an inn, had to be skirted unless well water was needed. Settlements grew more numerous. Chinese burial grounds created mazes to entangle the herd. Unlike the Mongolians, whose dead were left out in the open, the Chinese covered their coffins with mounds of dirt, creating a unique landscape. These "dragon's teeth" looked like military obstacles that could stop tanks in the war raging in Europe. Having horses mixed up in that confusion with the dead was no good. Some mounds had eroded, and the guides wanted nothing to do with these areas. The men of the 15th Infantry had no trouble with them. They had seen plenty around Tientsin, where they used the mounds as convenient rest areas. A person could sit or recline against a mound or use it as a picnic table on an otherwise flat prairie. Such burial grounds posed intermittent barriers for Barton all the way from here to the end of the drive.

The prairie ended as Barton faced coming off the Mongolian plateau. Ahead, they faced the mountain pass marking the lip of the plateau. The land going to the pass looked like a painted desert. Sand wasn't too bad to ride on, but a shower had soaked into the deep dust of the trail churned by hundreds of years of camels and carts. The sunken surface had turned to Montana gumbo. The low rumble of the moving herd changed into the sucking sounds of thousands of hooves being pulled from the morass. The horse's legs became heavier with each step as the gumbo stuck. The landscape was riven with deep erosional canyons and jumbled rocks in every direction. Ruined towers of the Great Wall snaked across the skyline and out of sight. At Mt. Pisgah and the Great Wall, the view from the top was breathtaking. Mountain ranges appeared in nearly every direction, some still capped with snow. Soon the men would be headed south into China past these same mountains.

Now the Orlovs used the same rocky trail as did all caravans and began the steep plunge to Kalgan. There was only one way down, consisting of a partially dry streambed that careened pell-mell down the mountain. It took a leap of the imagination to comprehend that the Gobi sat at a higher elevation than most of the mountains. In the American West, deserts normally behaved themselves and conformed to human expectations: a person rode up on mountains and rode down to deserts. Mongolia reversed that.

The path down proved torturous. Huge rocks had fallen from the surrounding cliffs, creating obstacles in the streambed. The trail was not wide enough for thousands of horses to meet caravans going up and down. Fortunately, horses found few places where they could stray. The worse danger was rain. Even a small amount of rain could send water cascading off the plateau, down the trail, and into Kalgan. With no place to go, caravans caught between canyon walls on the trail coming off the pass could be simply washed away. Kalgan had seen its share of human bodies and camel and oxen carcasses flushed down its main street during flash floods. Whole caravans had perished.

The pass was not all rock, however. Loess hills on the decline served as homes for some Chinese. Whereas the Great Plains had sod houses that melted in downpours, China's cave houses simply collapsed. Blue-clad families had carved caves into the brown hills. The Chinese had a saying about those who lived troglodytic existences in these earthen dugouts. They enjoyed three things that cannot happen. They cannot be hot in summer. They cannot be cold in winter. And when the cave falls in, they cannot be found.[5] Barton's men saw such habitations most of the way through Shansi Province to Barton's ranch. Earthquake cave-in deaths in China came easy.

Two natural bridges sat on one side of the gorge. Mongols told the story of how Genghis Khan formed them when he shot arrows through the rock on his way to conquer China. Others said he used a gun. Either way, one of the holes was big enough to drive an automobile through. After twelve miles of descent, the path down from the pass took a turn. For the first time, Kalgan could be seen hanging onto the steep sides at the bottom of the valley. Descending off the steepest part of the descent, Barton's herd passed a flat area, which served as Kalgan's cattle market and staging area for many of the camel caravans.

Timing needed to be right to move through Kalgan. The huge wooden doors to the north gate were barred and closed at sundown to everyone and were not opened until morning. A good friend and a big bribe might get someone through the gate from inside the city, but travelers outside the city were just out of luck if they arrived too early or too late. Barton gained entry. Moving through the gate was treacherous on the wet paving bricks, but once all the Orlovs streamed through, they had escaped the Gobi.

• Ten •

Final Leg
Kalgan to Taiyuanfu, 1917

The country is much like Montana and the Cascade Mtns ... rolling valleys, herds of sheep, cows and ponies grazing on the mountain slopes, and then steep mountains, ridge on ridge.[1]
—Mabel H. Cabot, *Vanished Kingdoms:
A Woman Explorer in Tibet, China and Mongolia, 1921–1925*

Kalgan existed as a border trading center on the fringes of China and Mongolia. The railroad from Peking ended at Kalgan, so Chinese merchants were plentiful. Frans Larson made his home here when he wasn't in Urga or Ta-Bol. This was the first real town in terms of population since Urga. Its main street was not now flooded with streambed carcasses, but rather with hordes of people on foot, on horseback, on camels. Their dust coated everything in the merchants' stalls, so that all of Kalgan was a uniform brown, despite the colorful Mongolian and Chinese clothing. Camels were dust brown, as were oxen, sheep, dogs, and now the Orlovs. Although Kalgan was used to large herds of horses passing through to be sold, the thousands of Barton horses made quite a sight. It drew attention away from the traveling theatrical troop performing a classical Chinese play in the open air and distracted scores of old Chinese men taking their daily stroll with their pet singing birds housed in elaborate cages.

Kalgan's cramped buildings clung to the steep valley walls. Unstable boulders threatened to fall and turn stores into rubble. Since a river ran through the town, rock breakwaters protecting the town from floods created even steeper crossings to get from one side of town to the other. Cart-pulling animals strained to get up and down the ramps. Floods caused merchants to erect grooved timbers or stones on the sides of their businesses. Planks inserted into the grooves kept out the waters when the torrents came.

Barton did not have to be concerned with Chinese etiquette yet. Kalgan was a border town teaming with Mongolians, so Chinese customs did not always apply. In most of China, riders were expected to dismount while passing through a town. This of course was not the Mongol way, nor Barton's. Trying to walk a herd of thousands of hot-blooded horses through a crowded town filled with recalcitrant camels and bullocks was a good way to get yourself killed.

Much like what Barton's group had witnessed in Hilar, Kalgan caravans carried hides, salt, soda, tea, wool, and silk. Some cargo, especially wool, was placed on trains.

In just a matter of days, it would arrive in Tientsin near the Chinese coast to be loaded on ships bound for the United States and other countries in this time of war. Strings of camels also set out to follow the same route Barton took to reach the ranch at Taiyuanfu in Shansi Province. The Shansi mountains and loess hills confined the route mostly to well-defined defiles. Barton would not have the freedom of making up his own route as he did in crossing the desert.

At least the number of camel caravans moving out of Kalgan was diminishing. Camel caravan season was partially suspended between April and November. Animals were given a chance to heal, put on weight, and restore energy supplies in their humps in readiness for the next season. While this may have seemed like a boon for unclogging the road out of Kalgan for Barton, it was not. Mid-spring to fall was prime time for the Chinese oxen caravans to pick up the slack. The 100-cart oxen caravans moved slower than the camels and were harder to negotiate around in narrow defiles. Oxen required more water and more grass than the camels, pressuring even more the areas around wells. At least Barton could capitalize on the several streams that ran through Shansi Province's central valley, instead of having to depend on wells alone.

Kalgan had declined. It served as the terminus for the caravan route that for centuries had carried tea and silk to Siberia and on to Moscow. This transcontinental trip took as much as eighteen months. At one time, hundreds of businesses had set up shop in Kalgan. Before the Trans-Siberian Railway cut into its business, 5,000 cases of tea a day passed out of the town by camel during the height of caravan season. Russia consumed millions of pounds of tea each year.[2] No wonder the track into Kalgan had been carved so deeply into the soil and even into the grooved rock. While the golden age of the camel had given way to the iron horse, many caravans still left for Mongolia from Kalgan's crowded streets. Some Russians still preferred tea carried by caravan rather than by train or boat. They believed the smoke from caravan campfires infiltrated the tea cakes, giving tea a most desirable smoky under taste. Without Kalgan, that classic Russian icon, the samovar, would not exist.

The Chinese repeatedly wanted to push the railroad through to Urga, but caravan interests and China's continuing fractious wars curtailed those thrusts. The caravan route from Kalgan to Urga still bore a lot of traffic, as did the route south to Taiyuanfu. The route served as a thoroughfare for commercial traffic and a pilgrimage route to the many sacred Buddhist sites in Shansi. Barton's herd would not be alone on the desert anymore. Although bandits plagued travelers, the danger was not as great as in Manchuria or outside Kalgan, for now Barton pushed the horses into the province run by, and under the protection of, Yen Hsi-shan and his army. Of course, sometimes the army was the bandit.

The drive meandered down the heart of Shansi Province. There really was only one road, if it could be called that, running north to south through the central valley. No guides were needed here. A mountain barrier framed the eastern side of the province, a mountain and loess hill barrier the west. All transport was channeled onto the central loess plateau. Most of trip proceeded over flat plains, deeply cut by erosion in the soft loess. One mountain pass had to be crossed where a mountain spur crisscrossed the valley.

More agriculture appeared. Classic Chinese terraced fields climbed up some mountain flanks. Villages here served the influx of pilgrims heading for Buddhist holy sites tucked away in the mountains. Gone the high altitude ozone smell of the desert, replaced by the familiar smell of China. Every Westerner who went to China knew it. It sat heavy in the air, mostly a product of human waste that thickened around human habitation. Poverty knew no bounds.

Even though trail hands were accustomed to using "outdoor facilities," it took some doing to get used to seeing men and women squatting wherever they happened to have the urge. Even life on the range enjoyed some modesty, particularly when it came to the fairer sex. Mongols, in contrast to the Chinese, had what amounted to a sanitary sewer system. The system was called dog. Mongolian dogs delighted in human excrement as a favored delicacy. This worked in favor of the Mongol version of a Montana teepee creeper. If a man wanted a romantic dalliance with a Mongol woman, he had a way of sneaking into her yurt without being torn apart by the guard dogs. As soon as the dogs were ready to light into him, he could squat and utter constipated grunts. The dogs would stop their attack and patiently wait for him to finish his duty. By moving forward and using several of these squats, he could gain access to the yurt for his tryst.[3]

While a few Mongols as well as numerous Buddhist monks tramped or rode along the way, the rural Chinese population lacked their color. Most wore blue or colorless wraps or tatters. Though not as ornately dressed as the Mongolians, their diet and personal hygiene made a difference. Since Mongolians ate fatty sheep tail and never washed, they wiped their hands on their clothes. Over a lifetime these clothes could have made some very good oversized candlewicks or water-repellant rain gear. Chinese peasants in hock to the local landowners did not have this sleek appearance.

Also missing was the elaborate Mongolian footwear, the oversized felt riding boots with upturned toe. Shansi Chinese were farmers, not horse riders. Mares were purchased out of Kalgan and Mongolia to breed mules for the field, not for mounts to be ridden. While Chinese armies required horses for mounts, and foreigners in China wanted mounts for polo and horse racing, most Chinese wanted horses to pull heavy loads and till fields, a job done better by mules. When horses were used to pull heavy loads, their mistreatment appalled any good cowboy. Collapsed, overburdened horses were literally at times whipped to death. They seemed as expendable as unwanted Chinese girl babies. The man/horse relationship differed greatly between Mongolia and China, and between Montana and China. The Orlovs headed to a better future.

In contrast to the Chinese view of horses, Barton's Mongol guides sang of how Genghis Khan's slain warriors became free spirits, risen again as proud steeds crossing Mongolia for eternity. Likewise, at Urga, the Bogdo Gegen, or Living God, always kept eleven snow-white ponies that had never been saddled and had never tasted a bit, nor would they ever. These mountain ponies would never be beasts of burden. They represented Uri Hangrän, a shamanistic deity of the children of nature.[4] Such wildness was privileged and honored, even if such deities were not contained in the lamaist tradition.

How glorious it would be to describe the natural and architectural wonders that lay before Barton and his men on their way through Shansi Province. The region contained some of the most picturesque and sacred sites in all of China. These have been well chronicled by other travelers, photographers, and explorers. Cowboys had little or no time for that. Taking the herd through three different countries was work, not a

A U.S. 15th Infantryman sits in a Chinese graveyard, a version of the Maginot Line and obstacle for armies or a herd of 3,500 Orlov horses.

sightseeing trip. Time was money. The longer the horses were on the trail, the more chance for losses. Beating the monsoonal flow also had to be considered. Having the herd bog down in mud from rain in loess country could spell disaster. In terms of the men on loan from the 15th Infantry, furloughs lasted only so long.

After crossing the border into Shansi Province, Barton picked up the Sanngan River, which led to the town of Datong (Tatungfu). Like most Shansi (or "west of the mountains") towns, Datong sat in the central valley at the base of the mountains. Datong was renowned for its beautiful women. Wealthy Mandarins traveled here to buy wives. People also made pilgrimages to see the Yungang Grottoes, known as the Cloud Ridge Caves, just outside town. Over 50,000 images of the Buddha and Bodhisattvas had been carved into mountain walls. Some displayed tiers of small images, others monumental Buddhas. The mountain complex climaxed in the 1500-year-old Taoist hanging temple, or monastery, perched on the sheer side of Mt. Hengshan, one of the five great or sacred peaks of China. As a testament to its builders, the hanging temple had survived centuries of earthquakes.

From miles away on the valley floor, the drovers saw a large tumulus on a mountaintop. The human-form mountain appeared to be lying on its back, stomach to the sky. The tumulus was the popped belly button of a very pregnant mountain. Lower in the valley, eroded loess-covered volcanic mountains were scattered around the valley separate from the mountain chains. They opened at one end as if huge hoofprints had risen from the ground. The herd then crossed the Yanghe River south of Datong, began passing badlands, and headed for the next notable town.

Shuozhou, a fortress-like walled city, was accessed through a huge stone gate much like that of Kalgan. The city served as gateway to one of Shansi's few mountain passes to the outside world. Yanmen Pass, or Wild Goose Pass, was so named because the mountains were too high for the wild geese to fly over, so they had to go through the narrow pass walled with high cliffs. Not far from Shuozhou sat Fogong Pagoda. This nine-story, octagonal wooden pagoda climbed over 200 feet into the air. From any direction or distance, it was hard to ignore. The tower presented an optical illusion. It contained more floors inside than indicated on the outside.

About fifty miles out of Taiyuanfu, the herd bypassed the final major town or village, Xinzhou, just to the west of Mt. Wutai, or Mountain of Five Terraces. Wutai was actually a cluster of five peaks at the 10,000-foot level, the highest point in the province. Another of the sacred mountains of China and home of the bodhisattva Manjusri, Wutai's slopes sprouted hundreds of Buddhist temples. This mountainous country served both pilgrims and hunters. The upper reaches of Shansi's mountains yielded trophy mountain sheep and other animals. Hunters from coastal China, including U.S. military personnel, made their way to this wild part of China for lengthy hunts.

Though it was wild, people proved to be the country's biggest obstacle slowing Barton. As James Gilmore pointed out in *Among the Mongols*, "As Jerusalem to the Jews, as Mecca to the Mahometans, so is Wu T'ai Shan to Mongols."[5] Year round, pilgrims from all over Mongolia clogged the narrow trail on their way to sacred Wutai. While Mongols preferred the horse, many traveled there by camels, which were better suited to the long trip and carrying camping gear. Other Mongols walked hundreds of miles on foot until they collapsed at Wutai's Buddhist temples and had to be cared for, some never able to return to their homelands.

Many made the long journey again and again, and for good reasons. Any beast that ate Wutai's grass and drank of its water was to be born hereafter into a higher state. Each visit ensured happiness for the believer in a future life. A second visit ensured happiness in a second future life, a third—and so on. Lamas prescribed trips to Wutai to cure diseases and heal wounds. If the sick person could not travel, others could go in her stead to effect a cure. Ice from a high sacred spring held special medicinal properties.

Pilgrims built up merits here that worked in their favor in future lives. Since most non-lama Mongols could not read, Wutai's prayer wheels greatly helped in obtaining merit. At the base of one temple mound, pilgrims circling the grounds spun 300 prayer wheels. This sent all the contained prayers to heaven, even for the illiterate. Inside the temple, an immense prayer wheel some 60 feet high contained books and prayers that would take a lifetime to read. Pilgrims could go down into the cellar beneath the wheel, grab spokes, and turn the great wheel. That equated to having read all the books, said all the prayers, and bowed to all the gods contained in the spinning wheel. Such a deal!

Wutai also sent its lamas to the far reaches of Mongolia to collect money and goods, giving Buddhists a chance at even more merit by contributing to the temples. These caravans increased traffic on the trail as well while Wutai's great lama sat in his temple. Above his head, the draft of air from his charcoal warming fire kept an ingenious, great, inverted wheel of life spinning and sending its prayers to heaven. He did not even have to physically spin the wheel to accumulate his own merit when the scales of his life were weighed.

Along the trail, pilgrims left their herds and much of their caravans below to make the trek into the mountains. Whereas pasturage and water were free in Mongolia, the Chinese charged pilgrims for everything. Oats grown in terraces around the temple mounts sold at scalper prices. Not only did the Tibetan-style mountain temples make out like bandits, so also did Chinese business interests along the way. The great pilgrim fleece was on. Old West snake-oil salesmen had nothing on these marketers. When a particularly meritorious monk died and his body was cremated, small white pills were said to be found in the ashes. These were pills of merit that could be passed on at an exorbitant price to wealthy pilgrims. A light was believed to shine from the eyes of one temple's statues on certain days of the month, so it was important to stay, be there at the time, and purchase objects associated with the great event. Barton was all business too, but for him, it was Yeats' "Horseman, pass by!" And guard your purse.

Pilgrims and other travelers might have slowed Barton's progress, but the sight of an army of several thousand big Russian horses supported by armed riders tended to clear most of the obstructive traffic. At last Barton began the final run into Taiyuanfu, past terraced farms, graveyards, and poppy fields. He was not sure what he would find. He had been away for months.

Shansi was feeling the throes of major changes. Warlord and governor Yen Hsi-shan had decided to overthrow the old ways and usher in the new. To do this, he instigated draconian measures to wage war on symbols of the past. He forbade the wearing of queues. His soldiers cut them from the heads of anyone they could get their hands on—a terrible loss of face for the tearful unfortunates. Taiyuanfu's central square filled with baskets and bales of human hair, which, of course, government officials sold at a profit. A smart soldier kept one of these queues handy. If he had to change sides quickly and found himself fighting for a general that required queues, he could quickly attach the hairpiece. Such was loyalty.

Symbols for women also changed. Their feet could no longer be bound. Traditional lily feet, just a few inches long, were not to be considered signs of beauty anymore. While missionaries and diplomats praised Yen, "the Model Governor," for his modernity in banning barbaric practices, Chinese girl babies now bore the shame of having feet like barbarians from the West.

A more cynical, if not realistic, interpretation of this modernization would read this as a way of not just freeing people but of increasing productivity of women in the field and Yen's factories. Yen bounced back and forth between idealism and power greed. More productivity through a more mobile workforce meant a stronger Shansi Province able to be more self-sustaining and impervious to outside forces. Since Yen controlled exports and taxes, this resulted in more loot in Yen's coffers—a classic case of trickle-down economics without the trickle-down.

On the surface, banning opium smoking seemed one of the governor's oddest reforms. Opium profits funded much of his treasury, which supported his army. Again missionaries and western diplomats were drawn to Yen for taking such a stand against what they saw as a family-destroying and production-destroying drug. Not to worry. Just because opium smoking was banned in Shansi did not mean the opium poppy ceased to be grown. Nor did opium cease to be exported to other provinces, with taxes collected. The ban had the desired effect of driving opium prices up in Shansi, but it had the same effect as Prohibition in the United States. At the same time Yen pursued his reforms, in December of 1917 the U.S. Senate proposed the Eighteenth Amendment banning alcohol. In hindsight, results were predictable.

As Henrietta Harrison pointed out in "Narcotics, Nationalism and Class in China," Yen's prohibition on opium was catastrophic. Farmers and merchants depended on the crop for local sales and survival. Contrary to the popular image of seedy opium dens whose occupants smoked their way to dissolute destruction, Chinese farmers and workers used opium for the treatment of pain in enduring hard labor. It was needed to continue production, not escape from it. Its use resembled that of Andeans chewing coca leaves. Obviously some opium den smokers were doomed. Most were not. The merchant class used opium as a means of socialization at meetings, much as Europeans would share a smoke or a social drink would be used today after concluding business. They usually were not habitual users. Yen risked turning workers and merchants against him.

Yen's opium banning quickly assumed the same negatives as U.S. Prohibition. Gangs moved in to control distribution of the product, whose price doubled. Dangerous substitutes replaced what had been legal, just as bathtub gin, wood alcohol, bad-recipe moonshine, and even formaldehyde sometimes replaced what had been mass-produced spirits in the States with deadly results. Snake-oil salesmen marketed opium substitutes as medicine, even cures for opium addiction. Such cure-alls as Golden Grain Pills hooked people on morphine. For workers, the morphine seemed a godsend. It left no smell, was easy to hide, and was quick to use. The pills also contained strychnine. It would not be long before Shansi would be back in the opium business more than ever.[6]

For Barton, none of this much mattered. His ranch was fenced, away from the city, and contained no villages. After the Orlovs were safely grazing at the ranch, the men of the 15th Infantry left to resume their military duties. For the thirsty men, the best way to beat Prohibition was to remain in the army, remain in the 15th, and, above all else, remain in China. Barton now turned his attention to the next stages of his breeding program. This included finding some cowboys to work the ranch away from world turmoil. Horses were not concerned with queues, foot binding, and opium. Before war closed in around the men of the 15th, the horses, like the men, just wanted to eat, drink, and roll around a bit.

• **Eleven** •

Montana Cowboys in the Celestial Empire, 1918–1920

The war in Europe and the drought in Montana are collapsed into a single catastrophe.[1]—Jonathan Raban, *Bad Land*

How the Montana cowboys came to China leads us to the story of the Morgans. Barton needed 650 Morgan studs to begin his breeding program. He bought them in small groups throughout the West and set up a temporary headquarters in Reno, Nevada, at a large pasture rented from George Winfield. At the time, Winfield owned much of Nevada. Horses came in from Montana, Wyoming, Utah, Nevada, and Oregon. Once the 650 were gathered in Reno, veterinarians examined them before the herd was shipped by rail to San Diego.

The trip went well at first for the Montana contingent. The horses traveled by boat to Manila. There, they were off-loaded for a week, then taken the rest of the way to China, landing at Shanhaikuan about 250 miles east of Tientsin. They went by Peking-Mukden Railway to Peking. Here plans for the ranch almost met with disaster. The train stopped about fourteen miles outside of Peking so the horses could be watered. Just at dawn, a Chinese man passed near the train with a caravan of fifty camels. The Western horses had never heard or smelled a camel before. One whiff of the strong caravan and the whole herd scattered, as Barton put it, "to hell and gone."[2] A week would be needed for the cowboys to find all the horses and bring them back to the railroad siding.

After that disaster, they switched trains at Peking to the French-run Peking-Hankow Railroad to Chentai. They transferred again for the trip into Taiyuanfu at Shihchiachuang, where the route changed to narrow-gauge tracks only three meters wide. From that fairly nondescript junction and its old hotel, the train began its eight-hour gradual climb to the Niangtzekuan Pass and its swift mountain streams. Beyond, on the high plateau, sat Taiyuanfu, the provincial capital. The land had been constantly rising since the coast. Beyond Taiyuanfu, on an even higher plateau, lay the ranch. The entire trip was accomplished by rail in China, except for the last miles from Taiyuanfu out to the ranch.

Assembling the components of Barton's ranch in China did not happen overnight. In 1919 and 1920 Barton picked up supplies, horses, and Montana cowboys he needed for China. Stories about Barton, the ranch, and his Montana recruits began to appear in the *Miles City Independent* and the *Miles City Daily Star*. A May 16, 1919, story in the *Independent* stated,

> Fred Barton, a former Custer county cow puncher, is at Tientsin, China. He has ordered two saddles with complete outfits from the Miles City saddlery company. Barton went to China about 10 years ago. He was here on a visit four years ago.[3]

The saddles mentioned above probably were some of those dedicated to Mongol princes discussed earlier.

The next year, the *Star* ran a May 24, 1920, article headlined "Hittin' for Unfenced Land of the Orient." Its subheadings stated, "Bunch of Untamed Cowpunchers Leaving Here Tuesday for China" and "Fred Barton Riding Close Herd on Some of Custer County's Star Riders." The article contains some of the creative spelling of the time, but it is worth quoting:

> Many of the visitors to the Miles City Round-Up this year will miss some of the best riders and ropers who have contributed largely to the success of similar celebrations in the past, they having decided to cross the Pacific and conquer the fastnesses [of] the mysterious east.
>
> Since the return to his old stamping grounds a month ago of Fred Barton, once known as one of the best cowpunchers that ever forked a bronk, has interested a number of his former stirrup partners in the possibilities of China, and more particularly in that part of the country in which he has made a spectacular success since leaving Miles City for the Orient ten years ago.[4]

Notice the article reports the ranch as already hugely profitable. Perhaps he had already made money selling Mongol ponies to the warlords or had been heavily bankrolled on the Chinese warlord dime. Or, perhaps he was making the venture sound good to attract men. In any case, Barton did have the money to purchase horses, train fare, and supplies. The article continues:

> Bert Putnam, Tut Camblin, John C. Oster, Jesse Perkins, Curley Wood, all splendid riders and ropers, and every one of them former star performers in the roundup celebrations held here in the past, are among those who have decided to tackle the land of the oriental of whom Bret Hart once asked, "For ways that are dark and tricks that are vain the heathen Chinese is peculiar." While Mr. Barton states that in his dealings with the celestial he has found them to be peculiar in many whys [*sic*], still there are splendid opportunities in that country for one who can ride and knows the ways of western ranges.
>
> The party, including Mr. Barton, expects to leave here tomorrow for the west coast to embark on their long voyage, which usually takes about 25 days to complete. They will go to Mr. Barton's large holdings in Tien Tsin, North China. It is reported that Denver Sherman is also seriously considering going across with the "gang," all of whom express the hope that he will so decide.

The Montana nucleus for the ranch was forming. More was revealed a few days later. The *Star*'s May 26 follow-up carried the headline, "Barton Party Starts for Chinese Ranges." The article read:

> Fred Barton, representative of the Chinese government, with his crew of future Chinese range riders, consisting of "Tut" Camblin, Jess Perkins and John Oster, left last night on Milwaukee No. 17 for Butte. Colie Ward, another member of the party, is enroute to San Francisco in charge of a consignment of American saddle horses, and within the next few days all will meet with Bert Putnam, who has charge of a large number of brood mares, the whole outfit embarking from San Diego on the Pacific steamship Dix for the Orient.

They expect to go via Honolulu and Guam. Mr. Barton stated that he did not expect to return again from China, that he has selected for his permanent home.[5]

The "American saddle horses" were Barton's Morgans on their way over. The article also shows Barton not claiming the ranch as his own, but states he is a "representative" of the Chinese. No longer is he a merchant from Shanghai as formerly stated on his passport.

The story gained national traction as well, as newspapers across the country picked up on a Helena, Montana, byline. For instance, Wisconsin's *Eau Clair Leader* covered Barton's China project in "Montana Cowboys Head for China: Cattle Raising in the Land of the Celestials Will Take Wild West Flavor":

> "Powder River—let 'er buck"—the battle cry that carried the Montana fighting men through the late war will soon be heard in the land of pigtails and pagodas.
> Fred Barton, in the old days a cow puncher on the Montana plains, who more recently took over the business of raising cattle in China, is here organizing a party of old time punchers who are due to ride in the celestial empire, where Barton has large cattle interests.
> According to Barton, the methods of herding and cattle raising in China aren't up to the general standards of the west and a few modern methods in that country should put the cattle raising business on the plane it should occupy.[6]

As seen in that press story, Barton used subterfuge to disguise what he was doing in China, going so far as to list on passport applications and passenger lists that he was in the cattle business or private livestock business when he was actually raising horses for the warlords.

What was not subterfuge was Barton's picking of the very best cowhands. Barton stated, "If a roundup boss on the roundup had as many as five top bronc riders and five or six top ropers with his crew of twenty-five men, he was lucky, but the rest were all good cowhands and did their work well."[7] Not even Barton's hero, Charlie Russell, considered himself a top rider or roper. As roundup boss of the Far East, Barton made sure his small team would be nothing but top fives.

Cowpuncher names mentioned in the newspaper articles represent men who did go to China. Their written and oral family histories, photographs taken in China, and obituaries corroborated the newspaper accounts of their departure. As the *Star* pointed out, the men who were mentioned were well known in the community as proven roundup stars and cowboys. What happened to them made news. They would be missed at the Miles City Round-Up.

Take the case of Tut Camblin, often referred to in print as "Tute" Camblin. The year before, on July 11, 1919, the *Independent* announced that Tut, whose real name was Custer, had headed in from Wason Flats for the roundup and was "enthusiastic in his attitude toward the event and took occasion to visit the Slippery Gulch, where he broke the crap game and nearly ruined the management of the roulette games."[8] The games of chance must have inspired him, for he made another $25 on the last day of the roundup by placing third in the steer roping contest. Earlier he had also placed first in the cowboy race. In the bulldogging contest, the paper said he had made a good catch right in front of the grandstand crowd, and he led the event at one point.

Tut was best known as a bronc rider. Some called him *the* best. Paddy Ryan, who earned the World's Saddle Bronc Riding Championship in Madison Square Garden in 1923 and was inducted into the Cowboy Hall of Fame in 1978, worked on the same ranch as Tut and learned how to ride from him. When Ryan was asked what kind of cowboy Tut was, he replied, "I was just a kindergartner, and he was a graduate when it came to cowboying."[9] Later Tut would be the honored grand marshal for the Miles City Round-Up and Bucking Horse Sale.

Gambling caused Tut to go to China in the first place.[10] Prior to his China excursion, he bought his own ranch near Miles City. The ranch was so successful that he sold it, thinking he could retire on the money he received. But after two years of playing the ponies, particularly at racetracks in Mexico, he was already cleaned out. He had to go to China to support his family. Tut would bet on anything, and bet big. Sometimes he bet big on the very small. Once he walked into a Miles City drinking establishment where a very pregnant pussycat reclined on the back-bar. One of the other imbibers announced that he believed the cat would have a certain number of kittens, whereupon Tut bet $500 on a different number. History has not recorded how many kittens made up the litter or whether Tut won, but the story reveals how Tut loved to bet on anything. Going to China was one of those gambles.

Earlier he had gambled on marriage. His first wife was a Miles City madam who may have helped Tut achieve a kind of immortality in another way. He and his wife went out in a buggy one day so Tut could apply for a job at a ranch. Tut was decked out in his city suit and laced yellow shoes. There was nothing cowboy about him. After sizing up this dolled-up gent from the buggy, the foreman said Tut would have to mount a horse and prove he could ride. Then—just maybe—the foreman might think about whether to hire him or not. Of course Tut could see they were giving him the rankest horse that had never been ridden. He asked the foreman, "Don't you think I ought to have spurs?" The man reckoned he did, so loaned him his. Tut put them on upside-down!

Furthermore, once the horse was saddled, Tut made sure his right foot never reached the stirrup by hooking his leg on the bronc's right shoulder instead. To the foreman, this city slicker clearly had no idea of what he was doing. Tut proceeded to prove he was, as others described him, "one heck of a bronc rider." Tut's family to this day remain convinced that someone either heard about this event or was there to witness it resulting in the Marty Robbins song "The Cowboy in the Continental Suit." Actually, by going to Asia, Tut became intercontinental.

Others who went to China or thought about it also participated that year in the 1919 Miles City Round-Up. "Little Pinkie" was listed in the bareback contest as well as other events. Charles Albert "Bert" Putnam, who went by the name of Pinkie, was photographed in China among the Montana riders. His image also appeared on roundup or rodeo postcards. He maintained his Western roots, dying in Edgemont, South Dakota, in 1935.

"Germany" John Oster (sometimes referred to as J.C. Osler in the newspaper) was also photographed working at the Shansi ranch in China. Germany could speak German because his German-Russian family came from Odessa to settle in Colorado. He competed in the Cowboy Catch and Saddle and Steer Roping events in the 1919 roundup. After he helped Barton start the Shansi ranch, Germany returned to Montana to become captain of the guards at the Montana State Prison at Deer Lodge. The prison needed someone dependable who knew how to handle himself and others, given the deplorable conditions at one of the most unprogressive prisons in the nation. The prison used convict labor on its own ranch, made famous in the closing scene of *Rancho Deluxe* (1975) starring Sam Waterston and Jeff Bridges as cattle thieves. As a single man and aging cowboy, Germany had done all right for himself, despite the Great Depression and his lack of education.

In 1931 the captain was found slumped dead in his car a mile outside of Butte with a bullet in his head. His revolver lay on the floor. According to news coverage in the May 25–26, 1931, issues of the *Greeley Daily Tribune*, Butte authorities ruled Germany's death a suicide and sent his body back to Greeley, Colorado, near where his family's home ranch was located. Before his body could be interred, the local sheriff, German's family and his friends questioned the circumstances of his death. They called in their own medical examiner, who took photographs of the corpse.

The Coloradoans did not believe that this cowboy who had survived China had died by his own hand. For one thing, he had been communicating with friends about how he was looking forward to taking time off to visit Alaska. The coroner also observed that the bullet's entry point in Germany's skull did not match that of a suicide attempt. In addition, two other severe scalp wounds revealed where bullets had grazed his head. They also learned his car had five bullet holes in its roof. As handy as Oster was with a six-shooter, it would not have taken him five or six shots to kill himself with a revolver aimed at his own head. Hard to miss at that range. The sheriff sent the results back to Butte and asked to be kept informed of the results of an inquest. But Butte was Butte, and authorities there stuck to the party line that Germany had committed suicide. Butte police maintained that Germany had tried to shoot himself several times but missed! To Coloradoans, corrupt Butte mined copper but paid little mind to the credibility of its coppers.

Denver Sherman, who thought about going to China, had competed in saddle bucking contests in earlier Miles City Round-Ups as well as in other events. He had won the wild-horse race, and in 1917 also showed his four-hoofed acumen by riding a bull backwards. In lieu of professional rodeo clowns, these cowboys provided their own antics and skill for the crowd.

In terms of longevity, Tut Camblin outlasted the other cowboys who worked in China. After their China years, Barton knew where Tut was too, for in Barton's interview with the Montana Historical Society in 1955, he stated that only one cowboy of the China bunch was still living, and that cowboy lived in Boise. According to Camblin's obituary in the *Idaho Statesman*, Tut C. Camblin was 92 when he died on the last day of December 1977, having been born August 13, 1885, in Falls City, Nebraska. This agrees with Barton's knowledge of his cowboys. Barton said he hired only cowboys older than himself so he could be sure he had responsible hands who would stick to their jobs. He wanted seasoned men from ages 35 on up. Camblin would have been just that in 1920.

Camblin rode the ranges in both Wyoming and Montana before marrying his second wife, Ida Hauck, in 1919 and going to China in 1920. He was not alone in China, for he took Ida and his baby girl, Betty, with him. According to the Camblin family, Ida and Tut had previously lost another child at their Miles City ranch. The girl had slipped into the corral, and before anyone could save her, the stud killed her. Everyone thought very highly of Ida, and Tut "wasn't afraid of God, Devil, or death, but he was afraid of Ida."[11] What would Tut have to fear from the Chinese? He had Ida. The Chinese learned that Ida and Betty were indeed forces to be reckoned with, as will be seen shortly. The presence of Ida and Betty may have been the encouragement needed for the Shansi ranch to import a dairy cow from Australia and to put in a typical American vegetable garden. The cow was said to be the only milk cow in all North China and a source of pride for Barton.

Tut Camblin's obituary claims that he chartered the USN *Dix* to transport 150 horses to Shansi, China, for breeding. The facts do not seem quite right compared to those given by other sources, but they are close enough. The *Dix* was not a navy ship, and the number of horses may be off. Likewise, how could he have chartered the *Dix* when he was leaving Miles City at the same time as Barton to rendezvous with the ship? On another occasion, he recollected that he had gone over to China on the *Dix* with eighty mares and six studs out of Miles City, and that only one horse was lost at the port of San Pedro. The horse was dropped during the loading process when the horses had to be lifted aboard and lowered into the hold. Despite some inconsistencies, his obituary corroborates the China story.

Recent family members also have made mention of Tut's China trip, again with some inconsistencies, as understandably the story has been bent a bit over time. Generally, most of the story passed down in the family to Tut's great-great niece and youngest daughter of Tut's namesake, holds true to the known facts. Tiffany Schwenke reported that Tut met representatives of the Chinese government in Montana, where he agreed to their horse breeding program. Along with two other cowboys, he gathered a large band of "big saddle horse type mares," buying them as they moved from Miles City through Idaho, Nevada, and California. The horses went by boat from San Francisco and up the Yangtze River 1,200 miles into the interior of China, where they were entrained the rest of the way to the ranch.[12] Barton was the "Chinese representatives." Although the boat carrying the horses did not come very close to the Yangtze, the horses were moved by rail across China.

Tut and his family did not stay long in the Orient. At the end of two years, local governor Yen Hsi-shan lost a big battle against one of the other warlords in an adjoining province. In full retreat, Yen's army took shelter in Taiyuanfu, leaving the countryside undefended. This included the horse ranch. Tut and his family fled for their lives, leaving with only the proverbial shirts on their backs. Fortunately Tut had sent earnings back to the U.S. This provided them with a nest egg to start again. Ironically, Tut went to China gambling he would make a fortune, but he left with none in his pocket.

The Camblins became residents of Idaho in the early 1920s. Instead of visiting clubs as he had done in Miles City with the Slippery Gulch, Tut owned his own clubs. His first nightclub, complete with dance hall, pool tables, and bar, opened up in the Idaho mining town of Placerville. He owned and operated the Placerville Club from 1931 to 1941, followed by the Sawtooth Club from 1941 to 1946. Of the latter, he said he made more money "than he thought there was."[13] Afterwards he owned a dairy farm from 1946 to 1957, when he retired. Before he died, he passed on to his namesake a few items. To his nephew T.J. "Tut" Camblin of Gillette, Wyoming, he presented the spurs, bridle, and bit he had used in Montana and then in China. He also passed on the trophy saddle he won in Haynes, Oregon, for first place in saddle bronc riding during his first year back from China.

Ida lived until May of 1981, attaining the age of 93. Her obituary differs somewhat from Tut's in terms of the China account. The *Idaho Statesman* reported that she had spent "several years" in China after marrying Tut on November 11, 1921, rather than the earlier reported date of 1919. Again, the reported facts seem educated guesses or slips in memory common to obituaries, but the China story is there. Ida was born just a few years before Barton on October 3, 1887, in Perham, Minnesota. She attended telegraphy school in St. Paul, Minnesota. Obviously Tut and Ida were mature adults when they married and set out for China.

As Tut and Ida would later describe it to relatives in Wyoming, Ida's life on the ranch near Taiyuanfu was not that hard. Just as the Fifteenth Infantry in Tientsin had its own servants, so did Ida. She did not have to concern herself with washing, cooking, and mending. Christian Chinese did that work. Non-Christian Chinese never posed a threat to them because of their daughter, Betty. The Chinese feared red hair, a sign that the person contained the devil. Betty had devilishly red hair. Shopping became easy for Ida because the merchants quickly sold her anything to get rid of her and her daughter. People crossed the streets in Taiyuanfu to avoid meeting not only the foreign devil woman but also her daughter, a foreign devil in name on the outside who contained a real devil on the inside squeezing out through the hair roots. Ida and Betty could go anywhere without fear of being physically harmed or robbed. Ranch staff, who were Christians, did not share these fears and carried on good relationships with the Camblins.[14]

Tut Camblin also produced a short autobiography for *Fanning the Embers*, a book which gives thumbnail sketches of historical people in the Miles City area. The book contains an excellent photo of Tut wearing chaps and standing with his horse. Most of the autobiography discusses ranches and people he knew and worked for. Highlights include his telling of working with a herd of longhorns in Wyoming that was so big it took two days to load them into train cars. They even branded 1,500 calves after supper. He thought he might have been the youngest cowboy to run an outfit in Montana, and he remembered bringing one of the last trail herds from Wyoming to Miles City.

He discussed his China experience briefly in this account. He had been in charge of a boatload of "seventy-eight" head of breeding horses (the number has shifted again). These horses were shipped in "1902." His reference to 1902 has caused a problem in dating and seems to be an impossible date. If the last two numbers are transposed to make up for typographical error, the date becomes 1920, which agrees with newspaper accounts. Camblin goes on to say that they used the "Transport Dickes Lines." There wasn't such an animal, but this does conform to using the U.S. Army Transport *Dix*. He recalled four cowboys in total going over with the horses on the *Dix*.

In orally recounting the China trip in later years, Tut also remembered having to switch the Montana horses onto the narrow-gauge railroad for the final leg into Shansi Province. Tut had familiarity with railroads. Just before he worked in Montana and went to China he had worked in Wyoming with his brother. After working on some Wyoming ranches, Tut started his own freighting business with string horses. With his brother, he freighted for the railroad survey team between Douglas, Wyoming, and either Billings or Miles City, Montana. When the survey team reached Buffalo, Wyoming, Tut had had enough. He quit the business and went on to Miles City to cowboy and to find his yellow-laced shoes while his brother returned to Gillette, Wyoming.

As youths, Tut and his older brother Edwin Earl "Cam" Camblin both fled their abusive father in Nebraska. Cam ran away first, trying to get on with the Dalton gang, but he was rejected as being too young.[15] He took work with the Ogallala Cattle Company, where he sharpened his cowboy skills. Then came the horrible winter of 1886–1887 and accompanying drought. Charlie Russell's painting *The Last of the 5000* didn't apply just to Montana. Wyoming and other states also suffered. In what survived of the herds, every cow now counted. Sneaking your brand onto someone else's cow could keep a ranch afloat. The struggle for rangeland was on. The Johnson County War broke out in 1892. It was also called the Wyoming Range War or Powder River War, and Cam ended up in the middle of it. The war went beyond just a struggle for grasslands and cattle. Water rights became just as precious. Homesteaders were killed for the precious liquid.

Cam became a shotgun guard for W.C. "Bill" or "Billy" Irvine. Irvine, a stockman, led a contingent of over fifty big stockmen and hired Texas gunslingers as "Regulators." This armed force from the Wyoming Stock Growers Association sought to rid what they considered to be *their* ranges of rustlers and other interlopers. They shot, lynched, and burned out anyone seen as threatening the monopoly of the WSGA. At the time, a cowboy could not start a ranch for himself. The WSGA saw to it that bonds were set so high for cattle bidders that no cowboy had enough money to even bid on a steer. The war set small ranchers and nesters against the big, established interests who saw public lands as their own.

The Johnson County War provided everything that would appeal to Hollywood, novelists, and television—vigilantes, hired guns, corrupt judges, shoot-outs, women being killed, sheriff's posses, cavalry, Horse Soldiers, rustlers, small farmers and ranchers vs. moneyed interests, and "get a rope." Its themes have been mythologized in such motion pictures as *Shane, The Virginian, The Redhead from Wyoming, True Grit,* and *Heaven's Gate,* to name a few. From Paladin's *Have Gun Will Travel* to Matt Dillon's *Gunsmoke,* at least one episode of just about every Western television series took something from the Johnson County War.

The Banditti of the Plains (1893), one of the most suppressed books in the history of U.S. publishing, resulted from the war. Its author, Asa Shinn Mercer, was one of the founding fathers of Seattle. He had moved to Cheyenne, Wyoming, to publish the *Northwest Livestock Journal*, an organ basically supportive of big cattle interests in the West. This all changed when Mercer saw what those interests were doing to smaller ranchers. As an eyewitness to the violence of the Regulators, he wrote his nonfiction book to expose what had taken place. The Livestock Growers sued, and for a time Mercer was jailed for sending what was considered obscene matter through the U.S. mail. Such was the political power of the WSGA. Its members tracked down and destroyed nearly every copy of the book's first printing. Even the Library of Congress copy disappeared. The printer's second edition was hijacked and destroyed. Mercer's offices were burned down and the book plates destroyed.[16]

With bloody retributions continuing on both sides, it is no wonder that Tut's brother was employed as a shotgun guard during and after this war. Strangely, Cam's boss, Bill

Postcard for the 1919 Miles City Round-Up.

Irvine, remained a Democrat. Other Regulator leaders and ranch bosses were Republicans, including some politicos who joined the WSGA small army. Public outrage became so great over the misdeeds of the Regulators and their perceived help from Republican president Harrison that Wyoming uncharacteristically went Democratic in the next election.

By then, the time of the open range ruled by a few large ranchers had passed. Cowboys such as the Camblins now had a chance to have their own outfits. Tut established himself as a cowboy in Montana, and his brother created a ranch out of some purchased or relinquished homesteads around the Pumpkin Buttes out of Gillette, Wyoming. While Tut went with Barton to China to breed a new kind of horse, Cam succeeded in doing a similar thing in Wyoming. He wanted a faster horse than his excellent Texas cow horses, so he brought in a thoroughbred from Kentucky. The results were fast, cow-savvy horses that worked equally well as polo horses and U.S. Cavalry remounts.

Barton could have used both horsemen brothers in China, as Cam loved nothing more than playing cards. This was a handy pastime to have in negotiating with Chinese warlords, but Tut was no slouch when it came to gambling either. Taking his family to China was playing a big hand. Tut would face conflict in Shansi far bigger than the Johnson County War.

Jess Perkins' past also sheds light on the China ranch experience. Perkins was another of Barton's Miles City cowboy acquaintances. The Range Riders Museum in Miles City displays a photo of Perkins on a bucking horse in 1917. His family left Texas to homestead in Stoneville, now Alzada, Montana, in 1905. When Barton asked Jess to sign on, Jess wired his brother Newt, who was on the rodeo circuit in Iowa. Newt decided not to go, but Jess did. However, once Perkins reached China, a squabble broke out over pay. Apparently

Eleven • *Montana Cowboys in the Celestial Empire, 1918–1920*

he was neither getting paid nor being given the money he demanded for a ticket back to Miles City. Being very big, he presented a strong, physical case. He received his ticket. That was enough travel for him. He cowboyed the rest of his life in Montana. His lack-of-pay story coincides with the time the Camblins fled from China.

Samuel "Colie" Washington Ward, like Perkins, was photographed in China. Barton hired him shortly after Colie returned from World War I, during which time he served in Battery D of the 347th Field Artillery of the 91st Division, American Expeditionary Force. The 91st, or Wild West, Division was known for its war whoop, "Powder River: Let 'er Buck," attesting to the cowboy nature of the unit. Ward fought in the St. Mihiel, Meuse-Argonne, and Ypres-Lys offensives. He was certainly prepared for whatever China had to throw at him, especially postwar, when cowboys needed work. After China, this "Let 'er Buck" cowboy would claim the American West as home the rest of his life. He died in Tucson in 1956.

An accomplished cowboy, Ward had worked for the L.O. Ranch on Mizpah Creek, a tributary of the Powder River in southeastern Montana. The L.O., principally a cattle ranch, at one time ran as many as 15,000 head. The L.O. also ran several hundred stock horses and worked an area from the Tongue River to Box Elder Creek (about 80 miles as the crow flies). Colie was what his L.O. saddle partner, Casey Barthelmess, called a fellow "bronc peeler." Casey was the son of Christian Barthelmess, the photographer stationed at Fort Keogh. Together in 1917 Colie and Casey participated in one of the great events of Miles City Round-Up history.

Just as roundups and rodeos boast their cowboy stars, every so often a horse comes along that becomes legendary. During the early years of the Miles City Round-Up that

Bert "Pinkey" Putnam shown bareback riding at Miles City before heading for Taiyuanfu.

Colie Ward (left) and unidentified friends (author's collection compliments of Elaine Rhea).

horse was Skyrocket. Just as Wyoming touts its iconic bronc, Steamboat, whose logo image graces the state's license plates, Montana's beloved equivalent was Skyrocket. Only five or six riders stayed on the big bay during his twenty years of putting cowboys in full-body plaster casts. If a cowboy drew Skyrocket as his ride, he was assured of winning the competition—if he could stay on. Some of those who did manage to stay up on the over half-ton of fury were able to do so only because they had an unfair advantage when a muddy arena softened Skyrocket's jarring moves. On hard ground, Skyrocket turned into a one-horse Book of Revelation. His antics caused nosebleeds, blackouts, and ribs to break, despite the rider wearing a corset.

Skyrocket was a natural performer. He'd lower himself almost down to his belly while the rider swung on. Then he skyrocketed straight up into the air, twisting and turning while doing so, only to land stiff-legged to jar the rider into insensibility. Skyrocket made sure he did this in the very middle of the arena so that everyone could see the carnage. He even tested Yakima Canutt, pioneer stuntman and mentor to John Wayne. Other roundup standouts with Hollywood stars in their eyes learned humility and were given healing lengths of time from Skyrocket. Skyrocket's owner at the time, Ray Warner of the 71 Ranch on the Tongue River, sent a postcard to his girls showing Skyrocket making quick work of a Miles City bronc rider. On the card he wrote, "Write girls to me if you can find time. This is a rodeo man trying one of my horses out. He wouldn't show this one in the moovies [sic] when he went to California, but many of our boys can ride him."[17]

With Colie Ward's help, Casey became the last to ride the legend. Some said it was the greatest ride ever. Skyrocket had good breeding and was intelligent. The first problem was just getting on him. Although Miles City used chutes for the first time that year to make mounting easier, Skyrocket was the featured horse for the roundup. That meant he needed to be mounted in front of the grandstand without use of the chute.

Ward was able to "ear" Skyrocket down so that he could be blindfolded and saddled. Casey said that Skyrocket was "proud and honest." Generally he would "wait while the rider pulled the wrinkles out of his drawers and made other adjustments, and when his ears were turned loose, you realized why he was a horse of reputation."[18] As soon as the blindfold was removed and Casey was in the saddle, Skyrocket barreled into Colie and sent him flying in the dirt. Casey stayed on. Both Casey and Colie survived—Colie to go on to China—but Skyrocket shortly was not so fortunate. No one rode the horse successfully the following year. When he was turned out to pasture for that winter, it was the last anyone saw of Skyrocket. Today we can enjoy seeing this great performer only illustrated on postcards and photographs of the time.

Skyrocket's namesakes do live on. In the 1950s on the revolutionary afternoon television show Walt Disney's *Mickey Mouse Club*, the show featured within it a miniseries of *Spin and Marty*, in which the two young fellows vied for the affection of Annette Funicello. Marty's horse did not wear her sweaters or swimsuits, but made out with the name Skyrocket. On the rodeo circuit, Skyrocket's tradition continued when in 1974 another of his namesakes tied for top bareback horse honors at the National Finals Rodeo.

Just as photographs exist of Colie Ward, Casey, and Skyrocket at the Range Rider Museum, a later photo of another Skyrocket appears in a book at the Custer Country Library. Groneberg's *The Secret Life of Cowboys* described a grainy photo of a rider on Skyrocket at the 1960 Miles City Round-Up and Bucking Horse Sale. The rider is a blurry mess of "teeth, legs, and leather."[19] The blurry mess was Ted Kennedy, who came to town as his brother's western campaign manager in JFK's run for the presidency. In Ted Kennedy's autobiography, *True Compass: A Memoir*, he described how the roundup was in progress when he arrived. Kennedy knew a good thing when he saw it. He wanted to address the captive crowd. When he asked the rodeo announcer if he could have the microphone for a few minutes, in the usual laconic Montana cowboy manner the announcer said, "Nope." The announcer added that the only way the Easterner could be announced to the crowd would be for him to ride a bronc, since the current event of bronc riding was the last event of the day. If he rode, he would draw a horse named Skyrocket.

Kennedy agreed, but lacked equipment. An old-timer lent him hat, spurs, and boots, and took the ride in front of Kennedy's in order to show young Kennedy how to get on the horse, what to hang on to, and how not to get killed in the chute as the horse tried to bite him and splinter wood. When it came Kennedy's turn, he actually stayed on for seven seconds, earning him the time to address the crowd. All he needed to say was, "You know there's a horse called Skyrocket." The crowd went wild. "And he wants you to vote for John Kennedy."[20] Enough said.

Skyrocket would have had good, wild company had he gone to China with Colie Ward. All the horses shipped from the United States aboard the *Dix* were unbroken, so there were plenty of horses on which to practice "bronc peeler" skills in Shansi province. China was a new Old West, and 1919 and 1920 were good years to leave Miles City for a broader expanse if a person had the yearning. Shansi provided good escape from the influenza epidemic that continued the World War I killing. The Miles City newspaper listed the mounting family deaths, sometimes whole families. Many soldiers returned to find the herds they had left behind had strayed and disappeared, or the people left to care for them were dead. They had to start from scratch, only there was no scratch. As if that were not enough, the West became a tinderbox, and fires began blowing up. The gunsmoke of martial arms had been traded for forests and prairies going up in smoke, particularly in western Montana around Missoula. The smoke drifted east to Miles City. Most of all, being a cowboy and raising horses in eastern Montana had changed.

The end of World War I in 1918 provided the primary impetus for change. As late in the war as 1917, the army still advertised in the Miles City newspapers to purchase five- to nine-year-old horses. These solid-color horses had to stand fifteen to sixteen hands high. The government would pay $150 for a cavalry mount, $180 for light artillery, and $225 for heavy artillery. As can be seen from this, the small cow pony was on the way out. At war's end, ranchers looked for heavier horses too as they turned from cattle ranching to mixed agricultural farms. The range began to fill up again with excess light-weight scrub horses.

End-of-war prices exacerbated the whole situation. Horse prices at Miles City in 1919 fell to $12 a head. Many horsemen refused to sell at those prices. They simply drove their horses from the auction pens back onto the open range. J.H. Dion described one such incident. One of the big English outfits near Glendive, Montana, was contracted to sell horses at $100 a head. When Hadley Robinson, in charge of delivering the horses, bunched them up on the other side of the Yellowstone River ready for delivery, the buyers said they could give only $90 a head. Hadley then turned the whole bunch back out on the open range. Later the horses sold to the canners at $10 apiece. Around 1927 almost all the horses went out of Dawson County, and as Dion described it, "every kid with a rope went down to the stockyards and roped himself a colt and took it home."[21] Horses went for practically nothing.

Making matters worse, Oregon's changing agriculture severely impacted Miles City. Oregonians shifted from rangeland to wheatland and farms, replacing draft horses and cow ponies with mechanical tractors and harvesters. Excess horses streamed into Miles City from Oregon by the trainload. Nearly all were headed for canneries. For Barton and his cowboys, this was the optimal time to choose good stock at a low price.

The CBC outfit operated the biggest business in eastern Montana, even though it was not a Montana enterprise. Cowboys lucky enough to find work hired on as CBC cowboys working for the Chaple Brothers Cannery of Illinois. At one point they ran 60,000 horses over the eastern third of Montana between the Yellowstone and Missouri rivers. Through the U.S. government, the cannery exported most of its horsemeat to Russia.[22] Like Cam Camblin, Philip Chaple had started out selling remounts to the army. Unlike Camblin, he quickly changed to selling Ken-L-Rations for dogs. A good horse was a canned horse.

The end of the war brought a glut of military horses, while the range filled up with unwanted scrub. Upon being discharged, some former cowboys serving in the military purchased their army mounts at cheap rates and returned to Montana. This applied to horses that remained in the States during the war. Only a handful of horses sent overseas returned. Most were killed in the fighting. Those lucky enough to survive were left to feed starving Europeans. Returning soldiers made a booming business for the saddle makers but not for horse dealers.

One soldier, John Glickman of Custer County, bought his army horse when he was discharged from Fort Dix. Giving roping exhibitions and performing other stunts, Glickman began riding the horse across the continent from New Jersey back to Montana— a 1,900-mile ride. Sometimes his performances were impromptu, as when he just happened to appear at the Minnesota State Fair. Glickman's qualifications to put on a good show stemmed from his work on ranches and performances with Buffalo Bill and Pawnee Bill. He worked with Douglas Fairbanks during the filming of *The Good Bad Man* in the Mojave Desert in 1915. Before volunteering for the military in 1917, he served as a guide in Yellowstone. Now all the roosters, human and otherwise, were coming home from the war to roost.

The range did not need all these cowboys and did not need the scrub. Arguments waged over what to do with the small horses that glutted Montana. The Montana Livestock Association wanted them driven off the range. Some proposed building a rendering plant in Miles City. Light range horses would be turned into food that could be shipped abroad, particularly to a starving postwar Europe. Chaple Brothers Cannery of Illinois had the answer. Horses that had made the cattle drives possible met a sad end. Quite the reverse was occurring in China.

At the same time Miles City newspapers bemoaned the fate of scrub horses and ran articles in which old-timers reminisced about the Old West, these same papers headlined articles that ran "China in Turmoil Again." Warlords needed horses. Go west, young man. Go west. Way west. Why reminisce when the memory could still be lived? Lucrative work on a ranch in an Old West setting, albeit a Far East Old West one, made economic sense.

• Twelve •

When to Hold 'Em, When to Fold 'Em, 1920–1937

Even the blind open their eyes (like saucers) at money.—Chinese saying

All this fighting is just a rehearsal in case war is declared.—Charles M. Russell (Cable from China)

In addition to the Orlovs and Morgans, Barton initially needed 2,000 ponies supplied by the Mongol princes via Kalgan. He quickly found out he needed more, many more. The ranch required a constant supply every year from Mongolia. The deal concocted between Yen His-shan and the Department of War in Peking required that Barton provide several thousand horses a year to the Chinese, friend or foe. As Owen Lattimore put it, "The horse business in ancient China was like the munitions business today. You bought from and sold to your enemies."[1]

Just as at Miles City auctions, sale horses needed to be four-year-olds. Facing these staggering numbers in the thousands, and the lack of four-year-olds in his breeding program for years, Barton told Yen the plan was preposterous. Yen laughed and told him not to worry. Yen schemed to supply the other warlords with around 500 horses bred at the ranch per year. The balance would be made up with Mongol ponies; however, the Chinese government would be billed as if the horses were all Morgan/Orlov crosses. Barton would buy ponies from the Mongols at twelve dollars a head, then sell them for $350.[2]

Shades of Barton's earlier coffin-making scheme! Only this scam could put him in a coffin. But this was the way business was done in China. Such a sweet deal, except a person would have to be careful if he valued his life. There was absolutely no competition, and Barton and his bosses planned to keep it that way. The ranch was kept secret, which explained why travelers passing through Taiyuanfu never heard of Barton or the ranch located off the beaten path. Barton and the cowboys stayed out of town. Yen came to them. When Ida and Betty Camblin shopped in town, they could easily be mistaken by any outsider for a Shansi missionary wife and child.

Working with the warlords, with this much money and with this kind of slippery deal, worried Barton. His life could be endangered by any misstep, so he turned to his earlier British-American Tobacco experience. That insight and lessons into Chinese business dealings gave him a winning poker hand. He had been told to "never let a

Chinaman owe you more money than he thinks you are worth," because if that happened, you would be invited to your last meal. It would be lavish, and you would be the special guest. Poison would lace the soup.

Despite the huge sums of money to be transferred each year, when it came time to ship horses, Barton made sure the Chinese never owed him more than $10,000 at any one time. He felt he was worth at least that much to them. Replacing him would cost more. Barton must have estimated his figures accurately, or else he came in with a very conservative figure. If ever there was a time to be conservative, this was it.

To ensure a steady supply of ponies, Barton got on the good side of the Mongols right away. Since the time of Genghis Khan (1167–1227), Mongolia had been ruled under separate princes with their own hereditary banners. Barton invited the twelve Mongol princes to his ranch for ten days of entertainment. Come they did. They rode in complete with families and advisory staffs. Barton played the good host by putting on a Wild West show. His Montana wranglers put on roping, shooting, and riding exhibitions. Although the visitors were accomplished riders born in the saddle, they had never seen anything like the cowboys.

The Montanans performed trick shooting with their Colts and Winchesters. Anything thrown in the air came down with a hole in it. The men's roping skills seemed magical. Lariats made loops overhead, double loops, and loops to dance through while spinning like prayer wheels. The cowboys could rope more than one horse at a time with a single rope. They could rope casually anything with just a flip of the wrist. They could also ride anything. At full gallop, riders could stand on two horses, or crawl all the way underneath a horse and come up the other side.

Their demonstration of breaking a wild horse differed completely from the Mongol way. At first the princes were taken aback when seeing pictures of horses being roped, wrestled to the ground, cruelly branded, and broken. Mongols captured horses by using a 16-foot birch pole with a snugging loop attached to its end. Riding up to an unbroken horse, they would reach out with the pole, slip the loop around its neck, and then twist the pole until the loop tightened and choked the horse to a stop. Some would then use the "horse-whisperer" approach to gentle the animal. If that did not work, a pony was small enough to be thrown to the ground. While it was down, a dismounted man grabbed the horse's tail and held on to it. When the horse was released, it was like tying tin cans to a dog's tail or firecrackers to a cat's. The frightened horse tore off. Behind the horse, the man imitated water skiing, using his thick, slick, felt boots with upturned toes as skis to skid over the steppes. When the small horse soon tired, it was easily thrown down and saddled. The tail-dragger then mounted him. After the exhausted bronc made a few moves in protest, the horse was considered broken.

Montana cowboys would have none of that. High-plains skiing behind a mustang through Miles City prickly pear and yucca would not have worked. Besides, it was beneath a cowboy's dignity to work from the ground rather than the saddle. The only time worth grabbing a horse's tail was when a cowboy faced drowning while crossing a river. Choking down a big Orlov or Morgan with a Mongol version of a fishing rod and a loop was foolishly impractical, even deadly. The cowboys demonstrated to the princes that they cut through the Mongolian preliminaries. Each simply roped a horse, climbed aboard, and held on until the horse gave up. To save time, selecting horses that had been

Top: World Champion Paddy Ryan on Skyrocket. Wars in China may have been safer than Skyrocket. *Above:* Arrow indicates Colie Ward's leg sticking out of the dust as Skyrocket tries to pile drive him out of his misery after Ward removed the bronc's blindfold. Casey Barthlemess stays on board for the 1917 epic ride at the Miles City Round-Up.

half-broken the week before may have helped. Of course, the princes need not know about that. It was an old trick pulled on Wyoming and Montana ranches to hoodwink dudes. Nevertheless, the Americans' skills and toughness were impressive. The bucking horse rodeo put on quite a show.

Despite these differences, Mongols and Montanans shared much. This could be seen in the 1920s when the National Geographic Society sent groups on assignment to Mongolia and Shansi Province. These expeditions included magazine contributors Adam Warwick and Frederick and Janet Wulsin. Frederick Wulsin, an intelligence officer in World War I, mounted an expedition that passed through Taiyuanfu and by Barton's ranch. While the Wulsin expedition focused on the Chinese, Warwick focused on the Mongols. Both expeditions occurred in 1921, followed by others, at exactly the same time as Barton's cowboys showed what they could do.

In *National Geographic* magazine's "The Mongols: The People of the Wilderness," Adam Warwick's description of Mongolians applied equally to these horsemen and their American open range cowboy counterparts. He said these men cherished things other than money since there was little place to spend it on the range. City affairs and the rising cost of living really did not interest them. Both American and Mongolian spent so much time in the saddle that they had a rolling gait while walking. They did not need highways; they had the prairie instead, a natural uncrowded highway. They required little water, except the Mongol had to have his strong tea, the cowboy his strong coffee. Neither needed electricity. After a tiring day in the saddle, they turned in when darkness fell. They lived a free and elemental life with their animals, removed from police and courts, abiding instead by their own code.[3] Barton could not have said it better.

To top off impressing the Mongol princes, Barton presented gifts. He had purchased saddles from Coggshall in Montana and Visalia in San Francisco. Each prince received one of these saddles, a rawhide rope, a hackamore, a bridle, a Winchester repeating rifle with scabbard, and a Colt revolver with holster. The princes particularly took to the firearms because they had no access to such weapons in Mongolia. When a man is outnumbered, a Winchester can be "mighty comprehensive."[4]

From accounts of the cowboys who worked in Shansi, the ranch had its ups and downs. Barton said that the ranch did experience a turnover of Montana cowboys, but that a few stayed on through the whole period until 1937 to see an estimated 5,000–6,000 horses delivered to the Chinese army. Barton took his own bumps with the ranch and had to be careful of his position. In January 1921, newspaper articles datelined Taiyuanfu read as follows:

> Mr. Fred Barton, an American citizen, has resigned from the managership of the Shansi Government Live-Stock Bureau on the first day of January, 1921. From now on he will be personally responsible for all his future dealings with others and the management of the above Bureau will be taken over by the former director, Mr. Guey Shing Nan. G.S. NAN, Director of the Shansi Government Live-Stock Bureau. Taiyuanfu, Jan. 4th, 1921.

The Shansi Livestock Bureau suffered nearly complete corruption. It was a futile position. A cowpuncher could not expect to fix it and live. Barton may have tried. Being a nononsense cowboy and respectful of his own life, Barton gave it a good try because of his relationship with Yen Hsi-shan, but then he resigned to save his own skin. He did not really have to fix the livestock bureau, for he had already served his purpose. His tenure as director stretched just long enough for Yen to send Barton to the U.S. with official status as a representative of the Chinese government to collect horses and seek U.S. approval for their transport to China. Once the Morgans from the American West arrived in Shansi, Barton's task centered on breeding horses, not directing other livestock breeding programs involving sheep and pigs. Thus, Barton's serving as livestock director became a brief matter of subterfuge and political expediency.

Aside from the Japanese invasion of Shansi in 1937, the worst time for the ranch occurred in 1922 when the Camblins escaped. Realize that Barton did not always face what his cowboys faced. He did not spend the whole year at the Shansi ranch but alternated back and forth between his home in Los Angeles and Shansi. He attended to the stock shipments for three months of the year at the ranch, but the rest of the time he would often be absent from China. This left hired hands on their own to face whatever came.

In 1922 it came. Joseph W. Stillwell, later appointed commander of all China's armed forces, was caught up in events near the ranch. Stillwell had worked with Shansi governor Yen Hsi-shan in 1921 to build an 82-mile road in the province using 6,000 Chinese laborers. The International Relief Committee of the Red Cross requested his services, so, similar to the soldiers furloughed to Barton, Vinegar Joe was detailed from the U.S. Army to Shansi Province. Here, on horse and on foot, he supervised the work. Because severe famine had struck China the year before, the road gave people work so they could earn money to feed themselves. It also provided a quicker means for moving emergency supplies and food into the area for future disasters.

Stillwell appreciated Barton's frequent houseguest, Yen Hsi-shan. The "Model Tuchun" or "Model Governor" was cordial, cultured, and keenly interested in improving the lot of his people. Since Yen controlled both the military and civilian government, he could call all the shots, assisted by his Oxford-educated Chinese secretary, who

---

——WAR——

HORSES

We will receive Horses for the U. S. Government the Last of Each Week at the Miles City Horse Sale Company Yards.

These Horses must be five to nine years old and stand fifteen to sixteen two hands high, solid colors and will accept dark greys.

    PRICES FOR CAVALRY - - $150.00
    LIGHT ARTILLERY - - - $180.00
    HEAVY ARTILLERY - - - $225.00

We will receive pack mules fourteen two and up. Lead and draft mules fifteen hands and up.

THIS INSPECTION WILL BE IN EFFECT UNTIL JULY 31ST ONLY.

Miles City Horse Sales Co.

Guy Crandall, Manager.

Newspaper advertisement for Miles City horses needed for the U.S. Army in World War I (*Miles City Independent*, July 6, 1917).

also served as dean of the engineering department at Shansi University. Yen, described by some as a big man "with hard eyes in a puffy face"[5] and by others as "genial [and] sunburned,"[6] determined that more money was to be made by improving the standing of his people than by taxing them into destitution. Yen tried to hide his money outwardly by showing signs of simplicity. He wore simple cotton garments rather than silk. In contrast, many warlords of the time dressed lavishly while living on taxes. When their people were taxed out and the army could not be paid, the only move left was to either let the army attack its own people or raid adjoining provinces. These armies contained the worst of the worst. A saying in China at the time went, "One does not use good iron to make nails." Soldiers were nails.

As Barbara Tuchman has pointed out, Yen was a different kind of reformer.[7] Usually Chinese reform meant improving the morals of the people. It's a time-honored political ploy that still has a modern ring to it. If you do not want to spend money on the people but want it for your own pet programs, family, friends, or self-enrichment, turn arguments into a question of national or state morals. Blame the state of affairs on bad schooling, materialism, foreign influence or immigrants, and the media. The Chinese leadership did just this.

Yen, however, wanted to improve their material lot. He experimented with reforestation, imported varieties of grain seed, and created primary and trade schools. He wanted all ten million of his people to read. He invited his soldiers to live in town with their families so they had community involvement, a family life, and the furnishings that come with that. As mentioned earlier, he fought against repressive Manchu customs, waging campaigns against foot-binding, opium (which some generals used to pay their troops), and queues.

He sold the shorn queues to the West, especially the United Sates, which had an insatiable need for hair and still does. Besides being used for eyelashes and wigs as it was in Yen's time, today the United States and other countries use human hair from China to provide anti-weed mats for commercial gardeners, oil-spill soakers, and L-cysteine amino acid used in baked goods, as in pizza dough and bagels. (Enjoy.)

The U.S. government wondered if Yen Hsi-shan could finally be the leader that China deserved. But trouble was brewing. Across the Yellow River to the south in the adjoining province of Shensi (not to be confused with Shansi, which is spelled with an a), the warlord and Christian general, Feng Yu-hsiang, watched the road construction in Shansi and wanted his own road. Appealing to the Red Cross, he was able to have chief engineer Stillwell transferred to his province. In the same way the Fifteenth Infantry was collecting intelligence in China, warlords collected military intelligence from the U.S. military. As Stillwell said of Feng, "He cares not if I build the road or not; he wants the dope on military affairs."[8]

The generals involved in the fracas that threatened Barton's ranch were as colorful as the Montana cowboys who worked there. Feng Yu-hsiang was no exception. Stillwell remarked that the big forty-one-year-old man with the shaved head lived just the opposite of the way Yen lived. Instead of a palace, Feng lived in Spartan quarters and was "a slow spoken bird ... a solid sort of guy with no airs who makes friends."[9] Feng took his idea of Christianity seriously. His men sang hymns as they marched, had to learn two new Chinese characters before each meal, and even invited their wives and daughters to learn. He, too, initiated public works such as irrigation projects much like Yen's in Shansi. Drinking and smoking were frowned upon. Instead of the usual British-American tobacco posters everywhere, Feng put up messages encouraging his people not to buy cigarettes and wine. So far, he had not attacked the opium trade, fearing that could cause revolution against him. He encouraged improving both body and mind. Men not only studied the Bible and learned to make shoes, sew clothes, and become blacksmiths, but they also learned how to do giant swings from the horizontal bar, performing a mini-Olympics in front of Stillwell.[10]

Just as Barton shuttled back and forth between California and China, so did Feng. Years later, shortly after General Stillwell's death, Mrs. Stillwell was at her home in Carmel, California, when a visitor was announced as "the Christian." In walked Feng with his "cannonball head" to express his condolences and mourn the loss of his friend.[11]

But his friend would not build the road for Feng. According to Stillwell's diaries, just as he was leaving Sian, the capital of Shensi, with several of Feng's officers who would head the road crew, Stillwell's carts and men were recalled. Feng learned that the Mukden Tiger, Chang Tso-lin, was moving on Peking and was out to control all of North China again. This time he threatened another warlord, Wu Pei-fu, who controlled the area around Peking. Feng had made a pact with Wu. Together they wanted to end Chang's menace in the north, so Feng organized his army to rush to Wu's aid.[12]

Diplomats regarded Wu Pei-fu as another possible candidate for the strong man China so desperately needed to end its fragmentation into warlord zones. As Edna Lee Booker, a journalist in China, pointed out, many Chinese saw Wu as a national hero. His name, Pei-fu, meant Trust and Confidence. Wu kept a painting of George Washington on the wall of his residence to convince journalists that he wanted to do for his country what Washington had done for the United States. He also composed a poem expressing his admiration for what Washington had done to unite a nation.[13] Wu hardly looked the part. His slenderness, fine bones, narrow head, aquiline nose, and carefully cultivated Mandarin vocabulary all bespoke of his being well born. He regarded himself as a public servant rather than as an autocrat. Some other warlords disliked him because he paid his troops regularly. His troops were tightly disciplined rather than being marauding looters as seen under other generals.

Wu drank a lot, which displeased Feng, who tried to trick Wu into drinking water instead of wine. Feng, a teetotaler, had married the Chinese secretary of the YMCA in Peking, but it had been Wu who had appointed Feng as military governor of Shensi.[14] Now Feng was returning the favor by rushing to his aid. Stillwell left Feng at the Shensi border and crossed into Shansi Province to catch the train at Taiyuanfu to Peking. His road building was done. On the way into Peking, he met Chang's troops on their way south to attack. He arrived just in time to watch the artillery clashes that raged at night outside the locked gates of Peking. The great Tiger of the North was defeated by the combined forces of Wu and Feng and sent packing to Manchuria.

Back in Taiyuanfu, Chang Tso-lin's loss put Yen Hsi-shan and the ranch in a precarious position. Not only was the horse business deal in limbo, the whole province could have gone under. Opposing the combined armies of Wu and Feng would have been difficult, particularly when Wu had solidified his grip on Peking. Feng's army could return home by traveling directly through Shansi. Feng would have a road all right, but it would be Yen's.

Somehow Yen must have cut a deal promising an alliance with Feng and Wu, because Yen retained power and the ranch remained. Although often short-lived, such deals were common among generals not eager to expend more manpower and money by fighting. Even Wu hedged his bet during the battle with Chang. Wu's men wore red armbands to identify themselves as his troops, but these could easily be removed in case Wu decided to join some other side if the battle did not go well. Yen may have had the money and munitions at his arsenal that the other two warlords needed.

The changeable ties between Chang Tso-lin and Yen did not seem those of brotherly love in the first place. When writer and adventurer Harry A. Franck visited Yen and Shansi Province during the Barton years, he reported that Yen had been able to keep his neutrality by paying "squeeze" to those who could overthrow him. Franck said, "It is almost publicly known that he gave one million two hundred thousand dollars each to Chang Tso-lin and Tsao Kun in the 'Anfu' days as 'military assistance.'"[15]

Money talks when war costs. The battle against Feng and Wu cost Chang $24 million, and when he took them on again in 1924, the rematch cost the Fengtiens $50–60 million.[16] Between 1916 and 1927, Manchurian militarists (Chang and Wu) took out $23 million in high interest loans from banks and the Japanese government. Shansi had earned a reputation for its bankers, and Yen's pockets were deep.[17] Within a few years of Chang's defeat at Peking, Feng and Wu would fight each other. Yen would throw in with Feng against Wu, Chang would become strong again, and Barton continued to reap profits. But for a short time in 1922, the panic must have been acute. It was time to ride.

Civilians had more to fear than the generals. Generals cut deals and lived by a code that existed between them; civilians didn't. Barton's ranch consisted of civilians, and, except for servants, they were all foreigners to boot, mostly Mongolians. This was not good.

Mongols and Chinese differed in about every way imaginable. Mongols lived in part on kumiss or yak milk. Chinese would not drink any milk because they believed it came from a urinary organ. For Mongols, white symbolized nobility, magic, luck (a white horse showing up on its own volition with saddle galls at the yearly Genghis Khan ceremony signaled his imminent return). For Chinese, white indicated mourning. One did not ride to war on a white horse. One did accept white horses as tribute. During the Qianlong period (1736–1795), the Bogdo Gegen, or high lama of Mongolia, presented the Qianlong emperor of China with the Nine Whites—eight white Mongolian ponies and one white camel—in exchange for silver and cloth.[18] Mongols would herd adders out of the way with a cloth. Chinese would kill them. Mongols lived in circular yurts. Chinese lived in huts, caves, and houses.

And then there were the foreign devils from Montana. Fortunately the warlord generals used foreign military advisors and had become friends with some Americans such as Stillwell. The rank and file soldier had not had that chance. Generals distinguished between political relationships and personal relationships. This led to some strange battlefield occurrences. Opposing generals were known to meet socially on a hill overlooking the battle. As Ch'i described in *Warlord Politics in China, 1916–1928*, generals sat, chatted, and played board games while orderlies brought reports from the field.[19] In this way, they usually avoided personal harm and defeated generals were allowed to save face. "Battles" often were ritualistic affairs that began with both sides firing a few random cannon shots followed by troops popping their umbrellas and enjoying the rest of the outing. Warlords gave advanced warning of their impending invasions or attacks to reduce casualties. Telegrams would fly, and formal declarations of war were required. Hence, Feng knew when Chang would attack Wu at Peking: the invitations were in the mail.

In fact, correspondent Edna Lee Booker happened to be visiting Wu when he was drawing up the articles of war against Chang. Interestingly, she reported that seven other warlords also signed on against Chang. One of those was the Tuchun, or governor, of Shansi Province. Had Yen turned against Chang? Since Chang's defeat put Shansi into a bind, it doesn't seem likely that Yen was considered to be pals with Wu and Feng, unless he had shifted the blame for the ranch on to the foreigner cowboys. The ranch's business and social relationship with Yen do not seem to bear this out. More likely Yen Hsi-shan signed on either to hedge his bets or to go with the flow with Chang's understanding. The deal smacks of the one Fidel Castro offered Lyndon Johnson: Rail at me all you want—I understand, you need to appear tough and against me to win the election over the other candidate, and I want you to win. Chang had to know that Yen was sandwiched between Wu's and Feng's forces.

Booker watched the battle for Peking and North China unfold. The armies threw waves of thousands of men at each other. This time ritual was set aside. The armies brought coffins and intended to use them. Feng's Invincibles came in by train singing "Onward Christian Soldiers." They meant to kill. Wu's troops took the concept of being well equipped to a new level. They marched to the front with umbrellas, alarm clocks, fans, teapots, lanterns, and hot-water bottles hanging from their packs alongside the usual accouterments of war.[20]

But this was not the kind of battle warlords feared most. They could survive this type of confrontation. Warlords feared internal revolt or revolution in their own provinces most. Then their heads could be cut off. Civilians worried most about frustrated, bored, unpaid, hungry troops. Whether these troops were victorious or defeated made little difference. Usually the citizenry, not an army, was attacked. In some places in order to survive, men would leave their wives and daughters for the troops to rape while they hid in the hills to avoid losing everything. As Lattimore put it, this abandonment of the women was understood as a bribe. Soldiers could rape the women, kill whatever stock they needed, and rob the household. In return, they were not to burn the house or kill people. "Bandit Babies" would later be abandoned to die of exposure. Families not paying the price would be killed and burned out.[21]

In contrast to these dramatic years in war-torn China, Barton lived a comfortable, different life in the U.S. among the Hollywood set. Quite a number of former Montanans, including cowboys, ended up in the Los Angeles area where Barton kept his stateside residence. He was particularly fond of boasting of his friends and acquaintances in the Hollywood Western movie set and in the Western art scene. With profits made from the China ranch, he acquired Western art and artifacts.

When the Japanese occupied Shansi in 1937, the commander of the Japanese forces decided he liked Barton's ranch house better than Yen Hsi-shan's palace in town.[22] The ranch became Japanese headquarters, effectively eliminating its use as a ranch. Barton now had to spend all his time in the U.S. No more shuttling back and forth. The Far Eastern Wild West was closed to cowboys.

• **Thirteen** •

Poor Little Rich Boy and Princess Xenia, 1920

> *There is an immense class of exiled and ruined noblemen in Europe with little hope of escaping from common labor except by marrying American heiresses. Together with the marriages of American girls and foreign noblemen must be included the less common cases of rich American men who marry European girls of noble family. Most interesting and peculiar [is] that of the immensely rich William B. Leeds, Jr., and the exiled Princess Xenia of Russia.[1]*
> —Sandusky Register, June 19, 1921

Lester Barton was no cowboy. This other member of the Barton family went to China but did not become one of the cowboys at the Shansi ranch. Fred Barton's younger brother, Lester Emil Kottmeier (Barton), went but did not stay. Educated on the East Coast, he remained an Easterner. Unlike Fred, who claimed to have been born in Miles City, Lester usually claimed he had been born in New York City. Actually he was born in Germany when his parents were visiting relatives there. Being married and having served as a private and artilleryman in the New York 71st Infantry, he was exempted from induction in 1917.

Prior to going to China in September of 1920, he worked as a salesman for the Hudford Company of New York. He bucked trucks rather than broncos. Hudford opened factories and sales centers in several major cities. The company advertised widely in automotive magazines. In the mid teens the company supplied conversion kits, including gears and drive shafts, which allowed Ford automobile owners to convert their car chassis to trucks for less than the cost of buying a new truck. That way, Ford owners could own both a truck and a car for just what a new truck would cost. Some did just that. They converted their aging Fords into trucks and took the savings of $1,000 to buy a nice new car. Many fire departments and other small business entrepreneurs jumped at the chance. Hudford also supplied parts and trucks to the army during the war. Unfortunately, Hudford declared bankruptcy and was placed under trusteeship in October 1917 just after Lester was exempted from further military service. Litigation over the bankruptcy continued in 1919. Lester may have been looking for some much needed money and a new start.

Fred must have encouraged his brother to consider China, since in the spring of 1920, just as the Montana cowboys were headed to the Shansi Ranch, Lester applied for a passport to China. On his passport application, he at first said that he was going to China on personal business with his brother, but then he crossed out "with his brother." He planned to sail for China in May, the same month he applied for a passport, but he postponed departure until September. By this time, the Montana cowboys had already sailed on the USAT *Dix* with the horses for the Shansi ranch. Lester planned to stay for only six months, and that was what he did, returning in February 1921.

The delay made quite a difference, for it put Lester in China at the same time as his future employer. The press called William Bateman Leeds, Jr., "poor little rich boy." The boy was the original American poor little rich boy, a name later applied to William Randolph Hearst and others, culminating in the long-running comic book *Richie Rich, the Poor Little Rich Boy* (1953–1984+). Leeds inherited a fortune from his multimillionaire "Tin Plate King" father, for whom Maxim's of Paris renamed their famous mussel and white wine soup to "Billi B." His father sold his tin plating company to U.S. Steel Corporation. As a later tribute, a steel World War II Liberty boat was christened the *William B. Leeds*. He made more millions by becoming president of the Chicago, Rock Island, and Pacific Railroad. His other companies included such giants as National Biscuit, Diamond Matches, and American Can. The elder Leeds left his son a sizeable inheritance and trust, worth over six billion dollars in today's money.

Junior's mother, an Ohio beauty, remarried after the death of the elder Leeds. She wed Prince Christopher of Greece, whereupon she became Princess Anastasia. Heroine of a true American story, she completed her journey from being a lowly stenographer to becoming royalty and one of the richest women in the world. She was deemed the "Dollar Princess" after a popular musical playing in London and then New York (1909), with numbers by Jerome Kern.

By accident Lester Barton found himself in China at the same time as Leeds. Globe-trotter Leeds had been hunting tigers in Sumatra when he was bitten by a poisonous insect. He lay for weeks in a Shanghai hospital. Fearing that infection had worked into the bones of his left arm, doctors felt the arm might have to be amputated. Leeds made arrangements to see specialists in New York. While he was trying to recover, a cable arrived, saying his mother was seriously ill in Athens.

He immediately pulled himself out of the hospital to rush to his mother's side. He was accompanied by Mr. and Mrs. H.M. Greene, his uncle and aunt, who lived in Montclair, New Jersey, where William had attended school as a boy along with other offspring of the very wealthy. Along with him came Wang, a Chinese servant, and two monkeys he had collected in Sumatra. He arrived in San Francisco on February 22, 1921. Sailing with him was Lester Barton on the SS *Venezuela*. Lester was heading home. The next time Lester applied for a passport or his name appeared on a passenger list, he would be listed as private secretary to William B. Leeds, Jr. Lester came to China as a salesman; he left as something quite different.

As Fred Barton traveled back and forth across the Pacific between Los Angeles and the Shansi ranch in the 1920s, his brother crossed the Atlantic from New York to London in service to Leeds. In the early Roaring Twenties, Lester served as private secretary at a critical time in socialite Leeds' life. Against his mother's initial wishes, young Leeds married Her Highness the Princess Xenia Georgievna Romanov in 1921 in Paris after he and his mother had recovered from their illnesses. Fred Barton had seen Xenia's second cousin, Czar Nicholas II, when Fred had traveled to Russia to set up a horse breeding ranch. He observed the Russian royal court and family at the same time Princess Xenia was there. Now it was brother Lester's turn with the princess. It was Lester who traveled with Leeds and Xenia, one of the Romanovs who had escaped the Bolshevik's execution of the czar and much of his family in 1918.

The press ate up the storied marriage. Anything involving the super rich and royalty was sure to make headlines. Such headlines as "Great Bargains for American Heiresses in Titled Husbands: Poor Princes and No End of Royal Princesses Who Have Been Beggared by War Upheavals and Revolution" appeared. Of all the spousal movement across the Atlantic, the Leeds/Xenia story proved best.

Leeds was nineteen years old at the time of his marriage to the eighteen-year-old Xenia. Although Lester Barton was entering his thirties, Leeds and Barton had commonalities. Despite the difference in economic standing, they had attended rival New Jersey private schools close to New York City. While the pampered, isolated, asthmatic Leeds rode to school each morning in a horse-drawn carriage, attended by servants from his private upscale house, Lester boarded with his brother, Fred, and many other students. They walked to class. Both Leeds and Lester knew what it was to live apart from parents, which bridged the lines of social status.

Leeds used his need for speed and travel to express his independence. Picking up a traffic ticket in London, he was forbidden to drive for months. Helen Worden, in *Society Circus*, reported, "Willie Leeds has as many as one hundred Lincolns in his garage at Oyster Bay."[2] He owned motor boats and yachts, and tested speedy torpedo boats for the military. This led to his saving both his wife and Adele Astaire (film star dancer Fred Astaire's sister) from accidental boat infernos at the dock. He had his own airplane, named after his wife, and funded a transatlantic attempt from Ireland to the United States. Having befriended Sir Hubert Wilkins on the first round-the-world flight of the *Graf Zeppelin*, Leeds signed on to be mooring master for Wilkins' submarine, the *Nautilus*, designed to sail under the polar ice cap. As an automobile specialist and former parts salesman, Lester Barton was just the conversational ticket. Choosing Barton for a private secretary made sense.

On August 29, 1923, Leeds' mother, Anastasia, died. This set off a hectic chain of events for Lester Barton and the Leeds. Prince Christopher wanted the Leeds and his wife to live permanently in Europe after their return from Anastasia's funeral in New York. Lester did sail with the Leedses in October back to Europe, but in December William gave it up. They celebrated Christmas on the *Aquitania* as William, Xenia, and Lester steamed back to the United States to live for good.

Sometime after that, Lester Barton took another job as an automobile agent in San Francisco. Here he lived with his wife, Rose. Previously, and before meeting Leeds, Lester (then Kottmeier) and Isabelle Rose married in Manhattan in 1917. In 1920, under the name of Barton, she applied for a passport to sail on the SS *Columbia* with her husband to China. By 1930 they had taken in Fred and Lester's mother, Martha. Martha retained Kottmeier rather than changing to Barton as her surname. The elder Frederick Barton had died in 1920, and the stock market had crashed in 1929. Martha needed support. In the end, it might have been son Lester who needed support. He died in 1949. His mother outlived him by a year.

The story of William B. Leeds, Jr., became entwined with one of the more sensationalized events of the twentieth century. Anyone who has seen Ingrid Bergman's Academy Award–winning performance in the motion picture *Anastasia* (1956) already knows the fictionalized version of what happened. A woman claimed to be Grand Duchess Anastasia of Russia, the czar and czarina's youngest daughter, who somehow survived the slaughter. Many White Russians dearly wanted to believe her as they sought to hold on to their past. When they were children, Xenia had actually played with Grand Duchess Anastasia (not to be confused with William's Ohio mother who took the name of Anastasia when marrying Greek royalty). Xenia brought her to New York in 1928. She was convinced the woman was who she said she was, but, after six months, the frustrated William Leeds was not convinced and threw the woman out. "Anastasia" had important defenders and detractors in the New York social scene. The battle over whether the woman really was Anastasia or a lunatic imposter raged on for years until the advent of DNA authenticating. Lester avoided that mess.

He also avoided controversy surrounding the trophy marlin that became part of Ernest Hemingway's basis for his *The Old Man and the Sea*. Hemingway drank with his friend Leeds on the billionaire's famous yacht, *Moana*. For Leeds and Hemingway, the yacht's image appropriately graced the colorful labels of Gilbey's Gin bottles. At the time, Hemingway participated in a 1935 fishing tournament in Bimini. He spotted Leeds' Thompson submachine gun, wanted it, and finally got it.[3]

On his own boat, the *Pilar*, the competitive Hemingway was getting skunked fishing, but artist friend Mike Strater tied into a world record marlin. To scare the sharks away or to foul up Strater's chances, Hemingway sprayed them with machine gun fire from Leeds' gun, nearly wounding Strater and ruining a quick catch. The marlin sounded while all the blood attracted more sharks. The crazed sharks tore into the marlin as Strater tried to pump it to the surface. The 14-foot, thousand pound marlin was dead and a half skeleton when they pulled it on board. Of such stuff was *The Old Man and the Sea* made. Like Papa Hemingway, Leeds ended his life with a bullet. Leeds was one of Hemingway's "Haves." Lester would have been one of Hemingway's "Have Nots."

Although Lester chose not to involve himself in Fred Barton's ranch in China, another Barton, or Barton-to-be, did.

• Fourteen •

The Many Wives of a Lifelong Bachelor, Here and Abroad

[When J. Frank Dobie, the Texas folklorist, writer, and savior of the Texas Longhorn, interviewed Fred Barton in 1956, Barton spun the yarn that he was a lifelong bachelor.]

Love: a season pass on the shuttle between heaven and hell.[1]—Don Dickerman

No, sir, a woman can go farther with a lipstick than a man with a Winchester and a side of bacon.—Rawhide Rawlins

A man who tells the truth should always have one foot in the stirrup.[2]—Richard S. "Kinky" Friedman, the Good Ol' Texas Jewboy

Undeniably, the Chinese practice of beheading riveted the attention of Westerners. While not quite considered a spectator sport, visitors could not take their eyes from these public executions. Soldiers of the 15th Infantry and the Marine Legation Guards, as well as shore leave sailors, other foreign military units, and European civilians, crammed their souvenir scrapbooks with photos of the gruesome justice. Either on the killing grounds or right out on the street, beheading scenes became a most popular Chinese postcard subject. Illustrated news magazines tended to use garish head-lopping scenes as cover illustrations when reporting on China. A chromolithograph insert in French chocolate maker's Chocolat Inimitable bars graphically showed Tsong-Lie-Yamen parting ways with his head. Thus, children could better enjoy the bar's sweetness. If their parents bought them more bars, they could collect the full set of images from the 1900 Chinese war.

Criminals, rebels, and pirates—all often loosely defined—suffered the fate. It was indeed a rich police force or warlord army that could execute its prisoners with bullets. The sword was much cheaper, definite, and ceremonially professional. Even in more cosmopolitan cities, baskets containing heads were prominently displayed on poles or lampposts while streetcars and automobiles passed by underneath. Messages underneath the baskets warned others not to do what the owners of the heads had done. The grotesque death faces created a perpetual Halloween for Americans. China may have been one of the oldest civilizations, but the blood-spurting, head-rolling practice was seen as unciv-

Fourteen • The Many Wives of a Lifelong Bachelor, Here and Abroad 149

ilized, barbaric and ghastly, particularly when it sometimes took several blows to sever someone's head. Not everyone possessed the consummate skills of the Lord High Executioner.

When Boxers raged across China killing Christian missionaries, particularly in Taiyuanfu in 1900 near the future site of Fred Barton's ranch, beheadings became more abhorrent in the United States than ever. Wholesale slaughter of missionaries and Christians horrified the public. Even worse, letters, reports, and press accounts underscored that the victims had been beheaded. In some instances, Chinese Christian followers had been forced to lick the blood of the beheaded missionary men and women. The United States was above such barbarism. Or was it?

On December 9, 1885, the worst anti–Chinese massacre in the nineteenth century occurred in Rock Springs, Wyoming. The Union Pacific Railroad's coal mines near the town supplied coal for its trains on the transcontinental railroad where it crossed the Rocky Mountains. A labor dispute broke out because the mines paid the Chinese workers less than other workers. In a scene replayed several times throughout American industrial history, the local union organized against the Chinese immigrants who were seen as taking jobs away from whites by virtue of their being a cheaper source of labor.

Beheaded, scalped, mutilated, branded, and hanged—twenty-eight Chinese miners died horribly. One had his testicles and penis cut off. They were toasted at the local bar as trophies of the hunt. Many of the men tried to escape as the rampagers burned seventy-five Chinese homes to the ground. The event touched off waves of anti–Chinese rioting in the American West, especially in the Northwest. Violence became so bad that army units, including the 19th Cavalry, were deployed to Rock Springs. Word of the atrocities

Japanese propaganda print of the 1937 fall of Taiyuanfu near the horse ranch.

reached China. Outraged and horrified, some Chinese and family members of the dead threatened to come to Rock Springs to wreak vengeance on white miners. The Rock Springs Massacre became an international event at a time when the United States wanted China as a trading partner. President Grover Cleveland was compelled to address the issue in his 1885 State of the Union Address. Internally, in the United States, the massacre became somewhat of an Easterners versus Westerners affair.

Eastern newspapers railed against the slaughter, whereas Western papers and politicians rallied behind the white miners. The editors and politicos supported what had happened and demanded tougher enforcement of exclusion laws, very much like later arguments over immigration policy regarding Latinos. It is that mean streak in American culture that says when the economy gets tough blame immigrants, even though you may be one yourself. This same attitude in China led sword-wielding, bare-chested Boxers to blame foreign Christian missionaries for the drought, crop failure, and diminished finances.

Dubbed the father of the American cartoon, Thomas Nast used his cartooning cudgel to attack what had been done to the Chinese at Rock Springs. Known as the creator of the modern version of Santa Claus and the Republican elephant, he also popularized the figures of Uncle Sam, Columbia as a personification of American values, and the Democratic donkey. His editorial cartoon attacking the massacre drew on contemporary popular culture themes. Its caption read, "Here's a pretty mess (in Wyoming)." This combined a quote from *The Mikado* with Wyoming. Gilbert and Sullivan's comic opera with its Lord High Executioner and his sword was set in Japan rather than China, but that was a good enough Far Eastern reference for Nast. The sober cartoon used Goya's famous dark painting *The Third of May 1808* as its basis. Instead of Napoleon's firing squad liquidating helpless men, woman, and priests, Nast substituted white miners shooting helpless Chinese. The cartoon was a far cry from western state representations of the "Yellow Horde." Fury over the incident forced the United States to pay China indemnity.[3] Presaging the Johnson County Cattle Wars, local judges and politicians made sure the murderers avoided punishment, while the local press turned them into heroes. Such was beheading in America.

On that December 9, 1885, date of the Rock Springs Massacre, another event took place that involved Fred Barton and China. Barton's first wife was born in Detroit, Michigan. Not only would she marry this Westerner in the land of *The Mikado*, she would also live with him in China. Barton was a cowboy, not a miner—a big difference.

Just as Barton tried to choose more mature men for his China cowboys, he chose a more mature woman when marrying the already mentioned Mabel. She was in her early thirties, he in his late twenties. Prior to their marriage in Nagasaki on September 18, 1916, Mabel had lived in the Philippines in 1913 as Mrs. Mabel Blanche Newman, citing San Francisco as her permanent address. The Philippines were not without their own beheadings at the time. This was the year of the final major battles of the Moro Rebellion, a stage of the longer Philippine-American War. Both the Moros and forces under U.S. general John "Black Jack" Pershing were alleged to have beheaded their foes. While Mabel was in Manila, away from the atrocities, newspapers were flush with battle accounts. She then traveled alone to Shanghai and lived there in 1914.

At this time Fred still worked for British American Tobacco based out of Shanghai.

Fourteen • *The Many Wives of a Lifelong Bachelor, Here and Abroad* 151

Fred and Mabel met in April 1916 and married six months later. While Fred tended to business, Mabel set up shop as a housewife in Shanghai. For the marriage ceremony, she shed the name of Mrs. Newman and chose her maiden name of Mabel Roberts. She had married her cowboy, and Fred was not a bad example. He stood just under six feet tall. During summer, his auburn hair sun-bleached to a badlands sandstone reddish hue. His eyes were the rain-swept blue of Montana skies.

The Roberts family were blue collar and about as Scottish as one could get. Mabel's father had emigrated from Scotland to Detroit and had married into a Nova Scotia family. Alexander Roberts worked as a machinist turning out automobile axles for Detroit's burgeoning auto industry. Mabel's mother, Maria, died in childbirth when Mabel was seven, leaving behind four daughters and a son. Alexander then remarried and doubled the family. Seventeen-year-old Mabel worked as a chambermaid and boarded at the Normandia Hotel in downtown Detroit. She knew what work was, and she had become a seasoned traveler before the adventurous Fred Barton appeared in her life.

While Fred sought to set up his own business in China, Mabel was not one to stay at home in Shanghai. Her travels with Barton left a paper trail that included Shanghai, Hong Kong, Tientsin, Peking, and Vladivostok. The Bartons also sailed back and forth across the Pacific between China and the United States into the early twenties. However, by 1925 the sailing and the marriage had worn thin. Fred and Mabel parted.

Years later, Barton asserted his status as a lifelong bachelor with no remaining family members. Quite a quirk in his self-assessment! The more this "lifelong bachelor's" life comes under scrutiny, the more wives pop out of the woodwork. For wife #2, he did the opposite of what he had done in choosing Mabel. Barton chose a woman fourteen years younger than he. Enter another Anastasia, only this one did not claim to be a Romanov princess, as many had. What she and her family did have was a history in China.

Yafracina Anastasia (Ashia) Paschenko and Fred Barton met and married in Tientsin, China, in the spring of 1928. Ashia, a twenty-five-year-old White Russian, had been born in the Russian-created Manchurian city of Harbin. Her father was a Kamerstein and her mother a Kovton. In 1930 Barton brought her to San Francisco, where she became a naturalized citizen in 1932. They divorced in 1939 in Las Vegas but remained friends, even though Barton professed having never been married and having no close ties. Ashia would live in their house in Hollywood until remarrying. Fred and Ashia made a very attractive Hollywood couple. After the 1939 divorce, she still claimed Fred as her husband and Elizabeth Bistrisky as stepsister, all still living at that address for the 1940 census. This unusual circumstance might be explained by a later Barton marriage imbroglio, to be explained later.

Like many Jews, Ashia's family fled the bloodshed and pogroms in Russia, entering China by way of Siberia. Declared "stateless" and without rights, these refugees set up their own communities and businesses. The Russian Revolution stressed these communities as thousands of White Russians poured into China's overcrowded cities while fleeing the Bolsheviks. The destitute existed on aid or by whatever means available. What was called "the marketplace of heartaches"[4] sprang up along the railroad stops. On the walkways and streets, Russian families, rich and poor, offered their most cherished possessions for sale. That included their clothes, shoes, and hats—all of the articles needed for the winter. Torn between starvation and hoping no one would buy their keepsakes, they played with death.

Some had fallen to the lowest of the low, existing by picking through garbage dumps of the Chinese. The Chinese threw away little garbage. For many, finding a way to the United States represented hope and a future. During and after World War I, all Asian immigrants were barred, and Eastern Europeans were severely restricted. Marriage to an American represented about the only way a Russian woman in China could be admitted into the United States. Even then, she must pass the citizenship test for naturalization within a few years or be deported, married or not.

Ashia and her sisters made it. Their stories intermixed with much of the same times and places as Barton's in Russia, China, and Hollywood. Like Barton, they married in the Far East and then married again in the States. Like Barton, they ended up in Hollywood. They and their families were privy to Fred Barton's horse ranch adventure in China. The sisters led notable lives, ranging from serving in intelligence in China to raising a son who would become vice president of Boeing and an opera star to marrying a 20th Century Fox movie set builder and foremost authority on the early Russian colonization of Alaska, Hawaii, and California.

Barton's sister-in-law Elizabeth worked as a beauty shop operator when she stayed with Ashia in Barton's house in 1940. Ashia and Elizabeth were born in Harbin, China. Elizabeth spoke of their family's not having much. The family never got out of debt. As a Harbin schoolgirl, she trudged to class in the bitter North China subzero cold wearing nothing more than her one dress and a too-thin sweater.[5] Married to a violinist, Elizabeth Bistrisky first sailed to the United States from China in 1930 to visit sister-in-law Khassia and her family in Detroit. Khassia had come to the U.S. a few years earlier. Elizabeth's five-year-old son, Boris, accompanied her.

In his later years, Fred Barton entertained guests in his Hollywood apartment by picking at his guitar and singing old songs of the range. Boris, Fred's nephew-in-law, outdid Fred in both musical talent and travel. After he came of age in the U.S. and his mother remarried, he changed his name to Boris Mishel. Using this stage name, he enjoyed a stint with the Rockettes in New York City. His operatic experience included appearances in Germany and Italy, and he appeared with the Los Angeles Symphony and Seattle Opera. Meanwhile, he worked his way up to being vice president of Boeing. He traveled around the world for the company and entertained diplomats with his singing at the same time.

After staying with Fred's wife Ashia, Elizabeth married Vasilly V. Usharoff, who was born in Hilar, where Barton's Orlovs had crossed from Manchuria into Mongolia on the long horse drive. Usharoff's father worked as a telegraph operator on the Trans-Siberian Railway and then stationmaster at small outposts on the China-Eastern Railway that Barton's herd had followed, in part, across Manchuria. Usharoff entered the United States in 1922 to work in the sawmills and as a logger. Since few if any Russians were able to come to the United States during World War I, immigration quotas for Russians remained unfilled, so he was able to fill one of the few quota spots available. He married a Scots-English woman and had a son, but the couple later parted. Usharoff met and married Elizabeth, who helped him in his dental practice. As will be seen, he became even more involved in sister-in-law Ashia's life in later years.

Fourteen • *The Many Wives of a Lifelong Bachelor, Here and Abroad*

Just as Barton escaped the Japanese in China, so did Ashia's other sister, Olga (Olia). Sometime shortly after 1932, Olga fled to Shanghai. Large contingents of Russian refugees flowed into Shanghai from Manchuria and Constantinople. Since many were civic-minded professionals such as teachers, entertainers, and musicians, a vibrant Russian community was established. The charming, attractive Olga danced ballet. She married a Russian, who like many was employed by the Japanese at various professions after the Japanese occupied much of China. With the coming of the Flying Tigers and the U.S. entering the war, the tide began to turn against the Japanese. They quickly evacuated the area in which Olga's husband worked. Fearing that he knew too much about their operations and plans, they murdered him in a way too ghastly to describe.[6]

Olga's being his widow and also engaged in clandestine operations jeopardized her life, but then she met Lt. Irvin S. Layton, Special Operations, Office of Strategic Services (OSS). Teams from the OSS, the predecessor of the CIA, operated behind the Japanese lines in Burma and China, including in Taiyuanfu near the Barton ranch. The teams trained Chinese soldiers, sabotaged Japanese targets, rescued fliers, and gathered intelligence. Olga and Layton discovered they made a good team too. They married and Layton was able to get her out and to the United States after the war. Just as Barton saved Ashia from an uncertain future, Layton did the same for her sister.

Both the OSS and the Sino-American Cooperative Organization (SACO) had contacts with people Barton knew during World War II. SACO was a secret joint organization formed between the U.S. Navy and the Chinese. At the time Barton knew warlord Yen Hsi-shen during his years in Shansi, Yen chose Fu Tso-yi as his top general, even putting him in charge when Yen would have to make himself scarce. Yen brought his generals out to the ranch where Barton entertained them.

Yen put Fu in control of Suiyuan province, which bordered Shansi on the northeast at the edge of the Gobi Desert. During World War II, SACO established a navy meteorological station, Camp 4, its northernmost outpost, about twenty-five miles north of the Yellow River in Suiyuan. The station provided advanced weather reports of what was going on over the Gobi so the navy's Pacific Fleet would know what to expect as fronts moved eastward to Japan and the Philippines. That gave the U.S. Navy an edge over Japanese weather stations far to the east and in Tokyo. Attacks and eventually a possible invasion could then be planned. Camp 4 intercepted enemy radio communications and trained Mongols and Chinese to interdict Japanese forces.

The sailors lived far from supply lines. It took a three-month truck journey from Chungking just for the twelve original SACO men to establish Camp 4. Low on supplies and unequipped for the desert heat and frigid winter, the men were saved by Chinese generals Barton had known at his ranch. The sailors were given food and appropriate clothing. This was Mongol country, horse country, and Fu presented the men with twenty-six horses. The horses gave the sailors the idea of creating the navy's only World War II cavalry unit. One sailor hailed from Montana. Another had been a police horse patrolman. The Mongols they were training knew how to ride better than they did. Forming a cavalry unit seemed a natural idea, and it would be something to do besides cleaning sand out of equipment each day. The navy office in Washington was perplexed, however, when a requisition arrived from the camp for such critical equipment as western saddles, along with a request that they be airdropped into the Gobi desert.

This unorthodox unit led to one of the more bizarre events of World War II. Unit action prompted a Hollywood movie and a fictionalization of the event in *Collier's* magazine. Encountering a Japanese force while on reconnaissance, the unit attacked them at night with bazookas mounted on horses and camels. The strange sight of what seemed mythical fire-breathing dragons demoralized the Japanese and even scared the friendlies. Although the Japanese had pushed within twenty-five miles of the base, come morning they were gone.

Richard Widmark starred in the 1953 film *Destination Gobi*, based on the story of the navy weathermen at Camp 4. Some of the weathermen who saw the film said it did a good job of capturing the essence of what actually happened. Edmund G. Love's "Ninety Saddles for Kengtu," with a lavish two-page illustration, appeared in the September 6, 1952, edition of *Collier's*. Its storyline also pursued the creation of a Genghis Khan navy cavalry unit. Linda Kush's nonfiction *The Rice Paddy Navy: U.S. Sailors Undercover in China, Espionage and Sabotage Behind Japanese Lines in China During World War II* (2012) fleshed out the real events even more. Intelligence operations that went on in Barton's and Layton's time are now just slowly being revealed.

Ashia and Fred divorced on October 17, 1939. Barton married wife #3, Mamie Parker McElroy, the very next month. Therein lies another story with twists and turns involving Ashia and her family. Fred and Mamie's November wedding story appeared on the front page of the *Deming Headlight*, the local New Mexico newspaper closest to Mamie's famous NAN Ranch in southwestern New Mexico on the Mimbres River. The November 24 story appeared right under the gangster photo of a smiling Al Capone. Locals believed this a fitting juxtaposition. Barton was perceived as being a shyster who moved in on a wealthy, vulnerable widow. Apparently Barton did not win many friends in New Mexico, according to Salvador Parra, the foreman who worked under him.[7]

Other newspapers picked up the wedding story, making a point of saying the nuptials came as a complete surprise. The *El Paso Post* of November 30, 1939, focused less on the wedding and more on establishing the credentials of the mystery groom. Since the newspaper received Barton's story secondhand through "Mr. Barton's friends here," the account did, and did not, match up with reality. Titled "Widow's Mate Placed Range Pony in China: Fred Barton Introduced Breed in Land of Orient," it read as follows:

> How Fred Barton of Faywood, N.M., a Montanan, introduced the western cowpony to China, for breeding purposes on a large scale, was told today by Mr. Barton's friends here.
> Mr. Barton and Mrs. Mamie McElroy, widow of John T. McElroy, millionaire cowman and oil man, today were married in Silver City recently. They are at the famous Y-Bar Ranch at Faywood.
>
> **100-Mile Ranch**
> Mr. Barton was in China with the American Tobacco Co. under a five-year contract. Forming the acquaintance of high officials in the Chinese government, he succeeded in getting them to finance a project to raise saddle horses on a scale, patterned after the methods of the western ranges. The Montanan is an admirer of the western cow pony because of qualities of its sterling endurance.
> An area of 100 miles square was blocked out on the steppes of Shen-Shi province and prepared for breeding grounds.

Fourteen • *The Many Wives of a Lifelong Bachelor, Here and Abroad*   155

Assemble Stock

After completing his contract with the American Tobacco Co., Mr. Barton returned to the United States in the summer of 1919 and established headquarters in Miles City, Mont., to purchase breeding stock for export to China. The region along Mizpah, Tongue and Powder Rivers was scoured. By fall, a herd of 300 choice specimens of mares and studs was assembled at Miles City for shipment to San Francisco and export to China.

Fifteen top cowhands from Miles City area equipped with a Coggshall outfit (saddle and tack) at no expense to them accompanied the horses to China. They were to remain in the employ of the Chinese government under the supervision of Barton.

Due to losses incurred by marauding parties of the Mongols, the venture was a failure. The cowhands came home in 1922 [p. 2].

The figures cited were cockeyed, and the spurious Mongol invasion very curious.

Before Barton took over, Mamie's recently deceased husband, J.T. McElroy of El Paso, Texas, owned the ranch. During his tenure, Mrs. McElroy did extensive building at ranch headquarters, equipping the hacienda mansion's seventeen rooms with lavish interiors. Rooms featured hand-wrought lighting fixtures and brass and silver hinges. Mamie was known for keeping pet monkeys and exotic birds in the house—a weird blend of Victorian exoticism spiked with Old Mexico. Each bedroom included its own sleeping porch. A swimming pool was provided. This living quarters near Faywood, New Mexico, was renowned as a real showpiece, with building costs of over $1.3 million in today's money. Barton, described now in newspapers and family lore as a "California gambler" and "capitalist," heard about the rich widow McElroy after her husband died. He became her chauffeur and worked his way into her good graces.

Barton married into Texan legends. Both the Parkers and the McElroys represented quintessential Texas history, with stories too big for even the Lone Star state to hold. Combining television's *Rawhide* and *Dallas* with Hollywood's *Giant* and *The Searchers* might come close. Mamie's pioneer ancestors founded Fort Parker, site of the 1836 Fort Parker Massacre. After most of the Parker family had been killed, the Comanche rode off with nine-year-old Cynthia Parker. She married a Comanche chief and had a son, Chief Quanah Parker, who became the last great chief of the Comanche. Although she was later found, she resisted conforming to the white man's ways. Her life has become an iconic story of the Old West, being told over and over in short stories, books, movies, television series, and graphic novels. Most influential was John Ford's 1956 Hollywood version, *The Searchers,* starring John Wayne and Natalie Wood, which enjoyed enormous popularity. In 2008, the American Film Institute proclaimed it the greatest American Western of all time.

In her own way, Mamie also rose from humble beginnings, lost her family, was taken prisoner, and became the bride of a "chief." Tragedy struck early in her life. Her mother died when Mamie was young. Her despondent father deserted her and her younger siblings and headed off to the gold fields. Grandfather Peyton Parker, who ran a hotel in Pecos, Texas, took the kids in. Mamie swore on her mother's deathbed that she would take care of her brother and sister. This promise dictated the rest of her life, and perhaps explains her later agreeing to marry Barton.

Because of his ranch holdings in the area, and being major stockholder and president of the Pecos Bank, John T. McElroy often frequented the hotel. He saw the plight of the Parker children and assisted them financially towards their education. Thanks to

McElroy's generosity, Mamie was able to go from hotel worker to Grayson College student, where she met her true love, Walter Chandler.

As the story has been passed down in the Parker family over the years, McElroy also had his eyes on the now comely Mamie. He forced the deal. She would have to give up Chandler and marry him or else he would immediately cut off all financial support, leaving her younger brother and sister in quite a fix. In return, he would make her a rich woman, one of the richest. Chandler, a poor law student, had to step aside. He would never marry and never forget Mamie. True to the pledge she made to her dying mother, Mamie agreed to the marriage in order to ensure a future for her brother and sister. The blackmail worked. Although thirty years younger than McElroy, Mamie married one of the richest men in Sherman, Texas, in 1900.

Like Barton, John McElroy earned his spurs and knew what a desert was. He equaled Barton in moving animals long distances. He trailed cattle from Guaymas, Mexico, to Nogales to Hancock to Kansas, a three-year, 2,000-mile trip that crossed both the Sonoran and Chihuahuan deserts. Born the same year as the 49ers, his adventurous spirit carried him from family homes in Ohio and Iowa to exploits across the American West. He claimed to have driven mule teams for Brigham Young, survived a Montana mine collapse, bought his first cattle herd in Oregon, fought Indians, and traveled to the California gold fields. Cattle business on a large scale became his true love. He was trail driver on the Chisholm Trail and made his own trails in the early history of the big drives. When beef packers refused to give him a fair price for his herd, he created his own meat packing business.

In 1927, on one of McElroy's Texas ranches, the J.T. McElroy discovery, oil well #1, was brought in as the leading edge of the Great Permian Basin oil boom near Odessa, Texas. Today, the giant McElroy field perpetuates John's name and has been rejuvenated, not just as a historic site but also as a still-producing oil field. Being a cattleman rather than an oilman, McElroy sold the ranch for millions and invested in the NAN ranch in New Mexico. The NAN was already famous as a cattle ranch and key excavation site for the Mimbres Culture (AD 100–1140). As a true "power couple" of Texas and the Southwest, John and Mamie's comings, goings, and doings provided newspapers with grist. John's philanthropy aided local communities.

McElroy promised to make Mamie rich; he did so many times over. Just as he equaled Barton in cowboying, Mamie matched him in travel. She traveled to the Far East in 1930, and sailed first-class to France many times on the dream liners of the time. Sometimes it was for travel, other times for treatment of illness.

Her absence from the ranch resulted in a nasty lawsuit that foreshadowed an even messier lawsuit Mamie would level against Barton. In 1927 a young woman, Mamye, had gone to the NAN ranch, where her father had taken a job. She fell in love with Honeycutt, one of the ranch hands, and they married. Mamie was in Dallas at the time being treated for poor health. When she returned and discovered the wedding, she became livid. Apparently she was sweet on the ranch hand too. She kicked them all off the ranch, but she later wanted them back. This caused the Honeycutts to separate a few times, divorce, and remarry. After the Honeycutts moved off the McElroy ranch once again, Mamie contacted John Honeycutt and asked him to return. She stated she would split her affections between McElroy and Honeycutt, and he could split his affections between his wife and her. If Mrs. Honeycutt could not agree to that, "she could go to hell," according to the lawsuit petition filed by Mrs. Honeycutt.[8] She had endured enough and sued Mamie and McElroy for $140,000. The district court hearing was delayed, as Mamie had gone to Paris due to illness and did not plan to return soon.

Life took an even worse turn in 1935 when all of John's teeth were pulled, from which he never recovered. He and Mamie moved from the ranch to an El Paso hotel where he tried to convalesce, to no avail. Mamie then had him interred in a specially made copper casket encased in redwood. The only other person having a similar casket was William Wrigley, Jr., the chewing gum magnate. McElroy chose Mamie to be executrix of his estate. After he died, Mamie decided not to return to the ranch mansion, but to continue hotel life. She retreated to her childhood hotel roots, but in high style. She divided her time between El Paso, Dallas, Houston and trips abroad. John left everything to her—ranch, banking interests, even a 1,000-acre Fort Worth subdivision.

At nearly the same time, Walter Chandler left Mamie everything too. Her first love never forgot her. He flourished as a lawyer and three-time congressman from New York, leading fights on Capitol Hill against anti–Semitism and against the Ku Klux Klan. He was instrumental in convincing the U.S. government to recognize the Baltic countries. Mamie's coffers overflowed, but the fortune would go fast. She needed money management rather than spending skills. In 1939 Barton proposed marriage when her fiscal well-being was already trending downward, but the ranch was intact. Barton had plans for it.

Marriage convinced Mamie to move out of the Hotel Dieu in El Paso and back to the NAN Ranch, now called the Y-Bar. Always the horseman, Barton set about converting the Y-Bar into a horse rather than cattle operation. As he gained more control over their finances, Barton convinced Mamie to form a Nevada corporation with him called the Barton Land and Cattle Corporation. This gave Barton room to expand his interests back into his old stomping grounds along the Montana border, with their corporation having a Wyoming directory listing in Buffalo.

Mamie and Barton were sued for breach of promise in January 1946 by a local farmer who had a five-year contract to farm 700 acres on the Y-Bar Ranch. William Lankford had agreed that profits would be divided, with 60 percent going to him and 40 percent to the Bartons. Lankford was to furnish the labor while Barton furnished the oat seed, machinery, and materials. With payment not forthcoming during the final year of the contract, Lankford sued for over $155,000. Because the Barton Land and Cattle Corporation was formed under the laws of Nevada, and because of the amount of money involved, the trial had to be moved from New Mexico's Grant County district court to federal court. The judge ruled it was quite apparent that Barton had not cooperated in holding up his end of the bargain and that successful farming was impossible if he would not supply the equipment Lankford needed to farm. Nevertheless, since nothing was in writing, the judge, in a frustrating decision, could award Lankford only $8,000 for one year of damages. Apparently a man's word was no longer his bond. Mamie shortly came to the same conclusion about Fred.

Fred had dodged a bullet, but he had made himself even less popular with locals. Testifying for Lankford, who was seen as an underdog going up against the corporation, was Roy Vermillion. As one of the most famous Southwestern lawmen, the much respected Vermillion came out of retirement and traveled all the way from Washington

State to testify on Lankford's behalf. Roy was perhaps tougher than Fred. A rancher and cowboy, Vermillion knew right from wrong. He had started out as a bulldogger and rodeo performer. His ability to catch rustlers and murderers endeared him to the ranching community and resulted in his quick rise through the ranks of the newly formed New Mexico State Patrol. He traveled thousands of miles and spent months undercover breaking up rustling rings. Often he rode on the running board of a car while it bumped across a pasture so that he could lasso suspected rustled steers, bulldog them, and check their brands. He became the first captain of the New Mexico State Police in 1936.

NBC's radio program *The Big Story*, sponsored by Pall Mall Cigarettes, dramatized one of Roy's trickier double-murder cases. What looked like the accidental deaths of two young men struck by a train turned out to be a case of murderers placing the bodies on the tracks so that the locomotive could mangle them, destroying any evidence of foul play. The episode brought much publicity to Clovis, New Mexico, site of the crime. The Lankford trial brought unwanted publicity to Barton. His time in New Mexico had just about run out. Just before Christmas 1946, the *Las Cruces Sun-News* headlined, "Historic New Mexico Ranch Involved in New Legal Dispute."[9] For the press, it was, "Oh, no, not again." Mamie gave Fred a Christmas present in the form of a lawsuit. What followed involved Barton's first wife and some of the big legal players in Hollywood. With those components, the case edged toward the bizarre.

Barton had taken over liquidating his and Mamie's estate. He shipped their mansion's furnishings to Los Angeles, where they did not sit in warehouse storage for very long. The story he gave Mamie was that the furnishings could be sold for a lot more money on the West Coast. Mamie said he used that as a ruse to go to live in Los Angeles, that he had been living there since early that year. He had represented himself to her and the press as a Miles City cowboy, when he had actually been living with Ashia in Los Angeles. He had no intention of selling the furniture. Instead, he furnished Ashia's home with the shipment—and himself. On top of that, he had converted over a quarter of a million dollars in Mamie's jewelry, their bank accounts, securities, and automobiles to his name before taking off for L.A. Given research done by her attorneys, she sued both Ashia and Fred, implying the two had received a quickie divorce so that Fred could marry Mamie. The rumor spread that Ashia was even a warlord's daughter. Mamie sued to reclaim her furnishings, $15,000 in damages, and the quarter of a million dollars for the other holdings Barton had cashed in. Mamie did not mess around, hiring as her lead legal representative a well-known Hollywood attorney.

Because of the extensive holdings, lawsuits, and incorporation, Mamie was used to being lawyered up. She employed Paul D. Thomas, an attorney, judge, and president of the El Paso Bar Association. Just as John T. McElroy had been a philanthropist for El Paso, Thomas had donated the land for an El Paso school that became Radford School. (U.S. Supreme Court justice Sandra Day O'Connor would graduate from that school.) Thomas rose to fame from having been involved with the sensational Hipolito Villa Jewelry Case. Hipolito was Pancho Villa's son and financial agent for the Villa Revolution in Mexico that spilled over into the U.S. The case involved U.S. customs agents seizing $25,000 of Villa family jewelry at the border. Mamie employed the services of another L.A. attorney, Leo B. Ward, who was used to handling cases involving ranch assets in Mexico and the U.S. But it would be W.O. Graf she hired as her top gun.

W.O. Graf knew his way around the Hollywood scene, in which he handled some high-profile celebrity cases. He appeared frequently in the Second Appellate District, matching wits with state attorney general Earl Warren, later of U.S. Supreme Court fame. His cases ranged from the seemingly trivial, such as one involving a woman who was illegally keeping bees, to newspaper front-page material, the stuff of Hollywood— murders, divorces, rapes, suits and countersuits. He knew a thing or two about marital couples from out of state wrangling over property in California. Such battles cropped up when he handled Hollywood/Reno divorce settlements and their ugly fallouts. Mamie appeared to have hired the right fellow and the right firm.

Graf also had some connection to Barton's cowboy world of Los Angeles, where Barton touted Will Rogers as his friend. When working with the nearly 400-pound actor Martin Wolfkeil, Rogers dubbed Wolfkeil "Tonnage Martin." The name stuck and appeared in his movie credits when he was cast with Stan Laurel in several of Laurel's solo movie comedies such as *Oranges and Lemons*, *Brothers Under the Chin*, *Wide Open Spaces*, and *Short Kilts*. When Laurel was having trouble with his fourth wife, Tonnage became his bodyguard. Graf was called in when Laurel refused to pay Wolfkeil for his services. Later, when Laurel heard that Wolfkeil had died, Laurel made a joke of it, writing, "I just heard that 'Tonnage' died (heart trouble) glad I was'nt [*sic*] invited to be a Pall-bearer! Imagine carrying all that HEAP!!"[10]

Graf involved himself in other cowboy court battles as well. One such battle involved Ken Maynard, another of the Hollywood group of riders and cowboys Barton knew. This famous early Western cowboy actor had worked as a trick rider for the Buffalo Bill Wild West Show and the Ringling Brothers Circus. He also became a champion rodeo rider. Maynard punched out fellow cowboy actor and movie set rigger William Leon Edwards. Recovering from a back injury at the time, Edwards was unable to defend himself. Known off-camera for his drunken, egotistical meanness, Maynard allegedly beat Edwards so badly that Edwards was in danger of losing his eyesight. Once tempers cooled, the Edwards lawsuit was dropped and attorneys for both sides worked out a deal. Graf was able to extract some money from the dimming cowboy superstar that was Maynard. Graf knew about Hollywood cowboys, so Barton had to watch his step.

Graf owed much of his fame to one of the more oddball, complicated Hollywood affairs, one involving heartthrob Rudolph Valentino. Thanks to Graf, actress/pianist Marchen Jorgensen won a lawsuit against comedienne Fanny Brice's brother, Lew Brice, for $11,000. She charged that she had shown up at Brice's house to apply for a job as pianist, only to have the intoxicated Brice escort her to his boudoir to force his sexual favors on her. Forcing Brice to pay was a problem.

Shortly after Jorgensen had won judgment against Brice, she was arrested and charged with bunco along with two accomplices in a home high in the Hollywood Hills. A large portrait of the Great Lover and late movie idol, Rudolph Valentino, hung on the wall. Beneath the portrait, bowls of burning incense and freshly cut flowers served as a shrine for the Valentino cult. As Evelyn Zumaya pointed out in *Affairs Valentino: The True Story of Rudolph Valentino*, others were also trying to reach the soul of Valentino by mystically bridging the ethers. Jorgensen claimed she could fall into a trance. Valentino then spoke to her through his lips on the portrait. She transcribed his mysterious messages as they came in on her typewriter. The messages often guided Jorgensen's assistants to fill Valentino's psychic laundry, household, and grocery lists, which required a bit of forgery. All messages came through Jorgensen so she could control the purchasing. Such was Graf's client.

Meanwhile, Lew Brice had won over $150,000 at stud poker from wealthy English squire Harry Clifton, who was married to heiress Lillian Lowell Griswold of Boston's famous Lowell family. Just as Brice had refused to pay Jorgensen, Clifton would not pay Brice. The "super-colossal" poker hand squabble garnered international attention from Australia to Great Britain. Brice was to have walked away with $340,000. Clifton claimed he had been set up. He charged that Brice had led him to believe he was going to play a gentlemen's game of foursome bridge at the hotel room of a millionaire, who was actually actor George Lewis, a Western movie actor. The conspirators changed the game quickly on him from bridge to poker, with high stakes. Clifton was a bridge player, not a poker player. They also changed from playing for matchsticks to playing for IOUs. Clifton maintained that he did not have to honor his debts since the game was illegal to start with. California outlawed stud poker. The fleecers countered by saying they played draw poker, which was legal. According to Hoyle, Clifton needed to pay up.

Graf wanted in on the proceedings, hoping to get a part of Brice's poker winnings to settle the payment Brice owed Marchen Jorgensen. The involvement of another foursome player, Tommy Guinan, publicized the affair even more. Tommy and his famous sister, Texas, grew up on a Waco ranch. The sainted Texas became famous as being Broadway's most popular "Welcome, sucker!" hostess, symbol of speakeasy culture during Prohibition. The jewels she wore were said to be big enough to signal ships at sea, her feathers made peacocks cry, and her white fur-trimmed wraps could house the queens of Europe. Prohibition agents raided her establishments and padlocked them so many times that when greeting customers Texas wore a necklace of padlocks she had collected. She took in $700,000 (over $9.5 million in today's money) in one ten-month period and rode to and fro in her bulletproof armored truck, but she died young of ulcerative colitis one month short of the repeal of Prohibition. Her death led to one of New York City's biggest funeral processions.

As a young woman, Texas worked as a trick rider and roper for a Wild West show and worked in vaudeville. As the first movie cowgirl, she starred in or produced some 300 movies, ranging from one- to six-reel Westerns. Dubbed the "Queen of the West," her face was plastered on movie posters, sheet music, and silent-movie-star trading cards. As she transitioned to speakeasy hostess, she became "Queen of the Night." Her *Too Hot for Paris* revue was a hit. She and Tommy became famous for running the most popular speakeasies in New York. Prohibition made her a legend, so much so that Barbara Nichols played her in *The George Raft Story* (1961), Betty Hutton in *The Incendiary Blonde* (1945), and Phyllis Diller in *Splendor in the Grass* (1961). Gene Roddenberry named Whoopi Goldberg's Guinan character in the *Star Trek: The Next Generation* series (1987–1994) after Texas Guinan. Appropriately, as part of the crew aboard the USS *Enterprise-D*, she served as bartender and lounge hostess. Texas Gainan also lived on as characters based on her in several other motion pictures and television series.

Tommy's fame grew too. Known as Texas's "frisky" brother, he held the notorious record for the number of times being busted by the police, while never having to serve any serious time. He ran Texas Tommy Guinan's Playground on West Fifty-Second

Street, Club Napoleon, and Chez Florence, to name a few. These fancy, classic speakeasies were indeed the playground of the rich, famous, and criminal. Mobsters rubbed shoulders with movie stars and the Broadway elite. Tommy knew who the whales at cards and horse track betting were.

Tommy and Texas knew the visiting rich Texas cattlemen and oil men. Seeking illegal boozy fun, these wealthy exhibitionists were just dying to be parted from their money as fast as possible, in contrast to Barton's Western friends and acquaintances who did not enjoy Broadway and the canyons of New York City. J. Frank Dobie could only patiently endure the literary "teas" while waiting to be released back to the West. As Stanley Walker, city editor for the *New York Herald Tribune* said in his exposé *The Night Club Era*, Barton's fellow Montanan Will James did not fare well either. The cowboy artist was "puzzled and sick on his first trip to New York."[11] It was no place for a cowboy.

A notable exception was Miles City cowboy Paddy Ryan, friend to Barton's China crew. When the affable rodeo champion performed in Madison Square Garden, New York's Irish community embraced the redhead in his bright green silk shirt. How could they not like a champion named "Paddy" Ryan? The New York Police Department made him their honorary captain at the same time that gangsters proudly entertained him in their speakeasies. Ziegfeld girls asked him out. Everything was on the house.[12]

If Paddy had been able to bring along that old racketeer of the range, Skyrocket, the two Rodeo Hall of Famers could have topped the famous entrance Texas had made. Guinan rode her horse down an aisle through an amazed crowd and then leapt up on the stage. Skyrocket, of course, would have left more speakeasy damage than revenuers with axes, but Skyrocket had cashed in his horse chips a few years earlier. On the other hand, Tommy and Texas were used to the breaking of glass and splintering of wood. It was almost like being back in Waco.

Even larger than life than Paddy, Valentino was the Great Lover. Enter clairvoyance and Valentino again. *Photoplay* hosted a 1926 reception at Tommy's Playground for Valentino to celebrate the opening of his new movie, *Son of the Sheik*. Mae West and Tommy's sister served as hostesses, both being much taken with Rudolph. A month later, Valentino was dead. Like Jorgensen, Mae and her best friend Texas performed a séance right away to contact the Great Lover. They believed that his enemies had poisoned him. Other séances followed to contact the undead film star on the other side.

Graf might as well have been on the other side, as he certainly came out on the wrong side of the court case. Clifton did not have to pay up, so Brice received no money. But as the saying goes, even bad publicity was good publicity, for Graf. Mamie Parker Barton was playing her poker hand well by bringing in the attorney.

Graf and his law partner, the flamboyant S.S. "Sammy" Hahn, were the "go-to" attorneys in Los Angeles. They started out taking on high-profile murder cases but then moved to lucrative divorce cases. The more famous and controversial the people involved, the better. Hahn participated in the famous Black Dahlia murder case and defended Louise Peele, one of only three women executed by the State of California. His divorce cases were a casting-service dream—Stan Laurel, Errol Flynn, and, later, John Wayne, Julie London, Jack "Dragnet" Webb, Susan Hayward, Frank Sinatra, and others.

Like Ashia Barton, Sammy Hahn was a Russian immigrant who put down roots in Los Angeles. Sometimes referred to as a gangster mouthpiece, he was said to know all the show biz, political, and mob secrets of Hollywood. Actor Geoff Pierson played Hahn in Clint Eastwood's *Changeling* (2008), based on the story of Christine Collins. The motion picture, a horrific tale of LAPD corruption, followed the events of her son's being murdered and replaced by another child, and her being unjustifiably committed to a mental institution. In 1957, Hahn was found drowned at the deep end of his swimming pool at his cabin up one of the canyons. A rope was tied around his neck and attached to two cement blocks. He reportedly had a gash on his head. No suicide note was left. Whether his mysterious death reflected suicide or homicide, perhaps he knew too much.

In handling Mamie's case against Barton, Graf flexed his legal muscle from the get-go. A court order impounded the furniture Barton had given to his second wife, Ashia. Sheriff's deputies arrived at her house and took out the twenty Oriental rugs, the silverware, and the furnishings. They then locked it all up in a warehouse. This action must have grabbed Barton's attention. In just a little over a week from the time Mamie filed her two suits against Barton, the suits were dismissed. Werner Graf announced that the couple had adjusted property matters and had become reconciled. Again tales of the case appeared in newspapers across the country, drawing attention to Mamie, Barton, and Graf. Some newspapers, such as the *Kingsport Times* in Tennessee, even reported that Mamie was now Barton's ex-wife. If she did divorce him, she kept her name as Barton.

When Graf announced that Fred and Mamie had "reconciled," that was probably a polite mischaracterization. More likely cash was exchanged out of court, and, undaunted, they went their separate ways. Barton had faced possible life-and-death situations in China and Montana, so a little downturn in his affairs with Mamie was not going to mean much in the grand scheme of things. Barton's side of the story in the whole affair remains untold, if there is anything to tell. Mamie's earlier court battle, concerning breaking up her ranch hand's marriage, does not leave her behavior unquestioned either.

The Y-Bar NAN Ranch was sold to Bill Green, a citizen of Mexico, who in 1949 turned around and sold it to Clay Holland and W.B. Hinton. The heirs of W.B. and Clara Hinton still own the NAN as a functioning ranch and New Mexico landmark, but the great McElroy/Barton Empire is gone.

Mamie came to live for a while in Los Angeles. Though it was already a big city where people could become lost to each other, her presence seems a bit edgy considering that Barton, Ashia, and perhaps even Barton's first wife lived there. According to Parker family history, Mamie was said to have died penniless on her sister's couch. She ended where she started: poor, but having kept her promise to care for her siblings. The McElroy fortune had evaporated. Upon her 1968 death, she was carried home to Groesbeck, Texas, and buried in the McElroy/Parker pioneer cemetery next to J.T., which is to say she was not buried next to Fred Barton.

So far as is known, Mamie was Fred's last wife. Before their breakup, Mamie's ranch wrought some revenge on Barton. While newspaper headlines bespoke of the American Volunteer Group (AVG), or Flying Tigers, fighting the Japanese back in Asia, secondary headlines told of Barton fighting his own wars in his new home in the U.S. At the Y-Bar

Fourteen • *The Many Wives of a Lifelong Bachelor, Here and Abroad*

NAN Ranch in the spring of 1941, Barton fell trying to get out of the way of a horse. The horse stepped on him while he was on the ground, snapping Barton's arm. At the time, he still owned El Paso's McElroy Union Stockyards. Barton was in the process of liquidating it, which he did, only to be sued for nearly $50,000 by a former injured stockyard employee who had fallen on the stockyard's loading platform. Aside from that, Fred had done well as "a lifelong bachelor." Ashia, the woman he was always soft on, ended up with most of the impounded furnishings after all. Her family kept a high regard for Barton and his generosity, even after Ashia remarried.

Like Barton, Ashia married three times. When in 1970 she married Alexander F. Dolgopolov (Doll), the furniture moved with her from the Barton house to the house that her new husband had built over time with his own hands in Laguna Beach overlooking the ocean. To some visitors, this simple, California pioneer-style house seemed overwhelmed by the baroque furnishings from the NAN Ranch. Many of the Charles M. Russell reproduced paintings Barton had commissioned adorned the walls. Dolgopolov made do with his new wife's New Mexico and Montana accoutermental invasion.

As a White Russian who had fought against the Reds, this 20th Century Fox set builder was able to flee to Constantinople and then, in 1923, take passage to the United States. Alex was not just any Hollywood worker. He had been decorated for his heroics during the White Russian's tragic, and ill-fated, "Campaign on the Ice" against the Reds. Survivors had frozen feet that were permanently damaged. This led to an embolism and Alex's death six years after he married Ashia.

Dolgopolov could appreciate the places Barton had been in China and Russia. He knew them well. Alex's good friend Khan Razak Bek Hadjiev had emigrated to Mexico, and his daughter had become a nurse in Ontario, California. Hadjiev served as adjutant to General Kornilov, who became commander-in-chief of the Russian Army. Hadjiev had served in Siberia, Vladivostok, and Manchuria, sometimes at the same time Barton had been there.

The Hollywood set builder became the world's foremost authority on early Russian colonization in North America. Just as Fred Barton became an Old West historian and preservationist, Alex sought to document and preserve the history of Russians in America. He became an expert on the Russian-American Company and California's Fort Ross. Fort Ross represented the southernmost expansion of Russian colonization, the point where Russian expansion from the north and Spanish/Mexican expansion from the south met in California.

Alex Dolgopolov's dedication inspired his brother-in-law, Dr. Ushanoff, to catch the same history bug. Unlike Barton, who could hire an artist to reproduce C.M. Russell's Old West paintings, Ashia's sister's husband trained himself to be an artist. Using old illustrations for inspiration, he produced some 130 paintings of Russian colonization in North America, particularly Alaska. Both the Dolgopolov and Usharoff collections are now owned by the Alaska State Library in Juneau.

Barton pursued his own collecting. Tracking what he called the Fred Barton Collection of the Old West is a bit more problematic, and would carry dangers for the art world.

• **Fifteen** •

Life Without Warlords
C.M. Russell and the Fred Barton Museum of the Old West, 1937–1967

Most of the stalwarts have gone over the great divide. A precious few of them still linger to give with warm and honest handshake, the personal touch of those manly days of old. It is our hope that we may be able to keep their spirit with us always; for in the strength of these old cattlemen with that of other pioneers was the force that builded [sic] and that will save our America.
—Howard R. Driggs, *Westward America*

By the 1950s, Barton was ready to retire. Earlier injuries sustained from falling off a horse and the onset of osteoporosis had taken their toll, giving him a sizeable humpback, neither of which may have improved his disposition. He was ready to pursue his pet interests: the creation of the Fred Barton Museum of the West and playing the role of the old cowboy who knew everyone in the Old West. Many people were invited to his L.A. apartment to view his collection and to hear his opinion on world affairs and the Old West vs. modern times. He did appear at some meetings of the Westerners Corral to claim his Old West connections, but he did not seem to sustain any membership, though he was quick to sing the praises of such groups to others.

Despite some shadows cast by Barton's character, he also cast a lot of light. He generously donated some of his relics and knowledge of the West to magazines and museums. He made sure widows of old cowboys received copies of Western history magazines that he paid for out of his own pocket. He also published small brochures about the Old West through private printings.

Family members respected him, avoiding saying anything negative. Even at this late date, long after his death, they are surprised to learn of shadows in his past. Those whom he befriended also share warm feelings for Barton.

Folklorist Mary MacGregor-Villarreal remembers the kindness Barton showed her in the 1950s when she was a child in love with horses. Her father, Emerson "Mac" MacGregor, and her step-grandfather enjoyed Barton as a friend and client. They owned a photography studio specializing in black-and-white photo developing. Barton asked MacGregor to make photographs of his art collection for insurance purposes. McGregor probably reproduced the many black-and-white photographs of Charlie Russell and Barton that Fred glued into his book collection. Dr. MacGregor-Villarreal still recalls how her family owned horses, and how, when she met Barton, he encouraged her by giving her gear from his cowboy days, including a cherished set of spurs.[1]

He also shared with the Montana Historical Society in particular. His correspondence with the Montana Historical Society (MHS) began in 1954 and would run nearly until his death in 1967. Most correspondence streamed between him and K. Ross Toole and Michael S. Kennedy, directors of the MHS, or Vivian A. Palladin, who edited *Montana: The Magazine of Western History*. Though Barton was sometimes hard to please, those who dealt with him did so in a friendly, professional manner. But diplomacy taxed their patience. He knew how to run everyone else's business and knew what was wrong with the world.

Excluding family and close friends, just about everyone who visited his home or wrote him came away with similar impressions. Barton was an "odd bird" (J. Frank Dobie),[2] an "eccentric' (Brian Dippie),[3] "a character" (Harold G. Davidson),[4] an "old wind-bag type" (Vivian Palladin).[5] Or, since Barton lived only a few blocks north of Wilshire Boulevard, if he played the good host and took his guest over to the nearby Brown Derby for lunch, he could be "a dapper old fellow dressed immaculately in Western garb who preferred to dwell on the 'good old days' when there were Real Men striding the earth, including himself...." (Harold G. Davidson).[6] By this time, the Real Man had been reduced to ordering only a soft boiled egg at the Brown Derby. Likewise, when Fal and Ruth Koerner Oliver (Ruth was the daughter of Western artist W.H.D. Koerner) went to visit Barton, he sang them a few cowboy songs while playing his guitar. Then he showed them the nude above his bed and a casket of someone's ashes that he kept on a shelf under a bunch of disheveled clothes.[7]

To cite just one dimension of Barton's personality in the 1950s and 1960s, California bookseller Richard Upton got both barrels when he visited Barton's apartment in Los Angeles.[8] Upton had seen Barton's name in an Old West magazine, perhaps *True West*, so he called Barton to see if he could visit. Barton invited him over; however, Upton learned he had made a mistake when he knocked on Barton's door. He could hear Barton inside unlocking a whole series of locks that ran up and down the door. After unlocking them all, Barton took one look at Upton, said, "You're five minutes early," and closed the door on him. Upton waited for five minutes and knocked again. Again came the ritual with what Upton described as "unusual locks." This time he was admitted, but Barton was just warming up.

Inside, the apartment was immaculate. Barton retained his military prep school training. For an old cowboy bachelor, he kept an organized, clean apartment and prided himself in being so organized that he had always needed only a half hour or so each day to keep his books and do paperwork. While earlier visitors to Barton's apartment noticed the genuine Tiffany lamp in the front room, Upton was more concerned with Western artifacts. Fred displayed a saddle on a saddletree. A closet contained Sunday going-to-town cowboy clothes, what cowboys bought at the end of drives, including fifteen Stetsons. As a buyer and seller of Western books, Dick was most interested in Barton's book collection, but Barton was not about to show him that. Instead, the old cowboy deflected him to a photo album that contained Huffman shots of the West and he mentioned the ranch in China.

Barton turned the conversation to topics Upton found inappropriate, beginning with African Americans. When Upton ignored his racist comments, Fred tried to get a rise out of him by attacking the educational system and how it did not teach the truth about history. Having been a teacher, albeit a band instructor, Dick felt some obligation to defend his former profession. Barton asked him if he knew who really owned all the big ranches. Dick replied that he thought Scotchmen and their sons had owned them from what he had read about history. His informed answer annoyed Barton. Upton was not as dumb as Barton wanted him to be.

At this point, Barton showed off his bedroom. Most Barton guests commented on this infamous bedroom, for over the bed hung a huge barroom painting of a nude. Barton continued his racist talk, to which Upton did not respond, so they returned to the living room to look at some more photo albums. Then Upton was shown the door. Now the lock ritual began all over again. Barton could not rid himself of Upton quickly because he faced having to unlock all the locks again. To make matters even more awkward, he had not really locked the door when Upton entered the apartment. Instead of unlocking the door to whisk Upton out, he was actually relocking all the locks. Having completed doing the reverse of what he wanted to do, he had to undo the locks all over again while Upton waited. Very awkward. A trip to Barton's was a trip to be remembered.

Other guests recalled all the friends he claimed, a virtual Who's Who of the West: Charles Marion Russell, Will Rogers, Wallace Coburn, Ed Borein, Frank Linderman, Will James, Joe De Yong. Barton's character traits cast doubt on the accuracy of his statements. Everything he said had to be taken with a very large grain of salt, one about the size of Montana frosted with Hollywood glitz. On the other hand, Barton's meticulousness extended to his correspondence. He kept letters he exchanged with those he claimed as friends.

Assessing the depth and quality of these friendships remains tentative. This holds particularly true for the close friendships he claimed with Hollywood Western stars and artists. Anyone living even a short time in Montana knows that the concept of friendship can be interpreted quite loosely. A quick handshake with someone can later be claimed as a close friendship. And nearly everyone who knew the difference between a horse and a cow would like to claim some family relationship with Barton's favorite artist, Charlie Russell. More people in Montana claim to have known Charlie personally than people living during Russell's lifetime. That may be an exaggeration, but it has become a running joke. Many people claim to have posed for the same painting by Russell or claim that Charlie painted a certain painting just for them only to have his wife, Nancy, sell it to some Easterner for big bucks. Like Barton's telling of his own story, some truth does reside in these stories, but it takes a lot of wading through the feedlot or silage pit to reach it. We are about to enter the pit.

Consider Barton's relationship with the older Charlie Russell (1864–1926). Fred fanatically admired Russell's work. What he couldn't buy he had copied. He quickly criticized anyone he felt did not know the true Charlie Russell. Once, he ordered a series of books from the Montana Historical Society. When they arrived, he quickly returned one on Russell by Britzman, saying, "I never did like Homer Britzman or anything he did. He never knew Russell, and was only interested in making money. The dollar was his God."[9] Director Michael Kennedy diplomatically accepted the return, saying, "I understand your feeling about Britzman. The only reason of course that we sent this book to you was because you ordered it."[10] Barton then launched an attack on Austin Russell's book about his uncle Charlie.[11]

Barton's opinion about Britzman, though shared by some others, may also have been a case of the pot calling the kettle black. Barton claimed to be close friends with Russell, but as eminent Russell scholar Brian W. Dippie and other Russell specialists have pointed out, nothing in any of the Russell papers mentions Barton. The closest to anything pointing to a connection is through inconclusive letters between Barton and J. Frank Dobie and in events surrounding Barton's reproductions of Russell's paintings. Such lack of written connection does not preclude oral communication or visits, however.

J. Frank Dobie had always wanted to write a biography of C.M. Russell but never completed it. When John Taliaferro took up the task again to produce *Charles M Russell: The Life and Legend of America's Cowboy Artist,* he reviewed Dobie's manuscript collection and his correspondence with Barton. Since Barton claimed friendship with Russell, Dobie was interested in what Barton had to say.

Taliaferro's review of the Dobie collection reveals that Dobie and his bookseller friend Jack Reynolds visited Barton in Los Angeles on March 22, 1956. In Dobie's typed manuscript describing the visit, he reported Barton was a very eccentric, wealthy bachelor in his 60s whose father had been a prosperous rancher near Miles City. Barton knew Russell and owned reproductions of some of his painting. He also knew Will Rogers and befriended Western artist Ed Borein, one of Rogers' closest friends. In fact, Fred Barton said he had set up Borein as an artist by giving him $500 for twenty etchings. Barton then shared some of his Russell stories. According to Barton, and using Dobie's paraphrasing:

> He [Russell] never cared for money and she [Nancy Russell] didn't care for much else. He was in nigger heaven with his friends and she was always trying to cut him off from them.
> He liked giving pictures to people he liked. He kept [an] old cowpuncher comrade waiting for years for a promised picture, and then set about painting something extra good to make up for the long neglect. He had been working on the canvas for some time and it was about 99 percent finished when Nancy came into the studio, urging him to finish it.
> "I have sold it for $5000," she said.
> "Not this picture," Charlie said. "It's for my old friend John Blank."
> "It's sold for $5000, I'm telling you," Nancy said. "You can dash off something for John Blank."
> Russell seldom lost his temper. He lost it now, jumped up, dipped a big brush in a can of paint and smeared the painting all over, utterly obliterating the painstaking and loving work he had done.[12]

Barton would recount this same story in a July 5, 1963, letter to Dobie. This letter stated he heard the account directly from Russell in the presence of Will Rogers and Ed Borein. He added that Russell said he was so mad at Nancy that he didn't return to his Great Falls, Montana, studio for three days. Other particulars of the story had also changed a bit. Instead of ruining the painting with a brush, Barton said Russell had taken a rag, picked up all the colors on his palette, and then had smeared the painting.

This story was, and remains, a favorite story of the Russellianaphobes in the Nancy-hater camp. Barton could have heard the oft-repeated story without hearing it from

Russell himself. Dobie continued with his paraphrase of another Russell story Barton told:

> One winter while they were at Santa Barbara Nancy gave a big party to promote sales. She had in all the rich retired plumbers and bankers she could gather up. Charlie's pictures were well displayed and he was supposed to be. His only response was to grunt to some innane [sic] question. Nancy was keeping an eye on him all the time, fearing some breakout. After a while he signaled her that he was going to the bathroom. He locked the door on the inside, opened a window and crawled out. He went straight to the home of his old friend Frank Linderman, who was sick. Charlie knew his room and knocked on it.
> "You have to come with me, Frank," he said. "I'm in trouble."
> Linderman dressed and they went and sat on the beach, Charlie telling a good deal beyond his story of distress. About 2 a.m., he said, "You reckon those sons-of-bitches have gone home yet?" Linderman reckoned they had and Charlie went home to Nancy.
> Russell had illustrated two of Linderman's books, for small fees, and was going to illustrate the last one Linderman published but Nancy would not allow him. She had good paying commissions for him, she explained—and they could not afford cheap ones, even for friends.[13]

Again, Barton related an anti–Nancy story that he might have picked up through gossip. Since he claimed friendship with Will Rogers, Ed Borein, and others who were friends of Russell, he could easily have heard stories from them.

The same was true of *Charles M Russell: An Old-time Cowman Discusses the Life of Charles M Russell*. Barton privately reprinted this pamphlet from an earlier version entitled *An Old-time Cowman Discusses the Intellect of Charles M Russell* and an article in the Fall 1958 issue of *Western History* entitled "Man of Mind: An Old Time Cowman Discusses the Intellect of C.M.R." He dogged the Montana Historical Society as well as West Coast booksellers to sell the monograph printed by Times-Mirror Press and distributed copies freely to his acquaintances. Booksellers and the historical society did carry and advertise the short piece. When the Montana Historical Society included it on its list of pamphlets for sale, Barton was listed as author Fred. M. Barton. Since he had no middle name, the historical society caught hell.[14]

The short piece enjoyed some popular demand after receiving favorable press in the August 1961 issue of the *Cattleman*. According to Barton, the editor, Biederman, wrote him to say "that he liked the booklet so much that he thought everybody who loved the old West and admired Charlie Russell should have a copy in their library."[15] To separate himself, as he perceived it, from the money-grubbers living off the Russell legend, such as Britzman, Barton always made sure people knew he did not want to make any money from the pamphlet. Though Barton claimed a close relationship with Russell, nothing in the pamphlet indicated fresh firsthand impressions, which is not to say people did not enjoy what Barton said. Many did; it is just that there was nothing new.

Dobie continued cordial relations with Barton and shared the secondhand knowledge he received that continued themes Barton had addressed. Barton received a letter from Dobie dated July 9, 1961, that addressed "the Nancy issue" and an observation Barton had made about the Russells being oil and water:

> I've met quite a few people who knew Charlie Russell and Nancy but did not approve of her. She was thrifty. Put money in the purse. He was not only generous but prodigal.

Life is a compromise. If she hadn't come along to kind of ride herd on him, he very probably would have ended up without achieving more than a few spontaneous pictures. She made art his career. I don't think I should have cared bout being in her company.

Sid Willis hated her guts, as the saying goes. According to what he told me, not too long after they married there ceased to be any physical union between them. This should be nobody's business, but somehow people make it a business to know about the private life of artists, writers, and other public characters. You say they had nothing in common mentally. Sid Willis said they had nothing in common physically. What in the devil did they have in common?[16]

Though we only have Barton's word for it, another of Dobie's notes on his meeting with Barton does resemble firsthand experience with the Russells:

Fred Barton said that he went to see Nancy in Pasadena not long before she died. She was in a wheel chair with a nurse and an attendant both at hand. She dismissed them and said to Barton: "I want to tell you something private. I know now that I ruined the last years of Charlie's life. We had plenty, but I always wanted more and drove him to make more, keeping him from idling with the friends he enjoyed. Now for three years I have been using up everything we made. I have been so long dying that nothing will be left for Jackie. Life for me is torture and I made Charlie's life a torture."

After Charlie was buried at Great Falls and Nancy went to live permanently in Pasadena she let it be known that she wanted to be buried in California, not with Charlie, but she relented and was buried beside him.[17]

The discussion between Barton and Dobie about the Russell marriage continued. In the July 5, 1963, letter to Dobie, Barton added the following:

When Charlie and I were alone one time I remember telling him that I did not believe that he had ever proposed marriage to Nancy. I was convinced that she had set her cap to catch him when she heard the Roberts' (for whom she worked at Cascade, Montana) tell that he was coming down from Great Falls to visit them. I told him that I firmly believed that Nancy had suggested marriage and that he was too damn polite to say no. He did not contradict me, but merely smiled and said nothing. Mentally they had nothing in common.[18]

Barton did say he had direct contact with the Russells over the Russell reproductions. Barton either could not afford or did not want to pay Nancy's $5000 price tags, and some of his favorite Russell paintings were already in private hands. He wanted them badly, so he turned to Charlie to see if he could have reproductions made. Art critics experience a parting of the ways here. Some call these copies "reproductions"; others label them "forgeries." Depends on one's point of view. Barton's May 19, 1963, autobiographical sketch related events surrounding the reproductions. Since, as Barton said, "no ethical artist would duplicate any of his pictures," Russell suggested artist E.L. Boone (1881–1952) of Montana, adding that he would have no objection to Boone's reproductions since he knew Barton wanted the paintings out of true love for the West and would never put them up for sale. Boone agreed, stipulating that he would make only one copy of each desired painting and none for anyone else.[19]

Again, can Barton's word be taken as truth? Elizabeth A. Dear, curator of the C.M. Russell Museum in Great Falls, seriously doubted that Russell gave him permission. First, Nancy would never have allowed it. Second, there was a good chance the reproductions were done after Nancy died. Factor in Barton's propensity to put himself at the center of Russell and California movie cronies, without strong evidence that he actually was, and his story about Charlie's permission becomes suspicious.

On the other hand, Russell's permission makes sense. Boone and Russell painted together in Montana before Boone became well known as a Southwest artist. They painted similar range cowboy themes, leading some people to believe that Boone took lessons from Russell. For instance, Boone's oil *A Helluva Way to Start the Day*, also called *Bronc Buster*, sits squarely in the Russell tradition of humorous early-morning scenes on the range such as Russell's *Bronc to Breakfast, Camp Cook's Troubles*, and *When Horses Talk War*—all of which show recalcitrant horses ruining cowboy breakfasts and mornings with mayhem and destruction. On the back of his 1917 oil showing a bucking bronco, Boone wrote that it was painted with Russell at the Big Belt Ranch in Montana. Since both artists loved depicting broncs and bronc busters as symbols of the Old West and Barton was a bronc buster, Boone was the perfect, trusted artist for Russell to recommend to Barton.

The reproductions were not to carry Russell's signature. This worried people like K. Ross Toole, who after traveling to California to see the collection believed the reproductions of such quality that they could easily be mistaken for Russell originals and placed in the market by simply adding his signature. Toole went so far as to write Barton in 1958, emphasizing that the copies should be kept together, that Barton should stipulate the collection was never to be sold, and that he should consider placing a photographic inventory of the Boone copies in the Montana Historical Society Archives.[20] Should they be sold, they could seriously damage the Russell art market and Russell's memory. Others who saw the Boone copies thought them to be bad. Ginger Renner, the well-known Russell writer and authenticator, remembered when her husband, Frederic G. Renner, visited Barton and saw the Boones. Not only were they bad copies, but Renner also felt that anyone with the slightest knowledge of Russell's work would know they were not originals. He felt Barton should have settled for good prints rather than investing in the paintings. Like Toole, Fred predicted that "sure as shooting some day one of those copies would turn up with a Russell signature on it."[21]

In addition to the Boone copies, Boone painted another oil for Barton unrelated to Russell. Barton provided Boone with a 1906 photograph of himself taken near Miles City. Using this, Boone created an oil of the teenage cowboy Barton standing in his leather chaps, uncreased hat, and bandana, sagebrush and buttes behind him in the distance. Boone and Barton became friends. Barton wrote a tribute to Boone after Elmer's death in 1952.

After seeing the Boone copies at his home, guests to the Barton apartment had to make two other stops. Barton took them to see his former White Russian wife, who lived nearby. Ashia was described as a big, fine-looking, mature, dark-haired woman. When Barton died in 1967, his death certificate listed her as the informant, with the name Ashia Tarr. After she married Universal Studios propman Alexander Feodor Doll, her name as surviving spouse in 1977 was given as Ashia Bashenko.

Barton also took visitors to an area bank that displayed the Boone reproductions. What happened to the Boone copies of Russell's work remains a mystery that all serious admirers and collectors of Russell's work would like resolved. Boone's reproductions could easily have been converted to forgeries. Clearly that was not Barton's intent, for he worried what would happen to them upon his death. He did indeed try to heed Toole's advice to keep his collection intact; consequently, Barton contacted several possible venues for the collection, insisting on just that.

Placing the Boone copies and the rest of the Fred Barton Collection of the Old West became impossible because of his demand that the collection be on permanent display in a Fred Barton Room. Pressed for space, museums could not dedicate that kind of area just to highlight his collection. Most institutions depend on temporary displays that change throughout the year while the rest of the collection remains in storage. Barton really wanted the collection to find its home in Montana, where he visited nearly every year, since so much of the collection originated there. He surprised the Montana Historical Society by asking Director Kennedy if the society would take it. Kennedy responded, saying he had always been under the impression Barton planned to donate the collection to the Cowboy Hall of Fame in Oklahoma.[22]

Kennedy was willing to take the collection under condition that the display not be permanent. Since the society was out of space, Kennedy held out a futuristic plum. He mentioned that if the legislature approved funding for a new wing, the Barton collection might become permanent. Not satisfied with the arrangement, Barton traveled to Miles City to convince the city or the Range Riders Museum to display his materials. They faced the same logistical problems as the Montana Historical Society. Other galleries faced problems with the reproductions being reproductions, because they collected originals.

And so the 56-year-accumulating collection of 100 Boone copies, other oils, bronzes and photographs remained with Barton, along with the saddles, angora and leather chaps, spurs, boots, hats, rawhide ropes and hobbles, Winchester 30–30 carbines, Colt .45 six-shooters, scabbards, Navaho saddle blankets, and other artifacts. He would sell off his Western book collection through bookseller Glen Dawson in Los Angeles. Curiously, this took place a few months after the visit by Richard Upton, who was mentioned earlier and who had to fend off Barton's racist comments only to be shown a locked door. Had Barton sold his collection to Dawson to spite Upton? The collection contained few rare items. Barton thought the whole collection priceless, yet Dawson remembered the books as being mostly reprints. Barton doctored them by using photo and newspaper article paste-ins. These hybrids still appear on the book market.

A bronze set of spurs also connects Barton tangentially to Russell. When the Montana Historical Society needed a set of spurs to complete a Russell bronze in the fall of 1958, Barton volunteered to ride to the rescue. He claimed his Russell bronze superior to that owned by the society. His had been made by a New York artisan suggested by A.J. Bayer. Barton also volunteered to oversee any future bronze work the society might need to make sure it received the best craftsmanship possible. The pair of spurs cost Barton $25. He was concerned that people in Helena might not know where to attach the spurs, so he wrote, "Be sure the spurs are attached in the correct place. Shorty Shope will know the proper place."[23]

Barton trusted Shope. Unlike Russell, who had given the artist Shope his blessing, "Shorty" was Montana born and raised. Shope did not have to run away from home to become a cowboy. His 1925 visit with Russell resulted in Russell's telling him to skip more Eastern art training and instead stick with painting the West that was in his heart.

Despite being stricken with polio at an early age, the diminutive teenager became a working cowboy for several years. Furthermore, he shared the same cowpunching range with Barton, mostly south of Miles City. He worked the range there when Barton was recruiting cowboys out of Miles City for the China ranch. Being a bit young for China, Shope went on to cowboy throughout the late teens and 1920s. Afterwards he became a successful painter of the West, as well as a commercial artist for the State of Montana and Montana Power Company. Located in Helena, Shope had easy access to the Russell bronzes of the Montana State Historical Society located there. He certainly knew where to place spurs on the Russell bronze. He had all the cowboy credibility Barton desired.

Barton cherished most highly his Russell-autographed photo of Charlie. Canadian professional photographer Harry Pollard took the photograph at the 1919 Calgary Stampede, the last Stampede the Russells would attend and the last time Russell would be photographed with Native Americans.[24] The Russell photograph became Pollard's most famous photo. It adorns the 2014 cover of Larry Len Peterson's *Charles M. Russell: Photographing the Legend*.

Whether Barton requested the photo or Charlie freely gave it to him is unknown. Barton photographed it in its frame so that the Montana Historical Society would have a copy. After receiving the photo from Russell, Barton immediately placed it in a hand-tooled saddle leather frame and showed it to Charlie. Barton reported that Russell liked the frame very much. Barton took pride in the photo because "Charles Russell consistently refused thru life to autograph any of his photographs of himself. He always said that every ham actor and politician made a practice of this. He made one exception to this rule and autographed his best photograph for me."[25] Actually, Russell did sign a few other photographs for selected people.

Barton owned other unautographed Russell photos he donated to the Montana Historical Society Archives—almost as many photos as he gave of himself. He presented more than one view of himself taken in Fort Worth around 1940. One undated photo shows Russell with Buck Buchanon, John Matheson, and Bill Deaton at Chico Hot Springs near Yellowstone Park. They all lean on a fence railing or each other and look pretty duded up. Another photo shows Charlie on a horse holding his infant adopted son, Jack, on his lap. Barton donated these photos in 1954. Finally, an outdoor shot shows Russell with Con Price, who looks none too happy posing. All the photographs show Russell with his distinctive cloth sash that he used for a belt.

Other Barton photos have surfaced before the public. John Taliaferro's 1996 article, "Curse of the Buffalo Skull," in *Montana: The Magazine of Western History*, featured a photo of author J. Frank Dobie that Barton donated to the Montana Historical Society in 1960. Dobie had autographed the photo and dedicated it: "To Fred Barton." The photograph shows an elderly Dobie wearing his cowboy hat and smoking his pipe. Given the communication that existed between the two men, it is easy to understand Barton's having this photo.

• Sixteen •

Barton and the Hollywood Cowboys

My excuse for writing this book is money—and lots of it.—Cowboy Charlie Siringo[1]

When you call me that, smile.—The Virginian, in *The Virginian*[2]

Another one of Barton's stated Hollywood chums was Western movie star Wallace Coburn. Barton donated two photos of Coburn to the Montana Historical Society: one shows him around 35 years old, the other around 80 years old. Wallace ("Wallie" or "Walt") Coburn worked as a likeable Montana cowboy whose father, Robert, was one of the state's pioneer cattlemen. The Coburns first started ranching during the Virginia City and Last Chance Gulch gold rush. They switched operations from Prickly Pear Valley to Flatwillow, ending up on the Circle C south of Malta, Montana, in 1886. Wallace's half brother Walt was also quite well known. He chronicled their adventures on the Circle C for the pulp magazines of the time. Given the Coburn Circle C brand, one could say that half brother Walt was the only Western writer whose cows and stories were copyrighted. Later he produced *Pioneer Cattleman in Montana*, published by the University of Oklahoma Press in 1968. Walt called Wallace the top cowman that he knew.

Before Wallace went off to Hollywood, he had already received notoriety for his collection of poems *Rhymes from a Round-Up Camp*, published by Putnam in both the U.S. and England. Charles M. Russell illustrated the collection. Wallace had Charlie's seal of approval, so Barton would naturally want an association with him. Russell praised Coburn highly:

Wallace D. Coburn, the Cowboy Poet, is known the country over as the author of *Rhymes of the Round-Up Camp* and other delectable compositions in verse and prose. He is blue-eyed, stalwart, laughter—loving with a face like a Galway Blazer, and a smile that is worth going miles to see. Horseman of the plains, mighty hunter, ranchman, cowpuncher, scholar, wit, practician and poet, he rounds out his career as a Westerner by being the ONLY White Chief of the Assinaboine Sioux, his tribal name being Peta-kooa-honga, which means Cowboy Chief. He is familiarly known to half a dozen tribes as Heymus, or Iron Tooth.

Wallace (everybody calls him by his first name) is recognized as one of the best rifle, wing and pistol shots, he has had hundreds of stirring adventures by mountain and stream. He has whipped with bait and fly every notable fishing water in the Northwest, and he is probably entitled to the Montana record as a bear hunter, having killed four grizzlies with rifle and knife unaided and alone in a single fight.... We have been friends, he and I, for many years, friends as only men can be who love the same life, who have camped together like true comrades and who are aware of one another's fidelity, loyalty and courage without the need of a spoken word.[3]

In speaking of friendship, Barton's language resembled or tried to copy Russell's, such as the comments Russell made about comradeship on the range. However, Barton's writing lacked Russell's gentle wit and positive outlook. Often his writing functioned as a lead-up to some grievance. For instance, in his May 21, 1961, letter to Western artist J.K. Ralston in Billings, Montana, Barton meant to write a tribute to Ralston and drew on the comradeship theme:

Nowhere in this World, have I ever seen such good comradship [sic] among men as that which existed among cowboys. Men fight over money and women, Cowpunchers all had the same money and there were no women to fight over.[4]

Here Barton turns a good phrase. Sounds all right, even perhaps a touch of humor, right? Here it comes:

The Movies and Television today show cowboys riding saddles with little or no cantle, looks like an English saddle with a horn. Also they put cheese hats on the cowboys. I never saw a [sic] open-range cowpuncher with a cheese cake hat.[5]

Russell and Coburn would have continued the positive note, but not Fred. Barton launched into his usual gripes about changing times and the death of the Old West, praising Ralston by saying he was one of the last living artists to portray that Old West accurately. He wanted Ralston to hang in there to combat false versions of the open range. The new battle for the West was being waged on canvass and screen. Barton may have abhorred the Hollywood cowboy look, but he wanted to be as close to the cheese hats as he could. The same people he claimed as friends were often the people creating the Western movies and the images he railed against.

Like Russell, Coburn created an image of the West for others. Coburn's movie life began in 1916 before he went to Hollywood. Ralph Miracle captured his activities in his article, "Montana's First Movie."[6] Coburn formed a film company out of St. Paul and Chicago called the Great West Film Company. The company traveled by Great Northern Railway to Malta, Montana, where it filmed Montana's first movie, *The Golden Goddess*, based on Coburn's poem "Yellowstone Pete's Only Daughter." Coburn, of course, played the lead. Filming took place in and around Malta, Zortman, and the Missouri Breaks. The cast was supplemented by local cowboys and townspeople and featured such well known bronc riders as world champion Lee Caldwell along with hands from the Circle C.

While the movie obviously used the authentic settings of the Little Rockies, producing director C.W. Hitchcock called for "an ultra-spectacular man-hunt"[7] involving seven posses and hundreds of riders, all of whom would run down one man. This was the stuff of Saturday movie matinees and of course depicted "typical" events of the Old West! Bring on the cheese.

Though Malta was hardly Hollywood, the filming experienced the usual ups and downs of Tinseltown. The starlet playing the romantic interest left in a huff and was replaced by former Paramount star Marjorie Daw. Locals recognized her from her onscreen performances at the Bison Theater in Malta, owned by Coburn. Daw would go on to become Tom Mix's leading lady in such Western films as *Outlaws of Red River* and share screen time with Tony the Wonder Horse. Daw did not fare as well when the talkies came, but during the silent film era when cowboys wore rouge on the movie lobby cards, she was a star.

When filming moved to the old steamboat landing of Rocky Point on the Missouri, the script called for an actor to cross the river on horseback. Before the crossing, the locals so filled the thespian's head with horrible stories of all the Indians and cowboys who had drowned crossing there that when he did try to cross, he spooked his horse and nearly drowned. He was saved at the last moment by some old hands with river-wise horses. The tenderfoot did not appear for a reshoot. On a lighter note, romances blossomed between cowboys and Midwestern actresses who suddenly thought staying in Montana wasn't such a bad idea.

Coburn was romancing too. He romanced Hollywood. After the completion of the movie, the Coburn ranch, the Circle C, sold out to the larger, famous Matador Cattle Company. The Coburn family moved its ranching interests to Arizona while Wallace moved to Hollywood to begin his career there as a producer and movie cowboy actor appearing in *Rusty Rides Alone*, *The Westerner*, *The Return of Wild Bill*, and *Shoot Out at Big Sag*. As a writer he produced many stories and serialized novels for such pulp Western magazines as *Ace-High Western*, *Dime Western*, and *Big Book Western* of the "Spikes in His Boots, Iron in His Fists" variety. Barton and Coburn began to establish themselves in Hollywood at roughly the same time.

Barton also claimed artist Ed Borein (1873–1945) as a dear friend. When Borein biographer Harold G. Davidson heard that Barton had known Borein, Davidson drove from Santa Barbara to Los Angeles in the mid 1960s to visit with Fred. Barton appeared immaculately dressed in Western garb and proceeded to show Davidson his Western artifacts, extensive Western wardrobe closet organized with "mathematical precision," and albums of Huffman photographs of the Old West. Barton was obviously wealthy. As Davidson put it, the trip was "a dry run" in terms of Borein materials. Barton carried on about the good old days and Real Men, of which he thought himself one, but he could not be pinned down on any details about the artist. This left Davidson feeling that Barton's relationship with Borein had been only casual.

Instead of yielding Davidson any specifics about Borein, Barton handed his guest a sheet he had written about Borein upon his death.[8] Most likely it was the same piece he had written and sent to the Montana Historical Society in 1958. The society wanted to copy pictures out of a limited edition Borein book Barton owned, for a proposed article on Borein in *Montana: The Magazine of Western History*. The article planned to compare Borein with Russell. Some of the photographs in Barton's book were unidentified, so Barton sought the help of Dr. Irving Willis of Santa Barbara. Willis, one of Borein's best friends, was looking after the ailing Mrs. Borein. Willis told Barton that many of the photos were never identified.[9]

Barton asked the magazine to include his sheet in the article, word for word, but the whole project fell through. Dr. Willis and Edward Spaulding stated that the Borein Memorial members did not wish the article published. Concerned that the Borein people

Left: C.M. Russell gave Barton this autographed photograph taken by Harry Pollard at the 1919 Calgary Stampede. Barton pasted copies of the cherished photograph on the inside covers of books in his Western collection and used it as the frontispiece for his *C.M. Russell: An Old-Time Cowman Discusses the Life of Charles M. Russell*. *Right:* Texas folklorist J. Frank Dobie, instrumental in saving Texas longhorns from extinction, autographed this photograph of himself for Barton due to their shared interest in C.M. Russell and the open range (photograph 941-987, Montana Historical Society Archives).

were worried about copyright violations and a wrong slant to the article, the society offered to send them proofs that they could correct and cut as needed. When that failed, editor Vivian Paladin wrote Barton saying that if "you as a close friend of Ed Borein ... can reverse their decision and make our position more clear ... feel free to do so."[10] As Davidson suspected on his visit to Barton's apartment, either Barton was not a close friend of Borein or he did not get anywhere with the Borein Memorial people, because that was the last heard about the project. Another mind that didn't change was Barton's own. He kept referring to editor Paladin as Miss Vivian Paladin even though she made a point to sign in parenthesis that she was (Mrs.) Vivian A. Palladin.[11]

The sheet that Barton wrote about Borein read as follows:

> Ed. has left us now, but those of us who remain and had the good fortune to know him and enjoy his friendship thru the years will not forget him. Ed. was my friend for twenty-five years. Only the environment of the old West 1875–1900. (An environment previously non-existent in this World) could produce such men of his type.

> Charlie Russell, Will Rogers, Wallace Coburn, Frank Linderman and many others of this type were all my friends. The old West is gone forever and so are most of these fine men.
>
> Every Rancher and Cowpuncher who knew the old unfenced West will agree that two artists Ed. Borein and Charlie Russell have left for posterity a splendid and accurate record of the West as it was from 1875 to 1900 from the Rio Grande to the Canadian line. Those of us who knew and loved the old West and the fine men it produced have only our memories left.[12]

In letters written to the Montana Historical Society's Michael Kennedy, Barton also mentioned how much Russell admired the work of Borein and how close the two artists were. Barton called him second only to Russell in accuracy in depicting the West.[13]

Still another Barton friend was Frank Murphy (1858–1943). Murphy left Barton his Colt .45 revolver, belt and holster when he died. Barton donated them to the Montana Historical Society along with Murphy's note dated February 4, 1940:

> To my old friend Fred Barton
> try and keep this gun as long as
> I did fifty-eight years.
> I bought it in Sydney Nebraska in 1882.
>   Frank Murphy

Barton mentioned upon donating the gun that the Miles City museum also wanted the gun and letter, but that he would rather give them to the Helena museum, where they now reside. Miles City was an attractive choice, too, since Murphy was a Texas cowboy who worked six trail herds from Texas to Montana and the Miles City area, with the first occurring in 1882 when he purchased the gun. He also brought in the first trail herd to Montana from Oregon. Barton claimed to have known Murphy since his Miles City days in 1906. Though Murphy lived in Custer County, Montana, most of his life, he died in Los Angeles and is buried in the Valhalla Cemetery there. Barton paid for the funeral. Barton also donated to the society a photo of Frank Murphy taken in Texas around 1880 showing a well-groomed, mustached, and Sunday-dressed Murphy.

Barton's connection to Will Rogers remains as tentative as that with Russell. Nothing yet, on paper, ties the two together in any great friendship, so evidence is circumstantial. It does make sense that the two would have known each other, or at least met. Given the close cowboy community, they would have had trouble not meeting. While many books cite the impressive list of guests Rogers invited to his Santa Monica ranch to ride, rope, and play polo—William S. Hart, Clark Gable, Spencer Tracy, Darryl Zanuck, Walt Disney, Hal Roach—Rogers also welcomed unlisted cowpokes who knew their way around a horse and a roping arena. Barton certainly knew how to ride and rope and had arrived in Los Angeles to enjoy the "cowboy scene" just before Rogers, Russell, and Borein all arrived in 1919.

One of Rogers' close cowboy pals, Ray Bell of Cheyenne, Wyoming, won the 1920 riding contest at the Cheyenne Roundup. Rogers convinced Bell to go to Hollywood with him to become a movie star cowboy. Bell left the rodeo to do just that. As part of the elite group of bronc riders who made the rodeo tour, he must have at least been acquainted with some of the Barton group of cowboys who went to China, since they either were or had been some of the best riders on the circuit with him.

As Ben Yagoda pointed out in *Will Rogers: A Biography*, in the period when Barton began spending time in Hollywood, shortly before and after World War I, Hollywood was becoming a "capital of cowboy culture."[14] Doctors advised elderly Montana and Wyoming cowboys to relocate to warmer California for their health. That included Charlie Russell, increasingly feeling cold due to goiter-caused hyperthyroidism. Many working cowboys planned their year around the spring rodeos, fall roundups, and winter in California. They met at the "Waterhole" at the intersection of Cahuenga Avenue and Hollywood Boulevard. Rogers went there to meet friends.[15] Barton lived close by, only a block from property Rogers at one time owned.

Rogers also owned what Barton wanted—genuine Russells. At a time when most Russell paintings and bronzes were sold to rich Texas or Oklahoma oilmen or Easterners wanting a piece of the West, Rogers bought and kept his in California. He owned images Barton would later want copied. Rogers did exactly what Barton did in admiration of C.M. Russell: he wrote a tribute to him. His April 13, 1924, weekly newspaper article said that "he is the only Painter of Western Pictures in the World that a Cowboy can't Criticise."[16] Rogers also praised Nancy Russell for her clever marketing and praised his close friend Eddie Borein for being the greatest etcher of Western subjects. Except for the glowing report on Nancy Russell, Barton and Rogers echo each other in their apotheosis of Russell and Borein and their downplaying of the art of Frederic Remington. What they agreed on, they agreed on.

Barton and Rogers could share plenty of similar stories while leaning against the corral poles. Earlier, after a failed start as a cowboy in Argentina, Rogers worked his way on a freighter to South Africa. Here he saw the results of all those scrub horses Montana had sent over to help fight the Boers.

When Rogers found himself in the un-cowboylike position of driving a bunch of mules from Durban to Ladysmith, South Africa, in 1902, he needed a way out and into show business. He found it in Texas Jack's Wild West Show, a very minor Wild West show of the time, playing in Ladysmith. Ladysmith might not have been exactly the "sticks," but as they say, you could see the sticks from there. Jack dubbed him the "Cherokee Kid, Fancy Lasso Artist and Rough Rider—the Man Who Can Lasso the Tail off a Blowfly."[17] Plenty of blowflies looped the loop in Ladysmith, but it beat herding mules in northern Natal after someone had stolen his saddle. Remember Texas Jack? He did much better later in his career, as did the Cherokee Kid. Texas Jack's show held forth in Miles City just when Barton was organizing to go to Shansi.

As Rogers' fame grew, so did his wanderlust. He traveled to places in the Far East Barton had already visited. That included Moscow and Siberia. In 1931 he visited Harbin and Mukden in Manchuria, as well as Peking and Shanghai.[18] By this time, the press hailed Rogers as the United States' "unofficial diplomat." His mission to Manchuria echoed Barton's involvement with U.S. intelligence. Though it's not documented, the two men may have shared a great deal as Rogers readied for his trip. Rogers never did reveal the reason for his foray into China.

As Richard D. White pointed out in *Will Rogers: A Political Life*, secretary of war Patrick Hurley visited Rogers at his California ranch just weeks before Rogers' trip. Hurley and Rogers were best friends, having worked together as cowboys in Oklahoma before either became famous. Hurley had volunteered for Teddy Roosevelt's Rough Riders, had gone through training, and had gotten as far as Tampa on his way to Cuba before it was discovered he was only fifteen years old. That ended the boy's soldiering at that time. He did rise to the rank of brigadier general in World War I. Will stood next to Hurley when he took his oath of office to become secretary of war. They were very joined at the hip.

Hurley's visit to the Russell ranch occurred on his return trip from the Philippines. Outwardly, his visit seemed a case of old friends getting together and having a good time. The press captured photographs of the two jovial saddle partners touring the Fox Movietone Studios. But beneath the surface, Hurley was in crisis mode. Deeply concerned that the continuing Japanese invasion of Manchuria heralded wider Japanese intentions, he worried Japan would invade the Philippines. History vindicated his concern. He also realized the United States military was too weak to defend its interests in Manchuria as Japan carved it up. Due to the fighting and increasing Japanese control, sparse information came out of Manchuria. Just weeks after Hurley's ranch visit, Rogers packed his bags and headed to Manchuria.

Before he left, dumbfounded reporters kept asking him why, of all places, he was going to Manchuria and into a battle zone. In a Portland, Oregon, interview, he said he was not going over as a war correspondent or anything; he was just going over to "prowl around."[19] He was just as evasive in other interviews in California, saying that he did not know whether he could even get into the country (China). Betty Rogers in her book,

Fred Barton, always the dresser, at age 71 in 1960, with "whitewalls" on his feet and head to match those on his Cadillac (photograph 940-767, Montana Historical Society Archives).

Will Rogers, explained this evasiveness by saying Will always found planning ahead distasteful. This explanation might have worked were it not for the fact that Rogers set off for China in a hurry right before Christmas, leaving his family alone at the holiday for the first time. In addition to the fighting, the 30-below temperatures in Manchuria at the time should have dissuaded any traveler from wanting to prowl around.

There really were no people for Rogers to entertain in Manchuria, so the Japanese felt his trip was a cover. Suspicions increased when he stopped in Japan on the way over and wanted to meet with the Japanese war minister. He then traveled across front lines to meet Japanese and Chinese commanders and a Manchurian warlord.[20]

The warlord happened to be "Young Marshal" Chang Hsueh-Liang, son of Barton's old Manchurian Tiger boss, Chang Tso-lin. The Japanese had assassinated the old warlord three years earlier in 1928. Now they faced his son. As governor of Manchuria, the Young Marshal succeeded his father in commanding his army. He also served as vice commander-in-chief of the Nationalist army and navy. Before invading, the Japanese army waited until the Chinese warlords were again fighting each other. More importantly, they waited until young Chang was hospitalized for months at the Rockefeller Hospital in Peking with typhoid fever. They then moved on Manchuria, forbade his return, and planned a puppet state within China.

Upon returning to the States, Rogers went immediately to the White House, where he met for hours with President Hoover and Hurley. Rogers had seen enough to know that the Japanese army was highly trained, dedicated, and a definite threat. Rogers and Barton were more than cowboys. They had much to share as wranglers of information for the U.S. government.

Much that can be said about Barton's interest in Rogers can also be said about interest in William S. Hart. Like Rogers, Hart owned a ranch near Hollywood where many of his motion pictures were filmed. Hart's *The Money Corral* (1919) featured an opening rodeo scene set in a Montana frontier town. Many rodeo stars and Hollywood area cowboys put on a real rodeo for the camera. Whereas Will Rogers became America's beloved cowboy philosopher, Hart was Hollywood's first true movie star and its most revered silent-movie Western star. The Far East may have had soldier of fortune and Sun Yat-sen bodyguard "Two-Gun" Cohen, but the Hollywood West had "Two Gun Bill" Hart.

He became so famous that gangster Al Capone's brother Vincenzo changed his name to Richard "Two Gun" Hart. While Capone ran his illegal booze racket during Prohibition, "Two Gun" worked as a Prohibition agent; he dressed in a cowboy hat, wore a tin star, and slung twin holsters around his waist, mimicking William S. Hart. The ersatz Hart even served as personal bodyguard for Calvin Coolidge, the president who prided himself in his own over-the-top Western getup when retreating to his Black Hills getaway. In an age of tommy guns, speakeasies, and getaway cars, the Old West pretended to ride again.

Hart had more connection to Charlie Russell than to others in California. The Russell/Hart friendship began long before Hollywood. Hollywood was actually Hart's second successful career. He started out as a stage actor, travelling the country and making a mark in performances of Shakespearian plays and *The Man in the Iron Mask*. He made a splash in what would grow into Hollywood's greatest equestrian drama of all time, *Ben

Hur. Hart starred in the first stage production of this epic, which opened at the Manhattan Theater in New York in 1899. Audiences experienced the thrill of the Roman chariot race coming right at them on stage. Horses ran pell-mell on a treadmill while mechanical fans kicked up dust. A moving cyclorama created the illusion of the Circus Maximus flying by at such speed as to make the audience woozy. It would take another half century for Charlton Heston to cash in on the same spectacle in the Academy Award-winning 1959 film version. Hart had already starred in his own very early 1907 silent film version.

Any Westerner who had Russell's approval had Barton's approval, and Russell certainly approved of Two Gun Bill. Russell and Hart shared much. They were born the same year and had grown up in what became the Midwest. Just as Russell wished he were Native American, Hart spent his boyhood playing with Sioux children, learning their spoken language and sign language of the Great Plains. Both men sympathized with the plight of the Plains Indians and had intimate knowledge of the ways of the unfenced West in the 1870s and 1880s. Hart's family ranged from the Black Hills of Dakota Territory to the plains of Kansas and the Indian territories of Oklahoma. He knew what a horse was and had seen men shot to death (the truth of which he conveniently sometimes stretched later in life). As Ronald L. Davis pointed out in *William S. Hart: Projecting the American West*, the Old West became Hart's version of Orson Welles' Rosebud in *Citizen Kane*.[21] Barton, Russell, and Hart were all bonded by their celebration of the Old West while mourning its loss, a West colored by their nostalgia as much as by fact. A race of men and way of life were gone forever.

This longing and appreciation of the Old West marked the beginning of the friendship of the thespian and the cowboy artist in 1902. Hart played the Grand Opera House in Great Falls, Montana, when the cast was invited to meet Russell. Grieving a family death, Hart said little at the meeting. Russell wondered why the man was so taciturn when he could be so eloquent on stage. After the troupe moved on to Helena, Hart saw a Russell painting in a saloon and was hooked. He wrote to Russell telling him how much he was moved by what Russell represented. Recognizing a kindred spirit, Charlie wrote back, telling Hart to drop by anytime.

In 1909 Hart again played Great Falls, this time in the hit stage production of *The Virginian*. Russell had a surprise for him, a painting of Hart on a bronc riding through the sagebrush, which became Hart's cherished item. Hart hosted the Russells when they were in New York City trying to sell paintings. He showed them the sights and tried to set up contacts. Each time the Russells sold a painting, they celebrated with Hart.

A few years later, Hart's second career as a motion picture film star blossomed. That gave him a chance to do something else that fit the characters of Barton and Russell. No matter how moralistic or melodramatic his silent-movie Westerns were, Hart insisted on authenticity in portraying the old West. Russell pursued the same attention to detail in his paintings. Barton did likewise in preserving Old West artifacts and paying homage to the way things "really were" in his writing. For Hart, cowboys needed to wear working cowboy clothes, not Hollywood costumes. Instead of makeup, Hart rolled in the dust as if he had just come in from a tough, long ride. Tack had to be authentic. He filled his home with artifacts of the Old West. He reportedly purchased Billy the Kid's six-shooters.

Barton saw himself as an embodiment of the Old West, but Hart outdid him in that regard. Hart commissioned sculptor Charles C. Cristado to cast a monumental bronze statue of Hart standing next to Fritz, his horse. This was to be Hart's embodiment and Cristado's largest bronze. For over fifteen years the sculptor worked for Hart. Gutzon Borglum asked Cristado to work on Mount Rushmore, but he declined. He went on to work for Disney in the 1930s and 1940s, creating the original models for Pinocchio, Geppetto, and other Disney characters. He also designed the Fay Wray doll and dinosaurs for *King Kong* (1933). For Nancy Russell and the C.M. Russell Museum, he cast a bust of Charlie Russell.

Hart wanted the bronze of himself placed on the rim of the Grand Canyon so his eternal self could look out over the vastness where, as he said, life and death were created. The Park Service nixed the plan despite senatorial support. Instead, the statue moved north, way north. Hart settled for the statue's being donated and dedicated in 1927 to commemorate the forty-fifth anniversary of the founding of Billings, Montana.

The statue was sited atop the rimrocks on a sandstone pedestal overlooking Billings and the Yellowstone. The dizzying mile-high rim of the Grand Canyon had diminished to the paltry 500-foot high Billings rimrocks, but they suited the mood created by the piece. Named *The Range Rider of the Yellowstone*, it symbolized the old cattle and Texas trails that led over 2,000 miles from south Texas to Montana. The sculpture shows Fritz nibbling on some bunch grass at Hart's side. Leaning against his faithful companion and working on his "fixin's," the Old Time cowboy stares out across the Western infinity. Hart wanted his statue of Western solitude far from the madding crowds, but the next year at the statue site, Billings opened its airport, now Billings Logan International Airport, where the Range Rider still resides.

Barton drove through Billings each year on his yearly Montana pilgrimages as Hart looked down on, or we should say over, him from on high. Regardless of Hart's being Russell's friend, it must have rankled Fred to know Hart's statue was up there representing the Montana range cowboy. A range cowboy would have found wearing two guns an impractical burden. Not so for the movie screen range. On the positive side, Hart had paid tribute to Fritz. The pinto initiated the string of popular, named, Hollywood-star horses such as Rex, Tony, Diablo, Buttermilk, Champion, Silver, Trigger, and Fury. As a pinto, Fritz also broke the Western B-movie mold of Hollywood stars riding mostly solid-color horses. In the movies, pintos usually symbolized mounts for nonheroes relegated to sidekick or Indian status. Of course, in bronze, a pinto could not be distinguished much from a palomino.

Later to become a museum, Hart's mansion contained artworks of Russell, Remington, de Young, and others. With most of Russell's work sold on the East Coast in New York galleries, Barton's interest in Hart's collection on the West Coast magnified. Again, what Barton did not own he wanted reproduced from the originals. Hart owned originals. Like Rogers, he also lived conveniently near Barton. While Barton settled for an autographed photograph from Russell, Hart owned both an autographed photo Russell had given him and the painting of himself signed and dedicated to him from Charlie Russell. He had the goods.

Someone else who also had the Russell goods was Montana sheepman Charles M. Bair. By 1910 Bair owned the largest sheep operation in North America, with between

250,000 and 500,000 sheep. When a lawyer told of having 150 sheep on his Virginia farm, Bair famously responded that he had more sheepdogs than that. Bair came to Montana working on the Great Northern Railroad. After trying his hand at sheep raising, he went to Alaska and became a millionaire selling mining machinery during the Klondike Gold Rush. Returning to Montana, he resumed interest in the woolies, leasing land on the Crow Indian Reservation.

Having become one of the richest men in Montana, Bair frequently traveled to California to purchase artwork from the Russells. These trips also became excuses for the Montana cowboy contingent there to gather with Bair and the Russells to swap tales about the old days in Montana. These gatherings included a mix of Western artists and cowboys, ranging from Tom Mix to photographer Edward Curtis, who had also photographed Russell. Again, Bair was another person Barton had access to and who had kept Russell works in the West.

Although not really a member of the Montana Hollywood contingent, Harry Carey attended many of the cowboy get-togethers. Barton and Carey shared a similar childhood in that both attended military preparatory schools within hailing distance of New York City. Carey moved west when the film industry moved west. Before that, when Carey was a young man headed for a law career, Montana did give him some fame and fortune. Out of boredom he wrote his Western melodrama *Montana* while recovering from a long fight with pneumonia that weakened his lungs for life. The hit play toured for over three years, making him a rich young man with a profit of a quarter of a million dollars. That was as close to Montana as he came.

As one of the early successful silent-movie actors, Carey ended up in a record 350+ silent and sound movies, a record no one has been able to top. Almost 250 of these movies were Westerns. Like Rogers, Hart, and others, he too created a ranch which provided locale for filming, in San Francisquito Canyon just outside Hollywood. This provided another gathering place for cowboys and stars. The 1200-acre working ranch boasted a Navajo trading post featuring "the only Navajos outside the reservation," to appeal to Hollywood tourists. Despite the tourist hype surrounding the ranch, Old Westerners appreciated Carey's humble and deep-toned delivery in the face of flamboyant Hollywood Western cowboy stars. Carey also earned his stripes as an accomplished horseman, which wasn't bad for a kid who started out just admiring the mounted police in New York City. John Wayne went so far as to copy Carey's way of riding and other mannerisms as the Duke molded himself into cowboy roles.

For Barton, Carey may not have been in the same Russell collector league as Bair or Hart, but he was a close friend of Charlie Russell, which meant he had been blessed. Carey even built an adobe cabin on his ranch for exclusive use by Russell. Carey called his son Dobe because the color of his hair matched that of Russell's adobe cabin. The ranch provided a good getaway for Russell. He did do some painting there, as well as goof around with Carey, wearing Carey's hat, doing rope tricks, and eating out on the ranch's "open range" with other cowboys. Russell never quit creating while there. At the breakfast table, he created ephemeral art by dipping his fingers in drinking water and then molding a perfect horse out of the doughy heart of a loaf of bread. He would go on to draw, mold, and paint several pieces of art for the Harts.[22]

Finally, we come to Western movie star Tom Mix and his connection with the Montana bunch. As William S. Hart's star waned, Mix's shone brighter. He became Hollywood's first rhinestone cowboy and the #1 box office attraction in America by 1927. He will go down in history as perhaps the only cowboy ever killed by a piece of luggage. In 1940 his car sped off the road, which caused his flying aluminum suitcase to hit him in the head. Although his silent movies lacked realism, Mix possessed honest cowboy skills. He proved to be a crack shot, bronc rider, and excellent horseman for the 101 Ranch in Oklahoma before his Hollywood days. For Barton, Mix was enmeshed in many facets of his experience, not only through place but also people, particularly in terms of Miles City and such people as Will Rogers and saddle maker Ed Bohlin.

Rogers and Mix met early in their careers as Wild West show performers. At the 1904 Saint Louis World's Fair, Rogers introduced young Mix to the woman Mix would later marry. Mix wooed her by telling many tales about himself, such as how he had been in South Africa for the Boer War and how he served in China during the Boxer Rebellion and also in the Philippines—all stories he had "acquired" by listening to Rogers and other cowboys who had actually been in those places. Tom tended to be more than a bit on the windy side, neglecting to tell Olive Stokes that he was an army deserter who spent his time in service on the East Coast. Such is love and stardom. Nevertheless, the affable Rogers did not seem to mind having Mix appropriate portions of his life for his own aggrandizement. Telling tall tales served as cowboy entertainment in the Western tradition. Lying was reserved for criminal activity and poker.

Mix's pre–Hollywood working cowboy life intersected with Barton's through another one of Mix's Oklahoma cowboy acquaintances, Bill "Badlands" McCarty, who was certainly of Barton's ilk. Before cowboying in Dakota and Montana, McCarty drifted through Texas, New Mexico, and Arizona. At a swarthy 6'2", McCarty stood and rode ruggedly tough, always wearing a six-shooter on his hip while on the range and keeping it in a shoulder holster while in town. His great love of horses led him to establish a large-scale horse ranch in the badlands of North Dakota where Teddy Roosevelt tended his holdings. McCarty trailed horses all the way from the Southwest to start his ranch. An accomplished rodeo cowboy, he won a trophy saddle at Madison Square Garden in 1903.

Just as Barton later herded 3,500 Orlovs across Siberia, McCarty brought in 3,500 horses from Montana. McCarty had them shipped by train from the Columbia River Basin, offloading them in Wibaux, Montana. The shipment was epic. Three trains, with twenty-three horses per car, were required to move all the horses. There remained the challenge of trailing them from the railhead to the ranch. Three hundred head were lost along the way. Helping him move the massive herd in 1907 was one Tom Mix. Mix applied his skills that year to help Badlands Bill break the horses so they could be sold to homesteaders and the military. Next year, Mix helped McCarty with the roundup, herding and branding horses. Since Miles City was horse capital of the world at that time for horse buyers, McCarty and Mix became familiar with the town and its cowboys at the same time Barton established his cowboy credentials there.

Barton and all the area people came to know McCarty, although in Miles City he was sometimes referred to as McCarthy. As one of the big horse buyers and shippers, he was central in founding the first Miles City Round-Up in 1913. Badlands Bill furnished most of the stock and served as arena director. He and other city promoters planned to make the roundup bigger than Cheyenne's Frontier Days, Calgary's Stampede, and the Pendleton Roundup.

Traversing the far reaches of the Far East, Barton had to miss the first two years of the roundup while he worked off his four-year contract with British American Tobacco. While plans for the roundup crystallized and became a reality, Barton was registering for protection at U.S. consulates in such places as Harbin and Antung, China, about as far north as a person can get in that country. The treaty port of Antung sat across the Yalu River from Korea. Harbin lay even farther north, near Siberia. Barton was, however, around for the earlier, original celebration that gave people the idea for the roundup. In 1909 Miles City very successfully celebrated the Fourth of July and concurrent Elks Convention with parade and rodeo. Four years later, most of the same participants fostered the Miles City Round-Up, an expansion of the original Elks blowout.

The Miles City Round-Up also celebrated the thirty-fifth anniversary of the founding of Miles City. Consequently, the event brought in the governor, the military, and many of the old-timers, such as buffalo hunters, Indian fighters, and first settlers to march in the parade. Barton's favorite photographer, L.A. Huffman, led the Old Timers in the parade. Since Huffman had photographed life at Fort Keogh and life on the range around Miles City, Barton purchased his prints and showed them to guests in his Los Angeles apartment. The whole procession of bands, military, Crow and Cheyenne, and wagons was led through town by Governor Samuel V. Stewart. Escorting him came McCarty and a few of the other organizers such as the appropriately named Wagenbreth and Kenneth Mclean. Mclean's popular daughter Ina, called "Tot," led 119 cowgirls in the order of march. Tot's impressive mounted unit wore matched white shirts, neckerchiefs, and chaps.

Barton and area cowboys knew the Mcleans well. Mclean was one of the many Scots who came to Miles City to raise cattle, horses, and sheep. Many cowboys received their first range jobs and learned how to be cowboys from the old hands on Mclean's big S-I Ranch forty miles southwest of Miles City. Ranchers and cowboys traded in town at his merchandise store and at the local bank, which he directed. Mclean was a charter member of the Elks who hosted the forerunner of the Miles City Round-Up and was elected president of the Miles City Chamber of Commerce sponsoring the roundup. But for Barton and other horsemen, Mclean was known for his Hambletonians. These trotters and pacers had supplanted Morgans as the superior harness racing horse. Now called Standardbreds, these horses descended from a horse named Hambletonian. They retained the speed of their Thoroughbred ancestry yet combined it with the strength and easier disposition of the Morgans that Barton favored for China.

Tot Mclean was the same age as Barton. She too had been sent East for finishing school. Along with students from across the country, including others from Montana, she enrolled at the Lasell Finishing School for Young Women, where young ladies were courted by young men from nearby Harvard. As indicated in Lasell yearbooks, Tot must have been a handful for both her teachers and the Crimson boys. Like Barton, all she wanted to do was return to Montana and the horses. She certainly did not sound like a New Englander. Rather than just date young men preparing for the military, she professed she wanted to be a military man. All she could talk about were her horses. When an economics teacher asked her what was made in Belgium, she replied, "Horses."

Tom Mix had his hands full with a horsewoman too. When Mix's unsuspecting wife-to-be journeyed up from Oklahoma to buy horses from McCarty, Tom promptly married her at McCarty's ranch after not having seen her for four years. McCarty accompanied the newlyweds on their honeymoon to Miles City. Previously, during the Spanish-American War and Philippine-American War, Badlands Bill had volunteered for the 1st Montana Volunteer Infantry, which later created the confusion of people thinking he was one of Teddy Roosevelt's Rough Riders in Cuba. He was seriously wounded in the thigh in the Philippines. As he had with Will Rogers, Mix borrowed McCarty's past to impress his bride. Mix had no qualms about recounting his adventures with Teddy and the Rough Riders in Cuba. The High Plains was becoming windier and windier—good preparation for Hollywood.

In 1905 Mix rode with Seth Bullock's Cowboy Brigade of sixty-one riders to Teddy Roosevelt's inauguration. These cowboys were mostly Dakota and Montana friends of Roosevelt from his ranching days. Bullock, Deadwood's first sheriff and a close friend of Roosevelt, captained Troop A, Grigsby's Volunteer Cowboy Cavalry Regiment, held in readiness in Georgia to support the Rough Riders in Cuba during the Spanish-American War. Bullock's group shipped their horses by train to Washington, D.C., where the riders paraded and were received at the White House by the delighted president. Instead of the Washington Senators baseball team taking the field the next day, the cowboys treated Washingtonians, including the president, with a rodeo topped with a mock hanging showing what happened to horse stealers in the West—a good message for congressional types even then. Washington baseball fans might just as well have hanged themselves. The Senators would go on to finish next to the bottom of the American League. Mix made many friends among these ballfield cowboys, whose stories he could add to fleshing out his own biography for his bride.

And so it was in 1909 that Mix took Olive on their honeymoon to Bill Tambler's ranch outside Miles City. Tambler apparently was a cowboy friend of McCarty and Mix. Olive was not impressed with Miles City, but Tom wanted to show her off to all the cowboys he knew, since she was a real cowgirl who could ride, shoot, and spin a rope. He also kept his ulterior motives hidden. Mix wanted to stop at Al Furstnow's Saddlery in Miles City. Secretly he had ordered twin saddles trimmed with silver of the highest grade and of the best leatherwork for both of them. He also purchased a beaded buckskin skirt and jacket for his wife, not exactly what Olive was looking for in a trousseau. When she saw he also picked up a very range-impractical pair of batwinged chaps inlaid with silver, she knew something was up besides living in the cozy ranch house of her dreams in Oklahoma. Tom planned for her to appear in Wild West, circus, or ranch shows with him. The diamond he slipped on her finger came not from Furstnow's but from the local pawnbroker. He would have done better if he had ridden out with Olive to the romantic sandstone Heart Arch just outside of town.

Furstnow Saddlery and competitor Coggshall Saddlery of Miles City brought one other Miles City cowboy into the life of Barton and Mix. Ed Bohlin, the saddle maker Barton tried to entice to partner with him on a saddle-making adventure in Mongolia, came to the United States from Sweden in 1912 with visions of Buffalo Bill and the cowboy life in his head. After doing farm work in Minnesota on his way west, he reached Miles City in spring 1913 in time for the first Miles City Round-Up. Here, he set about learning English and becoming a cowboy. Like Barton, he started out as a horse wrangler, then moved up to cowpunching on local ranches and long cattle drives. One of his first jobs was working for Great Northern Sugar Beet Company with landholdings north of Miles City. Beets made good forage to fatten up range cattle before they saw the light at the end of the tunnel in Chicago. When cows were shipped out of Miles City by train, Bohlin took the job of "cowpunching," or poking the cows to keep them on their feet until being unloaded at the Chicago stockyards. In 1917 he married the daughter of the railroad foreman at Miles City: His railroad cowboy experience paid off.

Between 1913 and 1916 he worked cattle and horses out of Miles City but spent downtime learning leather and silverwork at the saddleries, collecting saddlery mail-order catalogs to get ideas and taking an art correspondence course. Barton recalled Bohlin doing that as early as around 1912, which sounds almost right, since Bohlin reached Montana in 1913. While he spent time working for Coggshall Saddlery (by then called Miles City Saddlery), Bohlin may also have spent time at Furstnow's. He was still single at the time, which is why Barton thought he might be eager for a Mongolian adventure. Another plus was that Ed (or Eddie) could also appreciate other cultures. Like Russell, Bohlin made friends with such Crows as Goes Ahead Pretty and Chief Plenty Coups. He literally achieved hands-on knowledge of the Old West when he took a short-term job moving graves at Custer Battlefield National Cemetery.[23]

Some recall Bohlin admiring the craftsmanship of his Furstnow saddle. Bohlin was fascinated by the art of making saddles and other leather and silver crafts. He combined that love with his Buffalo Bill Western dream by moving to Cody, Wyoming, in 1916, after which he did more cowpunching at the Pitchfork and Antler ranches and drove stages to Yellowstone Park. Most of all, he took the leap from being a cowboy to becoming a craftsman and artist when he opened up his saddlery across from the Irma Hotel built by Buffalo Bill, his hero. After a short stint working as a designer for the Northern Products Company in Minneapolis, where his daughter was born, Bohlin brought Leana, his wife, back to live in Cody, where he would stand outside his shop and twirl a rope to attract customers. A pet buffalo also helped drum up business. Cody at the time was a mecca for dude ranching and tourists wanting to see Yellowstone.

After the death of Leana from influenza in 1918, and another quick, failed marriage, Bohlin took a job doing rope tricks and riding a bucking bronco onstage for the Gus Hornbrook Vaudeville Company and working as a Hollywood movie extra.[24] As the legend goes, one night Bohlin was performing onstage when Tom Mix interrupted the performance to yell out, asking where Bohlin got his fancy duds. Mix literally bought Bohlin's fancy leather jacket right off his back, not to mention his fine-tooled boots and traveling bag. Mix became Bohlin's first great customer and friend in Hollywood, convincing him to open up his own leather and silver business in Hollywood. By 1922, Bohlin was on his way. Like Wild Bill Tuttle of the 15th Infantry in China, Bohlin posed in his cowboy outfit for a Camels cigarette commercial, becoming precursor to the Marlboro Man in the United States.

Barton may not have convinced Bohlin to come to China and Mongolia, but Mix convinced Bohlin to stay in Hollywood. Much the better choice. While Barton dealt with the vagaries of warlords, Bohlin's wars played out on the silver screen. He made Egyptian-style chariot harnesses for Cecil B. DeMille's *The Ten Commandments* (1923) and Roman chariot harnesses for MGM's *Ben Hur* (1925). He opened his saddle and tack store across from Furstnow, who had moved his store to Hollywood in 1919. Mostly Bohlin made saddles, bridles, bits, engraved guns, and everything Western for the working cowboy; but he became famous as saddle maker and engraver to the stars, the Pasadena Rose Parade, and royalty around the world, from Emperor Hirohito of Japan to the King of Saudi Arabia, Mae West, Ronald Reagan, and Lyndon Johnson. Most, if not all, Western movie stars owned Bohlin creations. Barton proudly displayed his Bohlin, resting over a saddletree in his apartment, and part of his planned Museum of the West.

Describing himself as an "old cowman," Barton faced dealing with the same love/hate relationship with Hollywood that the rest of the Montana contingent did, and other open range cowboys, for that matter. At the same time Barton railed at stupidly dressed Western stars and inauthentic screen versions of the Old West, he wanted to be a Western movie star.[25] Like his hero Charlie Russell, he begrudgingly cut Hollywood some slack to make it his home. Russell disliked the fact that filmmakers gave the real cowboy story short shrift. He too thought the melodrama and costuming absurd. At least movie dialogue was not bad, since there was none at first. But the more cowboy stars invited him on to the sets to watch actual filming the more Russell came to appreciate their skills at riding, doing incredible stunts, and risking their lives.

Hollywood's magnetic attraction for star wannabes also drew in cowboys at a time when range jobs grew scarce or they had no winter work. In the golden age of B-movie Westerns, Hollywood needed more cowboys than any other category of actors. This kept range skills alive, showcasing many. The motion picture industry whetted the public's taste for the Old West, attracting interest in preservation in both direct and indirect ways—exactly what Barton sought. What boy didn't want to be a cowboy? What girl didn't want a horse? Dude ranches flourished. Groups dedicated to the West sprang up. Los Angeles saw one of the earliest chapters of the Westerners Corral, which used Russell's iconic bleached buffalo skull as its logo and was an organization of which Barton approved. Western stories flooded the publishing market.

When "talkies" replaced silent movies, actors and directors had to give their versions of how the Old West sounded as well as looked. When University of Southern California football player Marion Robert Morrison lost his football scholarship due to a bodysurfing accident and became actor John Wayne, he turned to an Old Time Westerner for his secret dialogue coach. Learning how to sit on a horse was one thing. Speaking in the cowboy manner was another. Some actors had to pass off embarrassing lines from cheap Western pulps that even a drunken vaudeville performer in Butte on a bad night wouldn't have allowed air time. Others read lines culled from actual range cowboys, the real deal. Dialogue was as uneven as the Rockies.

Barton's and other cowboys' struggles with Hollywood authenticity, or the lack thereof, created interesting situations. The film industry depended on actors with authentic Western skills, yet this was all in the name of entertainment, deserving at least some modicum of glitz. For Barton, Russell, and others, this collision surfaced most in terms of cowboy dress. Veteran cowboys hired as extras or wranglers criticized Two Gun Hart's clothing, despite his horsemanship and desire for authenticity. In Hart's case it came down to his neckwear and hat. His neckerchief was "big as a Harvey House half tablecloth,"[26] and his overgrown hat could just about cover a spread tablecloth. Good for a summer picnic, but not for open range work. Tom Mix's hat drew derision with the comment "the wider the hat, the less the cowboy."

Headgear deviation from cowboy standards had long been a bone of contention in the West. When cowboy outfits rode into town after roundup to let off steam, townsmen had better watch their derbies, boaters, and cheesehats, as those hats frequently became ventilated. One of the reasons saddle maker Bohlin departed Cody for the vaudeville circuit and Hollywood may have been for his hat gunplay. He garnered a reputation as Cody's bad boy after serving time for getting into fights. Then he put some daylight in a visitor's new straw hat in his store. Only an ignorant honyocker would wear straw. Bohlin's shooting seemed to be the last straw, as the Cody newspaper announced that this cowboy needed at least to be spanked for his bad behavior.[27]

There was nothing wrong with a cowboy wanting to get all "duded up" to show off in a parade or a show. Cowboys took pride in owning a pair of fancy boots, a dress hat, or some fancy shirts. Some cowboys were said to be able to strut even while sitting down. Barton kept plenty of dressy clothes in his storage closet, including his big collection of Stetsons. The problem was not with showy clothes; it was with how Hollywood projected an image of working cowboys wearing such outfits on the range.

As mentioned earlier, Barton hated seeing film cowboys wearing unrealistic "cheesecake" hats. Like Russell, Barton wore Stetson's original Boss of the Plains style hat, with its very high crown and flat, broad brim. No cheesecake here, and no fancy adornments. Often a cowboy signaled where he was from by the way he put creases in his hat or the way he molded the brim. Barton was a purist. No creases, just a smooth high dome, and the hat had to be of tough waterproof felt, not straw or some other material impractical in rain, snow, biting sun, and bitter cold. Such a hat carried him through Montana, Siberia, China, Manchuria, and Mongolia. Although he sported more of the boater-style business hat when working for British American Tobacco, he quickly went right back to his Boss of the Plains when his BAT contract expired.

Barton stayed more of a purist than he knew. One theory about the origin of the cowboy hat suggests its origins lay with the Mongols. Just as many Northern Plains cowboys like Barton preferred high-crowned hats for increased insulation against the cold and a broad brim for increased protection from the high-altitude sun, nature dictated the same parameters for the Mongols.

When Mongol horsemen raced out of the Asian steppes and invaded the Middle East and Europe during the thirteenth century, their light cavalry units sported high-crowned, brimmed hats of felt, the same material used for their *gers*, or *yurtas*. Not being farmers, Mongols looked to their herds as a source of felt for hat material. Cowboys also chose animal over vegetable. The practicality of such headgear spread from the Mongols through horse-centric Spain and thus into Mexican sombreros, crossing the border into Texas and the Southwest, then traveling north to Montana and ultimately finding the heads of the Royal Mounted Police in Canada. Barton's hat was worthy of the Museum of the West and any Museum of the Far East. In going to China and Mongolia, Barton brought the hat full circle.

• Seventeen •

Ruminating on Guys, Gussies and Morons at Trail's End

About 2852 BC, Fu Hsi, First of the Five Virtuous Rulers ... instituted the first national code of marriage laws for the people of his domain. The Calendar of the Hsia Dynasty, 2205 BC, of which part of a copy was found buried in the tomb of Confucius, contains the announcement that at the advent of the middle month of spring youths and maidens shall be made happy in love and set up house.[1]
—Nora Waln, *The House of Exile*

Barton's legacy includes more than donated photos and other Western artifacts. Besides his thumbnail autobiography and biographies of others he knew, he left behind written, copied, and distributed musings on life. He made sure he hand-signed each copy that he gave to guests. Two tracts have survived. One shows an early response to something he had read at the time of the China ranch. The other is that of an older man looking back on life to see what he perceives as the truth. Both should be taken in the context of Barton's oral and written remarks that he never had any formal education. He did, of course, but to emulate Russell, he would not say that he had. In other words, his philosophy fits into the college of hard knocks, the college of the open range. As C.M. Russell was fond of saying, spending so much time in the saddle gave a man plenty of time to think, which is why so many cowboys fancied themselves as philosophers. Barton so fancied.

Fred Barton revived a 1920 philosophical tract and presented it to Fallis and Ruth Koerner Oliver.[2] Fred used the very original title of "Fred Barton." Kidding aside, the article reveals that his Chinese experience prompted him to make serious comparisons. Towards the end of his essay, he said an article by Sir Auckland Geddes, British ambassador to the U.S. in 1920, prompted his response. Barton's article begins:

In this day and age, it should be a great distinction to be called a Man or a Woman since few are qualified to be so distinguished. Manhood and Womanhood are sharply defined concepts. They signify a state of maturity, and that does not mean <u>partial maturity</u>. If one survives 21 years, they have automatically reached physical maturity, but still may be and often are mental infants. To be regarded as mature mentally, one should reach a state of mental maturity consistent with the highest standards of the age in which they live. Very few achieve this state, therefore, very few humans can be classified as Men and Women.[3]

Certainly Barton struck familiar notes here. Many writers before and after Barton have proclaimed how adolescence is prolonged into what should be adulthood or how physical maturity and intellectual maturity are not synonymous. He goes on to discuss a word that has achieved popularity again recently: *guy*, as in "Hi, guy!" and "You guys ready to order?":

> I term a mentally immature man a "Guy" and his counterpart of the female sex a "Gussie." Nature has endowed mankind with the capacity and ability to analyze everything one may hear, read about, or observe. Very few human beings develop this great capacity with which nature has endowed them. They merely accept without analysis any fallacy. Thru the ages, man has been condemned, tortured, and killed by the ignorant brutes in power for not accepting in blind faith that which would not bear analysis and insulted his intelligence. By what logic should a man be condemned for using the ability to analyze with which nature has endowed him? Nature has endowed birds with the capacity to fly—should they then be condemned for flying?[4]

These observations already point towards Barton's writing on Charles M. Russell, in which he wanted to focus on Russell's intellect. Barton also expressed his lifelong theme of freedom and not wanting to accept commands:

> It is impossible to exaggerate human stupidity. History has proven that the only way to enslave humanity is to keep them in ignorance. This is encouraged by the very foundation of our so-called civilization "Survival of the Fittest in Acquisition" which does not require human intelligence. Shrewd animal cunning plus abuse of confidence is all that is necessary. With such a foundation, our civilization never has been and never can be successful. From a human point of view, the most important word in any language is confidence and it is furthermore the only source from which real love can originate. Confidence is the very foundation of all human relations. Two thousand years of recorded human history indicate very clearly what type of humanity has been successful under such an animal code. The most cruel, cunning, ruthless, greedy, and acquisitive people have gained power, wealth, and recognition while the real human beings have struggled thru life and gone to their graves unknown. This World has never known A Human Civilization.[5]

Again this early tract foreshadowed future events in Barton's life. His definition of unsung "real" people, as opposed to greedy animals, propelled him to suggest names and topics for articles for Western history magazines. Frank Murphy, the early cowboy who left his .45 to Barton, was of course included in the Fred Barton pantheon of worthies. Another suggested by Barton was O.C. Cato, general manager in Montana for the famous X.I.T. ranch of Texas.[6] Barton urged the Montana Historical Society to include one such personality in each issue of its magazine.

He also suggested that the magazine could become more of an *Arizona Highways* magazine to increase tourism in the state.[7] At this point the society mentioned one of Barton's favorite themes in the quotation above—wealth—or the lack thereof. The magazine's budget could not sustain Barton's suggestions:

> As a young man, I realized that I had arrived in a world which was still primitive to a degree where I might be enslaved physically and economically, but I was determined that my greatest asset, my mind, with its ability to reason and analyze, would never be enslaved.
> The greatest marvel in our little world is the human mind if allowed to develop and function naturally and if not poisoned with fallacious teachings. Any individual who teaches that which cannot be substantiated is a criminal—a mind prisoner.[8]

No wonder bookseller and ex-teacher Richard Upton was put on the defensive while a guest in Barton's apartment.

> Likewise, any institution guilty of the same offense is a criminal institution; and if the offense be committed by a government, then that government is a criminal government, guilty of criminal neglect by even tolerating mind poisoning within its domain. Few of us take the time to study the origin of our cherished convictions. Indeed, we have a natural repugnance to so doing. We like to continue to believe what we have been accustomed to accept as true, and the resentment aroused when doubt is cast upon any of our assumptions leads us to seek every manner of excuse for clinging to them. We regarded the Chinese as extremely cruel because they bound the feet of their baby girls, making them semi-cripples for life, but we are guilty of a greater offense with our fallacious teachings and dogmas which poison the minds of our people and prevent them from ever thinking clearly and logically. A lifetime of unanalyzed impressional experiences inevitably results in complete and profound mental confusion.[9]

Barton took some pains in wording these thoughts and made use of what he had seen in China that was abhorrent to foreigners. Outside of his earlier mention of materialism, he refused to be pinned down here on exactly what he saw the fallacious teachings and dogmas to be. He remained as frustratingly general here as he was in discussing those he claimed as friends. In his conclusion, he stated specifically the origin of this tract:

> I was prompted to write this article in 1920 after reading an article by Sir Auckland Geddes which is herewith presented. "A realization of the aimlessness of life lived to labor and to die, having achieved nothing but avoidance of starvation and the birth of children also doomed to the weary treadmill, has seized the mind of millions," Sir Auckland Geddes, British Ambassador to the U.S.A. 1920.[10]

Geddes' comment became one of the more quoted expressions of post–World War I. It often was repeated in chapter headings to various books discussing peace, science and insanity, and the nature of mankind. When Geddes delivered his comments at the 99th commencement of George Washington University, newspapers carried his words to both sides of the Pacific. Barton could have read them either in China or in the United States.

Geddes knew how to appeal to North Americans, and particularly Westerners like Barton. Newspapers and books quoted the noted statesman's address to the Pilgrims Society of the United States when be became ambassador to the U.S. Geddes began by speaking of the awesome spectacle he saw as he stood on the edge of the Grand Canyon, relating what a bishop and a cowboy would say. The bishop proclaimed, "Oh, Lord! Mysterious and wonderful are Thy works, O Lord!" But the cowboy replied, "What a hell of a hole!"

Both Geddes and Barton had seen one hell of a hole. Geddes had seen too much during World War I and the Boer War, and warned of more dismalness and disaster ahead if people did not pursue beauty, service and truth to save civilization. Barton had seen too much as well. Like Stillwell, he had seen the millions in China fighting starvation, only to come home to millions in the U.S. living what he thought were aimless lives.

Barton also liked to stereotype, categorize, and name-call in one of his later tracts. He distributed this to guests with a title designed to enforce its importance on the world. In "Extremely Important Observation, Analysis and Conclusions Regarding Marriage By Fred Barton,"[11] he looked back on what he had learned from life and had accomplished:

> During my short lifetime (75 years) my personal and business affairs have been so well planned and organized that they required only about a half hour of my time each day. I have therefore had plenty of time to study and analyze World conditions and the many problems of mankind and I have arrived at many important, interesting and informative conclusions.[12]

In other words, he was practicing the analytical capabilities he discussed in his response to Ambassador Geddes. Those with aimless lives, "ignorant morons," should pay attention and learn. Unfortunately, the vast majority of humanity are ignorant morons who, according to Barton, "never analyze anything":

> They arrive at conclusions with the physical senses such as seeing, hearing, touching, tasting and smelling exactly as children and animals do. Such people, if permitted to choose their mates, will be attracted almost entirely by beauty and sex which does not last thru life and they are rarely happy. Such marriages will reproduce the human race (another crop of morons). Their decision to marry is arrived at with the physical senses as opposed to the mind. Most morons of either sex are inclined to be jealous, and it is impossible to live with a jealous person.
>   I regard jealousy as a form of insanity. It is not necessary for either mate to do anything wrong to arouse the jealousy of the other, their imagination will take care of that. Whenever one mate is out of sight of the other they will immediately imagine the absent mate in the arms of another person. He or she will then want to kill, ruin or divorce the former object of their so-called love.[13]

Barton was obviously familiar with divorce, including his own. How much autobiography can be read into these comments is debatable.

> Love to the moron, like our primitive cave-man ancestors, is merely the possession of the physical body of his or her mate, legal or otherwise. A child and a moron will use the word love in a ridiculous and absurd manner. I love cake, candy, pie, etc., etc. To my mind, from a human point of view, the most important word in any language is Confidence and it is furthermore the only source from which real love can originate. To any human being in whom we have complete and absolute confidence and respect, love and affection will automatically develop.[14]

In the above passage, Barton returns to his key word, "confidence," that he used in his earlier philosophical tract. Again, he seems to view people as the missing link between animals and human beings. Since he can analyze, he can define himself as talking from "a human point of view." But since his marriages did not last, nor the marriages of others, he concludes by explaining what happens to "superior" marriage partners who fail:

> Now let us turn to the marriage problem of the very few superior young men and women who have developed their natural capacity to analyze everything, and have reached a state of high intelligence and are very well informed. Such people will not indulge in self deception, but will call an ace an ace and a spade a spade. When they consider marriage, they think in terms of a lifelong beautiful companionship which they both desire.
>   They will not rush into marriage, but will study each other's mind and character, and when both are completely satisfied that a perfect companionship is possible and their confidence in each other is complete and justifiable then he will propose marriage to her. The only motive back of his marriage proposal is his desire to be allowed to contribute thru life to her welfare, comfort and happiness because he really loves her.
>   They have a wonderful life and enjoy each other's companionship until death if there are not children. If and when she becomes a mother, then they face an unforeseen problem for which Nature is to blame. Nature has imposed upon all normal girls and women a

problem which they do not realize or take into consideration until they become Mothers. Directly she becomes a Mother about ninety percent of all the love, affection and devotion she is capable of will be directed to the product of her own womb. This is true even if she should hate the husband and Father of her child. After motherhood there is only a little love left for the husband. He then becomes a provider for herself and child. If before marriage she was not mercenary and was quite content to get along with what her husband could provide a change takes place after motherhood. She becomes very ambitious for her wonderful child who must have the very best of everything, all of which costs a lot of money which her hard working husband cannot provide, so she becomes discontented with him.

Why doesn't he get a better job and make more money? During my lifetime I have met thousands of people, but the only married couples I have met who enjoyed perfect companionship and love until death were those who had no children. So, even the highly intelligent man often fails to realize before marriage that his marriage can be a failure when his wife becomes a Mother.[15]

Barton talks about how even a highly intelligent man finds himself entrapped in a problem. But what about intelligent women? To paraphrase a country western tune, his moral seems to be "Mommas Don't Let Your Cowgirls Grow Up to Be Mommas." The passage's focus on wanting wealth harks back to his earlier tract. Barton remained mum on the subject of children in his own life.

The tract can be read as one coming from someone who has been through the school of hard knocks or from one who puts on the guise of the wise, old bachelor. Mabel, Ashia, and Mamie could all be read into this. Mabel and Mamie could represent mates who cost a lot, Ashia the devoted one. Barton's comments on perfect marriages being ones that are childless seem ironic. His marriages appear to be childless, yet none lasted.

For Barton, distributing his philosophical tracts to selected guests was actually a way of flattering them by expressing respect and friendship. Although some receivers thought being handed these musings a bit disturbing, exhibitionistic, bizarre, or the result of old-age ruminating crankiness, Barton saw the giving as a positive act. It was another way for him to pattern himself on the Russell paradigm. Barton pointed out in the homage he wrote for Russell that the cowboy artist offered a cordial face to all people but saved his real feelings, "true mind," or intellect for his closest friends. Barton interpreted Russell as sharing only with those people who qualified intellectually to understand him. Most Easterners were excluded, except for Malcolm Mackay of New York, who admired both Russell and his work and whose sons became Real Men, meaning Montana cattle ranchers. As Barton saw it, only he and a few others who had the open range in them were admitted into the select circle. As a senior citizen, Barton was doing the same for people he thought might be near his intellectual equal and could understand the Old West. He wanted to be as frank, honest, and candid as he believed Russell had been with his closest associates.

For Russell's dealings with outsiders, Barton observed that Russell either remained silent or deflected any seriousness with just a few comments, usually humorous. Likewise, Barton tried to express some humor in his booklet on the life of Russell, since it was being written for both insiders and outsiders. In contrast, his more private philosophical tracts were devoid of humor. But in his Russell pamphlet, Barton cited a quotation that tickled him. He recalled a remark made by an old Montana cowman in describing a stupid man he knew: "That son of a bitch had no head at all, just neck growed up and haired over."

That picturesque image was not his, but Barton was trying to inject a bit of humor at the end of his writing as Russell would have done; only Russell would have done it throughout. The humorous remark harked back to Barton's theme of there being two kinds of people in the world, the dumb ones and the Real Men. Included in his list of the dumb or "ignorant morons" were what he termed irresponsible Western thriller writers and Hollywood filmmakers who misrepresented the cowboy. No rancher would ever hire any of the killers in these books, nor did two-gun cowboys ever exist except in the movies. Barton felt that Montanans "were both generous and broadminded in their criticism of others and were prepared to overlook many faults, but damn moronish stupidity could not be tolerated."[16] Barton did not tolerate it. It was hard trying to be Russell.

His disdain for the ignorant extended to inanimate objects as well. He could not stand modern cowboy equipment. Even though his equipment was over fifty years old, he kept it all perfectly maintained and useable in his apartment. Modern riding tack and equipment represented impractical, impermanent, or showy junk, designed for someone's pocketbook rather than for a working cowboy.

Barton remained mum on many topics and events in his life, or so it would seem. His trail ends here. Just as he tried to summarize his own philosophy and life, so too, perhaps, should a biographical conclusion. Such a task remains difficult. He hid his life much as did those Mongol kings buried in Manchuria while, much like all of us, showing only what he wanted others to see. The kings were not buried where their tombs were but rather out on the flats, the steppes, the high plains. After one's internment in a nondescript location, thousands of Mongolian ponies were driven back and forth across the gravesite and entire region to obliterate any sign of the deceased's location.[17] But grave robbers also respected feng shui. They knew burial sites were located at the intersection of harmonious lines in nature. Every once in a while, they could find the remains of someone's life and its treasures.

In later years, Barton rode over the graves of his own trails, only he did it with a Cadillac. He had become songster Marty Robbins' "The Cowboy in the Continental Suit," the outward, deceptive glitz disguising the real-deal bronc buster and his adventures. Barton loved his Montana, returning to the state every summer from 1948 to 1960, when poor health intervened. For Barton, the area the Sioux called *Paha Sapa*, "The Heart of Everything," truly contained his heart of everything. As he was proud to say, "I am older than the State of Montana." And he was.

In the end, Barton did parallel his hero Charlie Russell. Both stayed true to the Old West. Both stretched facts. Russell switched birthdates quicker than rustlers change brands, as did Barton. For artistic advantage, Russell told big windies about how much time he spent living with Native Americans and how he painted outside under the Big Sky. In reality, he lived only briefly, at best, with the tribes. Moreover, he painted and sculpted nearly every major work in a studio, often using photographs as reference. Barton marketed and painted his own story, one that included not being married, a story filled with diversions and misdirection. While decrying how progress destroyed the beautiful land God had made and the open range of real men, both of the men used modern

Typical photograph and signature paste-in Barton used inside the back cover of books in his library.

technology to their advantage. Charlie and Nancy Russell owned the newest and biggest automobiles. Barton did likewise, although he drove himself. Russell embraced photography, posing for professional photographers and attending movies. Barton went a step further, even getting into the film business on his ranch in China.

Both men owed much to the horse. Russell molded horses out of wax for his bronzes. Barton sculpted horses out of other horses, with a bronzed patina of Mongolia, Siberia, and Montana. Both knew when to ride by sneaking out through the back windows of their lives. Both lived bronc lives. They may have been broken, saddled, and ridden by the modern world, but underneath they remained broncs.

Russell described both Barton and himself best when he painted *When Horses Talk War There's Slim Chance for Truce* (1915) (later known as *When Horses Talk War There's Small Chance for Peace*). The scene captures dawn at the remuda around the chuckwagon. Except for a sliver of color on the horizon, a dark, troubled overcast covers the sky. Cowboys finish their last cup of coffee and are saddling their horses in the early morning cold. One horse will have nothing of it. With ears up and hooves planted, the outlaw squares off against the rider on the other end of the rope. The horse raises his head defiantly while snorting steam at the cowboy. It's a standoff. Between them sits an icy puddle. One or the other, or both, are likely to end up there as the old wild spirit reemerges.

Such has been the case in uncovering the enigma of Fred Barton's life. The grass had grown seventy-eight times since the stork had gotten tired and dropped him off in Montana. On May 8, 1967, as Will Rogers might say, Fred switched outfits and hired on with the roundup boss up on the Big Mountain. He crossed the divide to ride a new range. The horses of history have crossed and recrossed his real grave. Sometimes lines intersect, the river finds its old bed, a rock is uncovered where it has always stood, the mountains align, the Shansi and Montana wolves return to howl that one night on their ancestral hill an old saddle is found. And what of that and of him we still don't know and have lost? As a Jon Billman character says in *When We Were Wolves*, "The smell of wet sage has a way of evening out your losses."[18]

Seventeen • Ruminating on Guys, Gussies and Morons at Trail's End

> *Let cattle rub my headstone round,*
> *And coyotes wail their kin,*
> *Let hosses come and paw the mound,*
> *But don't you fence me in.*
> —from an old cowboy song
> by Badger Clark, Jr.

Epilogue

"Events that happen," so a rickshaw runner explained as he pulled me to market one morning, "are not put away in books. That would not be fair. Only a few folk have leisure to read, and history belongs to everyone. It flows in every mother's milk and is digested by every babe. Thus it becomes a part of everyone's experience to use when needed. That which happens is not past. It's all a part of our now."[1]
—Nora Waln, *The House of Exile*

    Strange reports came out of North China at the ends of World War II and the Korean War. American POWs swore they had seen what seemed hardly possible. Among the Peking area's donkeys, mules, and Mongol ponies that had not been either eaten or killed in the wars, they witnessed a few unmistakable shapes of home—living American Morgan horses. How could this be? Where had they come from?

    Prior to World War II, the U.S. Marine Legation Guard in Peking maintained a colorful mounted "Horse Marine" unit. But like the 15th Infantry's mounted unit in Tientsin, their mounts consisted of Mongol ponies discarded from the Peking and Tientsin racetracks; in other words, they were mostly Larson's horses, not Morgans. While some believe that a few Western horses imported from Australia may have been included, photographs so far do not substantiate that claim. Except for color variations common to Mongol ponies, the military mounts appear uniform and matched in size—Mongol pony size.

    The Horse Marines provided a centerpiece for parades. The very active Peking racetrack and polo field attracted these men. The unit also played the part of marauding Chinese cavalry during war games. Barton must have interacted with the Guards during his many visits to the U.S. Peking legation when he worked for BAT, needed to share information, or needed to clear paperwork to have horses shipped to China. It is possible that Barton dropped off a Morgan or two as a gift when the Morgans moved through Peking, but there is no evidence of that. It is doubtful that either Barton, the warlords, or the U.S. minister to China would have wanted the problems that might ensue if another Morgan breeding program were established in China.

    While Marines could not be furloughed for Barton's horse drive from Siberia, the unit exhibited a certain Wild West flair. This led to one of the more unusual popular culture connections between East and West. When Marines helped save the legation during the 1900 Boxer Rebellion, Buffalo Bill Cody was moved by reports of the heroic battle. He broke his tradition of having his Wild West show re-create only scenes from the Old West. Following his show's regular performance of the robbery of the Deadwood stage by Indians, he inserted the pyrotechnics of "Rescue at Pekin [sic]," documenting the legation fight using a cast of hundreds.[2]

A stickler for authenticity (except for plot), Cody assembled a mockup of Peking's Tartar Wall, which Marines climbed under fire. Audiences witnessed Gatling guns and more modern armaments for the first time. Actual returning veterans of the Boxer Rebellion stormed the ramparts. Cody's Sioux regulars played the part of the Chinese. They shot a lot of blanks and fell over dead many times. The action became too believable to some audiences, as they raced out of the stands to attack the Chinese. The show made for a noisy, spectacular hit, though it is little heard of today. The lesson: Even in modern times, the world still needed audacious Anglo-Saxon frontiersmen, such as Cody, to overcome threats.

In 1920 or 1921, the Marines returned the favor to Buffalo Bill. Marine Lt. Edward Osgood Bogert of the Legation Guards, or "Riders of the Peking Dust," dressed up as a cowboy to reenact the robbery of the Deadwood stage in Peking. He did not do badly on costuming. He found a big hat, a neckerchief, an appropriate vest, and some boots (pant legs tucked in). His big problem was that he had to use a military saddle on his Mongol pony, and it was no Morgan.

Shortly before the Japanese attack on Pearl Harbor, the mounted legation unit was detailed to Tientsin to take the place of the departing 15th Infantry. They were ordered to leave their mounts behind. Soon the Marines had to try to make their failed escape from China as Japan closed in. In Peking, the Marines sold off their horses to Americans living outside the legation for $10 a head, which included tack and a McClellan cavalry saddle. Quite a deal. A few horses went with the Marines to Tientsin, but the 15th had to unload its horses, too, as it was recalled.

Even in the unlikely event that by chance some Morgans somehow happened to be in the mix, their chances of survival would have been unpromising. As in Shanghai, people who cared about their horses had them shot rather than let them fall into Japanese hands. This led to heartbreaking family scenes, such as when the pony served as a young girl's companion and pet. Americans anticipated the Japanese military would treat horses as cruelly, or more so, as the Japanese had treated conquered people. Giving their horses over to the Chinese would not work either. Owners could not bear seeing their animals worked to death pulling Chinese carts too heavy for any beast of burden. The bond between horse and human was too strong to let that happen.

Given the World War II sightings, possibly some of Barton's Morgans or their descendants survived, though they had been reduced to pulling carts. Cold War sightings were another matter. Frank "Pappy" Noel, the Pulitzer Prize–winning Associated Press photographer, found himself imprisoned by the Communists for three years during the Korean War. This volunteer photographer had been captured in the battle for Chosin Reservoir. After trying to escape three times from various prison camps, he labored on a work detail before his prisoner exchange release in Operation Big Switch in 1953. Once, while eating wormy crabapples to survive, he watched two Chinese generals ride up on Morgans, strikingly different from smaller Mongol ponies prisoners were accustomed to seeing. When Pappy fed the horses some apples, the generals' orderly, to rub it in, proudly announced that these were American horses.[3]

History had repeated itself. Like the Morgans that survived World War II, these Morgans had avoided the bullets and meat cleavers of the Chinese Revolution. They were there because of the ground Barton had broken earlier. Barton whetted the Chinese taste for crossbreeding Morgans with Mongol ponies. What Noel saw had been set in motion in 1947, just after World War II and just before the Communist takeover of China in 1949 and subsequent Korean War in 1950. Major General S.S. Young, Major General P.C. Tsui, and Lieutenant Colonel W.Y. Chang came to the United States to buy fourteen Morgan mares and twelve stallions to breed with Mongol ponies. Through photo identification, Noel positively identified one of the Morgans he saw and tentatively identified the second. It was none other than Magellan from the U.S. Morgan Horse Farm. Magellan became the senior stallion at China's Military Min-Sian Stud in Gansu Province. The Chinese patterned their breeding plan after what Barton and the warlords had in mind. The Morgans were to be crossbred with native Mongol ponies in North China, which were larger than those used in the south. Morgan blood would allow the new horse to have a gentle disposition, be more adaptable to differing circumstances, and show good conformation and intelligence.

Reminiscent of Barton's Morgan shipment, Magellan and the other stallions, mares, and fillies shipped out in style on the *Philippine Transport* from San Francisco bound for Shanghai. General Tsui did not want the horses to spend six weeks in the cramped, stagnant, unhealthy hold of a ship. He ordered stalls specially built for them on deck. A little dousing with seawater would not hurt. There to meet the horses in China was Major General Y.C. Yu, appointed as the first chief of the Horse Administration Bureau when it was founded in 1936. Other top members of the military dating back to the time of Barton's ranch in China also were present. They knew what Morgans were and needed to try again, for "peaceful uses," of course. As J. Victor Pinnell pointed out, the Chinese government wanted to raise horses that would "have the depth of the ocean, the stamina of Hercules and the loyalty and companionship of a true friend."[4] As the mounted units of the U.S. Marines and Infantry in China found out, Mongol horses, although only the size of a good Welsh pony, all too often just wanted to take a chunk out of you. The horses knew the difference between Mongolians and everyone else, and they were not afraid to demonstrate their knowledge. The Morgan blood would help make them less hot blooded.

Pinnell ought to have known about the qualities of the Morgan. As secretary treasurer of the Morgan Horse Association of the West, he had China in his blood. For their 1920 honeymoon, he and his wife sailed for China. He lived with and among the Chinese, off and on, for some twenty-six years. Like Barton, he had his own faithful Chinese servant and interpreter. He made friends with some of the generals left over from Barton's warlord years. Also like Barton, he settled down in Los Angeles as a prominent member of the horse scene and one who had been somewhat of an adventurer.

His 1920 trip to China gave him newspaper coverage nearly equal to that of Barton's publicity about the creation of the Shansi ranch. Pinnell earned his notoriety differently, as a cowboy of another sort. Prior to the trip, he owned a lumber company in Indiana. His wedding stag party, dubbed the "Feast of Belshazzar," created quite a scandal. It played on the theme of the extravagant party Belshazzar, King of Babylon, threw for a thousand of his guests, as recorded in the Book of Daniel. Belshazzar profaned the gold goblets that the Babylonians looted from the temple in Jerusalem. A mysterious hand appeared and wrote an inscription on the banquet wall that only Daniel, as a Jew, could read. It foretold the fall of Belshazzar.

By the next morning Pinnell's guests had all fallen. Thanks to John Barleycorn, Pinnell's pronated guests were found strewn all over the Kokomo Country Club grounds, and they were not exactly lining up putts. Remnants of food fights splattered the club walls in homage to various pagan gods. The stag party was indeed biblical. Profanation was complete, as Sunday preachers railed at the debauchery from their podiums. After all, this was supposed to be Indiana, not the Divine Inferno. While Pinnell could survive a preacher's hellfire, the not-so-mysterious hand of the Revenuers was another matter. They pursued Pinnell for violation of the Volstead Act. Time to hit the trail. The king had fallen, with Hoosier Daniels hot on his trail.

Pinnell skipped town with his bride on the heels of the epic blowout. He also skipped out on the $2,000 note he had with the local bank. Babylon and world travel were costly. When he returned after a long absence, the judge gave him a wedding present of ninety days on the state farm and put his business into receivership. Like Barton, Pinnell was an irrepressibly good survivor and later did well in California. The two old China hands, linked together by the Morgans, cashed in just months apart in 1967.

Also under the category of "the more things change, the more they remain the same," China today still requires Montana horses. The Chinese government regularly buys Montana horses for border guard duties in China's rugged mountainous regions where weather and terrain curtail the use of airplane, vehicle, and the foot soldier. The days of the mounted dragoons, mounted rifleman, and cavalry may be over, but not quite. Fort Keogh may no longer be a remount station, but Montana is. Just as Barton's horses were checked in Reno for their long trip by boat to China, recently Animal and Plant Health Inspection Service (APHIS) veterinarians out of Helena, Montana, dealt with the complicated requirements for the international shipping of livestock as they cleared Montana horses for export to China.[5]

In 2009, just before the 100th anniversary of Fred Barton's epic ride across Siberia with Russian Cossacks on Mongol ponies, Doug Stanton's *Horse Soldiers: The Extraordinary Story of a Band of U.S. Soldiers Who Rode to Victory in Afghanistan* appeared. The book revealed that even though the U.S. long ago discontinued cavalry units, that did not mean U.S. soldiers no longer find themselves going to war on horses. After 9/11, the U.S. Army Fifth Special Forces Group became the first U.S. boots on the ground in Afghanistan to confront the Taliban and Al Qaeda.

With a few thousand Northern Alliance mounted troops, the small Special Forces units rode into battle on the same type of Mongol ponies Barton had ridden. They defeated a much larger force, as their cavalry charged and surrounded Taliban who were armed with Russian tanks, armored vehicles, rockets, surface-to-air missiles, and heavy machine guns mounted on Toyota pickup trucks. In the barren, mountainous terrain, nimble horses went where vehicles could not and traveled much faster. When the Special Forces team obtained an ATV military Gator, it had to largely stick to the valleys rather than go where cavalry could go. Afghani horsemen lassoed the industrial strength golf cart and pulled it out of a glacial stream when water flooded its engine and began to float it away.[6] Old horsepower was saving the technological age and winning the war.

Virtually none of the Special Forces fighters knew how to ride or mount a horse, so the men rode into battle trying to stay on diminutive wooden saddles with nonadjustable stirrups. This caused bloody backsides and a slipped disc. As the men hunched on their saddles, their jaws at times met their own knees. Horses initiated the Americans into the wonders of hard ground and dust upon the horses' discovering the riders' lack of horsemanship. Learning the hard way, the team persevered. It was either get on or be left behind by the Afghan riders.

Barton's China bronc busters would have been proud of Fred Fall. Fall's name befits his achievement. Northern Alliance commander General Dostum, who witnessed Fall's incredible ride, or fall rather, called Fall the finest horseman ever, even though the tall, gangly staff sergeant looked like a complete mismatch on a Mongol pony. As he wound down a sheer mountain switchback, his stallion suddenly plunged directly down the nearly vertical mountainside. Fall had no idea of how to stop the horse and prevent his own death. But a similar scene from the movie *The Man from Snowy River* flashed through his mind. Like the actor in the film, he leaned back in the saddle, so that his head bounced on the horse's rump and his boots gyrated above the horses' ears and his own screams of "I don't want to die" ripped the air. His horse was able to land on a ledge to slow their speed and then make it the rest of the way down at a gallop.[7] A movie saved Fall's life. The non-horseman unintentionally became the immediate best horseman in the world—the Man from Snowy Afghanistan. His stallion deigned not to talk about it.

In a reversal of Barton's crossbreeding program, Asian horses recently returned the favor to the U.S. They were brought to the West to be crossbred. One valiant attempt at this involved the Nez Perce in Idaho. The tribe tried to reestablish its horse culture, destroyed after the surrender of Chief Joseph in 1877.[8] Not until 1995 did the Nez Perce own horses again. After this 117-year horse breeding hiatus, the Nez Perce established their Young Horseman program to train youths age 14 to 21 in horsemanship and to run a breeding program. The goal was to produce a unique breed equal to the Nez Perce horses Meriwether Lewis admired during the Lewis and Clark Expedition in 1805. At that time the Nez Perce were the only North American Indians engaged in selectively breeding horses,[9] and it showed. Chief Joseph (*Hin-meh-too-yah-lat-kelkt*, or Thunder Rolling Down the Mountain) was born in 1840 at nearly the same time the Oregon Trail was opening up. After crossing deserts and mountains, early pioneers on that arduous route exulted over the rewarding sight that greeted them as they crossed Deadman Pass into the eastern valleys of Oregon. Loren B. Hastings in 1847 saw "the bottom and bluffs covered with ponies and horses, too."[10] Horses were unexpected, especially in large numbers and with excellent conformation. The Nez Perce hoped to return to that vision.

The horse known in Chinese legend as the Heavenly Horse or the Golden Horse of Asia, known today as the Akhal-Teke (AT), was crossbred with the Appaloosa, which the Nez Perce had originally developed from the wild mustang.[11] The Appaloosa was so distinctive that Charles M. Russell used the horse to good advantage in the story "Mormon Murphy's Confidence," in his *Trails Plowed Under* collected stories. Two trappers were approached by another rider who claimed to be a peaceful Gros Ventre, but one of the trappers figured the rider was lying and was really one of Chief Joseph's men on the run and out for blood. Confirmation came in the way of his horse. He rode an Appaloosa, so he had to be a Nez Perce far from home, as only Nez Perce from over in Umatilla country bred such horses.

Crossing the Akhal-Teke with the Appaloosa produced a new breed called the Nez Perce Horse, or *Ni-ni-pu Sik'em*, a horse designed to combine the solid features of the spotted Western Appaloosa with the elegant long neck, swiftness, and warm-bloodedness of the Akhal-Teke. Having been bred for 3,000 years, the world's oldest breed, the Akhal-Teke was prized by rulers from Alexander the Great to Chinese emperors.

The palomino color variation made the horse literally glow in the sun like molten gold, thus the horse of heaven analogy. Like the Mongol pony, the Akhal-Teke is known for its toughness. A desert horse from the region of Turkmenistan and the high Mongolian plateau, it can tolerate heat and go with little water. This was demonstrated in 1935 when some Akhal-Tekes achieved notoriety by covering a distance that rivaled Barton's own horse drive through Siberia and Mongolia. Twenty-eight riders on Akhal-Tekes and some Akhal-Teke/Thoroughbred crosses traveled from Ashkabad to Moscow, a distance of 2,580 miles, in eighty-four days. For 600 miles they traversed the desert of the Kara Kum virtually without water. The crosses did not fare so well, but the purebred Akhal-Tekes did. The Thoroughbreds and Akal-Tekes shared more than just that trip. Some of the first stallions used to create Thoroughbreds were Akhal-Tekes (ATs). So the past comes back, but not all of it.

The story about Asian horses in the West does not end there. More dramatic is the odyssey of two countesses and their Akhal-Tekes and Clovers that made it to Montana. Legend has it that horses bearing on their noses the mark of clover (a slate-colored clover leaf shape) descend from the earliest horses. These horses originated on the Asiatic steppes some 3,000 years ago. The Magyars used ATs when invading Hungary in the seventh century. Genghis Khan's grandsons did also when they invaded in the thirteenth century. In the twentieth century, some Clovers still existed in Hungary. Akhal-Tekes and Clovers share the same bloodline back to the ancient horse of the Mongolian plateau. The question arose whether, after several hundred years, they could be crossbred so that the handful of surviving Clovers could be brought back to their original AT base blood, re-creating the original golden horse of the steppes.

To save the few that were left, two Hungarian countesses risked everything in World War II. Though surrounded by Russian troops, Countess Judith Byurky was able to sneak villagers, her Clovers, and other Hungarian horses through to a zone controlled by Americans. She had endured much through both World I and World War II to save her horses. She had been tortured and escaped by disguising herself as "Miss Arizona" in a vaudeville troupe. Out of her herd of seventy-three of the finest horses in Hungary, she was able to ship thirteen to the United States by marrying a sea captain willing to transport her beloved animals. While on the run, she parted with her jewelry and other possessions in order to buy feed for the horses. Since the Clovers were riding horses rather than plow horses, the Communists saw them as of the gentry, not proletariat. They slaughtered such horses and sold them for meat without concern for exterminating a breed. Tanks now substituted for cavalry, tractors for plow horses. Stalin had no room for "fancy" horses.

While Countess Byurky was making her escape from what became the Iron Curtain, General George S. Patton recognized what was going on. Hungarian horses needed saving.

As a former Grand Prix and Olympian jumper in the 1930s, Patton knew Hungarian horses and their riders through competition. Countess Byurky had been such a competitor at the highest levels. She did everything as well as the men did, if not better. Like Ginger Rogers, who did everything Fred Astaire did on the dance floor, only backwards and in high heels, Judith was required to make all of her jumps riding sidesaddle.

The day the Russians were closing off the Russian Zone at the end of World War II, General Patton learned of a mounted unit of Hungarians trapped on the other side of the river in the Russian Zone. With his usual guts, bluster, and hoodwinking, he brought the men and their horses across a bridge to the American side. Patton saved thousands of horses and men from being liquidated that day. This included the famous Lippizzans. Although the Lippizzans have come down to us through history, other horses were less fortunate. Patton was killed shortly after the rescue of the men and horses. Having its mind on other matters, the army in its infinite wisdom did not understand the importance of what Patton had saved, so it sold off the horses to a meat-starved Europe.

A few Hungarian horses were brought back to the U.S. as spoils of war. The army hoped to improve remount breeding programs. That program ended before it could begin when the military decided it no longer needed cavalry. Again, horses were sold off. Hungarian Countess Margit Bessessyey, having become horse-raising friends with Countess Byurky (now Judith Kelly), luckily got in on the army sale before the rendering plant called.

While Judith lived simply in order to afford her herd in Virginia, Margit owned a ready-made stable in Montana, the Bitterroot Stock Farm. Margit was the daughter of Count Anthony Sigray and Harriet Daly, daughter of Marcus Daly. This made Margit heir to the Daly fortune. Barton and everyone in Montana from the late nineteenth century into the twentieth century knew of Marcus Daly. Known as the Copper King and one of the richest men in the world, his Anaconda Copper Company ruled Anaconda, Butte, and pretty much the whole state of Montana at one time, not to mention some South American countries. Reflecting who controlled state politics and economy, the state flag of Montana exhibits a miner's pick and shovel leaning against a plow. No horses, steers, or sheep. A banner contains the state motto: "Oro y Plata" (gold and silver). No horses or steers there either, just mining. Daly pursued the sport of kings, racing his thoroughbreds and winning the Belmont Stakes. Margit set her sights instead on breeding the eight Hungarian mares she had saved from destruction.

When the countesses died in the 1980s, Jolaine Cowherd of Darby, Montana, became guardian of Margit's Clovers. In 1995 an Akhal-Teke mare foaled a metallic gold AT colt. With the help of a well known pre–World War II stud farm manager, Laszio Monostory, a breeding program was designed to cross the then young stallion with the mares. The result was a cross that had not been made in perhaps hundreds of years, a horse that brought the Clovers back to the original AT base blood of centuries ago. All by accident, luck, and courage, the last herd of pure, true-to-type Magyar horses that originally came from Mongolia lives again in the West.[12]

Artifacts of the China ranch experience that were brought back to the U.S. have been lost to home fires, and the not-knowing garbage can becomes too handy and irresistible when people die. On the other hand, some objects have been preserved and passed on from generation to generation. Others probably remain sitting in people's barns, in people's homes, or in museums without their owners knowing that the smell of leather and the jingle of steel were also those of the warlords and some very well-traveled cowboys.

Recently, north of the old Shansi ranch, Motorola, along with other U.S. companies and the China Rocket Carrier Technology Research Institute, launched Iridium telecommunications satellites with Long March-2-III rockets from the Shansi launch site. Taiyuanfu serves as the nerve center for this Cape Canaveral of China. Taiyuanfu resembles many of the old cowboy towns that Barton knew—Billings, Gillette, Sheridan. If you go away even five years and think of returning, locals say "you won't even know the place." Taiyuanfu made the leap from animal dung, coal, and kerosene fuels to rocket solid fuel and liquid hydrogen, from Mongol ponies to corporate jets, from terraced hills to an orbiting terraced sky. Instead of balls of shed camel hair bouncing across the plains, former NBA players dribble basketballs down the court for Taiyuanfu's professional basketball team, the Shanxi Zhongyu Brave Dragons.

But just as a cold Siberian Express or a hot Gobi wind still blows through Montana and Wyoming, the past sweeps through Shansi, and life remains on the frontier. In August of 1999, U.S. newspapers carried the story of the Shansi criminal who secretly poisoned oxen in the area. He then appeared at the homes of the poor, ruined farmers to take the carcasses off their hands for a small price. He and his family butchered the carcasses and sold the poisoned meat to unsuspecting consumers at full meat value. Bon appétit. What's a few lives to get rich? Some wolvers tried a similar stunt around Miles City when Barton rode the range. They tried to "de-wolf" poisoned wolf meat to sell to the unsuspecting. In an ironic twist, some wolfers died horrible deaths when a bad winter snowed them in necessitating that they eat their own strychnine-laden wolf meat. Modern Taiyuanfu need not worry about wolves. It does still have to contend with the snow and dust storms that blow in from the Gobi, but even these help to clear out the choking, polluted air inversions plaguing China's cities.

Fred Barton's life also becomes ever more clear and confirmed. On October 12, 2013, the Academy of Motion Pictures Arts and Sciences hosted its annual celebration of amateur filmmaking at its Linwood Dunn Theater in Los Angeles. Of the seventeen home movies screened, one novelty, the earliest film, showed "amazing footage" of cowboy life on Fred Barton's China ranch in the 1920s. Had any doubters remained about the actual existence of such a ranch and Barton's story, here was proof. Fred Barton's great nephew brought the aging images that Barton had filmed. It is incredible that it still existed.[13]

Hollywood and Barton's filmmaking proclivity at General Yen Hsi-Shan's ranch must have given the old governor-general ideas. In 1935 Yen decided he needed a motion picture depicting his life.[14] After all, he had out-survived nearly all other warlords. The movie must naturally star him, so he established his own motion picture corporation and cast himself. One problem: he had aged. That meant hiring a younger man to play his role before the year 1928. Yen knew that motion pictures made effective propaganda in the modern age. He was indeed a modern model governor. He was getting into the fray ahead of his time, or at least early, in what became a cinematic fight between Nationalist and Communist filmmakers in China's 1930s first golden age of filmmaking.

Motion picture importance increased when Japan invaded China. Movie theaters were the first Chinese businesses to be reopened by Japanese occupying forces. Their propaganda films touched on how Chinese life would be so good under their boot rather than under the boots of Western powers. Yen had the last laugh after the Japanese booted him out of his own province. When the Japanese were defeated in 1945, their army in Shansi had to surrender to Yen. Rather than sending them back to Japan, he conscripted them into his own army to ward off the Chinese Communists. At the close of World War II, Japanese soldiers simply kept fighting and retained their own officers. Yen apparently planned to waste them on the battlefield. He was a sly survivor, as was Barton.

Besides the Barton film of the China ranch, thanks to Barton's extended family, his letters and family and China ranch photographs have been preserved. The personal heart of his Museum of the Old West lives on. He has ridden off, looking back over his shoulder like a bemused, wily coyote at those who doubted his story. Never been a horse that can't be rode, nor a man that can't be throwed.

A bronc might be broke, but that hoss still has money in the bank.

Chapter Notes

Introduction

1. John Keegan, *The First World War* (New York: Knopf, 1999), 71.
2. Norman E. Saul, *The Life and Times of Charles R. Crane, 1858–1939: American Businessman, Philanthropist, and a Founder of Russian Studies in America* (New York: Lexington Books, 2013), 152.
3. Lloyd Clark, *The Battle of the Tanks, Kursk, 1943* (New York: Atlantic Monthly Press, 2011), 72.
4. P.A. Westwood, "Soldier of Fortune: Amazing Life of General Frank Sutton," *Adelaide Advertiser*, 4 March 1933, p. 9.
5. Daniel S. Levy, *Two-Gun Cohen: A Biography* (New York: St. Martin's, 1997), 125.
6. Henning Haslund, *In Secret Mongolia*, trans. Elizabeth Sprigge and Claude Napier (Kempton, IL: Adventures Unlimited, 1995), 156–158.

Chapter One

1. Barbara Tuchman, *Stillwell and the American Experience in China, 1911–45* (New York: Macmillan, 1971), 26.
2. Michael Wallis, *The Real Wild West* (New York: St. Martin's, 1999), 153.
3. Frederic Remington, *Pony Tracks* (New York: Harper, 1895), 25–26.
4. Remington, 1–2.

Chapter Two

1. Fred Barton, "Old Miles Town, Cow Capital of the West," letters section, *Montana: The Magazine of Western History* 5, no. 2 (1956), 65.
2. Mona D. Sizer, *Outrageous Texans* (New York: Taylor Trade, 2008), 116.
3. John Taliaferro, *Charles M. Russell: The Life and Legend of America's Cowboy Artist* (New York: Little, Brown, 1996), 97.
4. Fred Barton, interview by J. Ross Toole, Michael Kennedy, and Sam Sulberg, 30 August 1955, Montana Historical Society, Helena.
5. "Prices Are High in Vladivostock," *Miles City Independent* 18, no. 35 (29 August 1919), 5.
6. *Miles City Independent* 10, no. 25 (23 June 1911).
7. *Independent* 11, no. 1 (5 January 1912).
8. Charles A. Siringo, *Riata and Spurs* (New York: Houghton Mifflin, 1931), 167.
9. Richard Alexis Georgian, *Cossacks, Indians, and Buffalo Bill: The Adventures of Georgian Riders in America* (Naples, FL: Barringer, 2011), 16.
10. Dee Brown, *The American West* (New York: Scriber's, 1994), 388.

Chapter Three

1. Harry A. Franck, *Wandering in Northern China* (New York: Century, 1923), 86.
2. Ferdinand Ossendowski, *Man and Mystery in Asia* (New York: Dutton, 1924), 98–99.
3. Ossendowski, 95.
4. Barton, interview, 1955.
5. Ibid.
6. Richard M. Ketchum, *Will Rogers: His Life and Times* (New York: American Heritage, 1973), 347–348.
7. Barton, interview, 1955.
8. James Reid Marsh, *The Charm of the Middle Kingdom* (Boston: Little, Brown, 1922), 31–32.
9. Franck, 76–78.
10. Tuchman, 107.
11. Hsi-sheng Ch'i, *Warlord Politics in China, 1916–1928* (Stanford, CA: Stanford University, 1976), 183.
12. Tuchman, 108.
13. James Lafayette Hutchison, *China Hand* (New York: Grosset and Dunlap, 1936), 63–64.
14. Barton, interview, 1955.
15. Simon Sebag Montefiore, *Young Stalin* (New York: Vantage, 2008), 210.
16. Barton, interview, 1955.
17. Tuchman, 109.

Chapter Four

1. C.G. Mannerheim, *Across Asia from West to East in 1906–1908*, vol. I (Oosterhout: Anthropological Publications, 1969), 677. Mannerheim covered the whole length of Shansi in his travels. His book gives a detailed description of Taiyuanfu and all the terrain stretching north to Kalgan where Barton brought the Russian Orlovs into China.
2. Quoted in Sherman Cochran, *Big Business in China: Sino-Foreign Rivalry in the Cigarette Industry,*

1890–1930 (Cambridge: Harvard University Press, 1980), 17.
   3. Cochran, 17.
   4. Gail Hershatter, "The Hierarchy of Shanghai Prostitution, 1870–1949," *Modern China* 14, no. 4, pp. 463–98.
   5. Ibid., 79.
   6. Ibid., 243.
   7. Ibid., 352.
   8. Ibid., 353.
   9. "And He Went Up on High; Chinaman Departs for Paradise in Style," *Oregonian*. September 28, 1919, p. 14.
   10. Hutchison, 353.
   11. Fallis L. Oliver, letter to author, 9 October 1995.
   12. Hutchison, 78–79.
   13. Cochran, 85.
   14. Paul French, *Through the Looking Glass: China's Foreign Journalists from Opium Wars to Mao* (Hong Kong: Hong Kong University Press, 2009), 125.
   15. Frans August Larson, *Larson, Duke of Mongolia* (New York: Little, Brown, 1930), 260.
   16. "Odd Bits of News," *Laredo Weekly Times*, 12 December 1915, p. 11.
   17. French, 127.
   18. Christopher Bo Bramsen, *Open Doors: Wilhelm Meyer and the Establishment of General Electric in China* (Richmond, Surrey: Curzon, 2001), 150.
   19. J. Wong-Quincey, *Chinese Hunter* (New York: John Day, 1939), 47.

Chapter Five

   1. Roy Chapman Andrews, *On the Trail of Ancient Man* (Garden City, NY: Doubleday, 1926), 352–353.
   2. Peter C. Perdue, *China Marches West: The Qing Conquest of Central Asia* (Cambridge: Harvard University Press, 2005), 354.
   3. Ibid., 139.
   4. James Palmer, *The Bloody White Baron: The Extraordinary Story of the Russian Nobleman Who Became the Last Khan of Mongolia* (New York: Basic Books, 2009), 72.
   5. Karen Judson, *Chemical and Biological Warfare* (Tarrytown: Benchmark, 2004), 68.
   6. Westwood, 9.
   7. Jack Sherwood, *Fond Memories of a Young Man in Old China* (Bloomington: Author House, 2009), 115.
   8. Robert Skidelsky, "A Chinese Homecoming," *Igud Yotzei Sin Bulletin* 54, no. 394 (November–December 2007), 20.
   9. Donald G. Gillin, *Warlord Yen His-shan in Shansi Province, 1911–1949* (Princeton, NJ: Princeton University Press, 1967), 91.
   10. Roger D. Arnold. "Annual Letter, Roger D. Arnold, Taiyuanfu, Shansi, China, September 1, 1919," University of Minnesota Libraries, http://umedia.lib.umn.edu//node/555798 (accessed 22 November 2013).
   11. Owen Lattimore, letter from Paris, France, to Ralph Miracle, 18 February 1976, Montana Historical Society (MHS).
   12. Gillin, 28.
   13. Mannerheim, 676.
   14. Barton, interview, 1955.
   15. Ibid.

Chapter Six

   1. Barton, interview, 1955.
   2. Charles G. Finney, *The Old China Hands* (Westport: Greenwood, 1973), 251. This book recounts military history of the 15th Infantry in China and should not be confused with another book about the diplomatic history called *The China Hands* by E.J. Kahn, Jr.
   3. Barton, interview, 1955.
   4. Edward M. Coffman, letter to author, 24 August 1996.
   5. Dennis L. Noble, letter to author, 14 September 1996.
   6. Tuchman, 100.
   7. Noble, letter to author.
   8. Finney, 100.
   9. Alfred Emile Cornebise, *The United States 15th Infantry Regiment in China, 1912–1938* (Jefferson, NC: McFarland, 2004), 103.
   10. Charles H. Harris III and Louis R. Sadler, *The Archaeologist Was a Spy: Sylvanus G. Morley and the Office of Naval Intelligence* (Albuquerque: University of New Mexico Press, 2003), 12.
   11. Katherine K. Reist, "State Department Soldiers, Warlords, Nationalists, and Intervention," in *American Diplomacy: Two Centuries of American Campaigning* (Leavenworth: Combat Studies Institute, 2003), 105–114.
   12. From the poem "15th Infantryman," quoted in Edward M. Coffman, "The American 15th Infantry Regiment in China, 1912–1938: A Vignette in Social History," *Journal of Military History* 58 (January 1994), 69.
   13. Roy Chapman Andrews, *Heart of Asia* (New York: Duell, Sloan, and Pearce, 1951), 62.
   14. Andrews, *Heart of Asia*, 110.
   15. Noel H. Pugach, *Paul S. Reinsch: Open Door Diplomat in Action* (Millwood, NY: Kraus-Thomson, 1979), 67.
   16. Ibid., 67.
   17. Ibid., 89.
   18. Ibid., 90–97.
   19. Gillin, 178.
   20. Noble, letter to author.
   21. "Path to Pearl Harbor," *Columbian*, 7 December 2013, pp. C1, C4.
   22. Leon Shulman Gaspard, letter to Rockford Art Guild, 18 March 1921, Rockford Art Museum files.
   23. John Dorfman, "A Painter's Pageant," *Art and Antiques* 36. no. 10 (October 2013), 42ff.
   24. Frank Waters, *Leon Gaspard* (Flagstaff: Northland, 1964), 47–48.
   25. Ibid., 48.
   26. Patrick Taveirne, *Han-Mongol Encounters and Missionary Endeavors: A History of Scheut in Ordos (Hetao), 1874–1911*, Leven Chinese Studies 15 (Leuven, Belgium: Leuven University Press, 2004), 320.

27. Roy Chapman Andrews, *Across Mongolian Plains* (New York: Blue Ribbon, 1921), 219.
28. John K. Fairbank, *The Missionary Enterprise in China and America* (Cambridge: Harvard University Press, 1981), 1.
29. Frederick Hoyt, "Junk Mail Is Not New; China Missionaries Used Direct Mailing," *American Philatelist* 110, no. 11 (November 1996), 1022–1029.
30. Shirley Stone Garrett, "Why They Stayed: American Church Politics and Chinese Nationalism in the Twenties," in *The Missionary Enterprise in China and America*, ed. John K. Fairbank (Cambridge: Harvard University Press, 1981), 290.
31. Barton, interview, 1955.

Chapter Seven

1. Michael B. Miller, *Shanghai on the Métro: Spies, Intrigue, and the French Between the Wars* (Berkeley: University of California Press, 1995), 259–260.
2. Julie M. Fenster, *Race of the Century: The Heroic True Story of the 1908 New York to Paris Auto Race* (New York: Crown, 2005), 277.
3. Jamie Bisher, *White Terror: Cossack Warlords of the Trans-Siberian* (New York: Routledge, 2005), 60.
4. David Wolff, *To the Harbin Station: The Liberal Alternative in Russian Manchuria, 1890–1914* (Stanford, CA: Stanford University Press, 1999), 79.
5. Mark Graham, "The Many Faces of Hotel Moderne in Harbin," *East Asian History*, no. 37 (December 2011), http://www.eastasianhistory.org/37/gamsa (accessed 2 May 2014).

Chapter Eight

1. Ossendowski, 292.
2. Charles M. Russell, *Trails Plowed Under* (Garden City, NY: Doubleday, 1927), 188.
3. Andrews, 75.
4. Nasan Dashdendeviin Bumaa, "The Twentieth Century: From Domination to Democracy," in *Modern Mongolia: Reclaiming Genghis Khan*, ed. Paula L. W. Sabloff (Philadelphia: University of Pennsylvania Press, 2001), 40.
5. Palmer, 72.
6. Ibid., 141.

Chapter Nine

1. Marco Polo, *The Travels*, quoted in "Marco Polo and His Travels," Silkroad Foundation, http://www.silk-road.com/art/marcopolo.shtml (accessed 2 May 2014).
2. William C. Summers, *The Great Manchurian Plague of 1910–1911: The Geopolitics of an Epidemic Disease* (New Haven: Yale University Press, 2012), 1.
3. Beatrix Bulstrode, *A Tour of Mongolia* (London: Methuen, 1920), 52.
4. Haslund, 37.
5. James Hudson Roberts, *A Flight for Life* (Boston: Pilgrim, 1903), 51.

Chapter Ten

1. Mabel H. Cabot, *Vanished Kingdoms: A Woman Explorer in Tibet, China and Mongolia, 1921–1925* (New York: Aperture, 2003), 49.
2. Masha Nordbye, "The Great Siberian Tea Road," *Russian Life* 56, no. 3 (May/June 2013), 33.
3. Haslund, 309.
4. Ibid., 196.
5. James Gilmore, *Among the Mongols* (London: Religious Tract Society, 1888; reprint facsimile, Elibron Classics, 2005), 159.
6. Henrietta Harrison, "Narcotics, Nationalism and Class in China," *East Asian History*, no. 32/33 (December 2006/2007), 166.

Chapter Eleven

1. Jonathan Raban, *Bad Land: An American Romance* (New York: Pantheon, 1996), 211.
2. Barton, interview, 1955.
3. "The Local News," *Miles City Independent* 18, no. 24 (16 May 1919), 8.
4. "Hittin' for Unfenced Land of the Orient," *Miles City Daily Star*, 24 May 1920, p. 8.
5. "Barton Party Starts for Chinese Ranges," *Miles City Daily Star*, 26 May 1920, 5.
6. "Montana Cowboys Head for China; Cattle Raising in the Land of the Celestials Will Take Wild West Flavor," *Eu Clair Leader*, 10 June 1920, p. 3.
7. Fred Barton, *Charles M. Russell: An Old-time Cowman Discusses the Life of Charles M. Russell*, 10–11.
8. "The Local News," *Miles City Independent* 18, no. 28 (11 July 1919), 8.
9. Mr. and Mrs. Earl "Early" Camblin, phone interview with author, 29 August 1999.
10. Ibid.
11. Ibid.
12. Tiffany Schwenke, "Agricultural Impressions," https://www.facebook.com/photo/php?fbid=101516933509677873&set=o.3547332045565398type=18relevant_count=1 (accessed 9 August 2013).
13. Camblin.
14. Ibid.
15. Julie Mankin, "Campbell County's Historic Ranches: The Zigler-Camblin Ranch," *Gillette News Record*, http:gillettenewsrecrod.com/detail.html?sub_id=204&print=1 (accessed 9 September 2013).
16. Carl Sifakis, "The Banditti of the Plains," *Encyclopedia of American Crime*, 2nd ed. (New York: Facts on File, 2001); American History Online, Facts on File, http//www.fofweb.com/activelink2.asp?ItemID=WE52&iPin=EAC0090&SingleRecord=True (accessed 9 September 2013).
17. "Skyrocket Going Some," Miles City, Foster Photo Company, NO-H 27, Postcard, author's collection.
18. "Casey Defends Himself," quoted from W.B. Clarke, *Dusting Off the Old Ones* (1961), Milescity.com.org.net.info (accessed 14 August 2013).
19. Tom Groneberg, *The Secret Life of Cowboys* (Norman: University of Oklahoma Press, 2004), 148.

20. Edward M. Kennedy, *True Compass: A Memoir* (New York: Hachette, 2009), 130–131.
21. J.H. Dion, letter to Ralph Miracle, 27 November 1978, Montana Historical Society Archives, Helena.
22. "The 30s: Era of the CBC," http://www.chazmatic.com/badgett/pages/cvc.pdf (accessed 9 October 2013).

Chapter Twelve

1. Lattimore, letter to Ralph Miracle.
2. Barton, interview, 1955.
3. Adam Warwick, "The Mongols, People of the Wilderness," *National Geographic* 39 no. 5 (May 1921), 516.
4. Wallace Stegner, *Angle of Repose* (New York: Penguin, 1971), 288.
5. Tuchman, 74.
6. Franck, 261.
7. Tuchman, 72–74.
8. Ibid., 80.
9. Ibid., 79.
10. Ibid., 80.
11. Ibid., 82–83.
12. Ibid., 81.
13. Edna Lee Booker, *News Is My Job: A Correspondent in War-Torn China* (New York: Macmillan, 1940), 63.
14. Tuchman, 69.
15. Franck, 263.
16. Ch'i, 168.
17. Gillin, 178.
18. Zhang Yuxin, *Quing zhengfu yu lamajiao* (Beijing: Xizang Renmin, 1988), 112.
19. Ch'i, 183.
20. Booker, 76. Booker gives a nearly blow-by-blow account of the battle between Wu's forces and those of Chang Tso-lin. Booker herself was shelled during the artillery duel.
21. Lattimore, *Mongol Journeys*, 17.
22. Barton, interview, 1955.

Chapter Thirteen

1. "Great Bargains for American Heiresses in Titled Husbands: Poor Princes and Seedy Noblemen and No End of Royal Princesses Who Have Been Beggared by War Upheavals and Revolution," *Sandusky Register*, June 19, 1921, p. 27.
2. Helen Worden, *Society Circus* (New York: Friede, 1936).
3. Milt Machlin, *The Hell of Ernest Hemingway* (New York: Paperback Library, 1962), 104.

Chapter Fourteen

1. Stanley Walker, *The Night Club Era* (New York: Frederick A. Stokes, 1933), 96.
2. Sizer, 124.
3. David T. Courtwright, *The Violent Land, Single Men and Social Disorder from the Frontier to the Inner City* (Cambridge: Harvard University Press, 1997), 157–158.
4. Junius B. Wood, "The Far Eastern Republic," *National Geographic* 41, no. 6 (June 1922), 566.
5. Vasilly Usharoff, interview, "Russian Emigré Recollections: Life in Russia and California, Oral History Transcript, 1979–1983," University of California Berkeley, Oral History Office, Bancroft Library, California-Russia Emigré Series.
6. George Vitt, "My Narrative–91," e-mail to author, 26 September 2012.
7. Salvador Parra, as told to C.A. (Andy) Hinton, one of the NAN Ranch owners, letter to author, 30 July 1997.
8. "L.P. Woman Charged with Separation," *El Paso Herald-Post* 51, no. 193 (13 August 1931), 1.
9. "Historic New Mexico Ranch Involved in New Legal Dispute," *Las Cruces Sun-News* 66, no. 125 (20 December 1946), 1.
10. The Stan Laurel Correspondence Archive Project, http://lettersfromstan.com/stan_1962-10.html (accessed 8 October 2013).
11. Walker, 320.
12. Gail Hughbanks Woerner, *A Belly Full of Bedsprings: The History of Bronc Riding* (Austin: Eakin Press, 1998), 47.

Chapter Fifteen

1. Mary MacGregor-Villarreal, e-mail to author, 9 May 2013.
2. Brian W. Dippie, letter to author, 30 July 1996.
3. Ibid.
4. Harold G. Davidson, letter to author, 17 May 1995.
5. Vivian Paladin, letter to Ralph Miracle, 26 August 1976, Fallis L. Oliver private collection. Also the same information was related to the author in a phone interview with V. Paladin, Helena, Montana.
6. Davidson, letter.
7. Oliver, letter.
8. Richard Upton, telephone interview with author, 16 August 1996.
9. Fred Barton, letter to Michael Kennedy, director, Montana Historical Society, 24 January 1961, Director's File, MHS.
10. Michael Kennedy, letter to Fred Barton, 30 January 1961, Director's File, MHS.
11. Barton, letter to Kennedy, 19 August 1961, Director's File, MHS.
12. Frank Dobie, typed manuscript summary of his visit with Fred Barton, 22 March 1956, John Taliaferro notes from J. Frank Dobie Manuscript Collection, Harry Ransom Humanities Research Center, University of Texas at Austin.
13. Dobie, summary of visit with Barton, 22 March 1956.
14. Fred Barton, letter to Michael Kennedy, 12 April 1962, Director's File, MHS.
15. Barton, letter to Kennedy, 29 August 1961.
16. Dobie, letter to Barton, 9 July 1961, HRHRC, University of Texas at Austin.
17. Dobie, summary of visit with Barton, 22 March 1956.
18. Fred Barton, letter to J. Frank Dobie, 5 July

1963, John Taliaferro notes from J. Frank Dobie Manuscript Collection, Harry Ransom Humanities Research Center, University of Texas at Austin.
  19. Fred Barton, "Fred Barton," position paper, Fallis L. Oliver collection.
  20. K. Ross Toole, letter to Fred Barton, 29 July 1958, Fallis L. Oliver collection.
  21. Ginger K. Renner, letter to author, 23 August 1995.
  22. Kennedy, letter to Barton, 5 June 1963, Director's File, MHS.
  23. Barton, letter to Kennedy, 4 December 1958, Magazine File, MHS.
  24. Larry Len Peterson, *Charles M. Russell: Photographing the Legend* (Norman: University of Oklahoma Press, 2014), 186.
  25. Barton, letter to Michael Kennedy, 7 September 1960, Director's File, MHS.

Chapter Sixteen

  1. Quoted in Dee Brown, *The American West* (New York: Scribner's, 1994), 196.
  2. Owen Wister, *The Virginian* (New York: Kensington, 2014), 24.
  3. Charles M. Russell, quoted in Ralph Miracle, "Montana's First Movie," 20 January 1975, pp. 1–2, MHS.
  4. Barton, letter to J.K. Ralston, 21 May 1961, Director's File, MHS.
  5. Barton, letter to Ralston, 21 May 1961.
  6. Ralph Miracle, "Montana's First Movie," 20 January 1975, pp. 1–11, MHS.
  7. Ibid., 4.
  8. Davidson, letter to author.
  9. Barton, letter to Kennedy, 18 January 1959, Magazine File, MHS.
  10. Vivian A. Paladin, letter to Fred Barton, 23 March 1959, p. 2, Magazine File, MHS.
  11. Paladin, letter to Barton, 9 December 1958, Magazine File, MHS.
  12. Fred Barton, "Ed Borein, 1873–1945," Harold G. Davidson collection.
  13. Barton, letter to Kennedy, 26 August 1958, Magazine File, MHS.
  14. Ben Yagoda, *Will Rogers: A Biography* (New York: Knopf, 1993), 174.
  15. Ibid., 175.
  16. Ketchum, 310.
  17. Ibid., 83.
  18. Yagoda, 289.
  19. "Will Rogers to Report What-a-Manchurian War," *Eugene Register-Guard* 81, no. 143 (29 November 1931), 1.
  20. Richard D. White, *Will Rogers: A Political Life* (Lubbock: Texas Technical University Press, 2011).
  21. Ronald L. Davis, *William S. Hart: Projecting the American West* (Norman: University of Oklahoma Press, 2003), 19.
  22. Mark Bedor, "A Western Life Well Lived: Harry Carey, Jr.," *Living Cowboy Ethics* 4, no. 2 (Summer 2008), 35.
  23. James H. Nottage, *Saddlemaker to the Stars: The Leather and Silver Art of Edward H. Bohlin* (Seattle: University of Washington Press, 1996), 21.
  24. Nottage, 27.
  25. Home Movie Day News, "HDM Report, Los Angeles," reported by Trisha Lendo and Sean Savage, 19 November 2013, http://www.homemovieday.com/news (accessed 6 April 2014).
  26. Davis, 66.
  27. Nottage, 25.

Chapter Seventeen

  1. Nora Waln, *The House of Exile* (Boston: Little, Brown, 1933), 130.
  2. Barton, "Fred Barton."
  3. Ibid., 1.
  4. Ibid., "Barton," 1.
  5. Ibid., "Barton," 2.
  6. Barton, letter to Michael Kennedy, 7 September 1960, Director's File, MHS.
  7. Ibid., 18 January 1959; also, 27 December 1961.
  8. Barton, "Barton," 2–3.
  9. Ibid., 3.
  10. Ibid., 3.
  11. Fred Barton, "Extremely Important Observation, Analysis and Conclusions Regarding Marriage," Fallis L. Oliver collection.
  12. Ibid., 1.
  13. Ibid.
  14. Ibid.
  15. Ibid., 2.
  16. Barton, *Charles M. Russell*, 14–15.
  17. Marsh, 77.
  18. John Billman, *When We Were Wolves* (New York: Random House, 1999), 105.

Epilogue

  1. Waln, 53.
  2. John R. Haddad, "The Savage East in the Wild West, Buffalo Bill's Boxing Uprising, 1900–1901," in *The Many Worlds of Circus*, ed. Robert Sugarman (Newcastle: Cambridge Scholars, 2007), 11.
  3. Long Riders Guild Academic Foundation, "The Mystery of the China Morgans," http//www.Irgaf.org/articles/morgans2.htm (accessed on 2 November 2011).
  4. Julius Victor Pinnell, "Morgan Horses Shipped to China," *Morgan Horse* 7, no. 2 (February 1948), 40–42.
  5. Frank Houle, Veterinary Services, USDA, APHIS, Helena, Montana, phone interview, 13 August 1997.
  6. Doug Stanton, *Horse Soldiers* (New York: Scribner, 2009), 228.
  7. Stanton, 149–150.
  8. Nez Perce Tribe, "Nez Perce Tribe Young Horseman Program," http://www.nezperce.org/Young%20HorselNPTYoungHorseman.htm (accessed 11 August 2000).
  9. Stephen E. Ambrose, *Undaunted Courage* (New York: Simon & Schuster, 1996), 298.
  10. Oregon Trail Coordinating Council, "Deadman

Pass: The Long Road Down," OTCC Interpretive Kiosk, http://members.aol.comlotkiosks/otcc/deadmanpass.html (accessed 12 August 2000).

11. "Equine Creation: Nez Perce Build on Tradition, Develop New Horse Breed," *Columbian* 7 (August 2000), C2.

12. Jolaine Cowherd, e-mail to author, 28 April 2011.

13. Trisha Lendo and Sean Savage, "HMD Report, Los Angeles," *Home Movie Day News*, http://www.homemovieday.com/news/2013/10/26/hmd_report_los_angeles_3.html (accessed 18 April 2014).

14. Otto Bremers, Jr., "Accent of News," *Benson High News* 7, no. 3 (4 October 1935), 1; also in *Santa Cruz Sentinel* 92, no. 139 (12 December 1935), 8.

Bibliography

Ambrose, Stephen E. *Undaunted Courage.* New York: Simon & Schuster, 1996.

"And He Went Up on High; Chinaman Departs for Paradise in Style," *Oregonian,* 28 September 1919, p. 14.

Andrews, Roy Chapman. *Across Mongolian Plains.* New York: Blue Ribbon, 1921.

─────. *Heart of Asia.* New York: Duell, Sloan, and Pearce, 1951.

─────. *On the Trail of Ancient Man.* Garden City, NY: Doubleday, 1926.

Arnold, Roger D. "Annual Letter, Roger D. Arnold, Taiyuanfu, Shansi, China, 1 September 1919." University of Minnesota Libraries. http://umedia.lib.umn.edu//node/555798 (accessed 22 November 2013).

Barton, Fred. *Charles M. Russell: An Old-time Cowman Discusses the Life of Charles M. Russell.* Privately published.

─────. "Ed Borein, 1873–1945." Private collection of Harold G. Davidson.

─────. "Extremely Important Observation, Analysis and Conclusions Regarding Marriage." Personal papers of Fallis Oliver.

─────. "Fred Barton." Position paper from Fallis Oliver private collection.

─────. Interview, 30 August 1955, by J. Ross Toole, Michael Kennedy, and Sam Sulberg. Montana Historical Society (MHS), Helena.

─────. Letter to J. Frank Dobie, 5 July 1963. John Taliaferro notes from J. Frank Dobie Manuscript Collection, Harry Ransom Humanities Research Center, University of Texas at Austin.

─────. Letter to J.K. Ralston, 21 May 1961. Director's File, Montana Historical Society, Helena.

─────. Letter to Kennedy, 4 December 1958. Magazine File, MHS.

─────. Letter to Kennedy, 18 January 1959. Magazine File, MHS.

─────. Letter to Kennedy, 19 August 1961. Director's File, MHS.

─────. Letter to Kennedy, 7 September 1960. Director's File, MHS.

─────. Letter to Kennedy, 12 April 1962. Director's File, MHS.

─────. Letter to Kennedy, 24 January 1961. Director's File, MHS.

─────. Letter to Kennedy, 29 August 1961. Director's File, MHS.

─────. Letter to Kennedy, 27 December 1961. Director's File, MHS.

─────. Letter to Michael Kennedy, 26 August 1958. Magazine File, MHS.

─────. "Old Miles Town, Cow Capital of the West." Letters section. *Montana: The Magazine of Western History* 5, no. 2 (1956), 65.

"Barton Party Starts for Chinese Ranges." *Miles City Daily Star,* 26 May 1920, p. 5.

Bedor, Mark. "A Western Life Well Lived: Harry Carey, Jr." *Living Cowboy Ethics* 4, no. 2 (Summer 2008), 34–37.

Billman, John. *When We Were Wolves.* New York: Random House, 1999.

Bisher, Jamie. *White Terror: Cossack Warlords of the Trans-Siberian.* New York: Routledge, 2005.

Booker, Edna Lee. *News Is My Job: A Correspondent in War-Torn China.* New York: Macmillan, 1940.

Bramsen, Christopher Bo. *Open Doors: Wilhelm Meyer and the Establishment of General Electric in China.* Richmond, Surrey: Curzon, 2001.

Bremers, Otto, Jr. "Accent of News." *Benson High News* 7, no. 3 (4 October 1935), 1.

Brown, Dee. *The American West.* New York: Scribner's, 1994.

Bulstrode, Beatrix. *A Tour of Mongolia.* London: Methuen, 1920.

Bumaa, Nasan Dashdendeviin. "The Twentieth Century: From Domination to Democracy." In *Modern Mongolia: Reclaiming Genghis Khan.* Edited by Paula L.W. Sabloff. Philadelphia: University of Pennsylvania, 2001.

Cabot, Mabel H. *Vanished Kingdoms: A Woman Explorer in Tibet, China and Mongolia, 1921–1925.* New York: Aperture, 2003.

Bibliography

Camblin, Mr. and Mrs. Earl "Early." Gillette, Wyoming. Phone interview, 29 August 1999.

"Casey Defends Himself." Quoted from W.B. Clarke, *Dusting Off the Old Ones* (1961). Milescity.com.org.net.info (accessed 14 August 2013).

Ch'i, Hsi-sheng. *Warlord Politics in China, 1916–1928*. CA: Stanford University Press, 1976.

Clark, Lloyd. *The Battle of the Tanks: Kursk, 1943*. New York: Atlantic Monthly Press, 2011.

Cochran, Sherman. *Big Business in China: Sino-Foreign Rivalry in the Cigarette Industry, 1890–1930*. Cambridge: Harvard University Press, 1980.

Coffman, Edward M. "The American 15th Infantry Regiment in China, 1912–1938: A Vignette in Social History." *Journal of Military History* 58 (January 1994).

_____. Letter to author, 24 August 1996.

Cornebise, Alfred Emile. *The United States 15th Infantry Regiment in China, 1912–1938*. Jefferson, NC: McFarland, 2004.

Courtwright, David T. *The Violent Land: Single Men and Social Disorder from the Frontier to the Inner City*. Cambridge: Harvard University Press, 1997.

Cowherd, Jolaine. E-mail to author, 28 April 2011.

Davidson, Harold G. Letter to author, 17 May 1995.

Davis, Ronald L. *William S. Hart: Projecting the American West*. Norman: University of Oklahoma Press, 2003.

Dion, J.H. Letter to Ralph Miracle, 27 November 1978. Montana Historical Society Archives, Helena.

Dippie, Brian W. Letter to author, 30 July 1996.

Dobie, J. Frank. Typed manuscript summary of his visit with Fred Barton, 22 March 1956. John Taliaferro notes from J. Frank Dobie Manuscript Collection, Harry Ransom Humanities Research Center, University of Texas at Austin.

_____. Letter to Barton, 9 July 1961.

Dorfman, John. "A Painter's Pageant." *Art and Antiques* 36, no. 10 (October 2013), 42ff.

Driggs, Howard R. *Westward America*. New York: Somerset Books, 1942.

"Equine Creation: Nez Perce Build on Tradition, Develop New Horse Breed." *Columbian* 7 (August 2000), C2.

Fairbank, John K. *The Missionary Enterprise in China and America*. Cambridge: Harvard University Press, 1981.

Fenster, Julie M. *Race of the Century: The Heroic True Story of the 1908 New York to Paris Auto Race*. New York: Crown, 2005.

"15th Infantryman." Quoted in Edward M. Coffman, "The American 15th Infantry Regiment in China, 1912–1938: A Vignette in Social History." *Journal of Military History* 58 (January 1994): 69.

Finney, Charles G. *The Old China Hands*. Westport: Greenwood, 1973.

Franck, Harry A. *Wandering in Northern China*. New York: Century, 1923.

French, Paul. *Through the Looking Glass: China's Foreign Journalists from Opium Wars to Mao*. Hong Kong: Hong Kong University Press, 2009.

Frink, Maurice, with Casey Barthelmess. *Photographer on an Army Mule*. Norman: University of Oklahoma Press, 1989.

Garrett, Shirley Stone. "Why They Stayed: American Church Politics and Chinese Nationalism in the Twenties." In *The Missionary Enterprise in China and America*. Edited by John K. Fairbank. Cambridge: Harvard University Press, 1981.

Gaspard, Leon Shulman. Letter to Rockford Art Guild, 18 March 1921. Rockford Art Museum files.

Georgian, Richard Alexis. *Cossacks, Indians, and Buffalo Bill: The Adventures of Georgian Riders in America*. Naples, FL: Barringer, 2011.

Gillin, Donald G. *Warlord Yen Hsi-shan in Shansi Province, 1911–1949*. Princeton, NJ: Princeton University Press, 1967.

Gilmore, James. *Among the Mongols*. London: Religious Tract Society, 1888. Reprint facsimile, Elibron Classics, 2005.

Graham, Mark. "The Many Faces of Hotel Moderne in Harbin." *East Asian History*, no. 37 (December 2011). http://www.eastasianhistory.org/37/gamsa (accessed 2 May 2014).

"Great Bargains for American Heiresses in Titled Husbands: Poor Princes and Seedy Noblemen and No End of Royal Princesses Who Have Been Beggared by War Upheavals and Revolution." *Sandusky Register*, 19 June 1921, p. 27.

Groneberg, Tom. *The Secret Life of Cowboys*. Norman: University of Oklahoma Press, 2004.

Haddad, John R. "The Savage East in the Wild West: Buffalo Bill's Boxing Uprising, 1900-1901." In *The Many Worlds of Circus*. Edited by Robert Sugarman. Newcastle: Cambridge Scholars, 2007.

Harris, Charles H. III, and Louis R. Sadler. *The Archaeologist Was a Spy: Sylvanus G. Morley and the Office of Naval Intelligence*. Albuquerque: University of New Mexico Press, 2003.

Harrison, Henrietta. "Narcotics, Nationalism and Class in China." *East Asian History*, no. 32/33 (December 2006/2007): 151–176.

Haslund, Henning. *In Secret Mongolia*. Translated by Elizabeth Sprigge and Claude Napier. Kempton, IL: Adventures Unlimited, 1995.

Hershatter, Gail. "The Hierarchy of Shanghai Prostitution, 1870–1949." *Modern China* 14, no. 4, pp. 463–98.

Hinton, C.A. (Andy). Letter to author, 30 July 1997.

"Historic New Mexico Ranch Involved in New Legal Dispute." *Las Cruces Sun-News* 66, no. 125 (20 December 1946), p. 1.

"Hittin' for Unfenced Land of the Orient." *Miles City Daily Star*, 24 May 1920, p. 8.

Home Movie Day News. "HDM Report: Los Angeles." Reported by Trisha Lendo and Sean Savage, 19 November 2013. http://www.homemovieday.com/news (accessed 6 April 2014).

Houle, Frank. Veterinary Services, USDA, APHIS, Helena, Montana. Telephone interview, 13 August 1997.

Hoyt, Frederick. "Junk Mail Is Not New: China Missionaries Used Direct Mailing." *American Philatelist* 110, no. 11 (November 1996): 1022–1029.

Hutchison, James Lafayette. *China Hand*. New York: Grosset and Dunlap, 1936.

Judson, Karen. *Chemical and Biological Warfare*. Tarrytown: Benchmark Books, 2004.

Keegan, John. *The First World War*. New York: Knopf, 1999.

Kennedy, Edward M. *True Compass: A Memoir*. New York: Hachette, 2009.

Kennedy, Michael. Letter to Fred Barton, 30 January 1961. Director's File, MHS.

———. Letter to Barton, 5 June 1963. Director's File, MHS.

Ketchum, Richard M. *Will Rogers: His Life and Times*. New York: American Heritage, 1973.

Larson, Frans August. *Larson: Duke of Mongolia*. New York: Little, Brown, 1930.

Lattimore, Owen. Letter to Ralph Miracle, 18 February 1976.

———. *Mongol Journeys*. New York: Doubleday, 1941.

Lendo, Trisha, and Sean Savage. "HMD Report: Los Angeles." *Home Movie Day News*. http://www.homemovieday.com/news/2013/10/26/hmd_report_los_angeles_3.html (accessed 18 April 2014).

Levy, Daniel S. *Two Gun Cohen: A Biography*. New York: St. Martin's, 1997.

"The Local News." *Miles City Independent* 18, no. 24 (16 May 1919), p. 8.

"The Local News." *Miles City Independent* 18, no. 28 (11 July 1919), p. 8.

The Long Riders Guild Academic Foundation. "The Mystery of the China Morgans." http://www.lrgaf.org/articles/morgans2.htm (accessed on 2 November 2011).

"L.P. Woman Charged with Separation." *El Paso Herald-Post* 51, no. 193 (13 August 1931), 1.

MacGregor-Villarreal, Mary. E-mail to author, 9 May 2013.

Machlin, Milt. *The Hell of Ernest Hemingway*. New York: Paperback Library, 1962.

Mankin, Julie. "Campbell County's Historic Ranches: The Zigler-Camblin Ranch." *Gillette News Record*. http:gillettenewsrecrod.com/detail.html?sub_id=204&print=1 (accessed 9 September 2013).

Mannerheim, C.G. *Across Asia from West to East in 1906–1908*. Vol. 1. Oosterhout: Anthropological Publications, 1969.

"Mark Arrives from Philippines." *Miles City Independent* 18, no. 32 (15 August 1919), 6.

Marsh, James Reid. *The Charm of the Middle Kingdom*. Boston: Little, Brown, 1922.

Miles City Independent 18, no. 28 (11 July 1919), 3.

Miles City Independent 11, no. 1 (5 January 1912).

Miles City Independent 10, no. 25 (23 June 1911).

Miller, Michael B. *Shanghai on the Métro: Spies, Intrigue, and the French Between the Wars*. Berkeley: University of California Press, 1995.

"MONTANA COWBOYS HEAD FOR CHINA; Cattle Raising in the Land of the Celestials Will Take Wild West Flavor." *Eu Clair Leader*, 10 June 1920.

Montefiore, Simon Sebag. *Young Stalin*. New York: Vantage, 2008.

Miracle, Ralph. "Asian Adventures of a Cowboy from Montana." *Montana: The Magazine of Western History* (Spring 1977), 44–53.

———. Letter to James H. Dion, 15 December 1974. MHS.

National Earthquake Information Center. USGS. "Geologic Hazards: Most Destructive Known Earthquakes on Record in the World." http://wwwneic.cr.usgs.gov/neis/eqlists/eqsmosde.html (accessed 2 September 1999).

Nez Perce Tribe. "Nez Perce Young Horseman Program." http://www.nezperce.org/Young%20HorsselNPTYoungHorseman.htm (accessed 11 August 2000).

Noble, Dennis L. Letter to author, 14 September 1996.

Nordbye, Masha. "The Great Siberian Tea Road." *Russian Life* 56, no. 3 (May/June 2013), 28–37.

Nottage, James H. *Saddlemaker to the Stars: The Leather and Silver Art of Edward H. Bohlin*. Seattle: University of Washington Press, 1996.

"Odd Bits of News." *Laredo Weekly Times*, 12 December 1915.

Oliver, Fallis L. Letter to author, 9 October 1995.

Oregon Trail Coordinating Council. "Deadman Pass: The Long Road Down." OTCC Interpretive Kiosk. http://members.aol.com/otkiosks/otcc/deadmanpass.html (accessed 12 August 2000).

Ossendowski, Ferdinand. *Man and Mystery in Asia.* New York: Dutton, 1924.
Paladin, Vivian A. Letter to Fred Barton, 9 December 1958. Magazine File, MHS.
———. Letter to Ralph Miracle, 26 August 1976. Fallis L. Oliver private collection.
———. Letter to Fred Barton, 23 March 1959. Magazine File, MHS.
Palmer, James. *The Bloody White Baron: The Extraordinary Story of the Russian Nobleman Who Became the Last Khan of Mongolia.* New York: Basic Books, 2009.
"Path to Pearl Harbor." *Columbian,* 7 December 2013, pp. C1, C4.
Perdue, Peter C. *China Marches West: The Qing Conquest of Central Asia.* Cambridge: Harvard University Press, 2005.
Peterson, Larry Len. *Charles M. Russell: Photographing the Legend.* Norman: University of Oklahoma Press, 2014.
Pinnell, Julius Victor. "Morgan Horses Shipped to China." *Morgan Horse Magazine* 7, no. 2 (February 1948), 40–42.
Polo, Marco. *The Travels.* Quoted in "Marco Polo and His Travels." Silkroad Foundation. http://www.silk-road.com/art/marcopolo.shtml (accessed 2 May 2014).
"Prices Are High in Vladivostock." *Miles City Independent* 18, no. 35 (29 August 1919), 5.
Pugach, Noel H. *Paul S. Reinsch: Open Door Diplomat in Action.* Millwood, NY: Kraus-Thomson, 1979.
Raban, Jonathan. *Bad Land: An American Romance.* New York: Pantheon, 1996.
Reist, Katherine K. "State Department Soldiers: Warlords, Nationalists, and Intervention." In *American Diplomacy: Two Centuries of American Campaigning.* Leavenworth: Combat Studies Institute, 2003.
Remington, Frederic. *Pony Tracks.* New York: Harper, 1895.
Renner, Ginger K. Letter to author, 23 August 1995.
Robbins, Marty. "The Cowboy in the Continental Suit." *In the Wild West,* Part 5. CBS, LSP-15751/BFX-15213.
Roberts, James Hudson. *A Flight for Life.* Boston: Pilgrim, 1903.
Russell, Charles M. Quoted in Ralph Miracle. "Montana's First Movie." 20 January 1975, pp. 1–11, MHS.
———. *Trails Plowed Under.* New York: Doubleday, 1927.
Saul, Norman E. *The Life and Times of Charles R. Crane, 1858–1939: American Businessman, Philanthropist, and a Founder of Russian Studies in America.* New York: Lexington Books, 2013.
Schwenke, Tiffany. "Agricultural Impressions." https://www.facebook.com/photo/php?fbid=101516933509677873&set=o.3547332045565398 type=18relevant_count=1 (accessed 9 August 2013).
Sherwood, Jack. *Fond Memories of a Young Man in Old China.* Bloomington: Author House, 2009.
Sifakis, Carl. "The Banditti of the Plains." *Encyclopedia of American Crime.* 2nd ed. New York: Facts on File, 2001. American History Online. Facts on File. http//www.fofweb.com/activelink2.asp?ItemID=WE52&iPin=EAC0090&SingleRecord=True (accessed 9 September 2013).
Siringo, Charles A. *Riata and Spurs.* New York: Houghton Mifflin, 1931.
Sizer, Mona D. *Outrageous Texans.* New York: Taylor, 2008.
Skidelsky, Robert. "A Chinese Homecoming." *Igud Yotzei Sin Bulletin* 54, no. 394 (November–December 2007), 16–20.
"Skyrocket Going Some." Foster Photo Company, Miles City, No-H-27. Postcard, author's personal collection.
The Stan Laurel Correspondence Archive Project. http://lettersfromstan.com/stan1962-10.html (accessed 8 October 2013).
Stanton, Doug. *Horse Soldiers.* New York: Scribner, 2009.
Stegner, Wallace. *Angle of Repose.* New York: Penguin, 1971.
Summers, William C. *The Great Manchurian Plague of 1910–1911: The Geopolitics of an Epidemic Disease.* New Haven: Yale University Press, 2012.
Taliaferro, John. *Charles M. Russell: The Life and Legend of America's Cowboy Artist.* New York: Little, Brown, 1996.
Taveirne, Patrick. *Han-Mongol Encounters and Missionary Endeavors: A History of Scheut in Ordos (Hetao), 1874–1911.* Leuven Chinese Studies 15. Leuven, Belgium: Leuven University Press, 2004.
"The 30s: Era of the CBC." http://www.chazmatic.com/badgett/pages/cvc.pdf (accessed 10 September 2013).
Toole, K. Ross. Letter to Fred Barton, 29 July 1958. Fallis L. Oliver collection.
Tuchman, Barbara W. *Stillwell and the American Experience in China, 1911–45.* New York: Macmillan, 1971.
Upton, Richard. Telephone interview, 16 August 1996.
Usharoff, Vasilly. Interview. "Russian Emigré Recollections: Life in Russia and California, Oral History Transcript, 1979–1983." University of California Berkeley, Oral History Office, Bancroft Library, California-Russia Émigré Series.

Vitt, George. "My Narrative–91." E-mail to author, 26 September 2012.
Walker, Stanley. *The Night Club Era.* New York: Frederick A. Stokes, 1933.
Wallis, Michael. *The Real Wild West.* New York: St. Martin's, 1999.
Waln, Nora. *The House of Exile.* Boston: Little, Brown, 1933.
Warren, Allen. "White Paper by Allen Warren." Habitat for Horses. http://www.habitatforhorses.org/white-paper-by-allen-warren/ (accessed 9/10/13, posted 8 August 2012).
Warwick, Adam. "The People of the Wilderness." *National Geographic* 39, no. 5 (May 1921), 507–551.
Waters, Frank. *Leon Gaspard.* Flagstaff: Northland, 1964.
Westwood, P.A. "Soldier of Fortune: Amazing Life of General Frank Sutton." *Adelaide Advertiser*, 4 March 1933, p. 9.
White, Richard D. *Will Rogers: A Political Life.* Lubbock: Texas Technical University Press, 2011.
"Will Rogers to Report What-a-Manchurian War." *Eugene Register-Guard* 81, no. 143 (29 November 1931), 1.
Wister, Owen. *The Virginian.* New York: Kensington, 2014.
Woerner, Gail Hughbanks. *A Belly Full of Bedsprings: The History of Bronc Riding.* Austin: Eakin, 1998.
Wolff, David. *To the Harbin Station: The Liberal Alternative in Russian Manchuria, 1890–1914.* Stanford, CA: Stanford University Press, 1999.
Wong-Quincey, J. *Chinese Hunter.* New York: John Day, 1939.
Wood, Junius B. "The Far Eastern Republic." *National Geographic* 41, no. 6 (June 1922).
Worden, Helen. *Society Circus.* New York: Friede, 1936.
Yagoda, Ben. *Will Rogers: A Biography.* New York: Knopf, 1993.
Yuxin, Zhang. *Quing zhengfu yu lamajiao.* Beijing: Xizang renmin Press, 1988.

Index

Numbers in ***bold italics*** refer to pages with photographs.

Academy of Motion Pictures Arts and Sciences 205
Ace-High Western Magazine 175
Across the Desert of Gobi 54
Adee, Alvey A 84
Affairs Valentino: The True Story of Rudolph Valentino 159
Akhal-Teke 202–204
Allen, Rex 44
Alzada, MT 128
American Art News 81
American Can 145
American Expeditionary Force Siberia (AEF) 87
"The American 15th Infantry Regiment in China, 1912–1938: A Vignette in Social History" 73, 208, 209
American International Corporation 78
American Legation (cabin) 83
American Museum of Natural History 78, 82
Among the Mongols 117, 209, 214
Amur River 2, 89, 105
Anaconda, MT 204
Anaconda Copper Company 204
Anadyr 37
Anastasia 147
Anastasia (Leed's mother) 146–147
Anastasia of Greece, Princess 145–147
Anastasia of Russia, Grand Duchess 147
Andersen, Meyer & Co. 55
Anderson, A.W.P. 28
Anderson, Roy S. 78
Andrews, Roy Chapman 5, 9, 53, 60, 78, 81, 83, 85, 103, 208, 209, 213
Antarctic 62
Anti-Narcotic League 67
Antler Ranch 187
APHIS 201
Aquitania 146
Archdale 27

Argali sheep ***85***
Argentina 178
Arizona 49, 72, 111, 175, 184, 191, 203
Arizona Highways 191
Arizona Rangers 111
Army of the Commonwealth in Christ 20
Arnold, Roger D. 66–67, 208, 213
art deco 12, 56, 58
Artificial Flower Trading Company 49–51
Ashkabad 203
Asiatic Fleet (U.S.) 80
Astaire, Adele 204
Astaire, Fred 204
Astor House 49, 56
Atchison Topeka & Santa Fe Railroad 20
Athens 145
Atlas, cigarette 47
Australia 38, 67, 78, 125, 160, 198

Bad Land 120, 209, 216
Bair, Charles M. 182–183
Baker, Newton D. 84
Baltic 157
Bandit Babies 142
Barthelmess, Casey 19, 48, 129, ***136***, 214
Barthelmess, Christian 14, 129
Barthelmess, Robert 48
Barton, Ashia 90–91, 151–154, 158, 161–163, 170, 194
Barton, Clara 58
Barton, Lester 19–21, 57, 144–147
Barton, Mabel Blanche 56, 58, 150–151, 194
Barton, Mamie Parker 154–162, 194
Barton, Martha Olive (Kottmeier) ***13***, 21, 146
Barton Land and Cattle Corporation 157
"Barton Party Starts for Chinese Ranges" 121–122, 209, 213
Bashkirs 101

Bass, W.R. 29
Battenburg *see* Mountbatten
Battle of Kursk 4, 63–64, 207, 214
Battle of the Wilderness 21
Baxter, Bruce 78
Bayer, A.J. 171
Bean, Judge Roy 96
Beaseley, Sen. W.W. 30
Beery, Wallace 58
Bell, Ray 177
Belle of China, cigarette 47
Bengal, horse 59
Ben Hur 188
Bergman, Ingrid 147
Bessessyey, Countess Margit 204
Best & Belcher Mine 58
Biederman, Henry 168
Big Horn County 12
Big Red Nose 18
The Big Story (NBC) 158
Big Tongue 41
Biglin, Frank 30
Billi B 145
Billings, MT 20, 69, 126, 174, 182, 205
Billman, Jon 196, 211, 213
Billy the Kid 181
Bimini 147
Bisher, Jamie 90, 209, 213
Bison Theater 175
Bistritsky, Elizabeth 91, 151–152
Bistritsky, Khassia (Kassia) 152
Bitterroot Stock Farm 204
Black Dahlia Murder 161
Black Hills 181
The Bloody White Baron 101, 28, 216
Blue Sky, Chinese general 41
Boer War 27, 184, 192
Bogdo Gegen (Living Buddha) 53, 54, 72, 82, 88, 94, 97–101, 104, 115, 141
Bohlin, Edward H. 42, 44, 49, 184, 186–189, 211, 215
Bohlin, Leana 187
Boise 124

219

Bolsheviks 45, 82, 87–88, 101, 146, 151
Bolt, Gen. Philip L. 74
Booker, Edna Lee 140–142, 210, 213
Boone, E.L. 169–171
Borein, Edward 2, 166–168, 175–178, 211, 213
Borglum, Gutzon 182
Bovey, Charles 48
Bowen, Arthur J. 84
Box Elder Creek 129
Boxer Rebellion 3, 4, 39, 53–54, 68, 71, 77, 83, 149, 150, 184, 198–199
Bozeman, MT 33
Brice, Fanny 159
Brice, Lew 159–161
British-American Tobacco Company (BAT) 42, 46–56, 65, 75, 78, 79, 134, 140
Britzman, Homer 166–168
Broadway Mansions 58
Brown Derby 165
Buchanon, Buck 172
Bulstrode, Beatrix 108, 209, 213
Buffalo, WY 127, 157
Buffalo Bill 44, 133, 186, 187, 198–199, 207, 211, 214
Buffalo Bill's Wild West Show *34*, 133, 159, 198–199, 211, 214
Burma Road 64
Buryats 101
Butch Cassidy and the Sundance Kid 9
Butte 20, 78, 121, 124, 128, 188, 204
Butterfield, Dr. Ferdinand 58
Butterfield, Lillian 58
Buttermilk, horse 182
Byurky, Countess Judith 203–204

Cabot, Mabel H. 113, 209, 213
Cadillac 51, *179*, 195
Cahuenga Avenue 178
Calgary Stampede 35, 172, 176
Camblin, Betty 124–126, 134, 138
Camblin, Earl "Cam" 127–128, 132
Camblin, Ida 124–126, 134, 138
Camblin, T.J. "Tut" 125
Camblin, Tut 121–122, 124–129, 138, 210, 214
Cambodia 95
Camp Bumpus 28
Camp David 69
Camp 4, Suiyuan Province 153
Campbell, C.W. 53, 92
Canada 6, 11, 64, 90, 189
Canutt, Yakima 130
Capone, Al 154, 180
Capone, Vincenzo 180
Carey, Dobe 183
Carey, Harry 183
Carrol, Matt 12
Cascade, MT 48
Casey, Lt. Edward "Ned" Wanton 8, 18

Casey's Scouts 8, 18, 41
Castro, Fidel 142
Cato, O.C. 191
The Cattleman 168
Chagall, Marc 82
Champion, horse 182
Chandler, Walter 156–157
Chang Hsueh-liang "Young Marshal" *43*, 64, 180
Chang Tso-lin 4, 6, 38–*43*, 48, 60–67, 70, 81, 85–86, 88, 90, 101, 140–141, 180, 210
Chang Tsung-chang "Dog Meat General" 38, 40–42, 45, 60
Chang, Maj. Gen. W.Y. 200
Changeling 162
Chao Kung, Abbot *see* Lincoln, Trebitsch
Chaple, Philip 132
Chaple Brothers Cannery 132–133
Charles M. Russell: An Oldtime Cowman Discusses the Life of Charles M. Russell 168, 176, 209, 213
Charles M. Russell: Photographing the Legend 172, 211, 216
Charles M. Russell: The Life and Legend of America's Cowboy Artist 26, 167, 207, 216
Cheka 6
Cherokee Kid 178
Cheyenne (Northern) 8, 11, 14, 18–19, 21, 33, 185
Cheyenne Frontier Days 35, 185
Cheyenne, WY 127, 177
Chez Florence 161
Ch'i, Hsi-sheng 141, 207, 210, 214
Chiang Kai-shek 7, 40, 53, 78
Chicago, Rock Island, and Pacific Railroad 145
Chien Chao-nan 52
Chihli 40, 79
Chihuahuan Desert 156
China-American Trading Company 72
China Hand 42, 49, 51, 207, 215
China Relief Commission 28
China Rocket Carrier Technology Research Institute 205
Chinese Eastern Railway 88–92, 101
Chita 92
Chocolat Inimitable 148
Chosin Reservoir 199
Christian, William B. 72
Christopher of Greece, Prince 145
Circle C 175
Cisco Kid 44
Citizen Kane 181
City on the Hill 9
Civil War 17, 21, 26
Clark, Badger, Jr. 197
Cleveland, Pres. Grover 150
Clifton, Harry 160
Cloud Ridge Caves *see* Yungang Grottoes

Clovers 203–204
Club Napoleon 161
Clubfoot, scout 41
C.M. Russell Museum 169, 182
Coburn, Robert 173
Coburn, Wallace 2, 166, 173–175, 177
Coburn, Walt 173
Cody, Buffalo Bill 44, 198–199
Cody, WY 44, 187–189
Coeur d'Alene Strike 26
Coffman, Edward M. 74, 208, 214
Coggshall Saddlery 42, 54, 137, 155, 186–187
Cohen, Morris Abraham "Two-Gun" 6–7, 180, 207, 215
Colby, Bainbridge 84
Collier's 154
Collins, Christine 162
Colt 7, 9, 135, 137, 171, 177
Columbia River Basin 184
Commander Islands 37
Communists 6, 53, 199, 203, 206
Comstock Lode 58
Conner, Brig. Gen. Willard Durward *43*
Constantinople 153, 163
Coolidge, Pres. Calvin 180
Cooper, Gary 9, 44
Cossacks 4, 18, 33–42, 57, 91, 101, 104, 207, 209, 213, 214
Cowboy Hall of Fame 51, 123, 171
"The Cowboy in the Continental Suit" 123, 195, 216
Cowherd, Jolaine 205, 212, 214
Coxey's Army 20, 26
Crazy Horse, Chief 11
Cristado, Charles C. 182
Crittenden, Lt. John J. III 18
Crow 183, 185, 187
Cuba 29, 110, 179, 186
"Curse of the Buffalo Skull," 172
Curtis, Edward 183
Custer, Gen. George Armstrong 11–12, 18, 187
Custer County 11–12, 121, 133, 177
Czarina 45, 57, 147
Czechoslovakian Legion 82

Dallas 155
Dallas, TX 156, 157
Daly, Harriet 204
Daly, Marcus 204
Danzan, Soliin 98–99
Darby, MT 204
Davidson, Harold G. 165, 175–176, 210, 211, 213, 214
Davis, Ronald L. 181, 211, 214
Daw, Marjorie 175
Dawson, Glen 171
Dawson, Major 27
Dawson County 132
Deadman Pass 202, 215
Dear, Elizabeth A. 169
Deaton, Bill 172
DeMille, Cecil B. 187

Index

Deming Headlight 154
Destination Gobi 154
Detroit 72, 150–152
de Wilde, R.P. **85**
De Yong, Joel 66
Diablo, horse 44, 182
Diamond Matches 145
Dickens, Charles 38
Dickerman, Don 148
Dickinson, ND 30
Diller, Phyllis 160
Dillon, Matt 9, 127
Dion, J.H. 132, 210, 214, 215
Dippie, Brian 165, 167, 210, 214
Disney, Walt 56, 131, 177, 182
Dix, USAT 71, 84, 86, 121, 125–126, 131, 145
Dobie, J. Frank 148, 161, 165–169, 172, **176**, 210, 211, 213, 214
Dodge, automobile 82
Dodge City 9, 37
Dolgopolov (Doll), Alexander Feodor 163
Doll, Ashia 163; *see also* Barton, Ashia
Dollar Princess 145
Donald, William H. 78
Doos Imperial Russian Dancers 33
Douglas, WY 126
Dragon, Gen. 41
Duncan, Maj. Charles M. 21
Durban 178

Eagle and Dragon: The United States Military in China, 1901–1937 73
Eagle Pass 76
Eagle's Nest 37
Earth and Its Inhabitants **74**
Eastwood, Clint 162
Eau Clair Leader 122
Edwards, William Leon 159
18th Amendment 118
Eighth Cavalry 18
Ekalaka, MT 11, 25, 29
El Paso 75, 154, 157–158, 163
El Paso Bar Association 158
El Paso Post 154, 210, 215
Empress Dowager 39
"End of the Trail" 15
Enterprise-D, U.S.S. 160
Erhlien see Iren Dabasu
Esterz Troupe of Russian Cossacks 33

Fairbanks, Douglas 133
Fanning the Embers 126
Faywood, NM 154–155
Feast of Belshazzar 200
Fen River **74**
Feng Yu-Hsiang "the Christian General" 75–76, 78, 139–142
Fenster, Julie M. 89, 209, 214
Fifteenth Infantry 1, 8, 71–77, 83, 86, **116**, 126, 139
Finney, Charles 75, 208, 214
Fisher, King 102

Flatwillow 173
Flying Tigers (A.V.G.) 67, 77, 153, 162
Flynn, Errol 161
Fogong Pagoda 117
Ford, John 155
Ford Model T 51, 53, 72, 144
Formosa 77
Fort Keogh 8, 11, 20, 27–28, 41, 48, 68, 75–76, 110, 129, 185, 201
Fort Parker 155
Fort Parker Massacre 155
Fort Worth 157, 172
Fouch, John 14
Franck, Harry A. 36, 40, 141, 207, 210, 214
Frankie 42
Fraser, David 59
Fraser, James Earle 15
Freehold Military School 21–22
Friedman, Richard S. "Kinky" 23, 148
Fritz, horse 182
Fu Hsi 190
Fubo, Gen. "Queller of the Deep" 60
Funicello, Annette 131
Furstnow's Saddlery 186–188
Fury, horse 182

Gable, Clark 177
Gall, Chief 11
Gamewell, Frank 84
Garry Owen 12
Gaspard, Leon Shulman 80–82, 208, 214, 217
Geddes, Sir Auckland 190, 192, 193
George V, King 58
George Borgfeldt & Co 5
The George Raft Story 160
George Washington University 192
Georgians 33, 90
Geppetto 182
Ghost Dancers 18–19, 68–69
Giant 155
Gilbert and Sullivan 150
Gilbey's Gin 147
Gillette, WY 125, 127–128, 205, 209, 214, 215
Gillin, Donald 66, 208, 210, 214
Gilmore, James 117, 209, 214
Glendive, MT 132
Glickman, John 133
Gobi Sun 75
Goes Ahead Pretty 187
Goldberg, Whoopi 160
The Golden Goddess 174
Golden Grain Pills 119
Golden Horn 37
Golden Horse of Asia 202–203
The Good Bad Man 133
Goya, Francisco 150
Graf, W.O. 158–162
Graf Zeppelin 146
Grand Canyon 182, 192
Grand Hotel 91

Grand Opera House 181
Grand Prix 204
Grayson College 156
Great Die-Off 15–17
Great Falls, MT 167, 169, 181
Great Game 2, 77, 83–84
Great Manchurian Plain 89
Great Manchurian Plague of 1910–1911 105, 209, 216
Great Northern Railway 174, 183
Great Northern Sugar Beet Company 187
Great Permian Basin 156
Great Wall 39, 52, 61, 65, 72, 80, 108, 111
Great West Film Company 174
Greater East Asia Co-prosperity Sphere 56
Green, Bill 162
Greene, Mr. and Mrs. H.M. 145
Griffith, D.W. 92
Grigsby's Volunteer Cowboy Cavalry Regiment 186
Griswold, Lillian Lowell 160
Groneberg, Tom 131, 209, 214
Gros Ventre 202
Guaymas 156
Guey Shing Nan 137
Guinan, Texas 160–161
Guinan, Tommy 160–161
Guinness World Record 15
Gunsmoke 127
Gus Hornbrook Vaudeville Company 187

Hadjiev, Khan Razak Bek 163
Hahn, S.S. "Sammy" 161–162
Hancock 156
Hara-Ossu 111
Harbin 48, 56, 62, 65, 88–92, 97, 151, 152, 185, 209, 214, 217
Harley Davidson X8E 99
Harrison, Pres. Benjamin 128
Harrison, Henrietta 119, 209, 214
Hart, Bret 121
Hart, Richard "Two Gun" *see* Capone, Vincenzo
Hart, William S. 2, 177, 180–184, 188, 211, 214
Harvard Military Academy 48
Harvey House 188
Haslund, Henning 110, 207, 209, 214
Hastings, Loren B. 202
Hataman, cigarette 47
Haymarket Riot 26
Haynes, O.C. 30
Haynes, OR 126
Hayward, Susan 161
Hearst, William Randolph 154
Heart of Asia 78, 208, 213
Heaven's Gate 127
Hedin, Sven 53, 82
Helena 15, 48, 122, 171–172, 177, 181, 201, 207, 210, 211, 213, 214, 215
Hemingway, Ernest 147, 210, 215
Henderson, R.E. 30

222 Index

Hilar (Hailar) 87–94, 96, 113, 152
Hinton, W.B. 162
Hipolito Villa Jewelry Case 159
Hirohito, Emperor of Japan 188
His Bad Horse 41
Hitchcock, C.W. 174
"Hittin' for Unfenced Land of the Orient" 121, 209, 215
Hogan, William 20
Holland, Clay 162
Hollywood 1–8, 13, 15, 27, 44, 58, 92, 104, 127, 130, 142, 151–163, 166, 173–189, 195, 205
Hollywood Boulevard 178
Homestead Mine Strike 26
Hong Kong 6, 51, 66, 151, 208, 214
Honolulu 51, 122
Hoover, Pres. Herbert 53, 180
Hopalong Cassidy 44
Hotel Dieu 157
Hotel Moderne 91–92, 209, 214
Hotel Oriant 91
The House of Exile 190, 198, 211, 117
Houston 157
Hsia Dynasty 190
Hsu Shu-tseng, Gen. "Little Hsu" 101–102
Hudford Company 144
Huffman, L.A. 14–15, 165, 175, 185
Huneycutt, John 156
Huneycutt, Mamye 156
Hungary 203
Hutchison, James Lafayette 49–55, 80, 207, 208, 215
Hutton, Betty 160

Idaho 124–126, 202
The Idaho Statesman 124, 126
Imperial Military Academy 66
The Incendiary Blonde 160
Indian Territories of Oklahoma 38, 181
Iowa 95, 128, 156
Iren Dabasu 107
Iridium satellites 205

James, Will 161, 166
Jin Dynasty 60
Johnson, Pres. Lyndon 142, 188
Johnson County War 127–128
Jordan, MT 29
Jorgensen, Marchen 159–161
Joseph, Chief (*Hin-meh-too-yah-lat-kelkt*) 11, 202
J.T. McElroy Discovery Well #1 156
Juarez, Mexico 30
Judith Basin 15, 23

Kaabah 99
Kahn, Jacques 12–13
Kalee Hotel 56
Kalgan 2, 7–8, 48–55, 72–73, 78, 81, 89, *91*, 92–93, 96, 101–116, 134, 207

Kamchatka 37
Kamerstein 151
Kansas 156, 181
Kara Kum 203
Keeley 29
Kelley 7–8
Kelly, Judith *see* Byurky, Countess
Ken-L-Rations 133
Kennedy, Edward "Ted" 131, 210, 215
Kennedy, Pres. John F. 131
Kennedy, Michael S. 165–167, 171, 177, 207, 210, 211, 213, 215
Kentucky 128
Keogh, Capt. Myles 12
Kern, Jerome 145
Kerulen River 93–96, 103, 109
Khan, Genghis 4, 12, 61, 87, 93, 101, 112, 115, 135, 141, 154, 203, 209, 213
Kharbarovsk 87–89, *91*
Khingan Mountains 87–93
Kingsport Times 162
Kirin Mountains 90
Kit Carson's Buffalo Ranch Wild West and Trained Wild Animal Exhibition *32*, 33
Klondike Gold Rush 183
Kobe 51
Koerner, W.H.D. 51, 165, 190
Kokomo Country Club 201
Korean War 198–200
Kottmeier, Alice 58
Kottmeier, Blanche 58
Kottmeier, Frederick Sr. (Fred Barton Sr.) 11–14, 21
Kovton 151
Ku Klux Klan 157
Kublai Khan 61
Kulun Nor 94
Kunming, Yunnan 67
Kush, Linda 154

Ladysmith, South Africa 178
Lama City 99–100
"The Lama's Motor Car: A Trip Across the Gobi Desert by Motor-Car" 72
Lame Deer, Chief 11
Lankford, William 157–158
LAPD 162
Larkin Brothers Furniture Company 30
Larson, Frans August "Duke of Mongolia" 7, 52–55, 59, 69, 72, 75, 76, 78, 81–84, 88, 92–93, 98–99, 101, 109, 113, 198, 208, 215
Larson, Duke of Mongolia 54, 208, 215
Larue, Lash 44
Las Cruces Sun-News 158, 210, 215
Lasell Finishing School for Young Women 185
Last Chance Gulch 173
Latvians 90
Laurel, Stan 159, 161, 215, 216
Layton, Lt. Irvin S. 153–154

Layton, Olga (Olia) 153
Leeds, William B., Jr. 144–147
Legation, cigarette 47
Legation Guards, U.S. Marines 74, 77, 148, 198–199
Le Munyon, Ethan C. 72
Lena Goldfields Massacre 44–45
Lewis, George 160
Lewis, Meriwether 202
Lewis and Clark Expedition 202
Leyte, Philippines 28
Lhasa 99, 108
Li 69
Library of Congress 127
Limerick, Ireland 12
Lincoln, Trebitsch 7
Lindbergh, Charles 8
Linderman, Frank 166, 168, 177
Linwood Dunn Theater 205
Lippizzans 204
Little Big Horn, Battle of 11, 12, 18, 109
Little Dorrit 38
Little Rockies 174
Living Buddha *see* Bogdo Gegen
LO Ranch 129
London, Julie 161
Lone Ranger 44
Long-Legged General 41
Long March-2-III rockets 205
Lord High Executioner 149, 150
Los Angeles 4, 44, 48, 51, 58, 138, 142, 146, 152, 159–162, 165, 167, 171–185, 188, 200, 205, 211, 212, 215
Los Angeles Symphony 50, 152
Love, Edmund G. 154
Loy, Myrna 58
Lukmanov 36
Lusitania, RMS 57

Ma Yuan 60
MacGregor, Emerson "Mac" 164
MacGregor-Villarreal, Mary 164, 210, 215
Mackay, Malcolm 194
Madision Square Garden 123, 161, 184
Mafia riots 26
Magellan, horse 200
Magyars 204
Malta, MT 173–175
Maltese Cross, brand 48
Man Bear 41
The Man in the Iron Mask 180
"Man of Mind: An old time cowman discusses the intellect of C.M.R." 168
Manchu Empire 1, 3, 6, 11, 28, 39, 48, 68, 71
Manchucko 40
Manifest Destiny 9, 28
Manila 56, 76–77, 120, 150
Manjusri 117
Mannerheim, C.G. 46, 68, 207, 208, 215
Marco Polo 103, 209, 216
Marlboro Man 75–76, 187

marmots 96, 104–105
Mars Task Force 64
Marshall, Gen. George C. 74
Master Horseshoer Protection Association 22
Matador Cattle Company 175
Matheson, John 172
Maxim's of Paris 145
Maynard, Ken 159
McCarty, Bill "Badlands" 184–186
McClellan saddle 37, 60, 199
McConnell, E.B. 29
McElroy, John T. 154–158, 162
McElroy, Mamie Parker *see* Barton, Mamie Parker
McElroy Union Stockyards 163
Mclean, Ina "Tot" 185
Mclean, Kenneth 185
Mecca 99
Mergen Ul 94
MGM 188
Mickey Mouse Club 131
The Mikado 150
Miles, Col. Nelson A. "Bear's Coat" 11
Miles City 11–37, 42, 44, 48, 55, 65, 68–69, 89, 96–97, **138**, 144, 155, 158, 161, 167, 170–187, **196**
Miles City Independent 25, 28–35, 121–122, 138, 207, 209, 215, 216
Miles City Roundup and Bucking Horse Sale 30, 55, 121–123, **128**, 131, 184–185
Miles City Saddlery 54, 121, 187
Miles City Star 27, 121–122, 209, 213, 215
Milestown 12
Military Information Division 76
Millennarianism 18, 68
Milligan House 30
Milwaukee No. 17 121
Mimbres Culture 156
Ming Tombs **5**
Minneapolis 187
Minnesota State Fair 133
Miracle, Ralph 48–49, 51, 174, 208, 210, 211, 214, 215
Mishel, Boris 152
Miss Arizona 203
Missouri 28
Missouri River 11, 28, 174–175
Mix, Tom 2, 44, 91, 175, 183–189
Mizpah Creek 129, 155
Moana 147
Mojave Desert 133
The Money Corral 180
Mongolian coffins 97
Montana 22
"Montana Cowboys Head for China" 122, 209, 215
Montana Historical Society 13, 39, 41, 73, 124, 165–179, 191, 207, 208, 210, 213, 214
Montana Power Company 172
Montana State Penitentiary 44
Montana Stock Grower's Convention 16, 25, 29
Montana the Magazine of Western History 22, 165, 172, 175, 207, 213, 215
"Montana's First Movie" 174, 211, 216
Montclair, NJ 145
Monte Blue, (George Montgomery Bluefeather) 92
Morgan Horse Association of the West 200
Morgans 1, 28, 70–71, **76**, 120–122, 134, 138, 185, 198–201, 211, 215
"Mormon Murphy's Confidence" 202
Morocco 90
Morrow, Stanley J. 14
Morrow, Col. William M. 86
Moscow 36, 38, 82, 92, 98, 114, 178, 203
Motor Age 72
"Motorizing the Buddha of Urga" 72
Motorola 205
Mt. Hengshan 116
Mt. Pisgah 111
Mount Rushmore 182
Mt. Wutai 117
Mountbatten 58
Murphy, Frank 177, 191
Museum of the West 164, 188–189

Nadam Fairs 55
Nagasaki 56, 150
Nagumba, Stazanim 81
NAN Ranch 8, 154–157, 162–163, 210
Nanking University 84
"Narcotics, Nationalism and Class in China" 119, 209, 214
Nast, Thomas 150
National Biscuit 145
National Finals Rodeo 131
National Geographic 73, 137, 210, 217
Nautilus 146
Navajos 183
New Jersey Military Academy 20, 27
New Mexico 38, 49, 107, 154–163, 184, 210, 215
New York (cigarette) 47
New York City 11–13, 21, 46–58, 81, 93, 144–147, 160–161, 181–183, 194
New York Herald 12, 78, 161
New York 71st Infantry 144
New York Style 12
New Zealand 62
Newchwang 55
Newell, Col. I. 86
Nez Perce 201–203, 211, 214, 215
Nez Perce Horse (*Ni-ni-pu Sik'em*) 203
Niangtzekuan Pass 120
Nicholas II, Czar 8, 33, 36–38, 45, 57, 82, 87, 111, 146–147
Nichols, Barbara 160

nighthawk 23–25, 46, 104
Nine Whites 62, 141
1904 Saint Louis World's Fair 184
Nissen, Greta 58
Noel, Frank "Pappy" 199–200
Nogales 156
Normandia Hotel 151
North Carolina 46
North China Amateur Track and Field Meet 67
Northern Pacific Railroad 11
Northern Products Company 187
Northwest Livestock Journal 127
Nottage, James A. 44, 211, 215
Nova Scotia 151
N.Y.P.D. 161

O'Connor, Justice Sandra Day 158
Odessa, Russia 42, 65, 123
Odessa, TX 156
Office of Naval Intelligence 78, 202, 214
Office of Strategic Services (OSS) 153
Ogallala Cattle Company 127
Ohio 145, 147, 156
Okhotsk Sea 37
The Old China Hands 75, 208, 214
Old Guard of the City of New York 12
Old Man and the Sea 147
Oliver, Fallis L. 51, 190, 208, 210, 211, 213, 215, 216
Oliver, Ruth Koerner 51, 165, 190
101 Ranch 184
120 Martyrs of China 68
"Onward Christian Soldiers" 142
Operation Big Switch 199
Oranges and Lemons 159
Oregon Trail 202, 211, 215
Orlovs 70–71, **73**, **76**, 86, 88, 95–119, 134, 152, 184, 207
Ossendowski, Ferdinand 36–37, 81–82, 94, 207, 209, 216
Oster, John C. "Germany" 121–124
Outlaws of Red River 175
Oyster Bay 146

El Palacio 81
Paladin 127
Palestine 90
Pall Mall Cigarettes 158
Palladin, Vivian 165, 176
Palmer, James 101, 208, 209, 216
Pan-kiang 108
paper hunt 59
Pappenheim, Major von 88
Para-hota 96
Parker, Cynthia 155
Parker, Mamie *see* Barton, Mamie Parker
Parker, Peyton 155
Parker, Chief Quanah 155
Parra, Salvador 154, 210
Pasadena Tournament of Roses Parade 44

Paschenko, Yafracina Anastasia (Ashia) *see* Barton, Ashia
Patton, Gen. George S. 18, 203–204
Paul S. Reinsch: Open Door Diplomat in Action 78, 208, 216
Pearl Harbor 199, 208, 216
Pecos Bank 155
Peele, Louise 161
Peking (Beijing) 2, *5*, 39–42, 52–60, 66–67, 71–83, 86–88, *91*, 92, 104, 113, 120, 134, 140–142, 151, 178, 180, 198–199
Peking-Hankow Railroad 120
Peking-Mukden Railway 72, 120
Peking to Paris Car Race 92
Pendleton Roundup 35, 185
Percherons 28
Perkins, J.G. "Jess" 30, 121, 128–129
Pershing, Gen. John "Black Jack" 150
Peta-kooa-honga 173
Peterson, Larry Len 172, 211, 216
Philippine-American War 28, 110, 150, 186
Philippine Transport 200
Philippines 28–29, 76–77, 150, 153, 179, 184, 186, 215
Photoplay 161
Pierson, Geoff 162
Pilar 147
Pin Head, cigarette 47
Pine Ridge 8, 18–19
Pinkerton 111
Pinnell, J. Victor 200–201, 211, 216
Pinocchio 182
Pioneer Cattleman in Montana 173
Pirate, cigarette 47
Pitcher, Molly 21
Pitchfork Ranch 187
Placerville Club 125
Plenty Coups, Chief 187
Poles 90
Pollard, Harry 172, 176
Ponderosa 9
Pony Tracks 172, 211, 216
Pope John II 68
Powder River 68, 122, 129, 155
Powder River War *see* Johnson County War
Power, Tyrone 58
Pratt, George D. 82
Price of the Crown W.J.H. 28
Prickly Pear Valley 173
Prince Botloine's Troupe of Russian Cossacks *32*, 33
Provincial Bank of Shansi 79
Pugach, Noel H. 78, 208, 216
Pullman Strike 26
Pumpkin Buttes 128
Purple Mountain, cigarette 47
Putnam, P.A. "Bert" "Pinkie" 30, 121–123, *129*
Putnam Publishing 173

Quiqihar 89

Raban, Jonathan 120, 209, 216
Race Club 58
Race of the Century 89, 209, 214
Radford School 158
Ralston, J.K. 174, 211, 213
Range Riders Museum 48, 128, 171
Rasputin, Grigori 45
Rawhide 155
Rawhide Rawlins 148
Reagan, Ronald 188
Red-Bearded Bandit 41
Red Cross 55, 58, 66–67, 72, 138–139
The Redhead from Wyoming 127
Reinsch, Paul, U.S. Minister 67, 78–85, 208, 216
Remington, Frederick 18–19, 26, 178, 182, 207, 216
Remuda 23–25, 196
Renner, Frederic G. 170
Renner, Ginger 170, 211, 216
Reno 85, 120, 159, 201
The Return of Wild Bill 175
Reynolds, Jack 167
Rex, horse 182
Rhymes from a Round-Up Camp 173
Rice Paddy Navy: U.S. Sailors Undercover in China 154
Richie Rich, the Poor Little Rich Boy 145
Ridge Walker 41
Ridgway, Gen. Mathew B. 74
Ringling Brothers Circus 159
Ritner, Laura G. 14
Roach, Hal 177
Robbins, Marty 123, 195, 216
Roberts, James Hudson 54, 209, 216
Roberts, Mabel Blanche *see* Barton, Mabel
Robinson, Hadley 132
Rock Springs, WY 149–150
Rocky Point 175
Roddenberry, Gene 161
Rogers, Ginger 204
Rogers, Roy 44
Rogers, Will 2, 159, 166–168, 177–186, 196, 207, 211, 215, 217
Roosevelt, Pres. Theodore "Teddy" 16, 26, 29, 48, 110, 111, 178, 184, 186
Rosenwald, Julius 82
Rotary International 55
Rough Riders 27, 29, 110, 178–179, 186
Royal Irish Lancer 12
Royal Mounted Police 189
Ruby Queen, cigarette 47
Russell, Austin 167
Russell, Charles Marion 8–9, 14–15, 20, 23, 26, 29, 122, 127, 134, 163–183, 187–191, 194–196, 202, 207, 209, 211, 213, 216
Russell, Jack 169, 172
Russell, Nancy 166–169, 178, 182, 196

Russian Revolution 3, 6, 45, 64, 65, 81, 87–88, 110, 151
Russo-Japanese War 3, 4, 40, 45
Rustad, Alfred 51–53
Ryan, Paddy 122–123, *136*, 161

St. Henry, R.C. "Lucky Bob" 33
St. Paul, MN 126, 174
St. Petersburg 38, 45
St. Vibiana Cathedral 58
Sam Beise Urgo 94
Sammons, U.S. Consul-General Thomas 55
Samoa 71
San Diego 120–121
San Francisco 28, 51, 58, 121, 125, 137, 145–146, 150–151, 155, 200
San Francisquito Canyon 183
The Sand Pebbles 79
Sandusky Register 144, 211, 214
Sanngan River 116
Santa Barbara 51, 168, 175
Santa Monica 177
Sassoon, Sir Victor 59
Saudi Arabia, King of 188
Sawtooth Club 125
Saxe-Coburg-Gotha, House of 58
Schneider 49–51, 80
Schwenke, Tiffany 125, 209, 216
Scotland 151
Scott, Robert Falcon 62
The Searchers 155
Sears, Roebuck & Co. 82
Seattle Commercial Club 28
The Secret Life of Cowboys 131, 209, 214
Seth Bullock's Cowboy Brigade 186
7 Royal Tokio Japs *31*, 33
Seventh Cavalry 18–19
71 Ranch 130
Shane 127
Shanghai 2, 6–7, 46–59, 75–81, 122, 145, 150–153, 178, 200, 208, 209, 215
Shanghai Municipal Council 47, 55
Shanghai Race Track 59
Shanhaikuan 72, 120
Shansi Government Livestock Bureau 137
Shansi International Famine Relief Commission 66
Shansi Zhongyu Brave Dragons 205
Shantung 40
Shavehead 41
Sherman, Denver 121, 124
Sherman, TX 154
Sherman Silver Act 20
Shihchiachuang 120
Shoot Out at Big Sag 175
Short Kilts 159
Shuozhou 116–117
Siberia, S.S. (*Siberia Maru*) 51
Sigray, Count Anthony 204
Silver, horse 44, 182

Sinatra, Frank 161
Sino-American Cooperative Organization (SACO) 153–154
Sioux 11, 18–19, 33, 68, 173, 181, 195, 199
Sitting Bull, Chief 11
Skyrocket 130–131, **136**, 161, 209, 216
Slippery Gulch 122
Sloan, Lt. Col. Albert Brevard 86
Smith and Wesson 7
Society Circus 146, 210, 217
Son of the Sheik 161
Sonoran Desert 156
Soochow Creek 56
South Pole 62
Spanish-American War 21, 28, 110, 186
"Spin and Marty" 131
Splendor in the Grass 160
Springfield, rifle 110
Springsteen, Bruce 22
Stalin, Joseph 38, 45, 203, 207, 215
Stamm, Julius 58
Standard Oil 47, 55, 78–79, 82
Star Trek: The Next Generation 160
State Department 77–85, 208, 216
State of the Union Address 150
Stewart, Gov. Samuel V. 185
Stillwell, Gen. Joseph W. "Vinegar Joe" 41, 74, 138–141, 192, 207, 216
Stokes, Olive (Mrs. Tom Mix) 184–186
Strater, Mike 147
Sumatra 145
Summers, William C. 105, 209, 216
The Sun 12
Sun Yat-sen, Dr. 6–7, 39, 55, 78, 180
Sunggari River 3, 89
Sutton, Francis Arthur "One-Arm" 6, 59, 64, 207, 217
Sweet Pea Festival 33
Sydney, NB 177

Tabo-Ol 54, 72
Taiyuanfu 65–69, 89, **91**, 113–129, 134, 137, 140, **149**, 153, 205, 207, 208, 215
Taku 71
Taliaferro, John 26, 167, 172, 207, 210, 211, 213, 214, 216
Taos 80–81
Tarantula Wine 95
The Ten Commandments 187
Terracotta Armies 60
Texas 16–17, 23, 29, 69, 75–79, 86, 88, 96–97, 107, 127–128, 148, 155–156, 161–162, 176–178, 182, 184, 189, 191
Texas Bill's Wild West and Congress of Rough Riders 30, 33
Texas Jack's Wild West Show 178
Texas Rangers 111

Texas Tommy Guinan's Playground 160
"The Third of May 1808" 150
Thomas, James A. 79
Thomas, Paul D. 158
Tientsin 1, 3, 28, 43–59, 67–77, 83, 86, **91**, 104, 111, 114, 120–121, 126, 151, 198–200
Tiffany lamp 165
Tiger Town *see* Para-hota
tigers 92, 96, 145
Tillson, Col. J.C.F. 86
Time 65
To the Harbin Station 90, 209, 217
Tobacco Products Corporation (China) 75
Tom Tom **31**, 33
Tongue River 97, 129, 130, 155
Tony, horse 175
Too Hot for Paris Revue 160
Toole, K. Ross 165, 170–171, 207, 211, 213, 216
Topper, horse 44
A Tour of Mongolia 108, 209, 213
Tournament of Shadows 77
Tracy, Spencer 177
Trails Plowed Under 202, 209, 216
Trans-Siberian Railway 36, 54, 65, 82, 87–92, 114, 152; Bridge 89
Treacy, Joseph 22
Trigger, horse 44, 182
True Compass: A Memoir 131, 210, 215
True Grit 127
Tsi-Tsi-har 89
Tsong-Lie-Yamen 148
Tsui, Maj. Gen. P.C. 200
Tuchman, Barbara 11, 74, 139, 207–208, 210, 216
Tuerin 105–106
Turkey Legs 41
Turkmenistan 203
Tuttle, Capt. "Wild Bill" 75–77, 187
Twain, Mark 89
20th Century–Fox 152
22nd Infantry 13
27th Regiment 12

Ude 107–108
Uganda 90
Ukrainians 90
Ulysses 72
Under the Chin 159
Ungern-Sternberg, Roman Nikolai Maximilian von "The Mad Baron" 81, 101–102
Union Pacific Railroad 20, 149
University of Oklahoma Press 173
University of Wisconsin 80
Upton, Richard 165–166, 171, 192, 210, 216
Urga (Ulan Baator) 3, 7, 42–44, 48, 52–55, 72, 78, 81–82, 89, 93–115
Uri Hangrin 115

U.S. Steel Corporation 145
Usharoff, Elizabeth *see* Bistritsky, Elizabeth
Usharoff, Vasilly V. 152, 163, 210, 216

Valentino, Rudolph 159–161
Valhalla Cemetery 177
Van Demon, Ralph Henry 76–77
Vanished Kingdoms 113, 209, 213
Vanity Fair, cigarette 47
Venezuela, S.S. 145
Vermillion, Roy 157–158
Viceroy of the Far East 36–37
Victory, cigarette 47
Villa, Pancho 110, 158
Virginia City, MT 173
Virginia City, NV 58
The Virginian 26, 127, 173, 181, 211, 217
Vladivostok 6, 29, 36–42, 47, 55, 58, 62, 65, 71, 78, 82, 88, **91**, 151, 163, 207, 216

Wagenbreth 185
"Waiting for a Chinook: The Last of the 5,000" 15, 127
Walker, Stanley 161, 210, 217
Walks Fanning 41
Waln, Nora 190, 198, 211, 217
The Wanderer 58
War Department 77, 84–86
Ward, C. "Colie" 30, 122, 129–131, **136**
Ward, Leo B. 158
Warlord Politics in China, 1916–1928 142, 207, 214
Warner, Ray 130
Warren, Judge Earl 159
Washington Senators 186
"The Waterhole" 178
Waters, Frank 80, 208, 217
Wayne, John (Marion Robert Morrison) 9, 44, 130, 155, 161, 183, 188
Washington, Pres. George 21, 140
Webb, Jack 162
Wei-Hai-Wei 66
Welles, Orson 181
West, Mae 161, 188
The Westerner 175
Westerners Corral 164, 188
Westwood Ranch 48
Whangpoo 56
Wheeler, Gen. Earle G. 74
When Horses Talk War There's Small Chance of Truce 170
White Russian Asiatic Cavalry Division 101
White Terror: Cossack Warlords of the Trans-Siberian 90, 209, 213
Wibaux, MT 184
Wide Open Spaces 159
Widmark, Richard 154
Wilkins, Sir Hubert 146
Will Rogers: A Biography 178, 211, 217
William B. Leeds 145

Williams, Mark 54
Willis, Sid 169
Wilshire Boulevard 165
Winchester 9, 83, 110–111, 135, 137, 148, 171
Windsor 58
Winfield, George 120
Wister, Owen 26, 211, 217
Wolf Voice 41
Wolff, David 90, 209, 217
Wolfkeil, "Tonnage" Martin 159
wolves 15–16, 23, 30, 54, 61, 66, 92, 97, 102, 109–110, 196, 205, 211, 213
Wood, Curley *see* Ward, Colie
Worden, Helen 146, 210, 217
World War I 4, 6, 27–29, 45, 55, 57, 58, 63, 67, 78–82, 87, 89, 100, 110, 129–133, 137–138, 152, 178–179, 192, 203, 207, 215
World War II 2–3, 4, 18, 40, 53, 64, 77, 146, 152–154, 198–206
Wounded Knee 2, 18–19, 23, 33

Wovoka (Jack Wilson) 18–19, 68
Wray, Fay 182
Wu Ting Fang 28
Wyoming Range War *see* Johnson County War

Xenia, Princess (Xenia Georgievna Romanov) 146–147
Xian (Sian) 60
Xinzhou 117
X.I.T. Ranch 191

Y-Bar Ranch 154, 157, 162
Yagoda, Ben 178, 211, 217
Yakima, Washington 29
Yalu River 185
Yangtze 7, 125
Yankee Robinson Circus *31*
Yanmen Pass (Wild Goose Pass) 117
Yeats, William Butler 118
Yellow Horde 2, 150
Yellow River 67, 139, 153

Yellowstone National Park 172, 187
"Yellowstone Pete's Only Daughter" 174
Yellowstone River 11–12, 29–30, 33, 69, 132, 182
Yen Hsi-shan, Gen. 65–69, 79, 85, 114, 118–119, 125, 134, 138–143, 153, 205, 206, 208, 214
Yen Hsi-shan in Shansi Province 1911–1949 66, 208, 214
Yersinia pestis 105
YMCA 67, 141
Yokohama 51, 55
Young, Brigham 156
Young, Maj. Gen. S.S. 200
Yu, Maj. Gen. Y.C. 200
Yungang Grottoes 116

Zanuck, Darryl 177
Ziegfeld Girls 161
Zion 90
Zumaya, Evelyn 160

www.ingramcontent.com/pod-product-compliance
Ingram Content Group UK Ltd.
Pitfield, Milton Keynes, MK11 3LW, UK
UKHW050108020225
454550UK00010B/47